Happy CAFE

VOLUME 2

KOU MATSUZUKI

TOKYOPOP®

HAMBURG // LONDON // LOS ANGELES // TOKYO

Happy Cafe Volume 2
Created by Kou Matsuzuki

Translation - Alethea & Athena Nibley
English Adaptation - Lianne Sentar
Copy Editing - Hope Donovan
Retouch and Lettering - Star Print Brokers
Production Artist - Rui Kyo
Graphic Designer - Chelsea Windlinger

Editor - Cindy Suzuki
Print Production Manager - Lucas Rivera
Managing Editor - Vy Nguyen
Senior Designer - Louis Csontos
Art Director - Al-Insan Lashley
Director of Sales and Manufacturing - Allyson De Simone
Associate Publisher - Marco F. Pavia
President and C.O.O. - John Parker
C.E.O. and Chief Creative Officer - Stu Levy

A **TOKYOPOP** Manga

TOKYOPOP Inc.
5900 Wilshire Blvd. Suite 2000
Los Angeles, CA 90036

E-mail: info@TOKYOPOP.com
Come visit us online at www.TOKYOPOP.com

SHIAWASE KISSA SANCHOUME by Kou Matsuzuki © 2003
Kou Matsuzuki All rights reserved. First published in Japan
in 2005 by HAKUSENSHA, INC., Tokyo English language
translation rights in the United States of America and Canada
arranged with HAKUSENSHA, INC., Tokyo through Tuttle-Mori
Agency Inc., Tokyo.
English text copyright © 2010 TOKYOPOP Inc.

ISBN: 978-1-4278-1731-0

First TOKYOPOP printing: April 2010
10 9 8 7 6 5 4 3 2 1
Printed in the USA

Happy CAFE

VOLUME 2

KOU MATSUZUKI

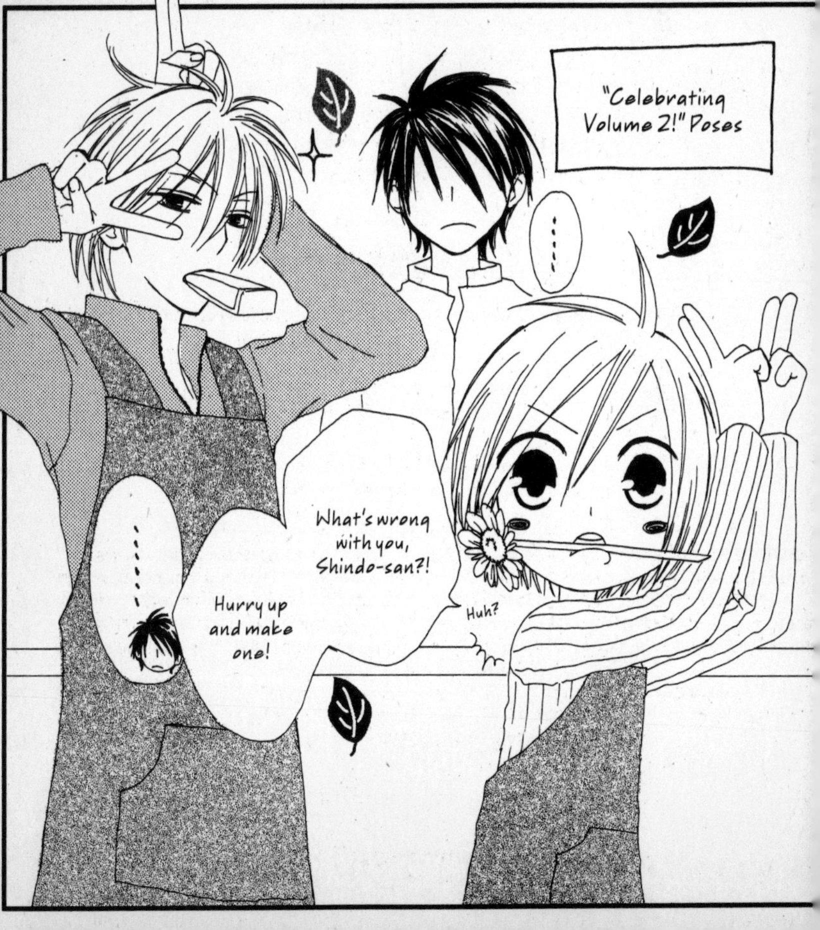
"Celebrating Volume 2!" Poses
......
What's wrong with you, Shindo-san?!
Hurry up and make one!
Huh?
......

CONTENTS

HAPPY CAFE

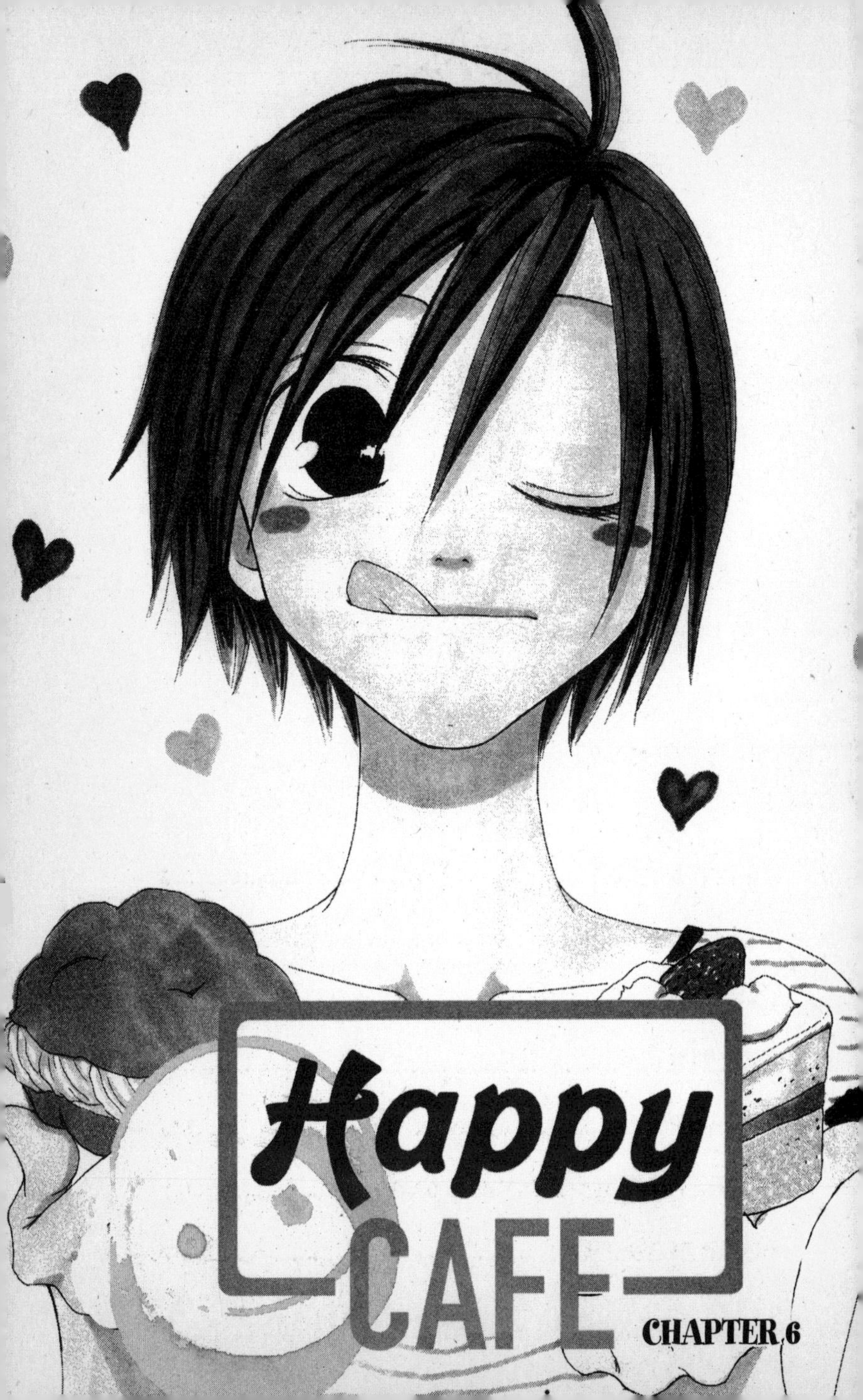
Happy
CAFE
CHAPTER 6

BIG INTRODUCTION: THE BONHEUR STAFF!

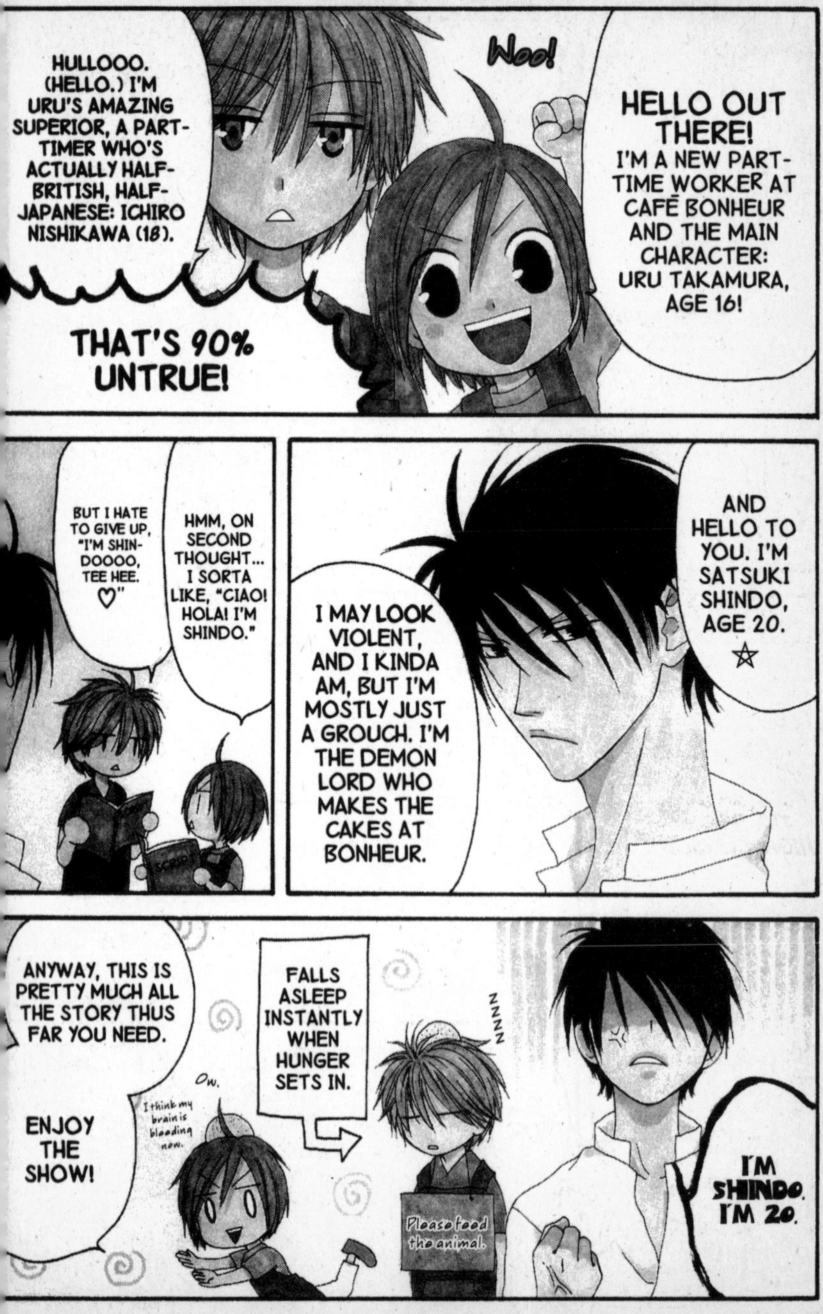

Woo!
HELLO OUT THERE! I'M A NEW PART-TIME WORKER AT CAFÉ BONHEUR AND THE MAIN CHARACTER: URU TAKAMURA, AGE 16!
HULLOOO. (HELLO.) I'M URU'S AMAZING SUPERIOR, A PART-TIMER WHO'S ACTUALLY HALF-BRITISH, HALF-JAPANESE: ICHIRO NISHIKAWA (18).
THAT'S 90% UNTRUE!
AND HELLO TO YOU. I'M SATSUKI SHINDO, AGE 20. ☆
I MAY LOOK VIOLENT, AND I KINDA AM, BUT I'M MOSTLY JUST A GROUCH. I'M THE DEMON LORD WHO MAKES THE CAKES AT BONHEUR.
HMM, ON SECOND THOUGHT... I SORTA LIKE, "CIAO! HOLA! I'M SHINDO."
BUT I HATE TO GIVE UP, "I'M SHIN-DOOOO, TEE HEE. ♡"
SCRIPT
I'M SHINDO. I'M 20.
ZZZZ
Please feed the animal.
FALLS ASLEEP INSTANTLY WHEN HUNGER SETS IN.
Ow.
I think my brain is bleeding now.
ANYWAY, THIS IS PRETTY MUCH ALL THE STORY THUS FAR YOU NEED.
ENJOY THE SHOW!

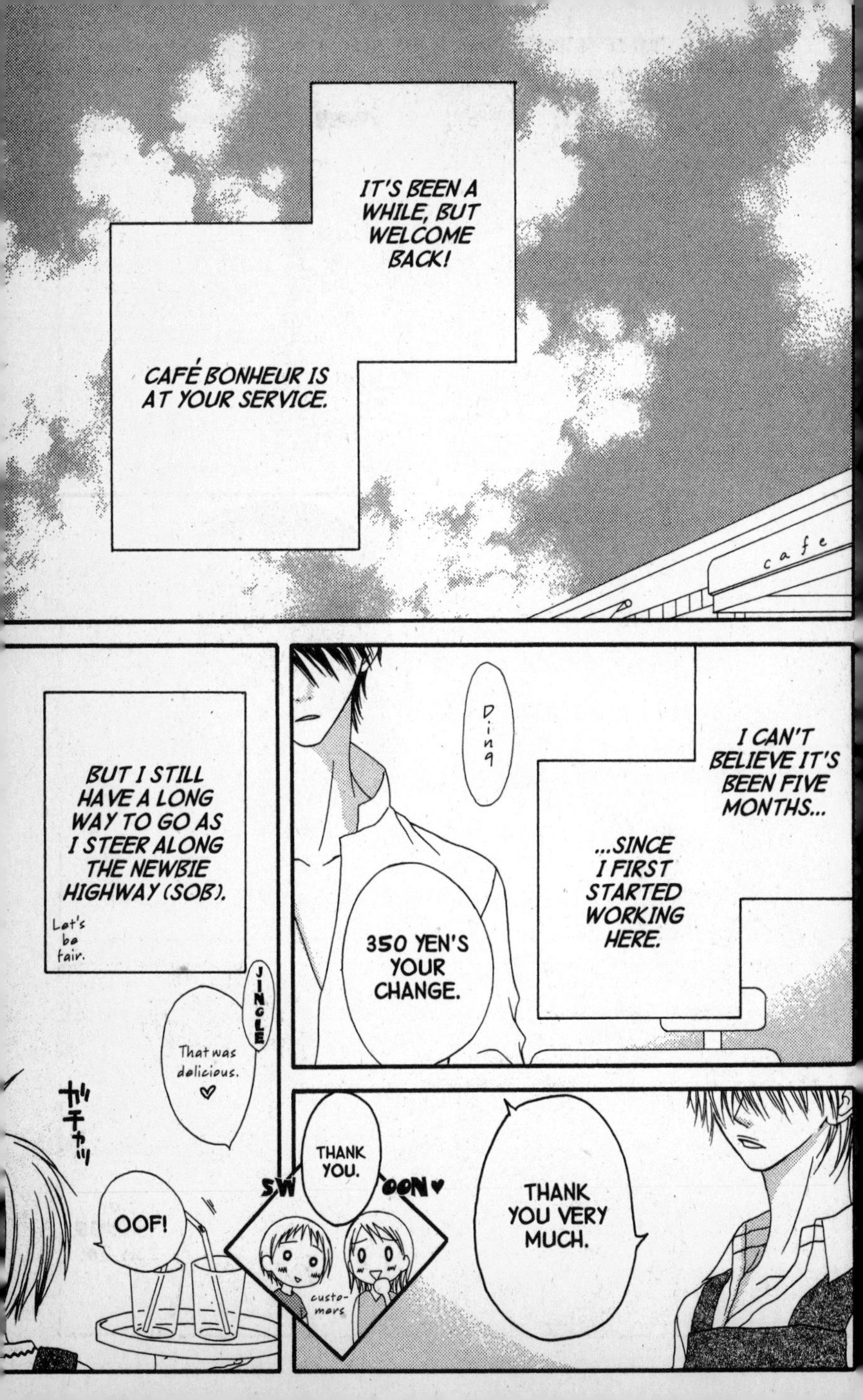
IT'S BEEN A WHILE, BUT WELCOME BACK!
CAFÉ BONHEUR IS AT YOUR SERVICE.
cafe
I CAN'T BELIEVE IT'S BEEN FIVE MONTHS...
...SINCE I FIRST STARTED WORKING HERE.
Ding
350 YEN'S YOUR CHANGE.
THANK YOU VERY MUCH.
THANK YOU.
SWOON♥
custo-mers
BUT I STILL HAVE A LONG WAY TO GO AS I STEER ALONG THE NEWBIE HIGHWAY (SOB).
Let's be fair.
JINGLE
That was delicious. ♡
ガチャッ
OOF!

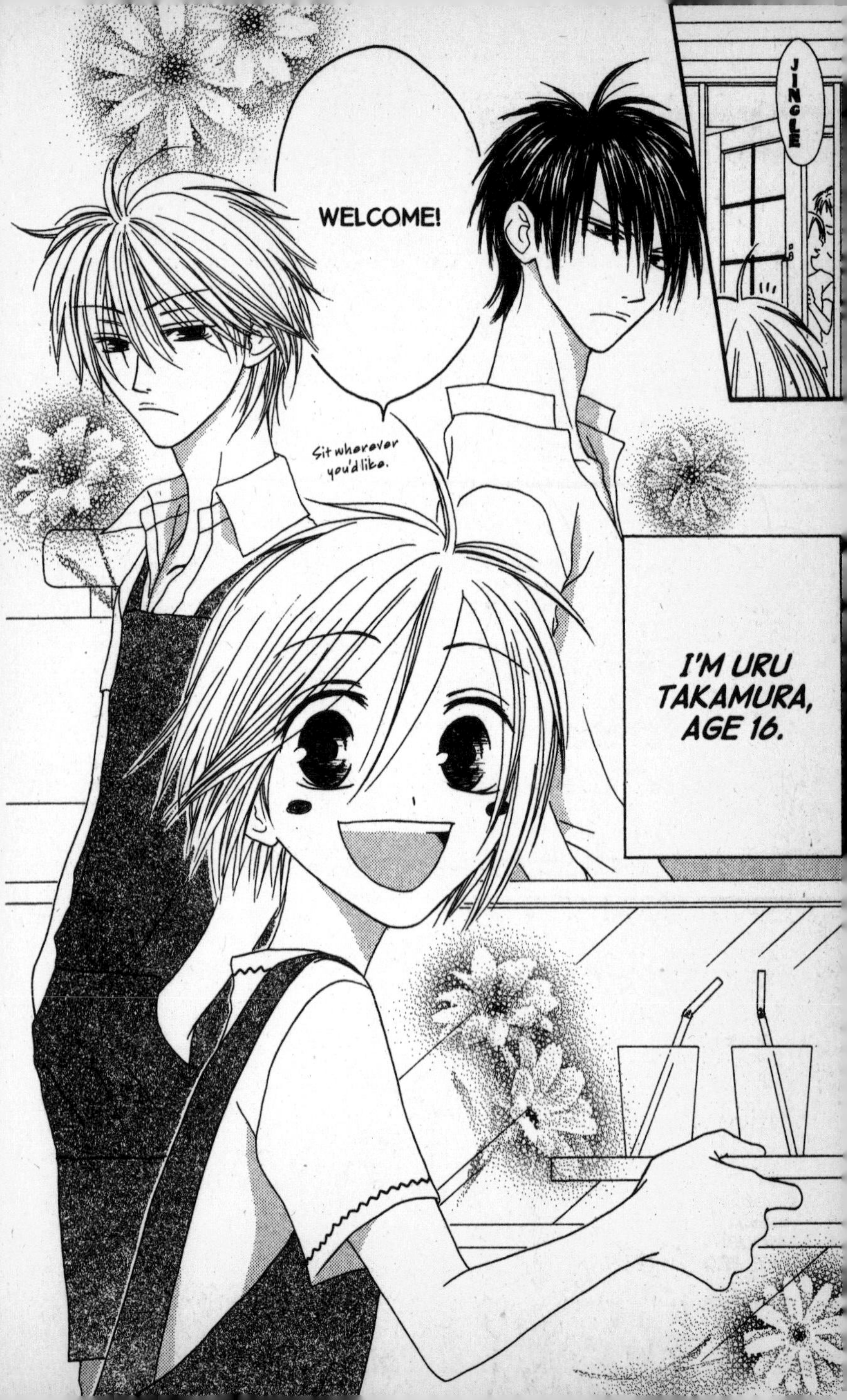
JINGLE
WELCOME!
Sit wherever you'd like.
I'M URU TAKAMURA, AGE 16.

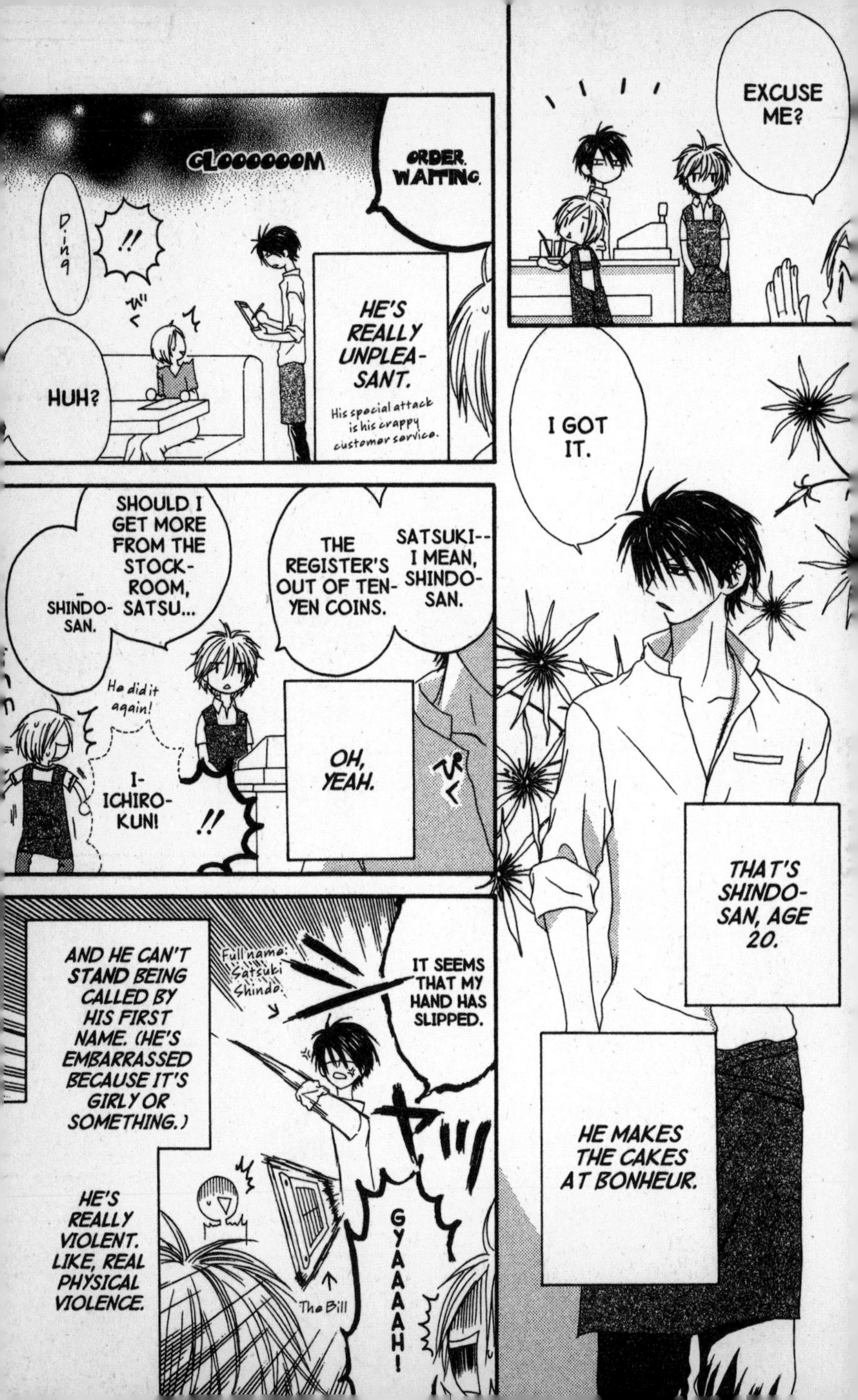
EXCUSE ME?
I GOT IT.
THAT'S SHINDO-SAN, AGE 20.
HE MAKES THE CAKES AT BONHEUR.
ORDER. WAITING.
GLOOOOOOOM
!!
Ding
HUH?
HE'S REALLY UNPLEASANT.
His special attack is his crappy customer service.
SATSUKI-- I MEAN, SHINDO-SAN.
THE REGISTER'S OUT OF TEN-YEN COINS.
SHOULD I GET MORE FROM THE STOCK-ROOM, SATSU... -SHINDO-SAN.
OH, YEAH.
!!
I- ICHIRO-KUN!
He did it again!
IT SEEMS THAT MY HAND HAS SLIPPED.
Full name: Satsuki Shindo
AND HE CAN'T STAND BEING CALLED BY HIS FIRST NAME. (HE'S EMBARRASSED BECAUSE IT'S GIRLY OR SOMETHING.)
HE'S REALLY VIOLENT. LIKE, REAL PHYSICAL VIOLENCE.
GYAAAAAH!
The Bill

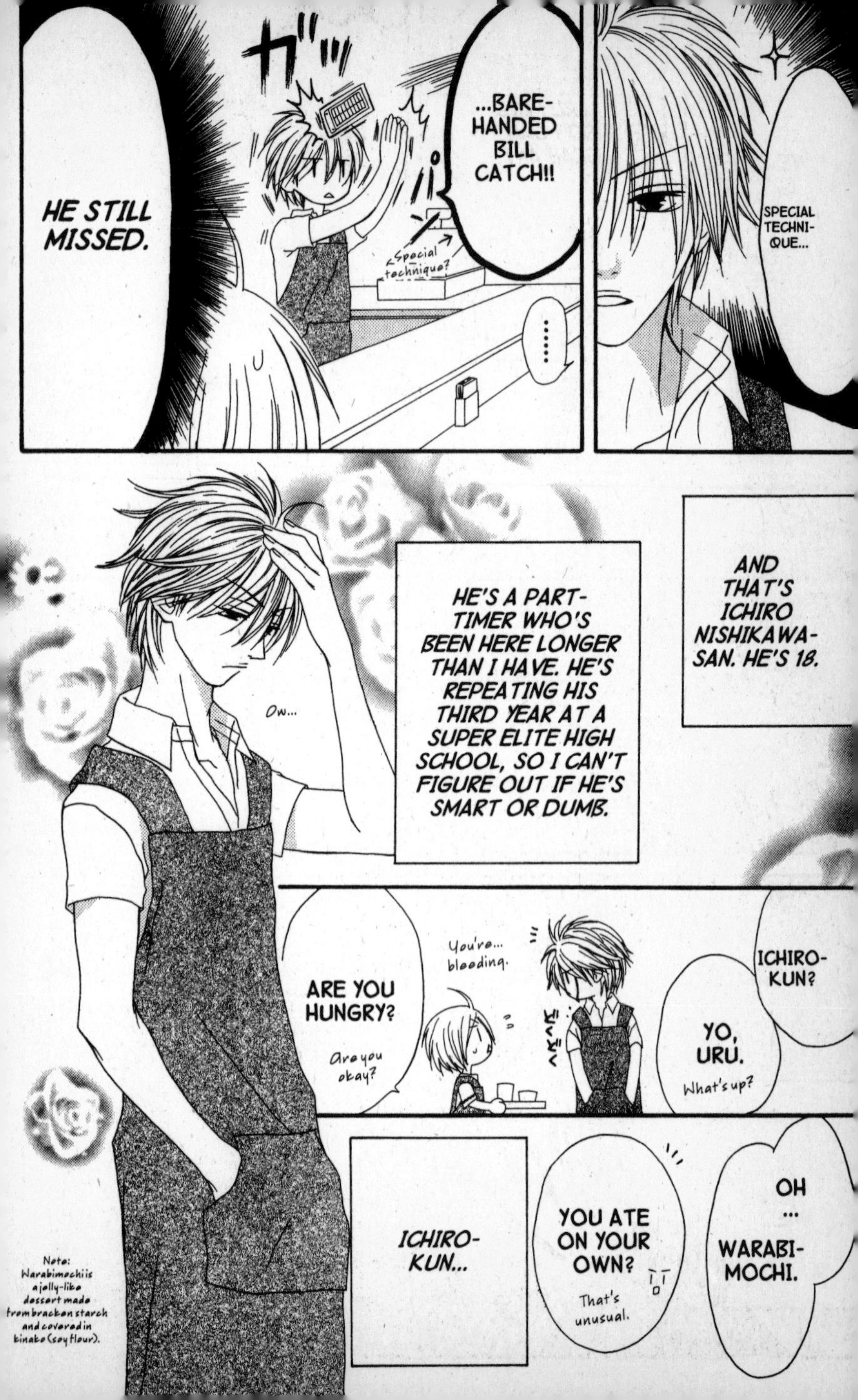
SPECIAL TECHNI-QUE...
ガッ
...BARE-HANDED BILL CATCH!!
Special technique?
......
HE STILL MISSED.
AND THAT'S ICHIRO NISHIKAWA-SAN. HE'S 18.
HE'S A PART-TIMER WHO'S BEEN HERE LONGER THAN I HAVE. HE'S REPEATING HIS THIRD YEAR AT A SUPER ELITE HIGH SCHOOL, SO I CAN'T FIGURE OUT IF HE'S SMART OR DUMB.
Ow...
ICHIRO-KUN?
YO, URU.
What's up?
You're... bleeding.
ARE YOU HUNGRY?
Are you okay?
OH ... WARABI-MOCHI.
YOU ATE ON YOUR OWN?
That's unusual.
ICHIRO-KUN...
Note: Warabimochi is a jelly-like dessert made from bracken starch and covered in kinako (soy flour).

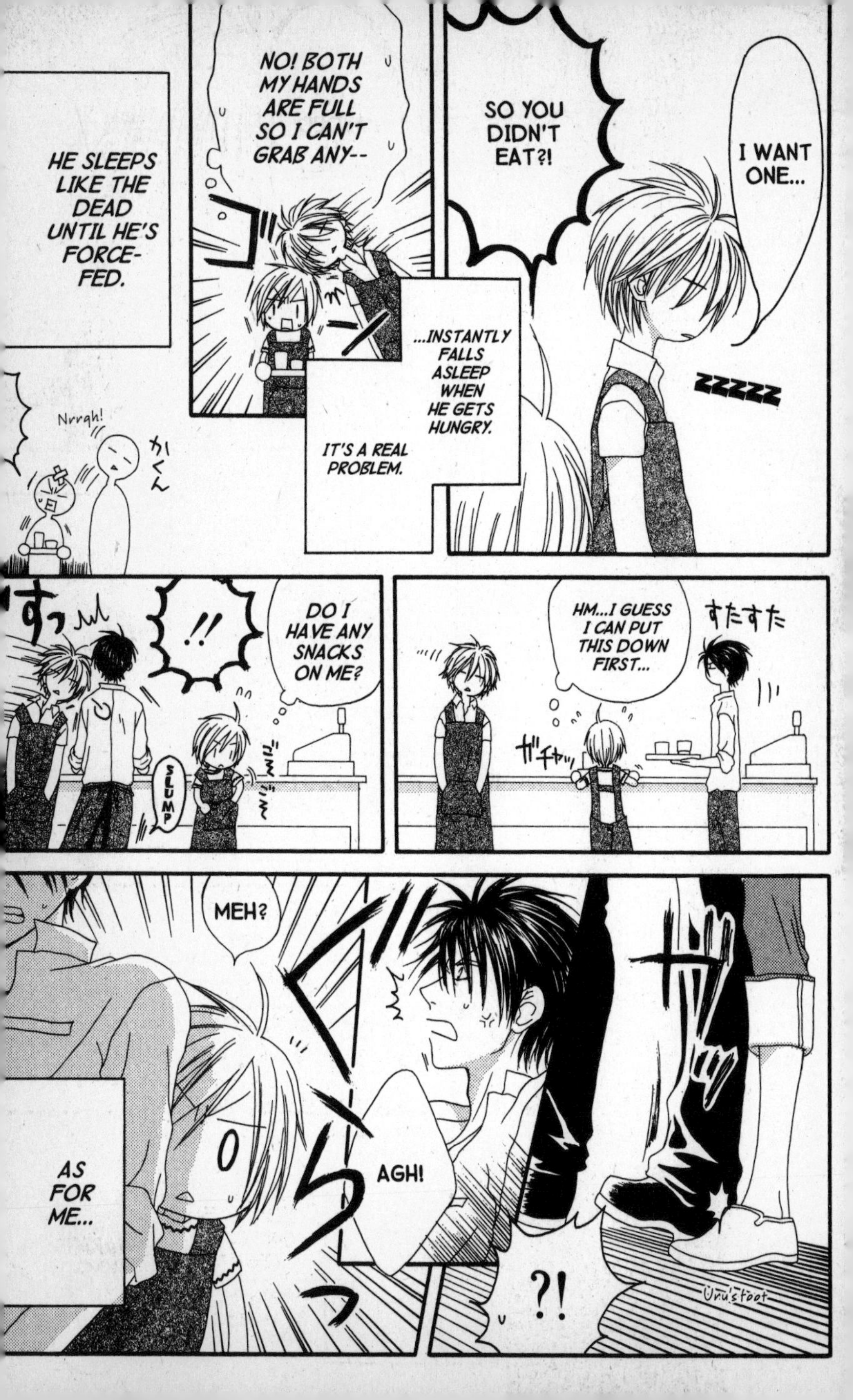
I WANT ONE...
ZZZZZ
SO YOU DIDN'T EAT?!
...INSTANTLY FALLS ASLEEP WHEN HE GETS HUNGRY.
IT'S A REAL PROBLEM.
NO! BOTH MY HANDS ARE FULL SO I CAN'T GRAB ANY--
HE SLEEPS LIKE THE DEAD UNTIL HE'S FORCE-FED.
Nrrgh!
かくん
すたすた
HM...I GUESS I CAN PUT THIS DOWN FIRST...
ガチャッ
DO I HAVE ANY SNACKS ON ME?
!!
すっ
SLUMP
?!
AGH!
MEH?
AS FOR ME...

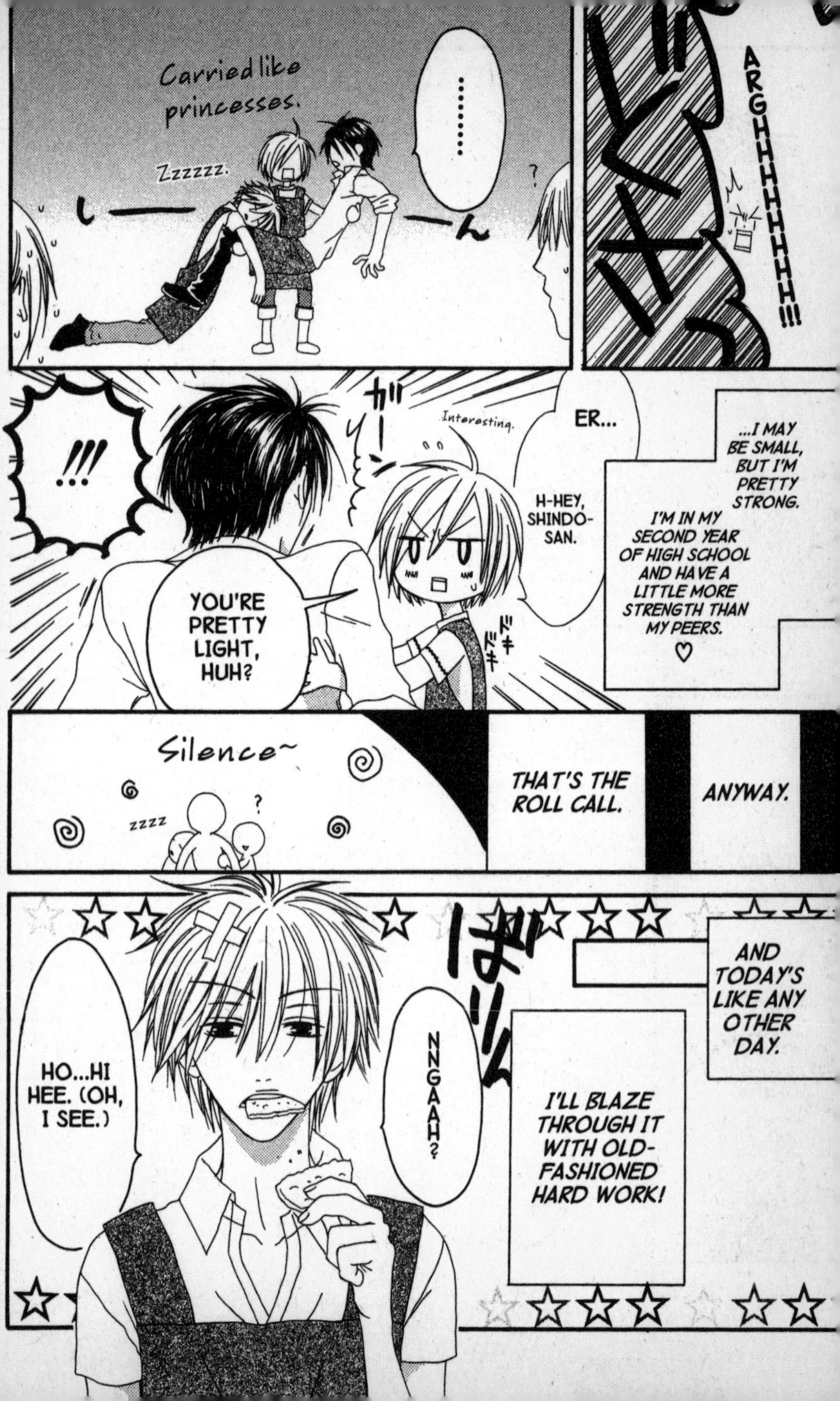

ARGHHHHHHHH!!!
....
Carried like princesses.
Zzzzzz.
?
...I MAY BE SMALL, BUT I'M PRETTY STRONG.
I'M IN MY SECOND YEAR OF HIGH SCHOOL AND HAVE A LITTLE MORE STRENGTH THAN MY PEERS. ♡
ER...
H-HEY, SHINDO-SAN.
Interesting.
!!!
YOU'RE PRETTY LIGHT, HUH?
ANYWAY.
THAT'S THE ROLL CALL.
Silence~
?
zzzz
AND TODAY'S LIKE ANY OTHER DAY.
I'LL BLAZE THROUGH IT WITH OLD-FASHIONED HARD WORK!
NNGAAH?
HO...HI HEE. (OH, I SEE.)

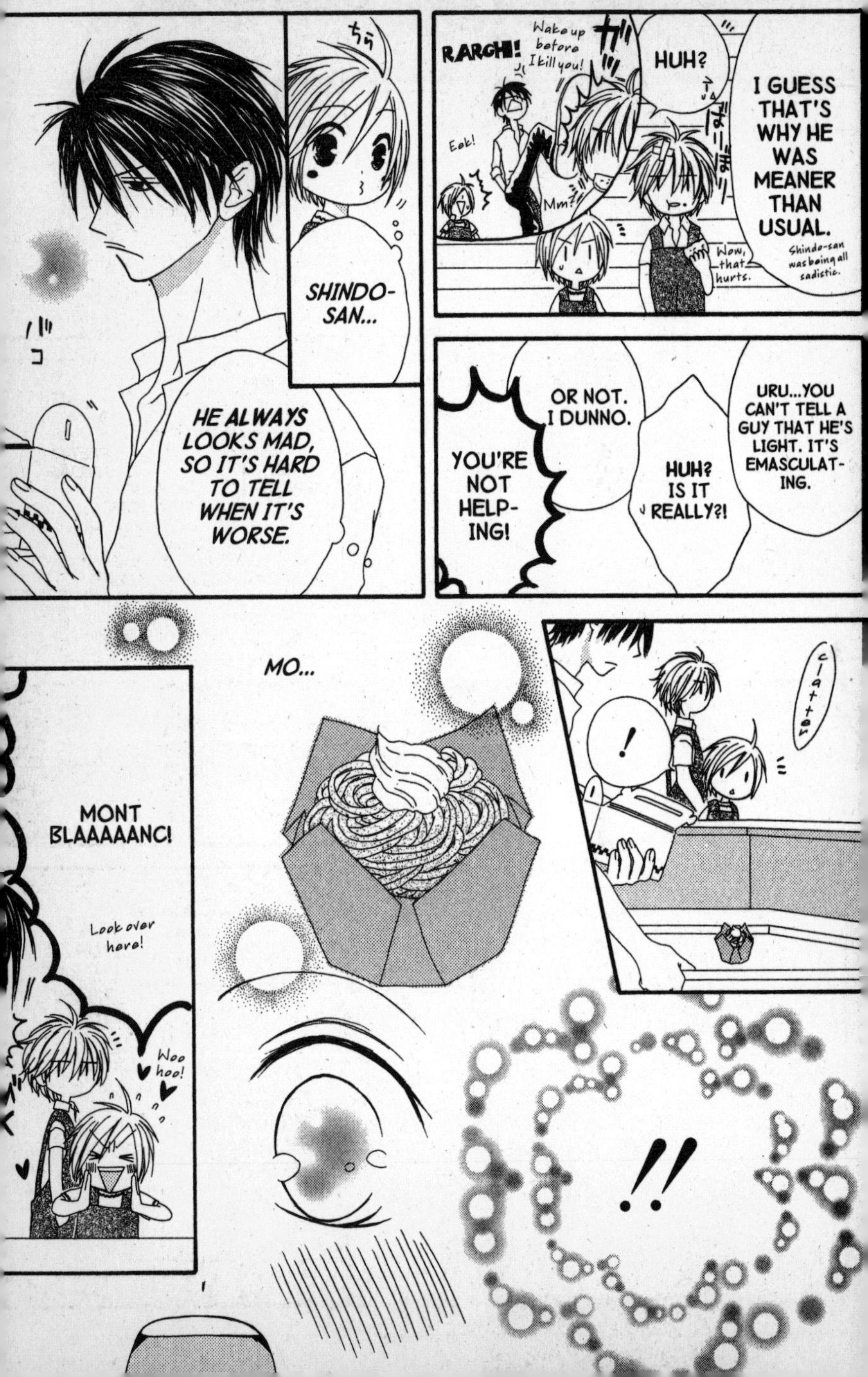

I GUESS THAT'S WHY HE WAS MEANER THAN USUAL.
Shindo-san was being all sadistic.
HUH?
Wow, that hurts.
Wake up before I kill you!
RARGH!
Mm?
Eek!
URU...YOU CAN'T TELL A GUY THAT HE'S LIGHT. IT'S EMASCULATING.
HUH? IS IT REALLY?!
OR NOT. I DUNNO.
YOU'RE NOT HELPING!
SHINDO-SAN...
HE ALWAYS LOOKS MAD, SO IT'S HARD TO TELL WHEN IT'S WORSE.
clatter
!
MO...
MONT BLAAAAANC!
Look over here!
Woo hoo!
!!

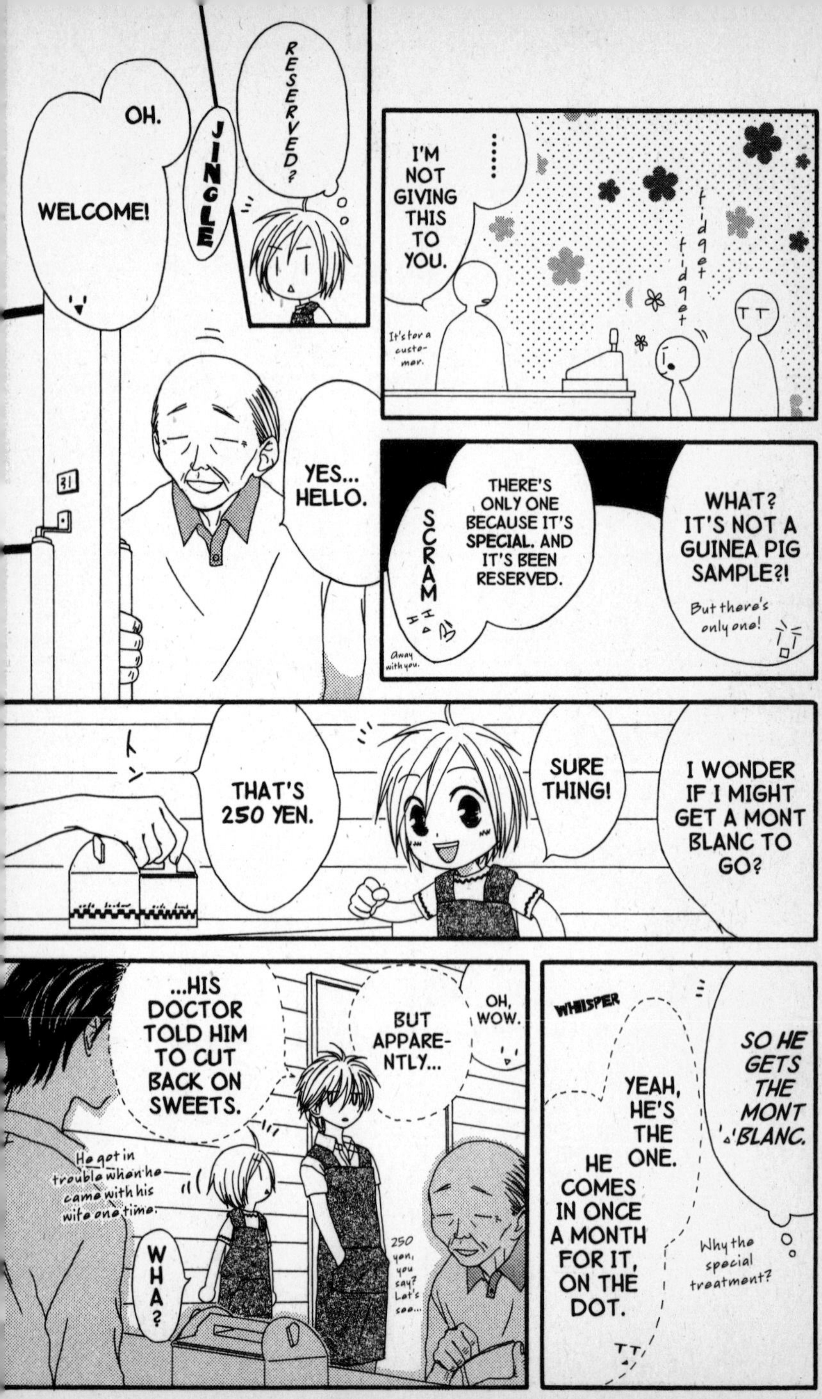
......
I'M NOT GIVING THIS TO YOU.
It's for a customer.
fidget fidget
WHAT? IT'S NOT A GUINEA PIG SAMPLE?!
But there's only one!
THERE'S ONLY ONE BECAUSE IT'S SPECIAL. AND IT'S BEEN RESERVED.
SCRAM
Away with you.
RESERVED?
JINGLE
OH.
WELCOME!
YES... HELLO.
I WONDER IF I MIGHT GET A MONT BLANC TO GO?
SURE THING!
THAT'S 250 YEN.
SO HE GETS THE MONT BLANC.
Why the special treatment?
WHISPER
YEAH, HE'S THE ONE.
HE COMES IN ONCE A MONTH FOR IT, ON THE DOT.
OH, WOW.
BUT APPARENTLY...
...HIS DOCTOR TOLD HIM TO CUT BACK ON SWEETS.
He got in trouble when he came with his wife one time.
WHA?
250 yen, you say? Let's see...

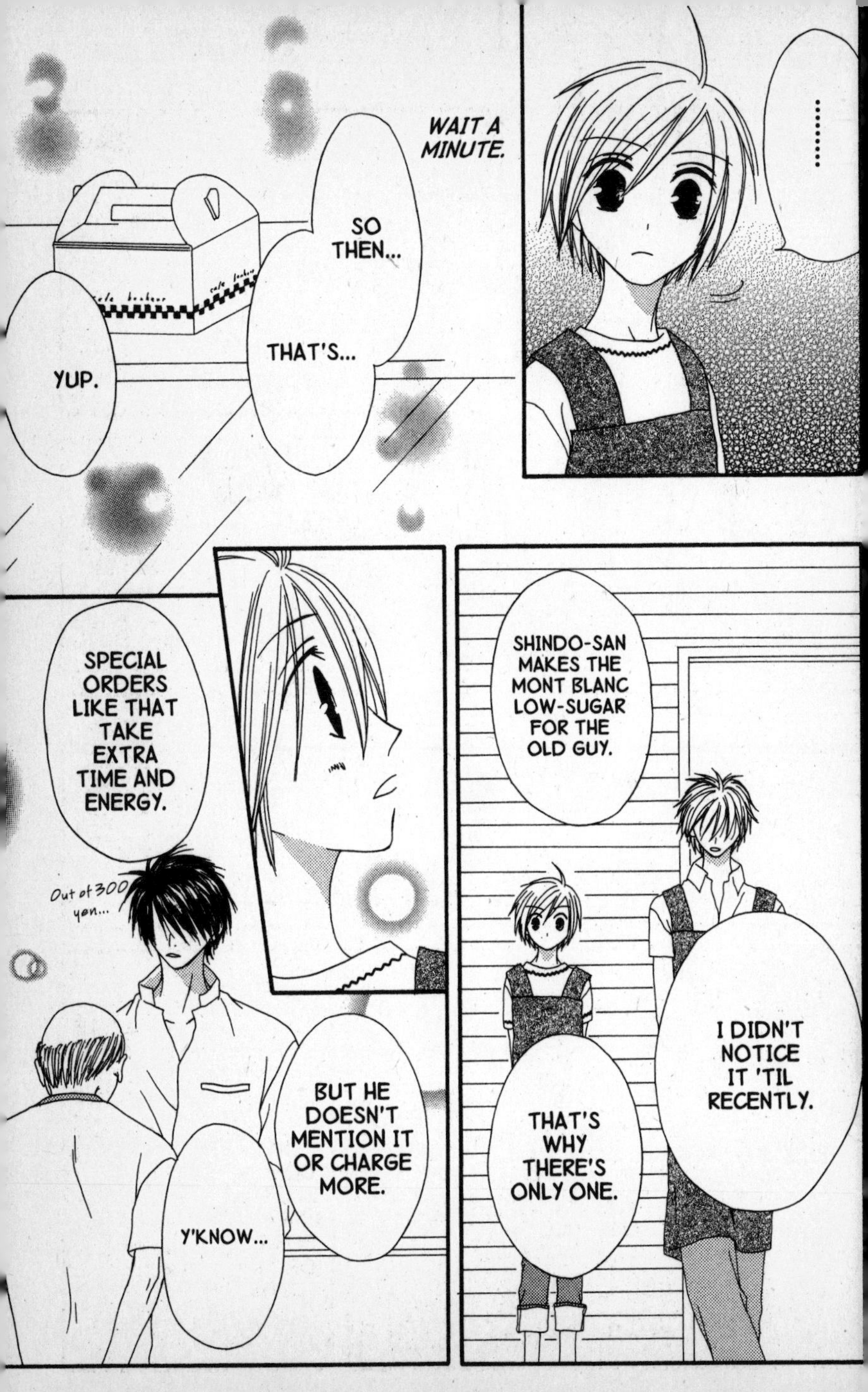
......
WAIT A MINUTE.
SO THEN...
THAT'S...
YUP.
SHINDO-SAN MAKES THE MONT BLANC LOW-SUGAR FOR THE OLD GUY.
I DIDN'T NOTICE IT 'TIL RECENTLY.
THAT'S WHY THERE'S ONLY ONE.
SPECIAL ORDERS LIKE THAT TAKE EXTRA TIME AND ENERGY.
Out of 300 yen...
BUT HE DOESN'T MENTION IT OR CHARGE MORE.
Y'KNOW...

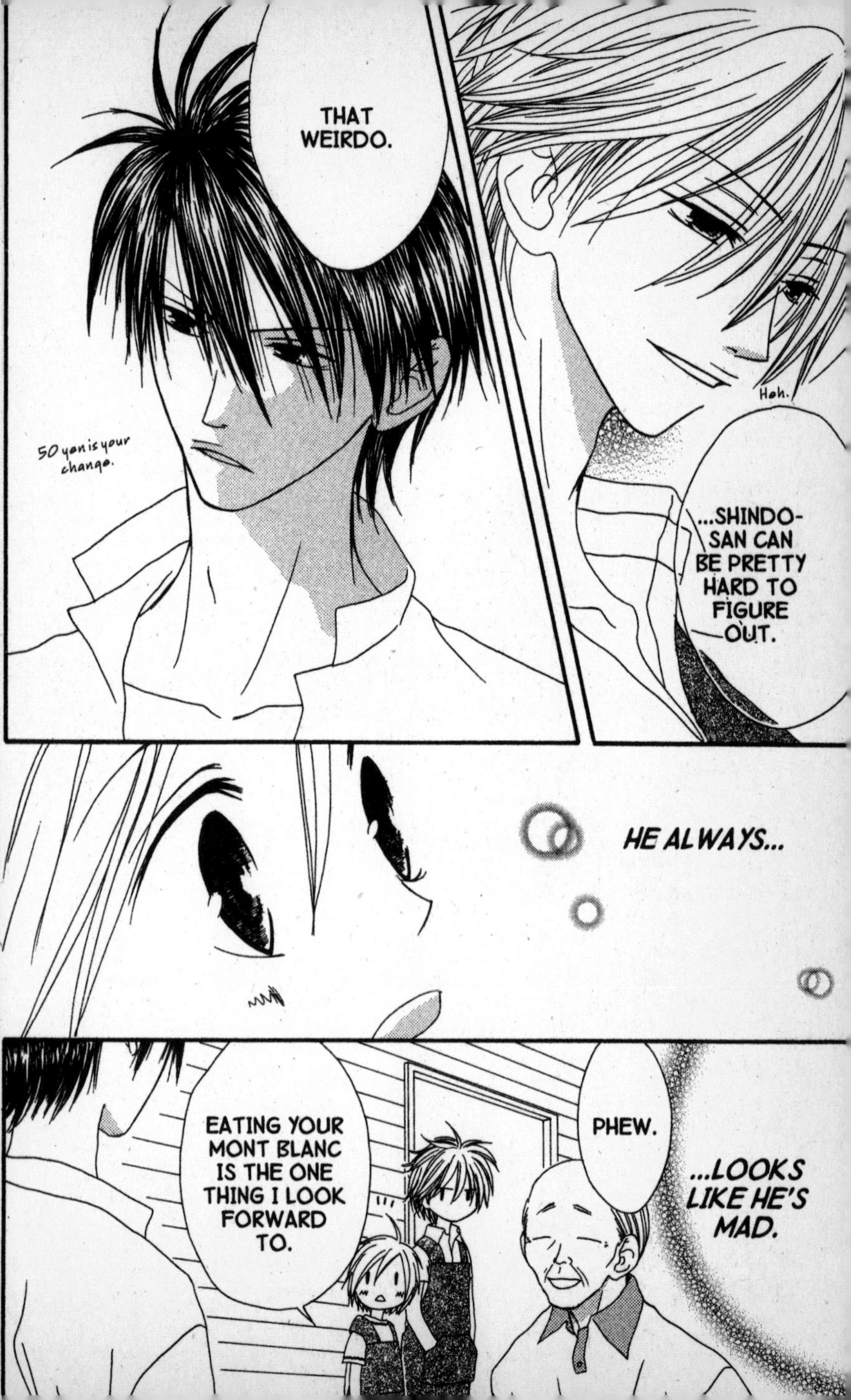

Heh.
...SHINDO-SAN CAN BE PRETTY HARD TO FIGURE OUT.
THAT WEIRDO.
50 yen is your change.
HE ALWAYS...
PHEW.
...LOOKS LIKE HE'S MAD.
EATING YOUR MONT BLANC IS THE ONE THING I LOOK FORWARD TO.

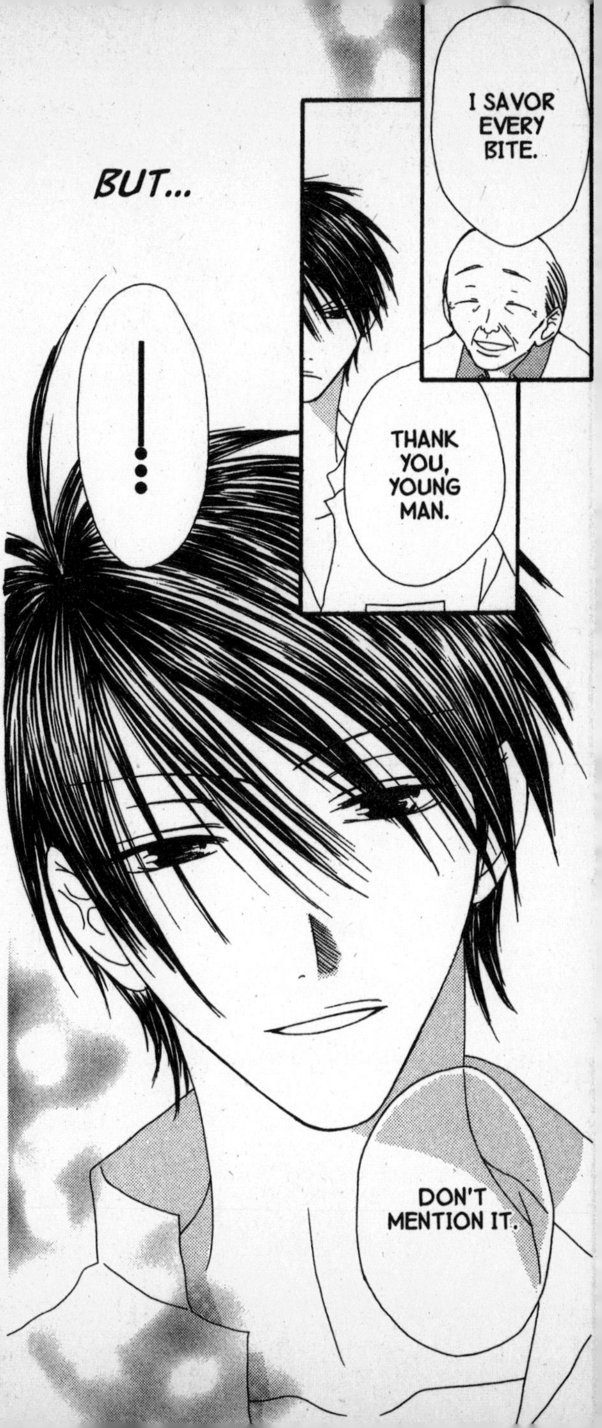
I SAVOR EVERY BITE.
THANK YOU, YOUNG MAN.
BUT...
!...
DON'T MENTION IT.

1

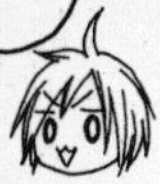

Hello! Matsuzuki here!

Thanks for buying volume two of Happy Café!

It's volume two! **Volume! Two!**

Volume twooooooo!

...Sorry.

There's a short story in the back of this book too.

It's my debut manga.

Anyway, enjoy!

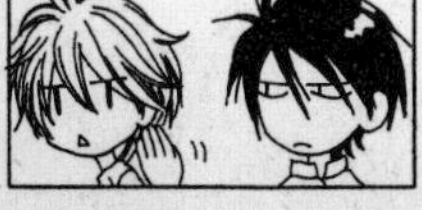
C'mon over.

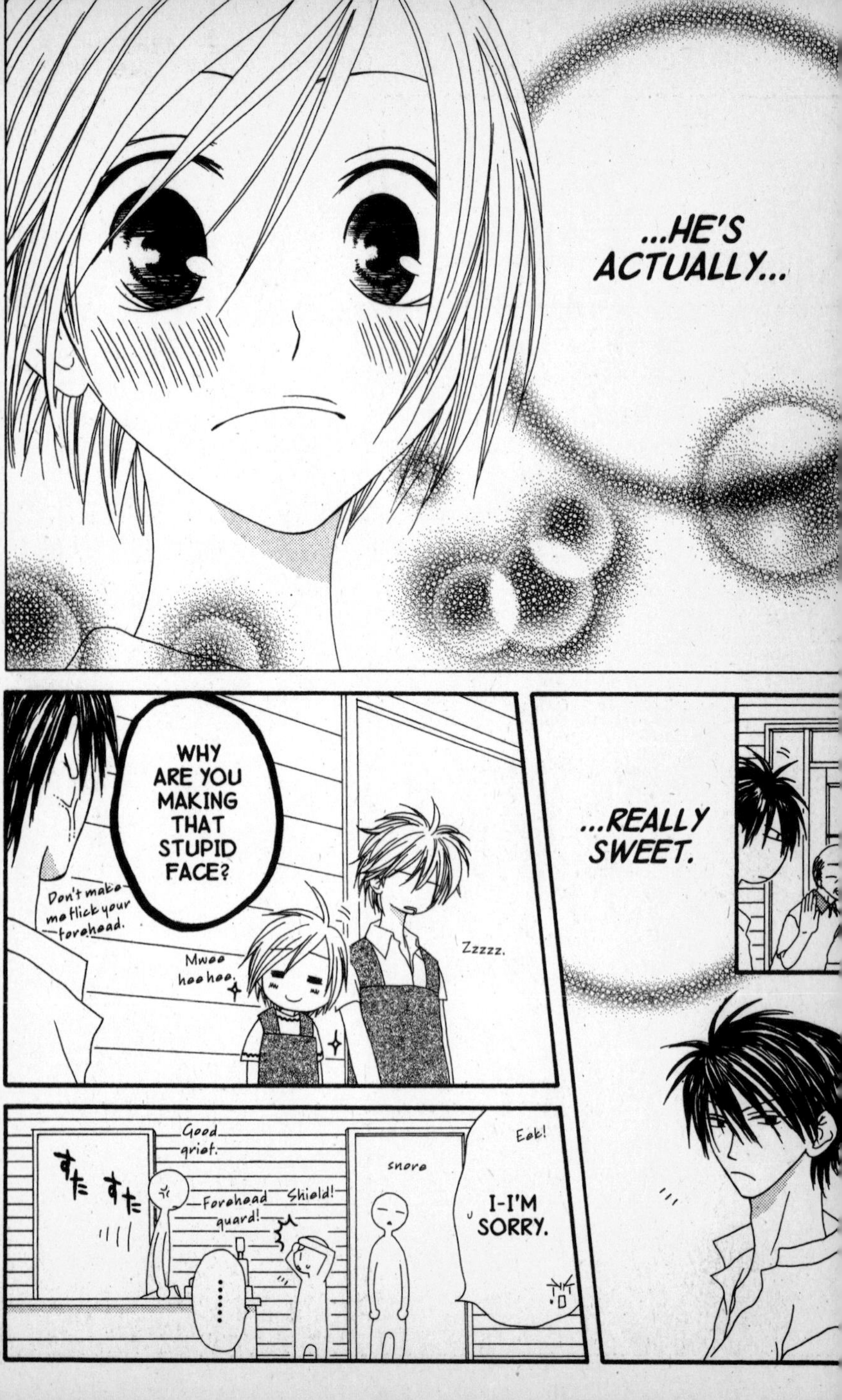
...HE'S ACTUALLY...
...REALLY SWEET.
WHY ARE YOU MAKING THAT STUPID FACE?
Don't make me flick your forehead.
Zzzzz.
Mwee hee hee.
Eek!
I-I'M SORRY.
snore
Shield!
Forehead guard!
Good grief.
すた すた
......

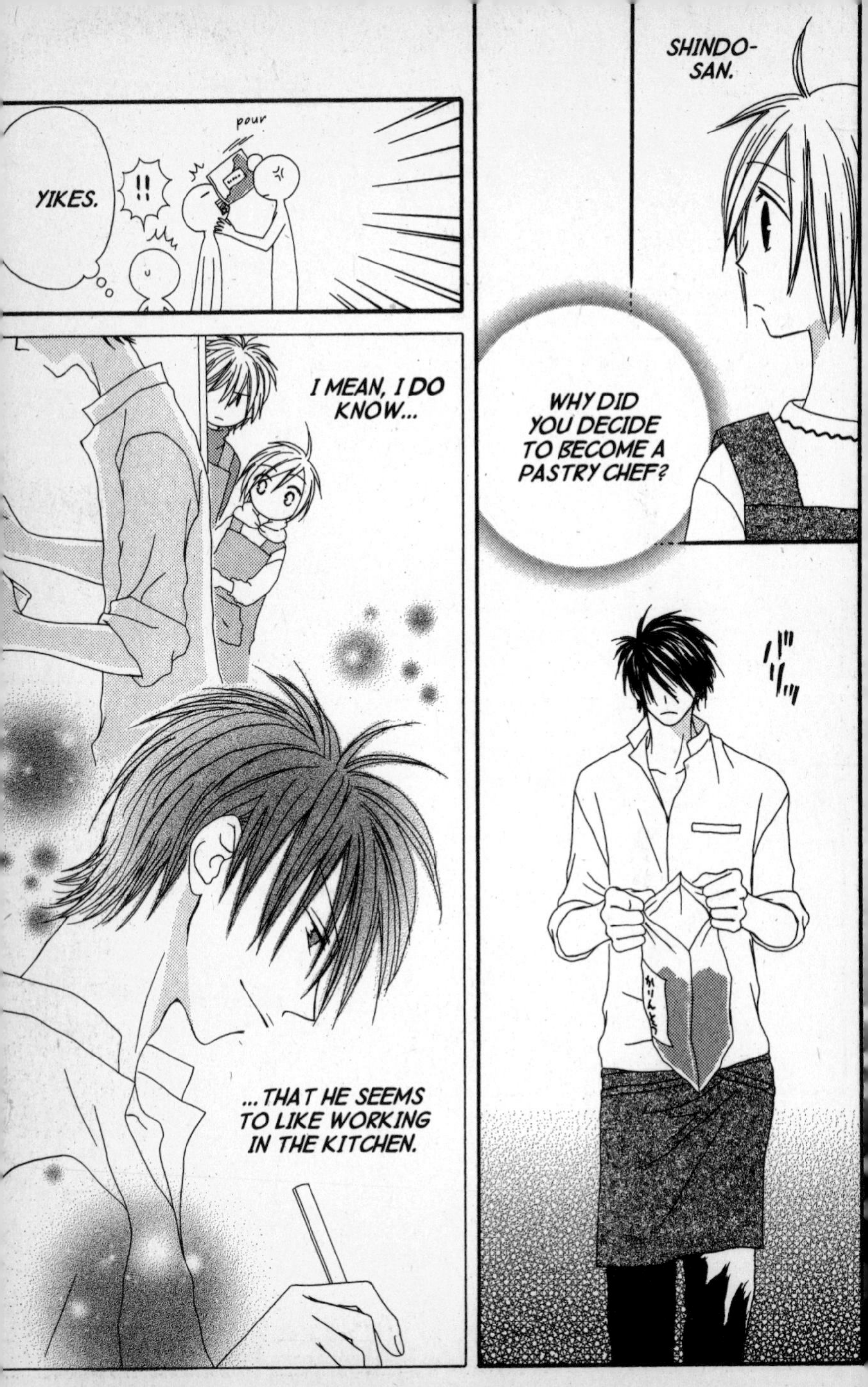
SHINDO-SAN.
WHY DID YOU DECIDE TO BECOME A PASTRY CHEF?
YIKES.
!!
pour
I MEAN, I DO KNOW...
...THAT HE SEEMS TO LIKE WORKING IN THE KITCHEN.

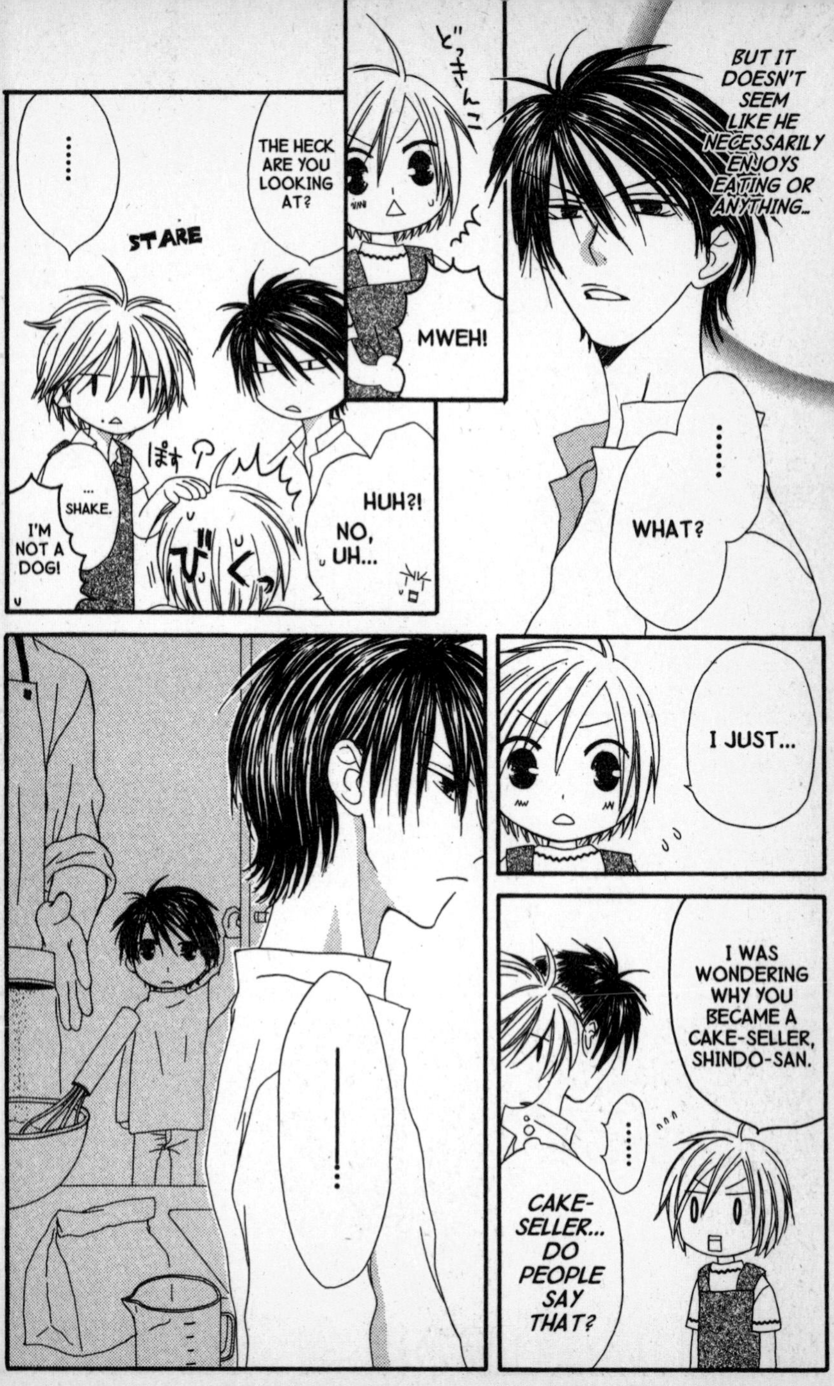
BUT IT DOESN'T SEEM LIKE HE NECESSARILY ENJOYS EATING OR ANYTHING...
......
WHAT?
どっきんこ
MWEH!
THE HECK ARE YOU LOOKING AT?
......
STARE
... SHAKE.
ぽすッ
びくっ
HUH?! NO, UH...
I'M NOT A DOG!
I JUST...
I WAS WONDERING WHY YOU BECAME A CAKE-SELLER, SHINDO-SAN.
......
CAKE-SELLER... DO PEOPLE SAY THAT?
......

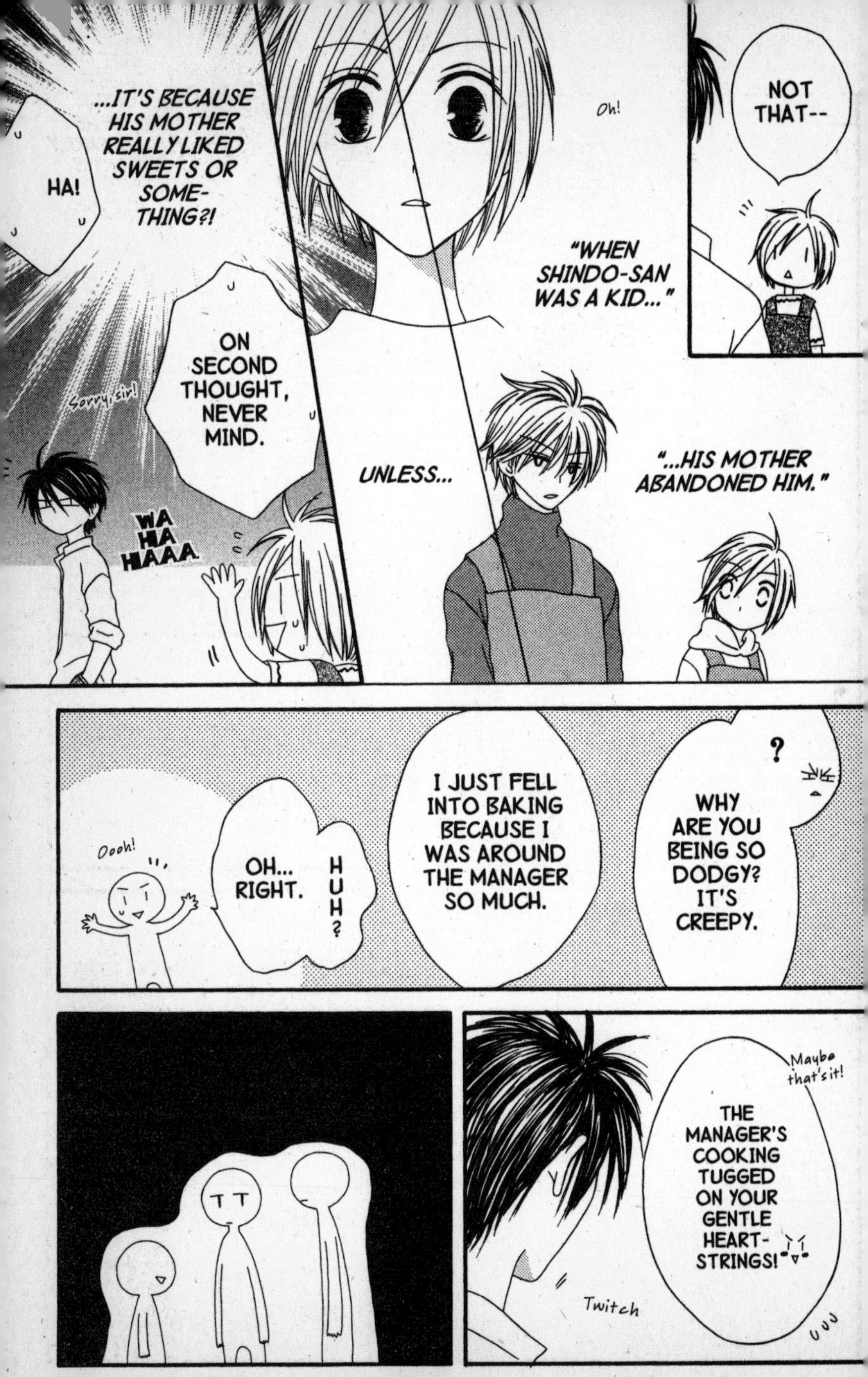
NOT THAT--
Oh!
"WHEN SHINDO-SAN WAS A KID..."
"...HIS MOTHER ABANDONED HIM."
UNLESS...
...IT'S BECAUSE HIS MOTHER REALLY LIKED SWEETS OR SOME-THING?!
HA!
ON SECOND THOUGHT, NEVER MIND.
Sorry, sir!
WA HA HAAA
?
WHY ARE YOU BEING SO DODGY? IT'S CREEPY.
I JUST FELL INTO BAKING BECAUSE I WAS AROUND THE MANAGER SO MUCH.
HUH?
OH... RIGHT.
Oooh!
Maybe that's it!
THE MANAGER'S COOKING TUGGED ON YOUR GENTLE HEART-STRINGS!
Twitch

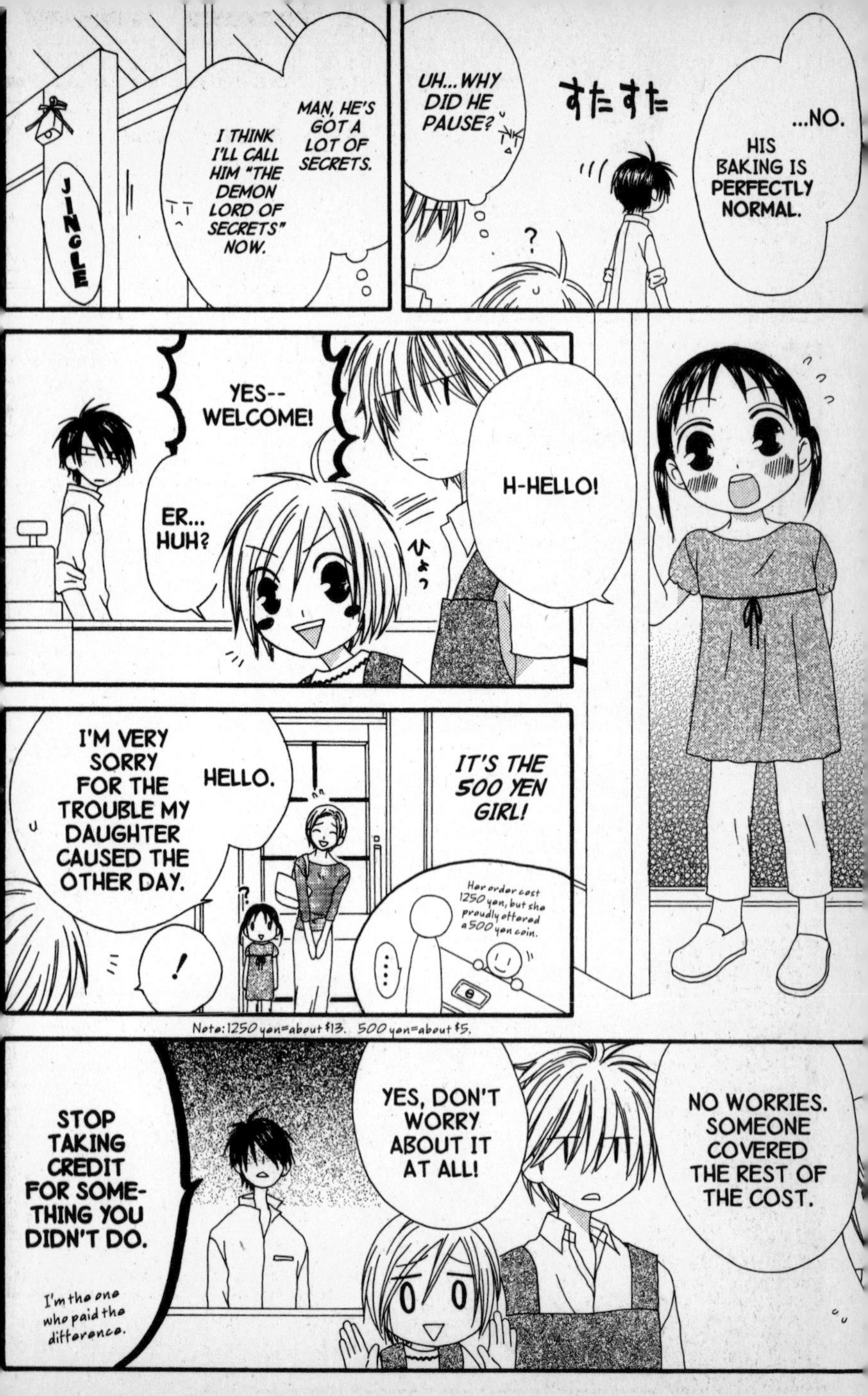
すたすた
...NO. HIS BAKING IS PERFECTLY NORMAL.
UH...WHY DID HE PAUSE?
?
MAN, HE'S GOT A LOT OF SECRETS.
I THINK I'LL CALL HIM "THE DEMON LORD OF SECRETS" NOW.
JINGLE
H-HELLO!
YES-- WELCOME!
ひょっ
ER... HUH?
IT'S THE 500 YEN GIRL!
Her order cost 1250 yen, but she proudly offered a 500 yen coin.
....
HELLO.
I'M VERY SORRY FOR THE TROUBLE MY DAUGHTER CAUSED THE OTHER DAY.
?
!
NO WORRIES. SOMEONE COVERED THE REST OF THE COST.
YES, DON'T WORRY ABOUT IT AT ALL!
STOP TAKING CREDIT FOR SOME-THING YOU DIDN'T DO.
I'm the one who paid the difference.

Note: 1250 yen=about $13. 500 yen=about $5.

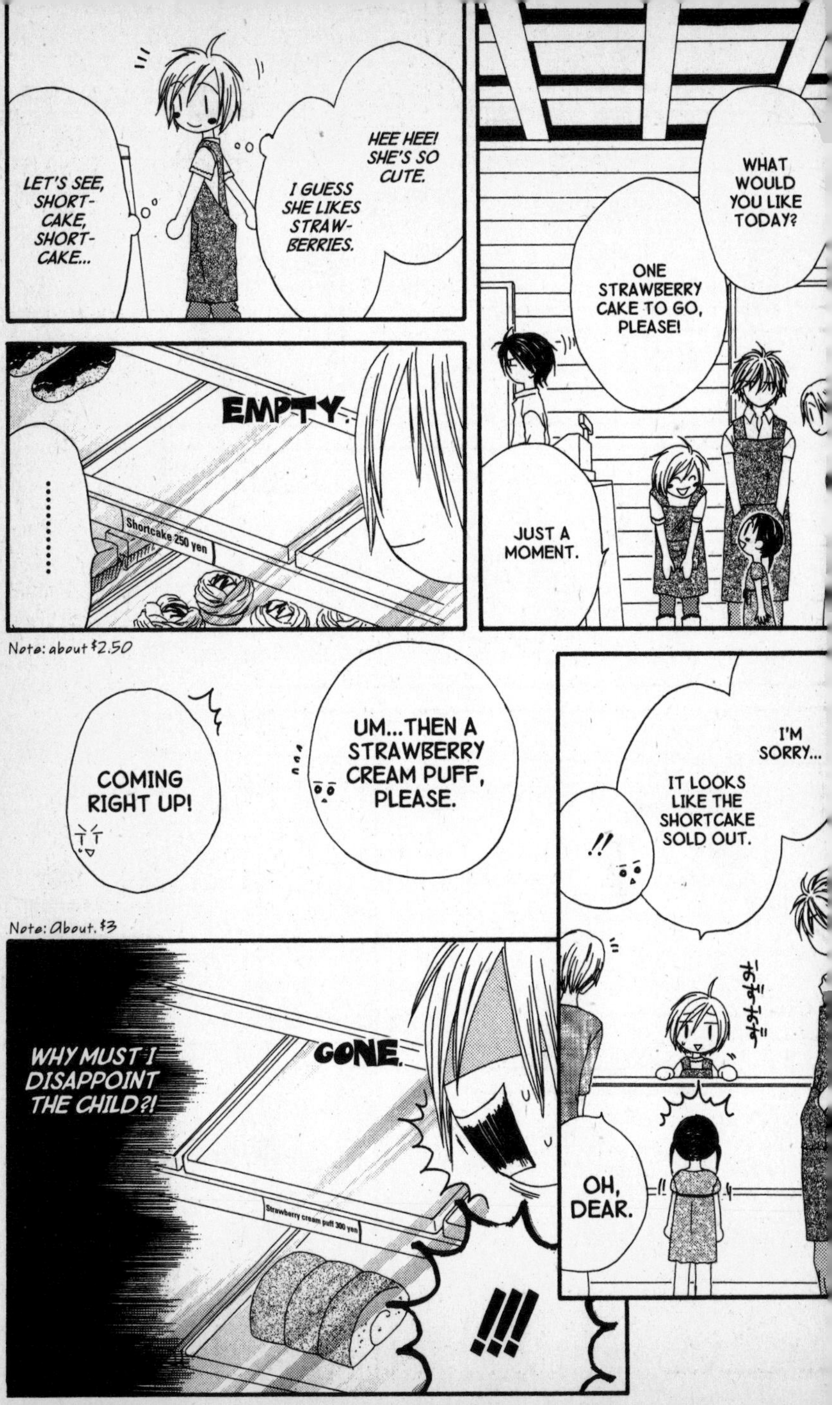
WHAT WOULD YOU LIKE TODAY?
ONE STRAWBERRY CAKE TO GO, PLEASE!
JUST A MOMENT.
HEE HEE! SHE'S SO CUTE.
I GUESS SHE LIKES STRAWBERRIES.
LET'S SEE, SHORTCAKE, SHORTCAKE...
EMPTY.
......
Shortcake 250 yen
Note: about $2.50
I'M SORRY...
IT LOOKS LIKE THE SHORTCAKE SOLD OUT.
!!
OH, DEAR.
UM...THEN A STRAWBERRY CREAM PUFF, PLEASE.
COMING RIGHT UP!
Note: About. $3
GONE.
!!!!
WHY MUST I DISAPPOINT THE CHILD?!
Strawberry cream puff 300 yen

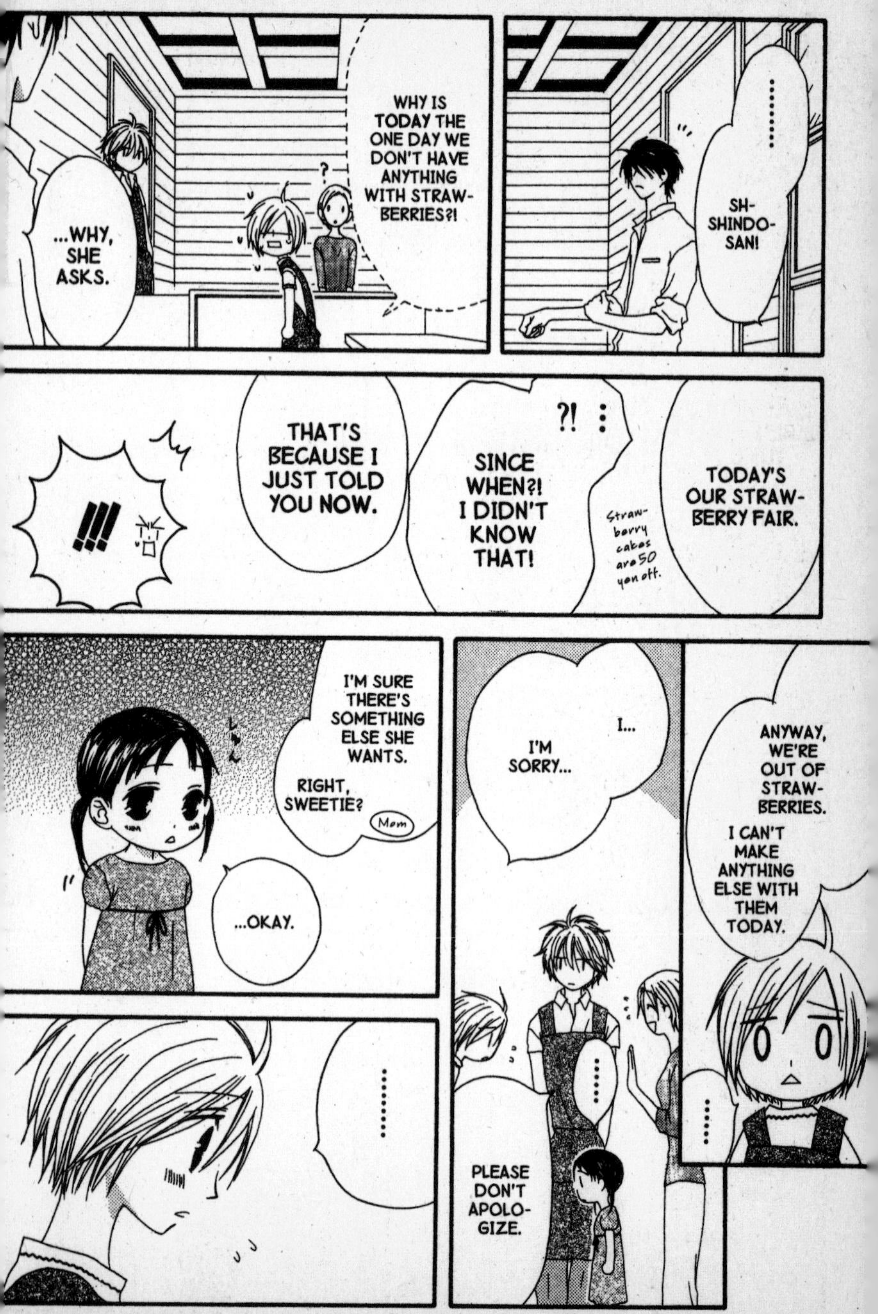
......
SH-SHINDO-SAN!
WHY IS TODAY THE ONE DAY WE DON'T HAVE ANYTHING WITH STRAW-BERRIES?!
...WHY, SHE ASKS.
TODAY'S OUR STRAW-BERRY FAIR.
Straw-berry cakes are 50 yen off.
?! :
SINCE WHEN?! I DIDN'T KNOW THAT!
THAT'S BECAUSE I JUST TOLD YOU NOW.
!!!!
ANYWAY, WE'RE OUT OF STRAW-BERRIES.
I CAN'T MAKE ANYTHING ELSE WITH THEM TODAY.
......
I...
I'M SORRY...
......
PLEASE DON'T APOLO-GIZE.
I'M SURE THERE'S SOMETHING ELSE SHE WANTS.
RIGHT, SWEETIE?
Mom
...OKAY.
....

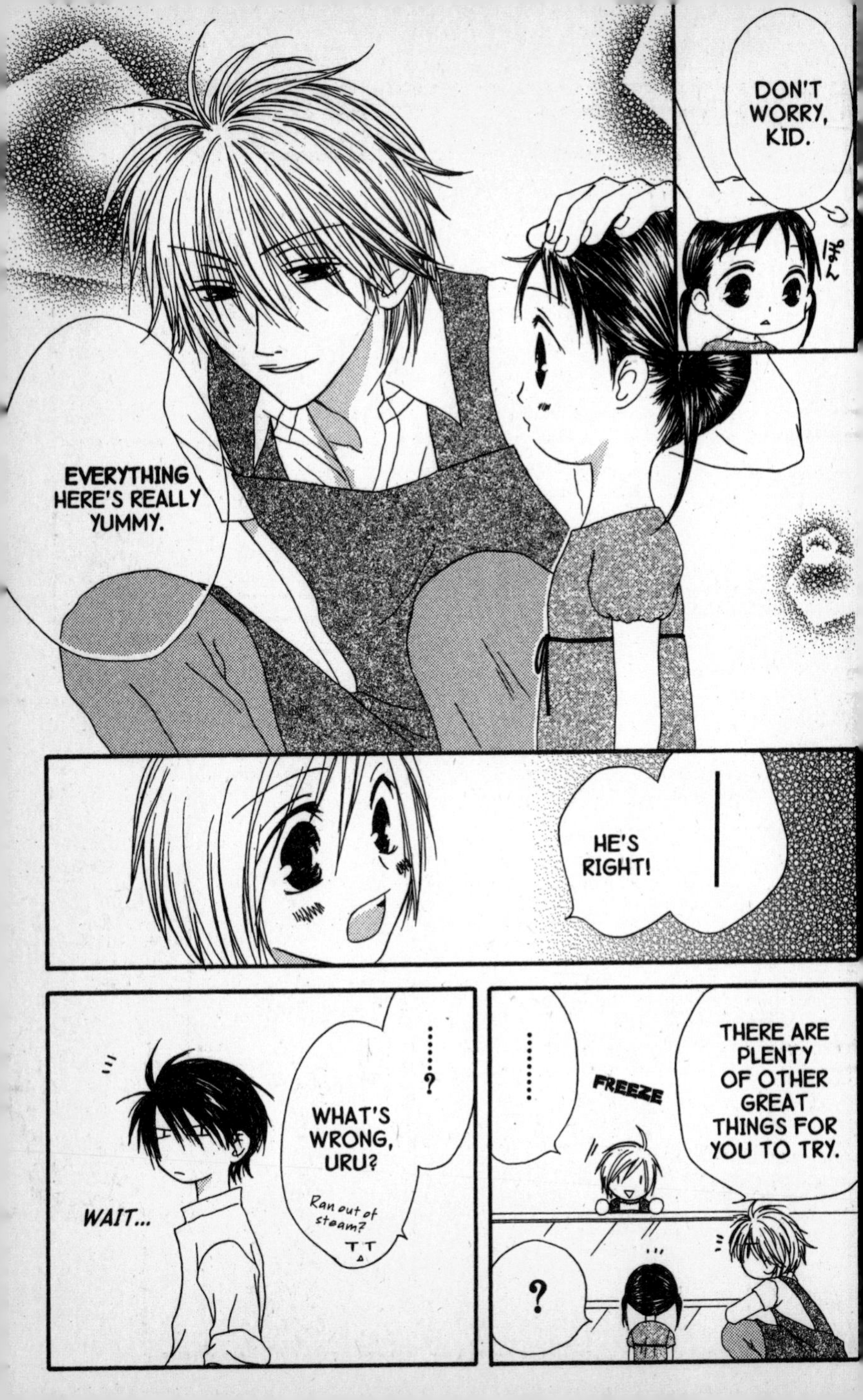
DON'T WORRY, KID.
ぽん
EVERYTHING HERE'S REALLY YUMMY.
HE'S RIGHT!
THERE ARE PLENTY OF OTHER GREAT THINGS FOR YOU TO TRY.
....
FREEZE
?
......?
WHAT'S WRONG, URU?
Ran out of steam?
WAIT...

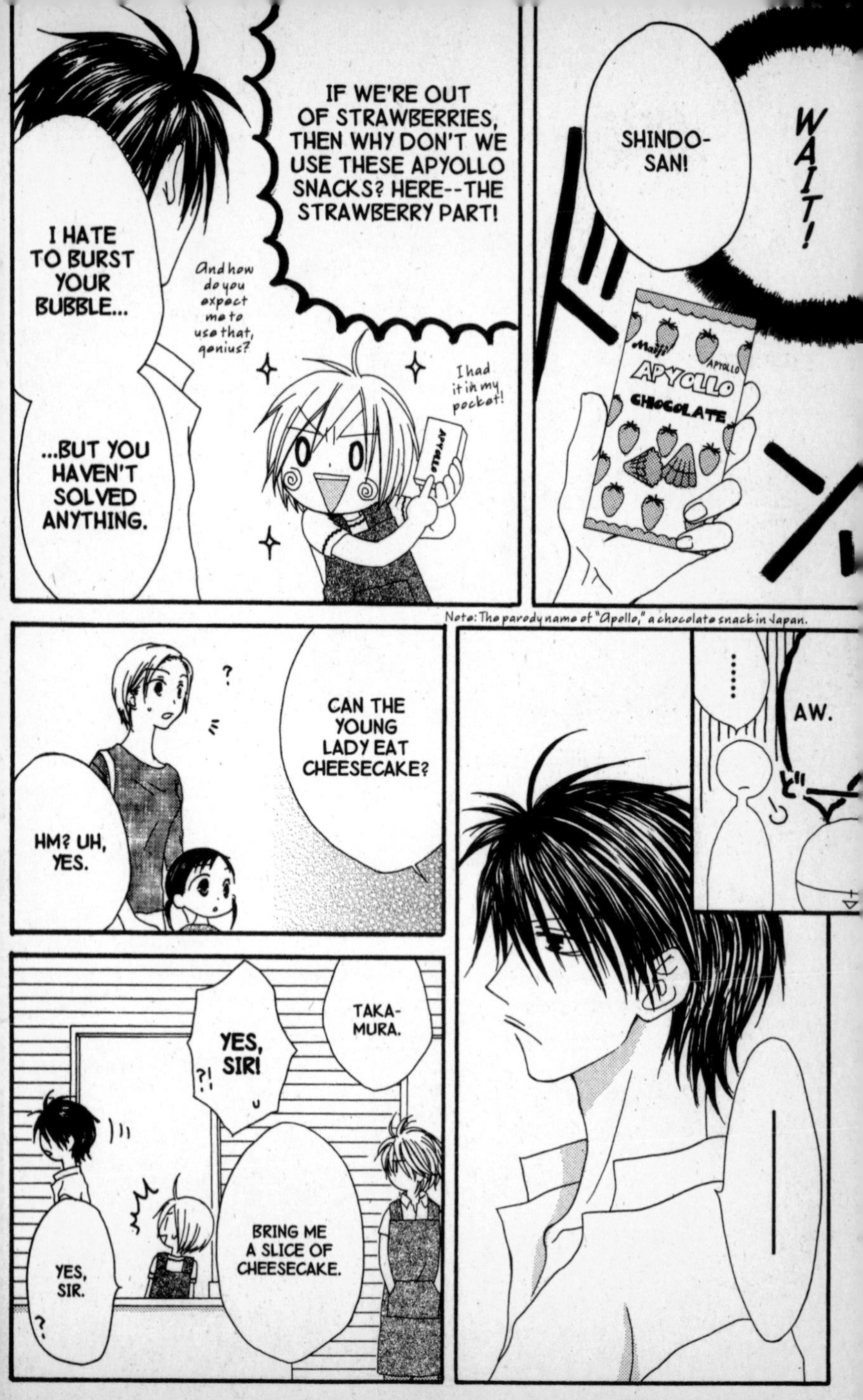
WAIT!
SHINDO-SAN!
Meiji
APYOLLO
APYOLLO
CHOCOLATE
IF WE'RE OUT OF STRAWBERRIES, THEN WHY DON'T WE USE THESE APYOLLO SNACKS? HERE--THE STRAWBERRY PART!
I had it in my pocket!
APYOLLO
And how do you expect me to use that, genius?
I HATE TO BURST YOUR BUBBLE...
...BUT YOU HAVEN'T SOLVED ANYTHING.
Note: The parody name of "Apollo," a chocolate snack in Japan.
......
AW.
CAN THE YOUNG LADY EAT CHEESECAKE?
?
HM? UH, YES.
TAKA-MURA.
YES, SIR!
?!
BRING ME A SLICE OF CHEESECAKE.
YES, SIR.
?

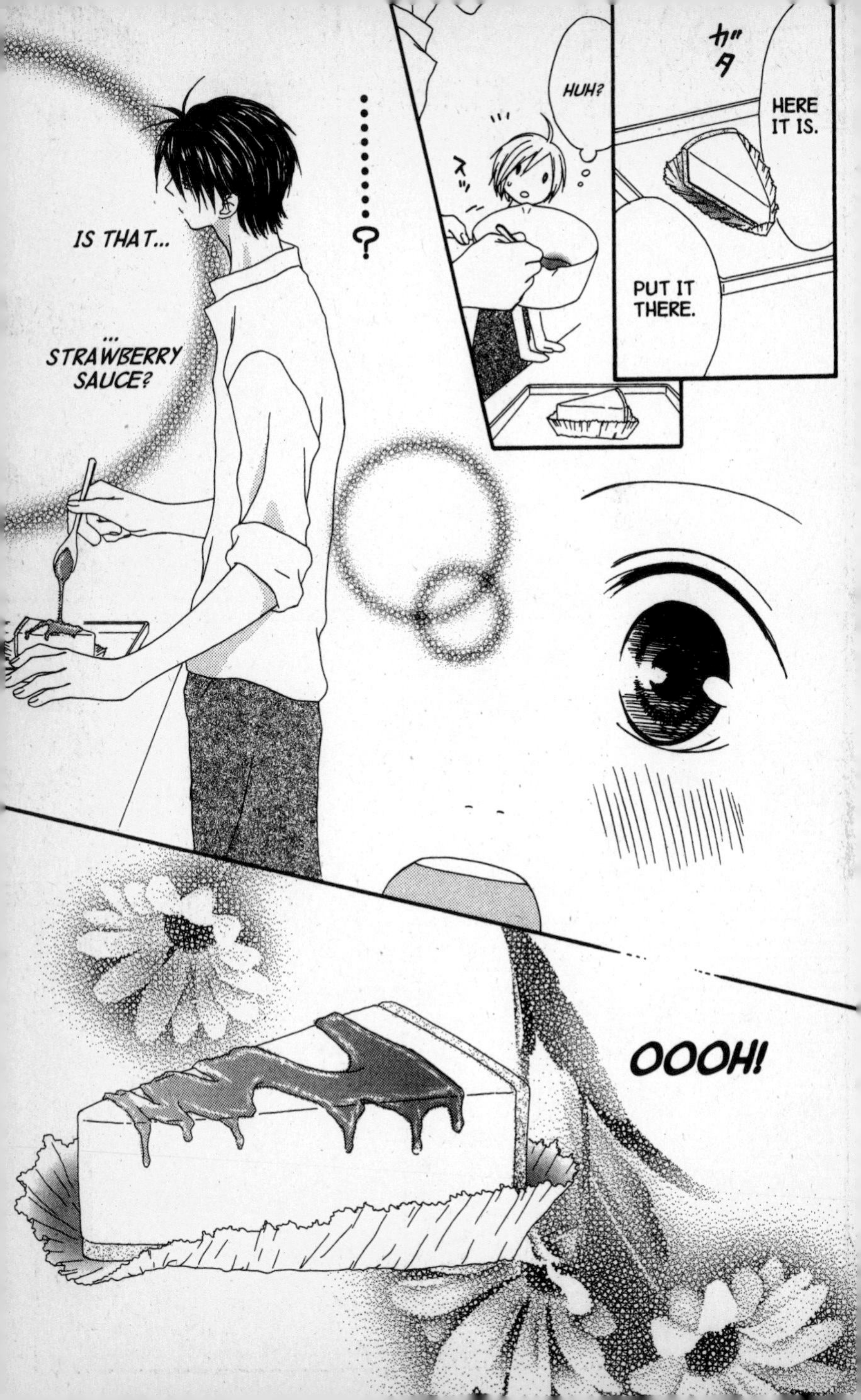
ガタ
HERE IT IS.
PUT IT THERE.
HUH?
スッ
......?
IS THAT...
... STRAWBERRY SAUCE?
OOOH!

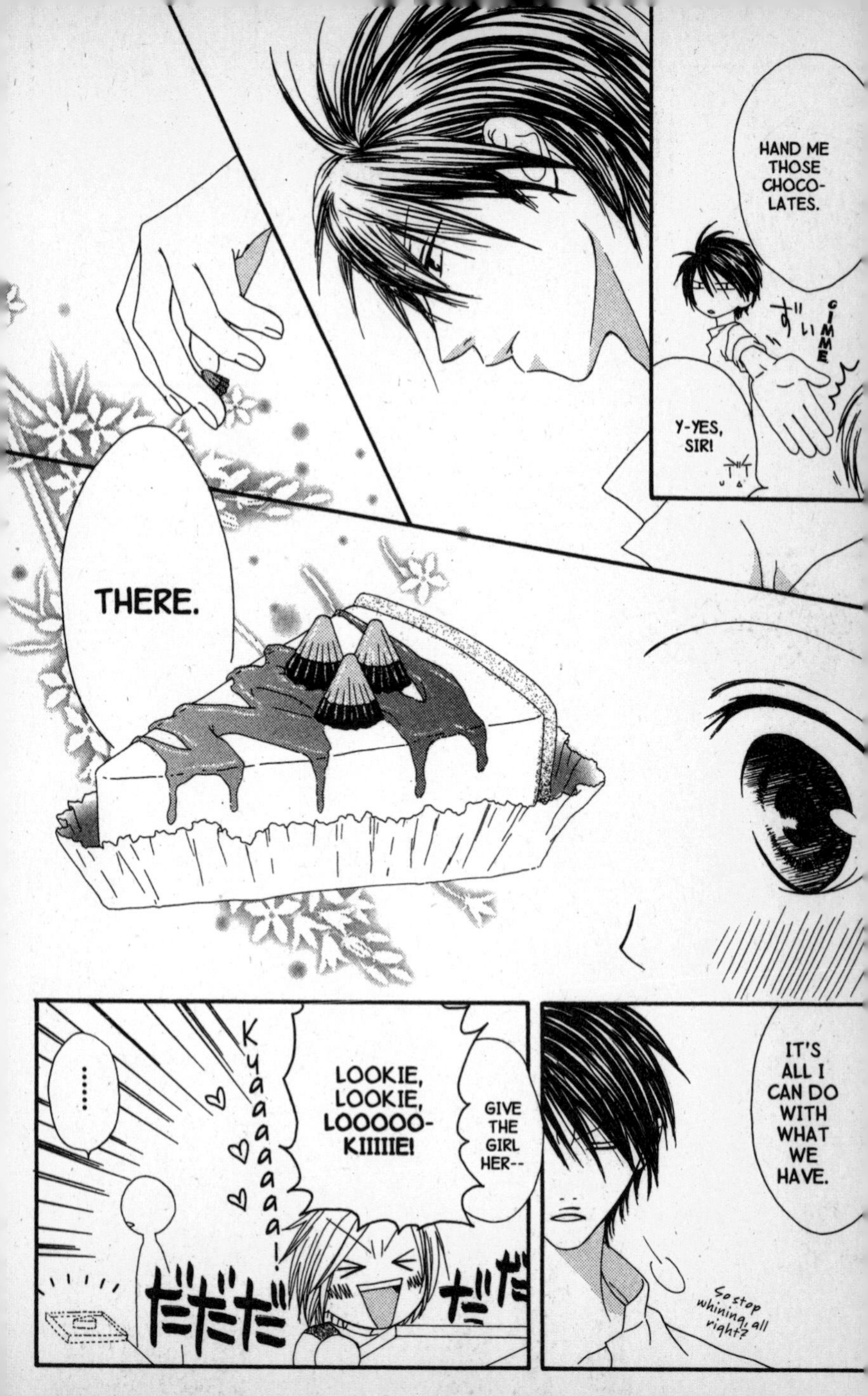
HAND ME THOSE CHOCO-LATES.
ずい
GIMME
Y-YES, SIR!
THERE.
IT'S ALL I CAN DO WITH WHAT WE HAVE.
So stop whining, all right?
GIVE THE GIRL HER--
LOOKIE, LOOKIE, LOOOOO-KIIIIIE!
Kyaaaaaaaaa!
......
だだだ
だだ

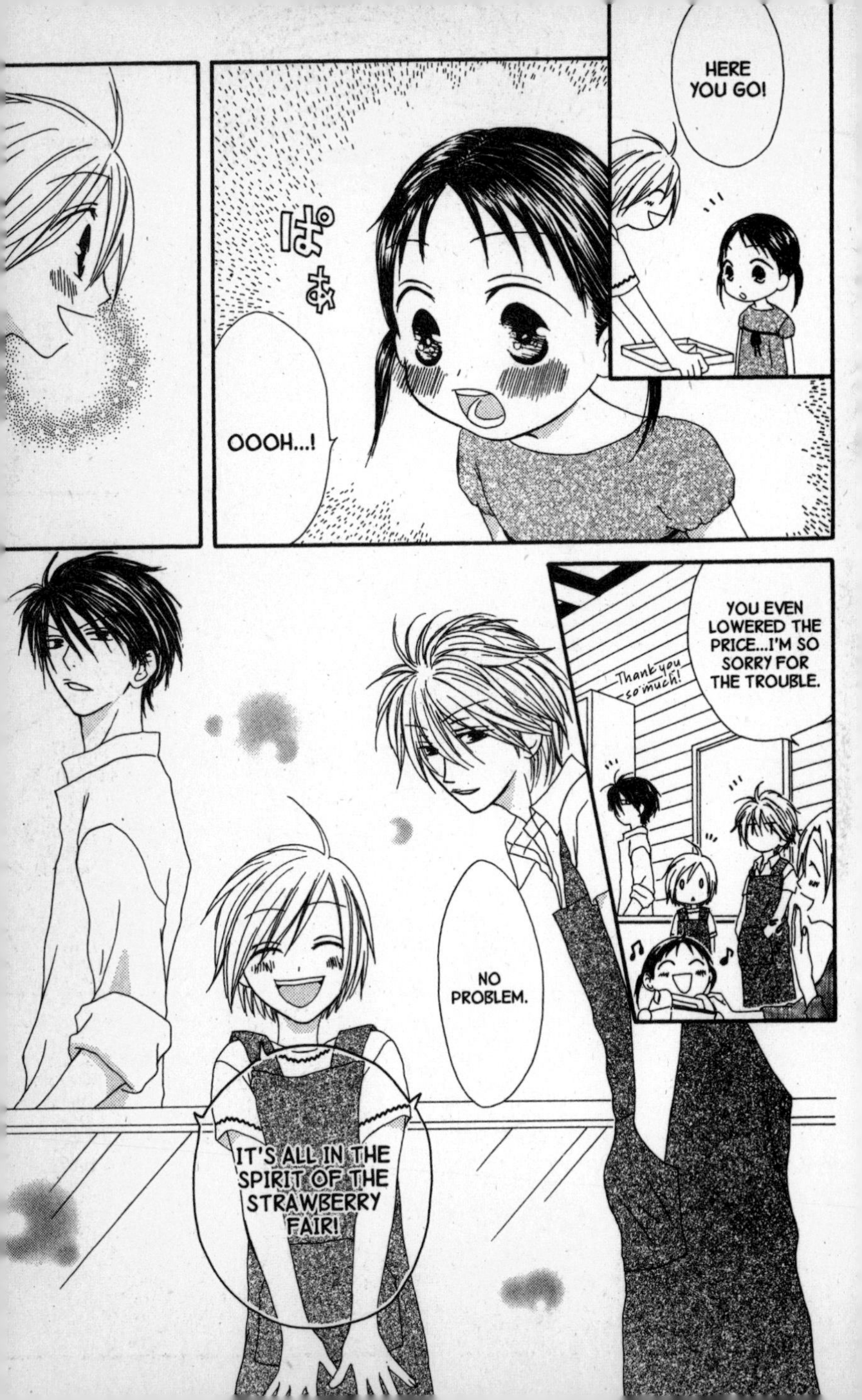
HERE YOU GO!
ぱぁ
OOOH...!
YOU EVEN LOWERED THE PRICE...I'M SO SORRY FOR THE TROUBLE.
Thank you so much!
NO PROBLEM.
IT'S ALL IN THE SPIRIT OF THE STRAWBERRY FAIR!

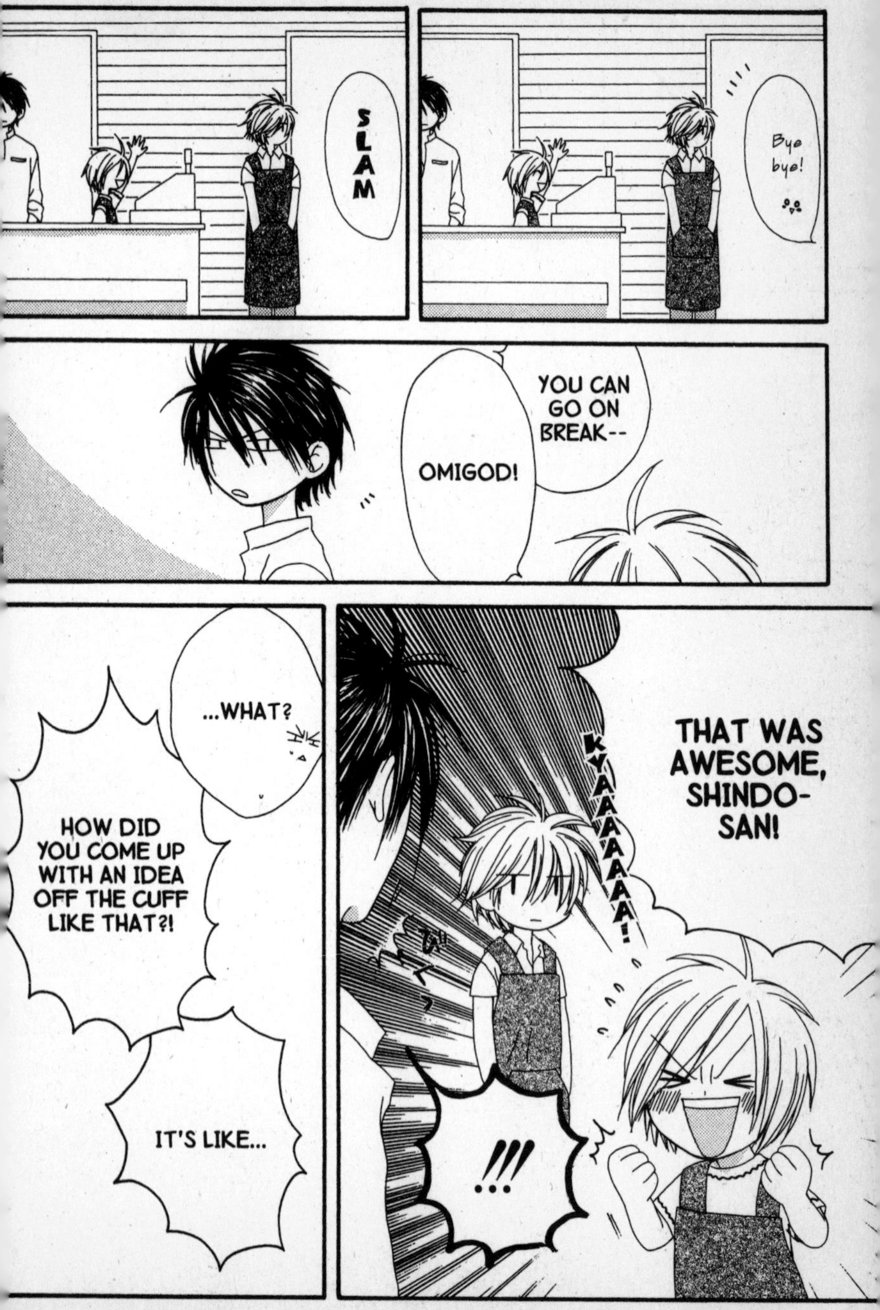
Bye bye!
SLAM
YOU CAN GO ON BREAK--
OMIGOD!
THAT WAS AWESOME, SHINDO-SAN!
KYAAAAAAA!
!!!
...WHAT?
HOW DID YOU COME UP WITH AN IDEA OFF THE CUFF LIKE THAT?!
IT'S LIKE...

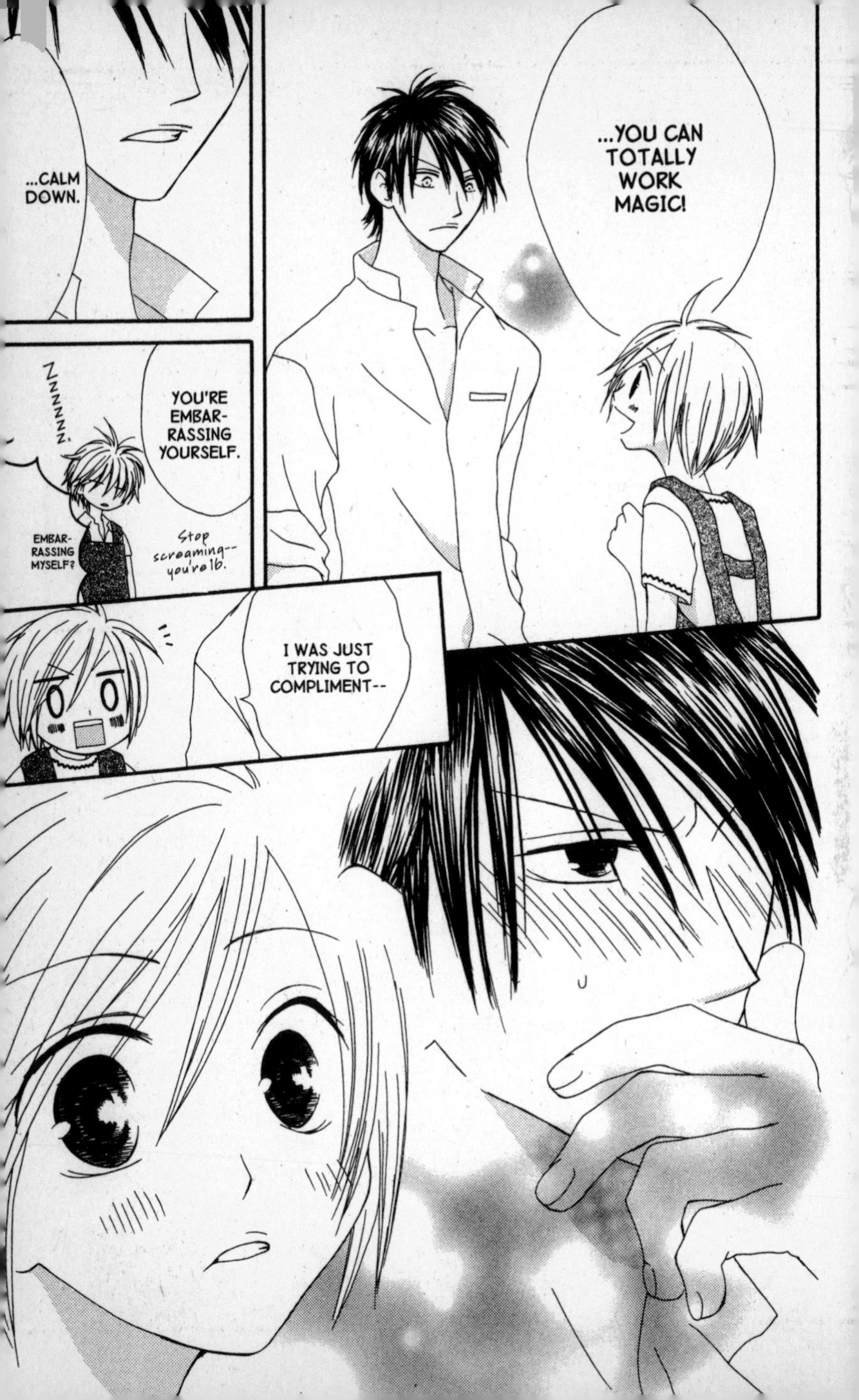
...YOU CAN TOTALLY WORK MAGIC!
...CALM DOWN.
YOU'RE EMBAR-RASSING YOURSELF.
Zzzzzz.
Stop screaming--you're 16.
EMBAR-RASSING MYSELF?
I WAS JUST TRYING TO COMPLIMENT--

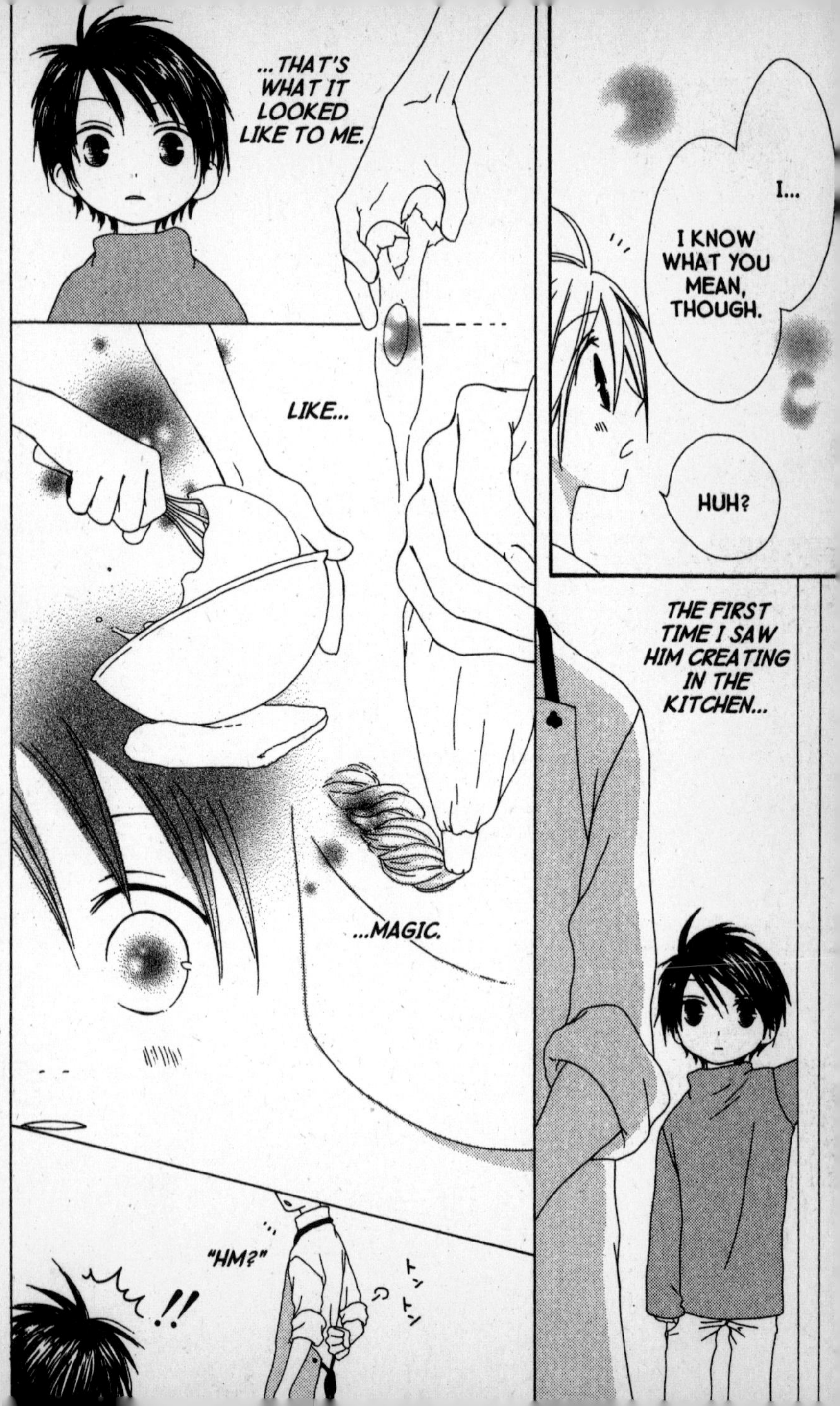
I...
I KNOW WHAT YOU MEAN, THOUGH.
HUH?
THE FIRST TIME I SAW HIM CREATING IN THE KITCHEN...
...THAT'S WHAT IT LOOKED LIKE TO ME.
LIKE...
...MAGIC.
"HM?"
!!

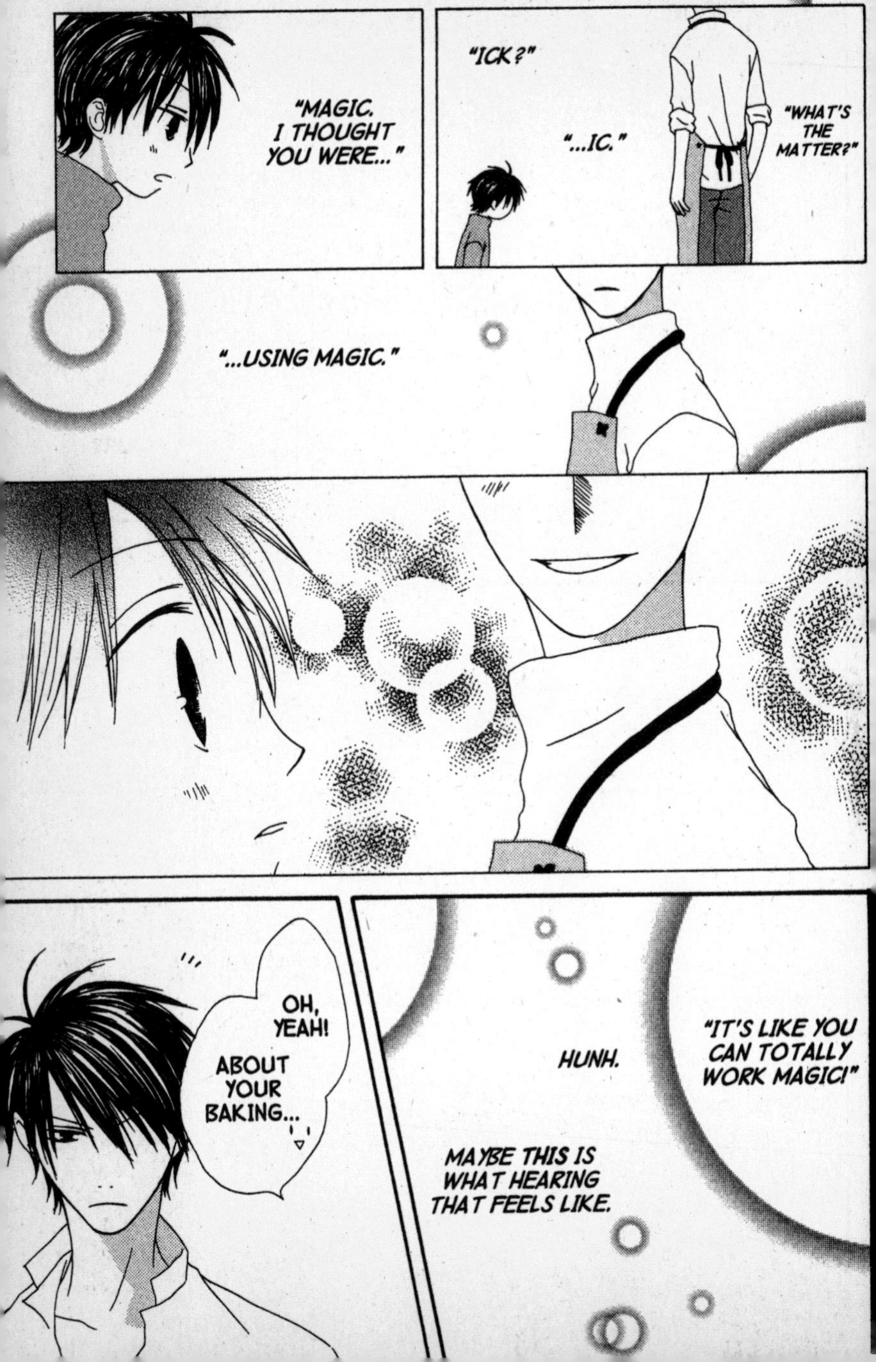

"ICK?"
"...IC."
"WHAT'S THE MATTER?"
"MAGIC. I THOUGHT YOU WERE..."
"...USING MAGIC."
"IT'S LIKE YOU CAN TOTALLY WORK MAGIC!"
HUNH.
MAYBE THIS IS WHAT HEARING THAT FEELS LIKE.
OH, YEAH! ABOUT YOUR BAKING...

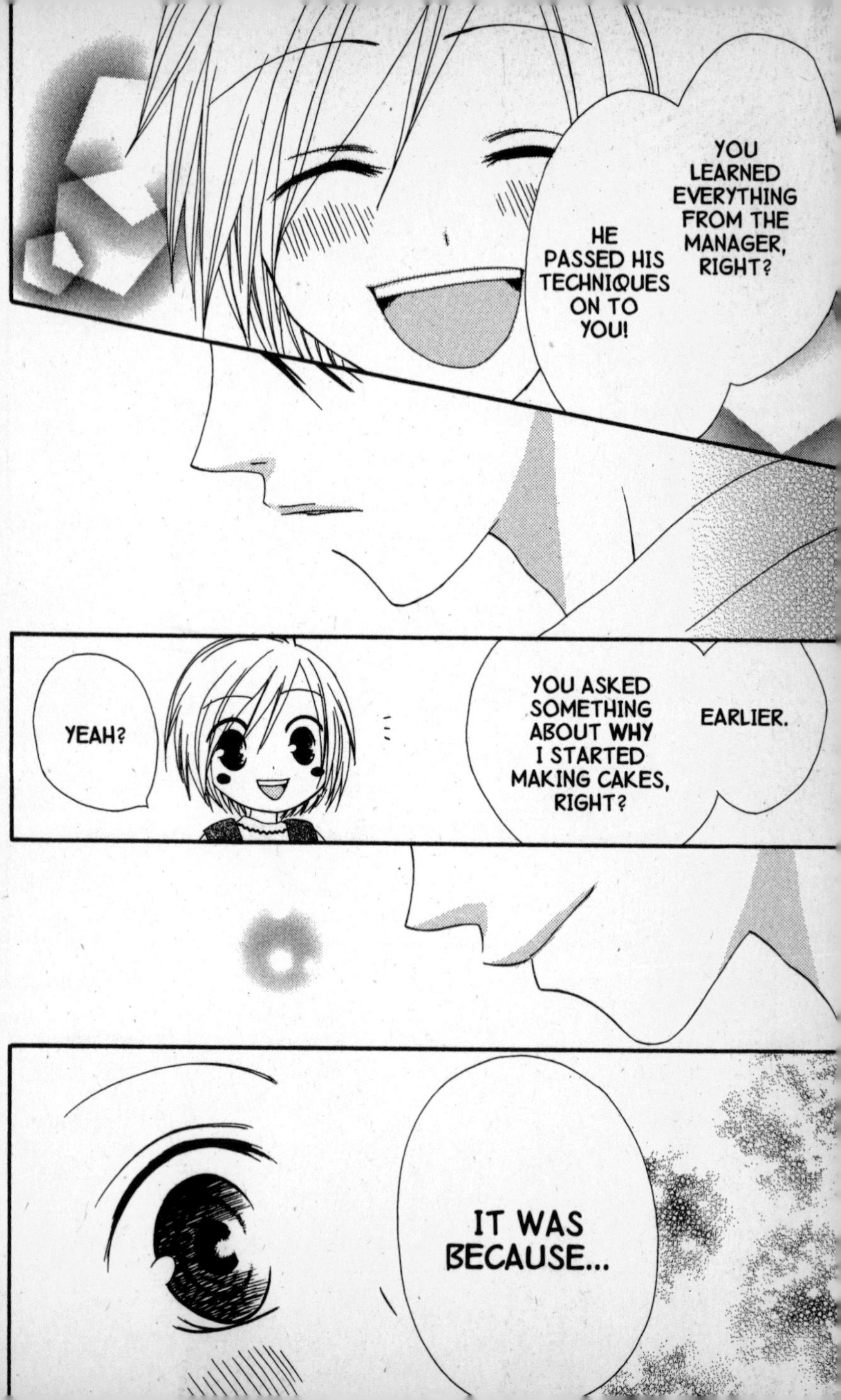
YOU LEARNED EVERYTHING FROM THE MANAGER, RIGHT?
HE PASSED HIS TECHNIQUES ON TO YOU!
EARLIER.
YOU ASKED SOMETHING ABOUT WHY I STARTED MAKING CAKES, RIGHT?
YEAH?
IT WAS BECAUSE...

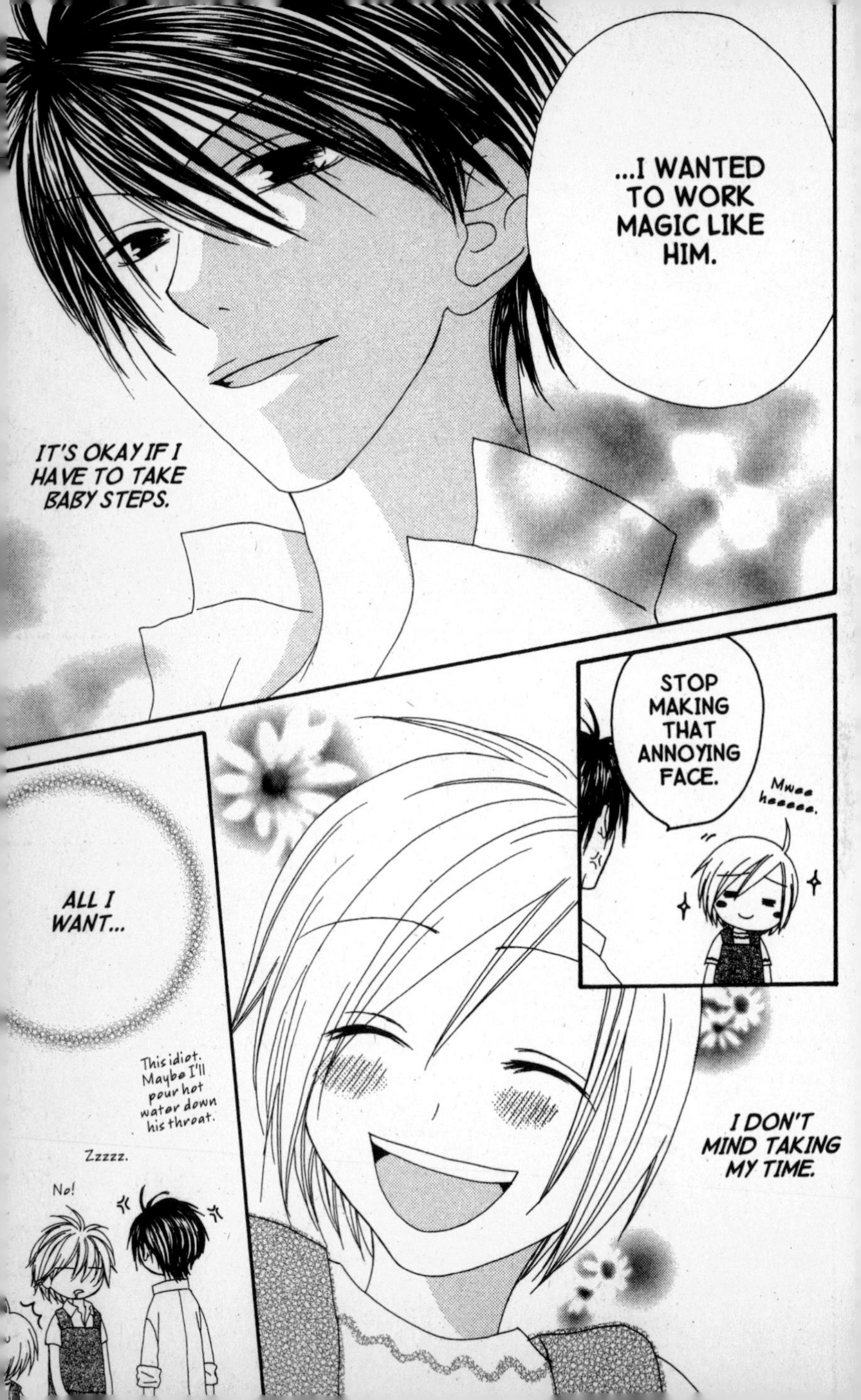
...I WANTED TO WORK MAGIC LIKE HIM.
IT'S OKAY IF I HAVE TO TAKE BABY STEPS.
STOP MAKING THAT ANNOYING FACE.
Mwee heeeee.
I DON'T MIND TAKING MY TIME.
ALL I WANT...
This idiot. Maybe I'll pour hot water down his throat.
Zzzzz.
No!

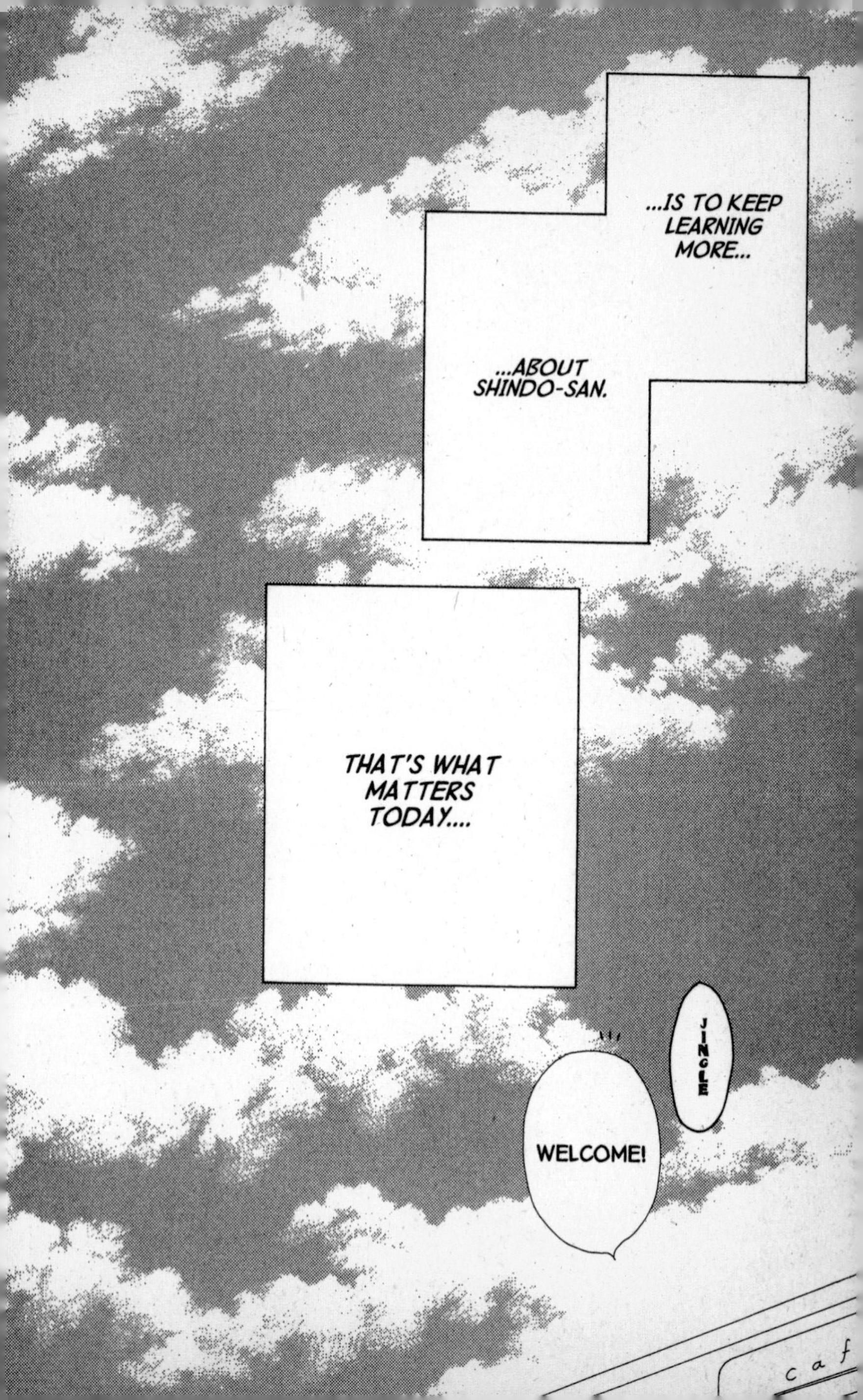
...IS TO KEEP LEARNING MORE...
...ABOUT SHINDO-SAN.
THAT'S WHAT MATTERS TODAY....
JINGLE
WELCOME!

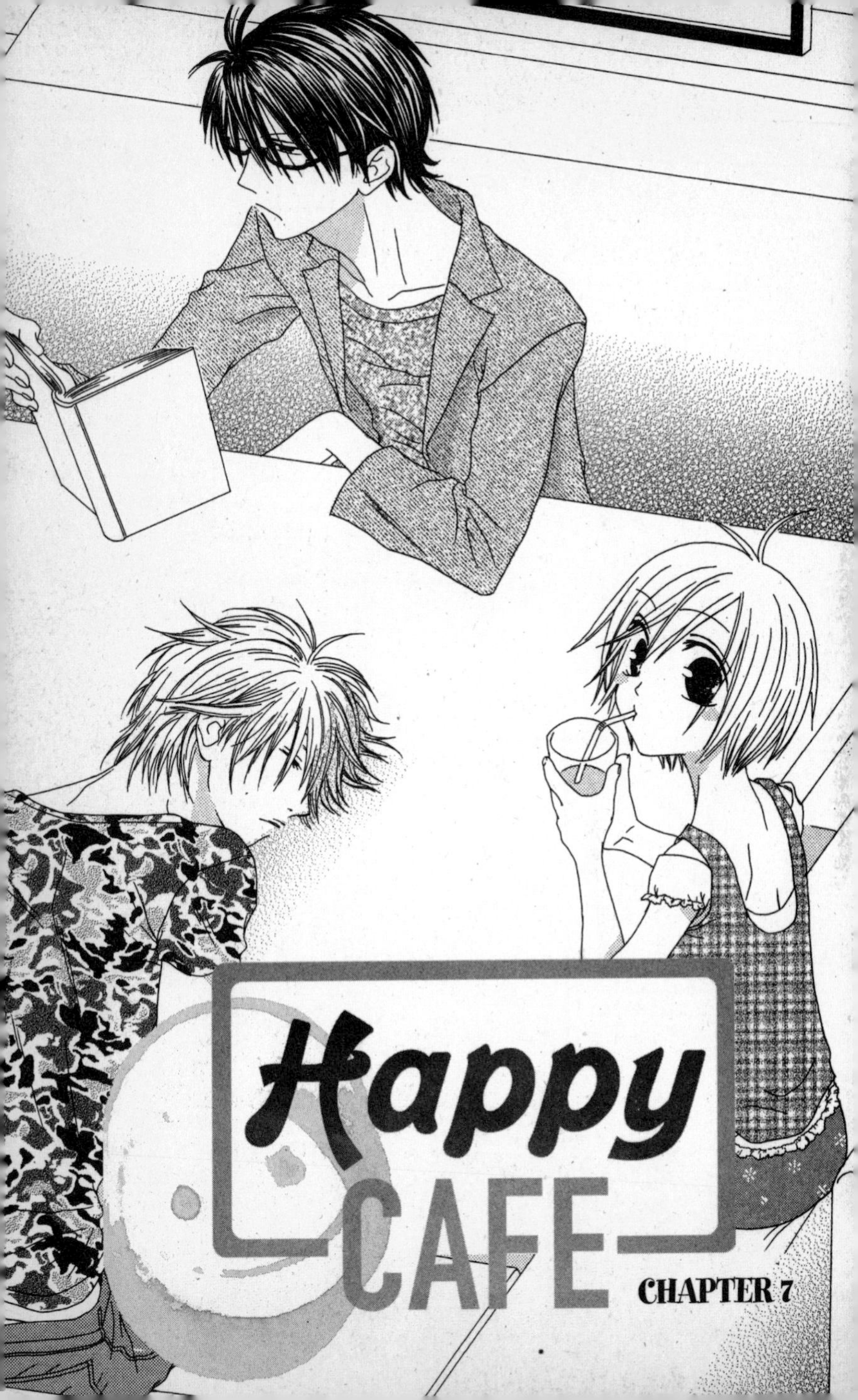
Happy
CAFE
CHAPTER 7

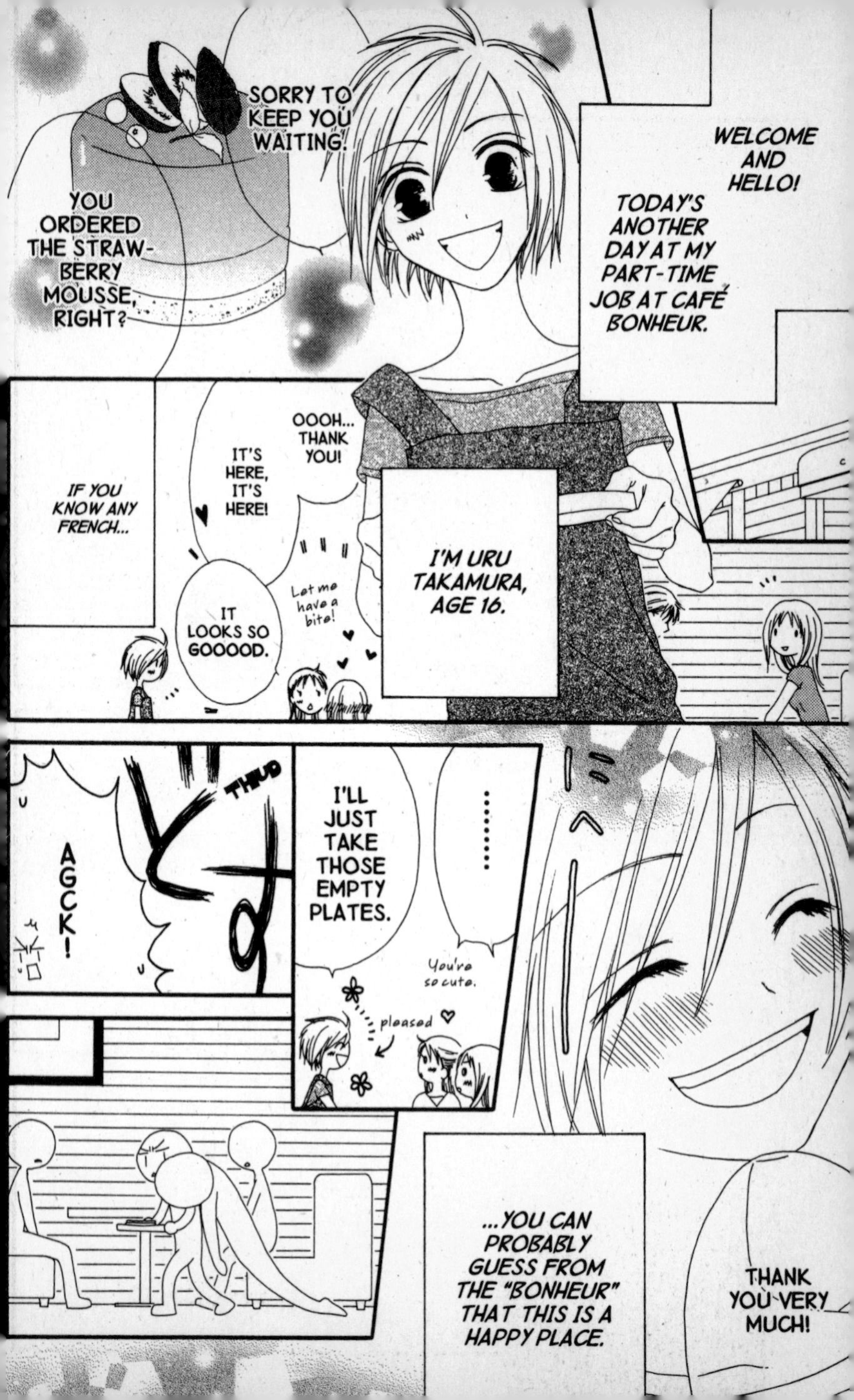

WELCOME AND HELLO!
TODAY'S ANOTHER DAY AT MY PART-TIME JOB AT CAFÉ BONHEUR.
SORRY TO KEEP YOU WAITING!
YOU ORDERED THE STRAW-BERRY MOUSSE, RIGHT?
I'M URU TAKAMURA, AGE 16.
OOOH... THANK YOU!
IT'S HERE, IT'S HERE!
Let me have a bite!
IT LOOKS SO GOOOOD.
IF YOU KNOW ANY FRENCH...
THANK YOU VERY MUCH!
...YOU CAN PROBABLY GUESS FROM THE "BONHEUR" THAT THIS IS A HAPPY PLACE.
....
I'LL JUST TAKE THOSE EMPTY PLATES.
You're so cute.
pleased
THUD
AGCK!

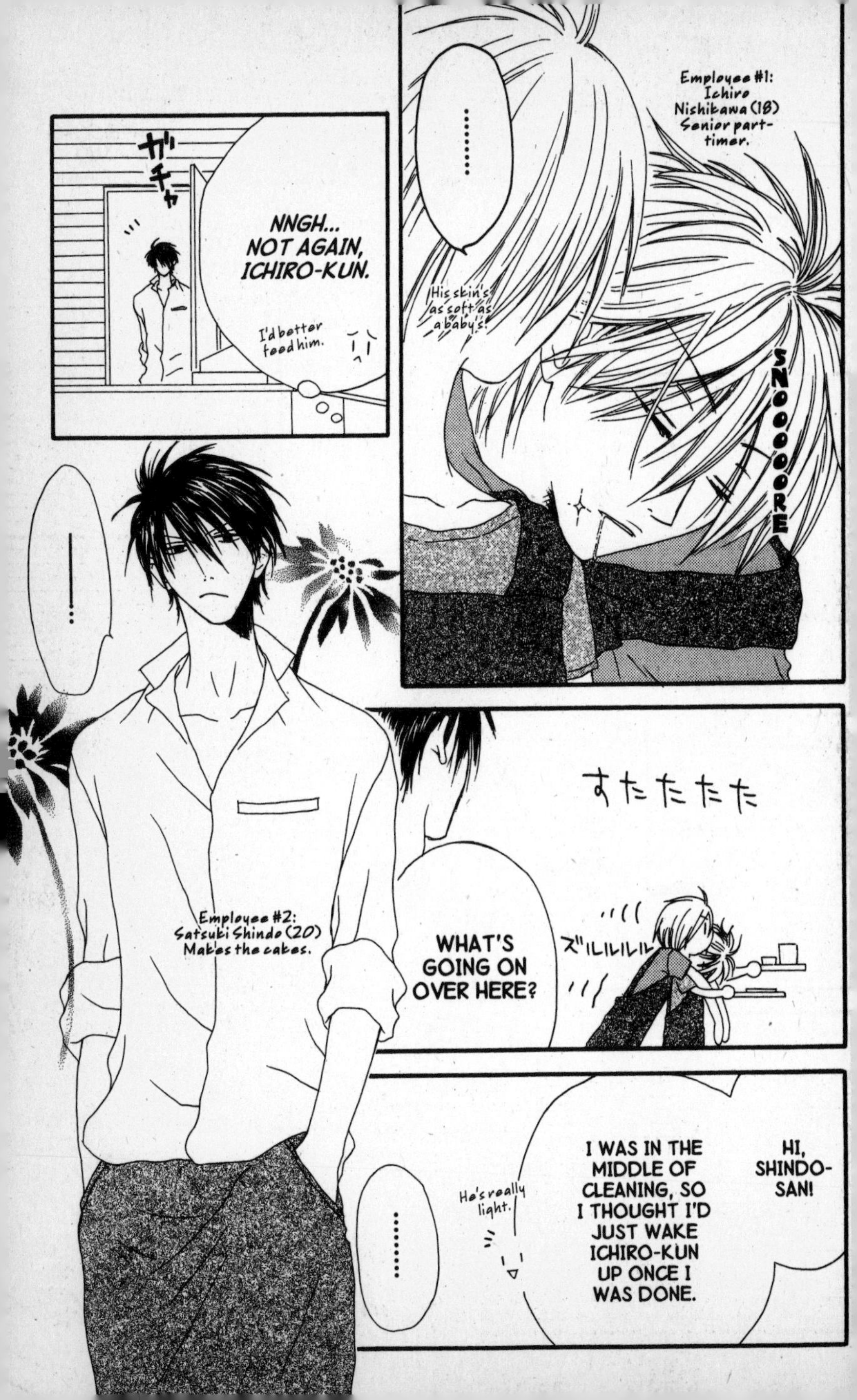

......
Employee #1: Ichiro Nishikawa (18) Senior part-timer.
His skin's as soft as a baby's.
SNOOOOORE
ガチャ
NNGH... NOT AGAIN, ICHIRO-KUN.
I'd better feed him.
すたたたた
WHAT'S GOING ON OVER HERE?
ズルルルル
HI, SHINDO-SAN!
I WAS IN THE MIDDLE OF CLEANING, SO I THOUGHT I'D JUST WAKE ICHIRO-KUN UP ONCE I WAS DONE.
He's really light.
......
—...
Employee #2: Satsuki Shindo (20) Makes the cakes.

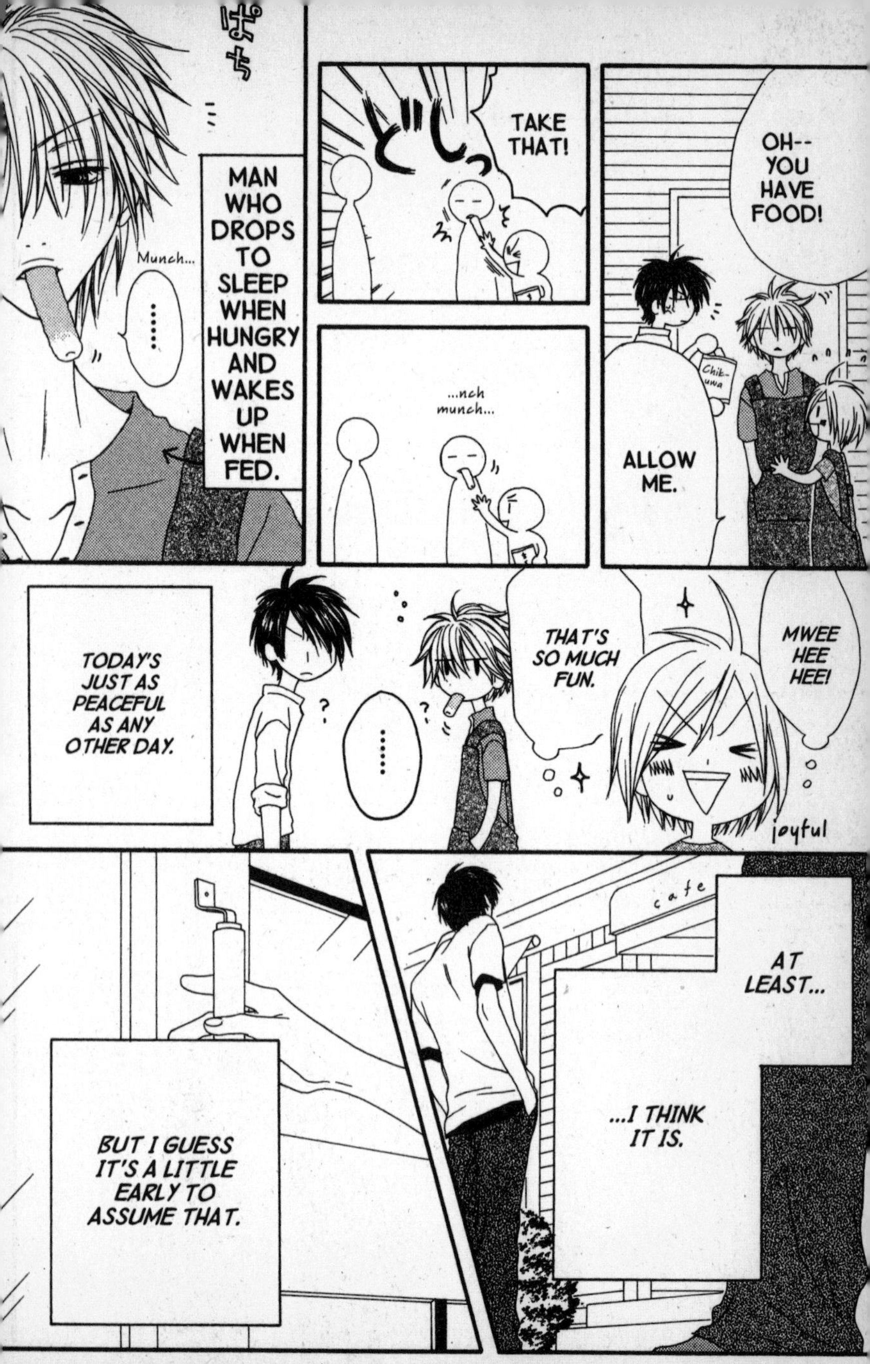
OH-- YOU HAVE FOOD!
Chik-uwa
ALLOW ME.
どしっ
TAKE THAT!
...nch munch...
ぱち
MAN WHO DROPS TO SLEEP WHEN HUNGRY AND WAKES UP WHEN FED.
Munch...
......
MWEE HEE HEE!
THAT'S SO MUCH FUN.
joyful
......
TODAY'S JUST AS PEACEFUL AS ANY OTHER DAY.
AT LEAST...
...I THINK IT IS.
cafe
BUT I GUESS IT'S A LITTLE EARLY TO ASSUME THAT.

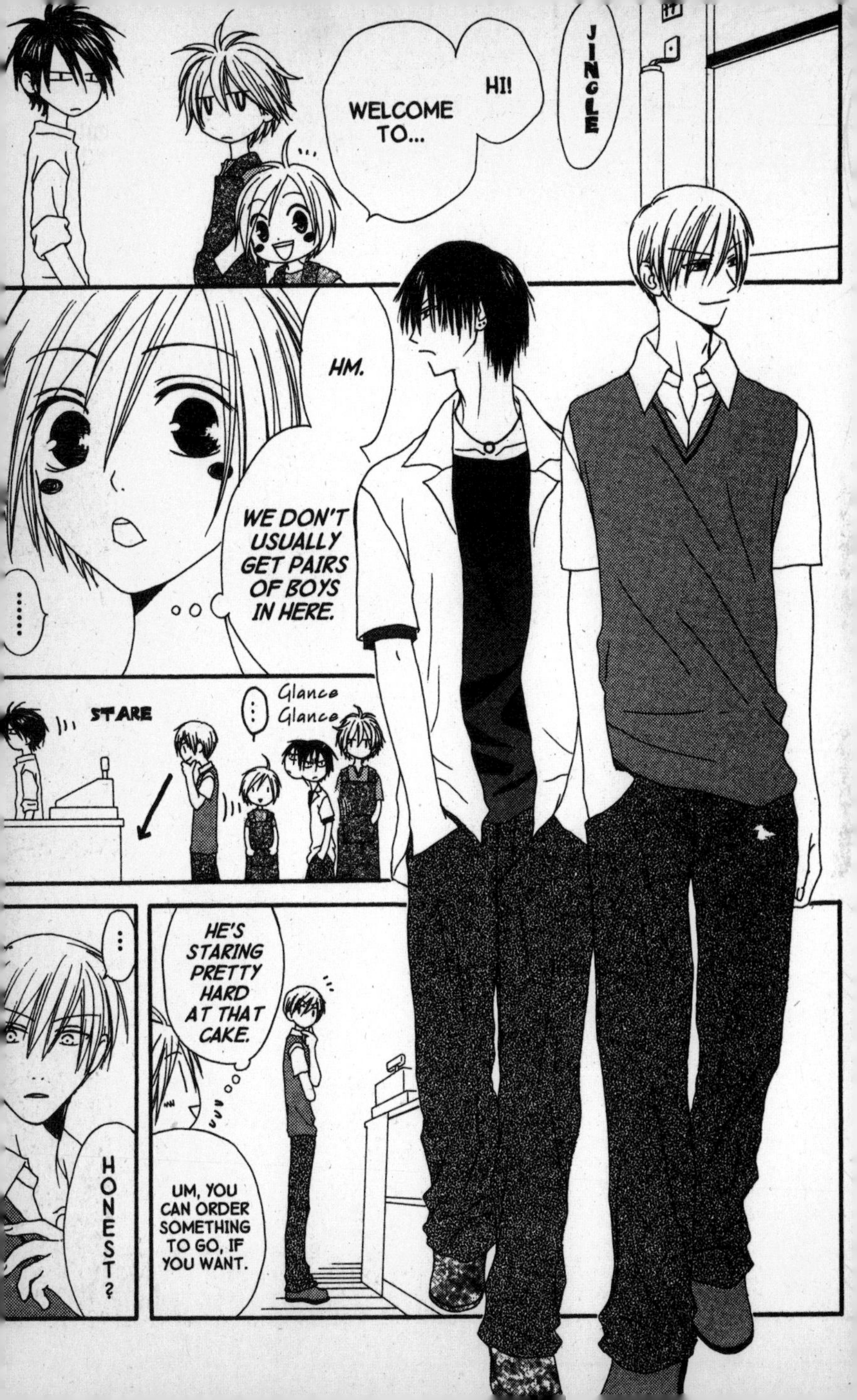
JINGLE
HI! WELCOME TO...
...
HM.
WE DON'T USUALLY GET PAIRS OF BOYS IN HERE.
......
Glance Glance
...
STARE
HE'S STARING PRETTY HARD AT THAT CAKE.
UM, YOU CAN ORDER SOMETHING TO GO, IF YOU WANT.
...
HONEST?

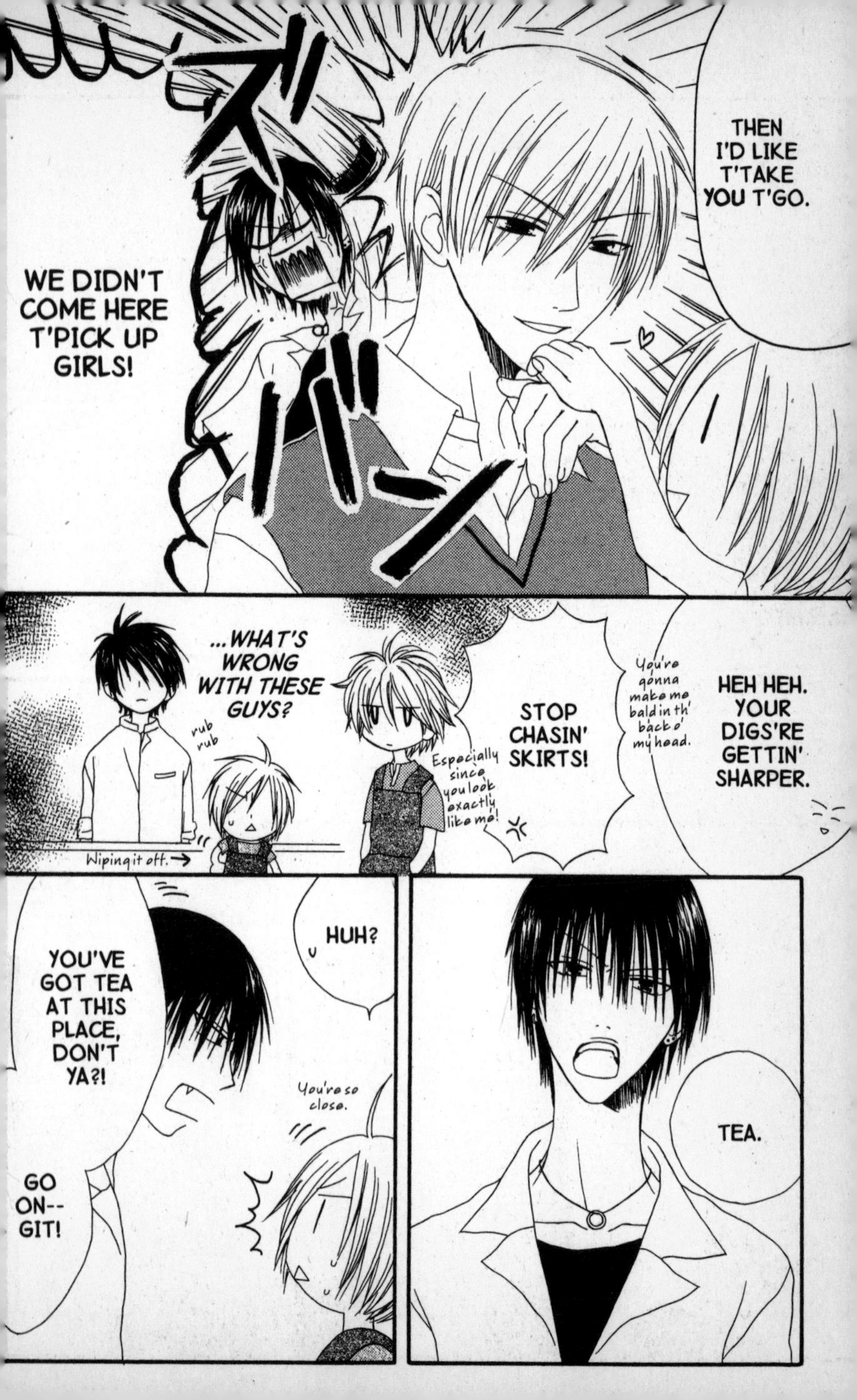
THEN I'D LIKE T'TAKE YOU T'GO.
WE DIDN'T COME HERE T'PICK UP GIRLS!
HEH HEH. YOUR DIGS'RE GETTIN' SHARPER.
You're gonna make me bald in th' back o' my head.
STOP CHASIN' SKIRTS!
Especially since you look exactly like me!
...WHAT'S WRONG WITH THESE GUYS?
rub rub
Wiping it off.
TEA.
HUH?
YOU'VE GOT TEA AT THIS PLACE, DON'T YA?!
You're so close.
GO ON-- GIT!

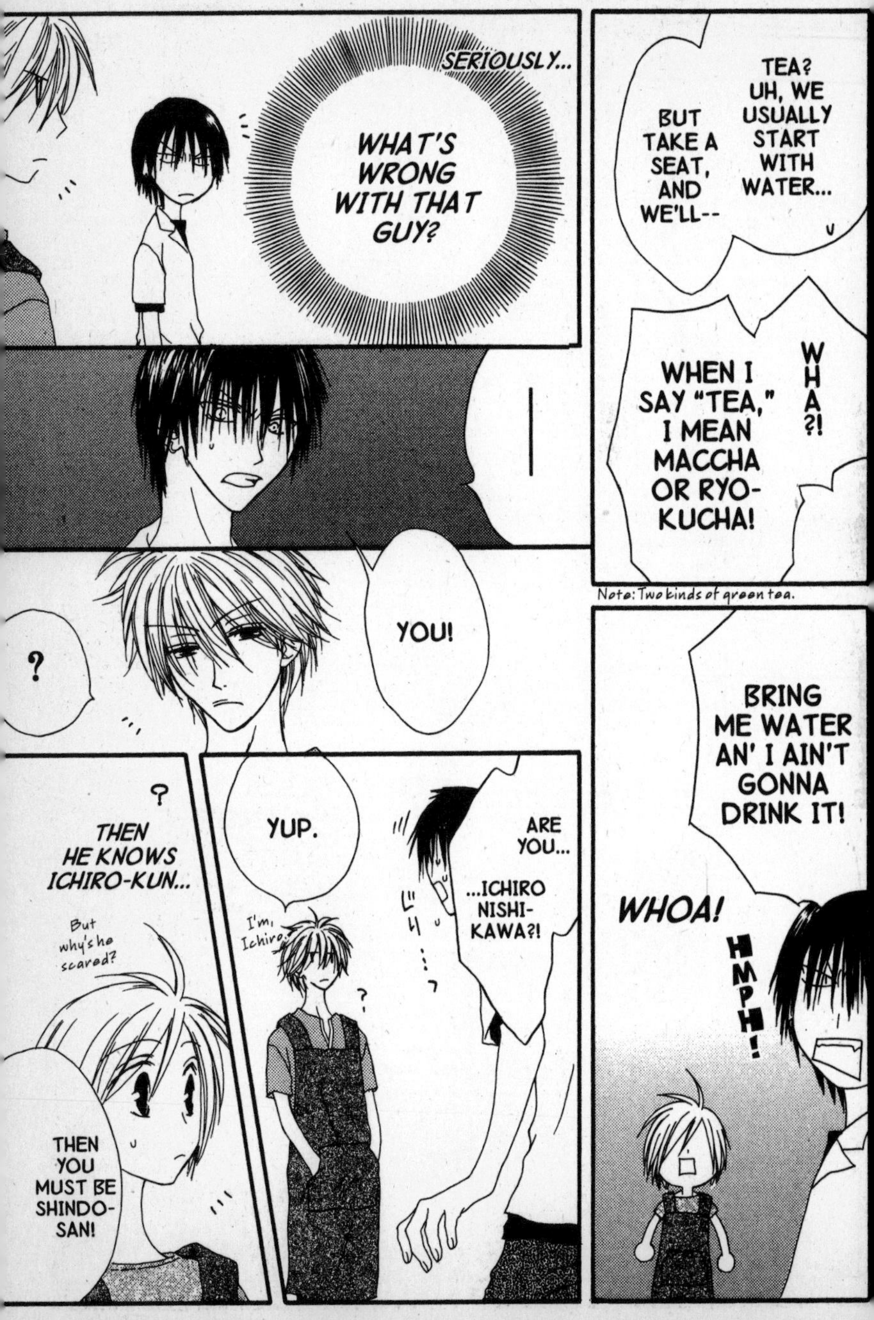
TEA? UH, WE USUALLY START WITH WATER...
BUT TAKE A SEAT, AND WE'LL--
WHA?!
WHEN I SAY "TEA," I MEAN MACCHA OR RYOKUCHA!
Note: Two kinds of green tea.
BRING ME WATER AN' I AIN'T GONNA DRINK IT!
WHOA!
HMPH!
SERIOUSLY...
WHAT'S WRONG WITH THAT GUY?
YOU!
?
ARE YOU...
...ICHIRO NISHIKAWA?!
YUP.
I'm Ichiro.
?
?
THEN HE KNOWS ICHIRO-KUN...
But why's he scared?
THEN YOU MUST BE SHINDO-SAN!

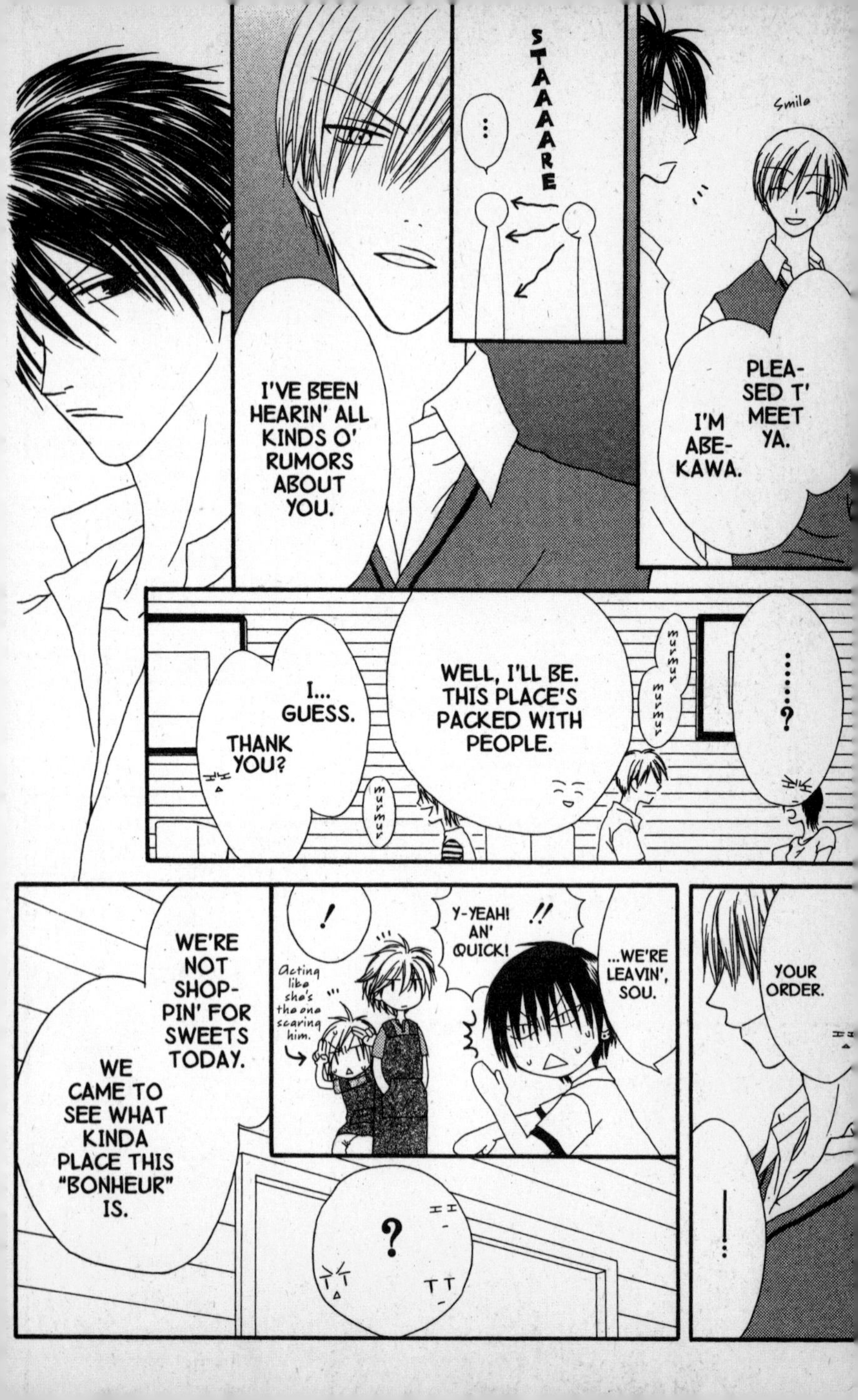
Smile
...
PLEA-SED T' MEET YA.
I'M ABE-KAWA.
STAAAAARE
...
I'VE BEEN HEARIN' ALL KINDS O' RUMORS ABOUT YOU.
......?
murmur murmur
WELL, I'LL BE. THIS PLACE'S PACKED WITH PEOPLE.
murmur
I... GUESS.
THANK YOU?
YOUR ORDER.
...!
...WE'RE LEAVIN', SOU.
Y-YEAH! AN' QUICK!
!!
!
Acting like she's the one scaring him.
WE'RE NOT SHOP-PIN' FOR SWEETS TODAY.
WE CAME TO SEE WHAT KINDA PLACE THIS "BONHEUR" IS.
?

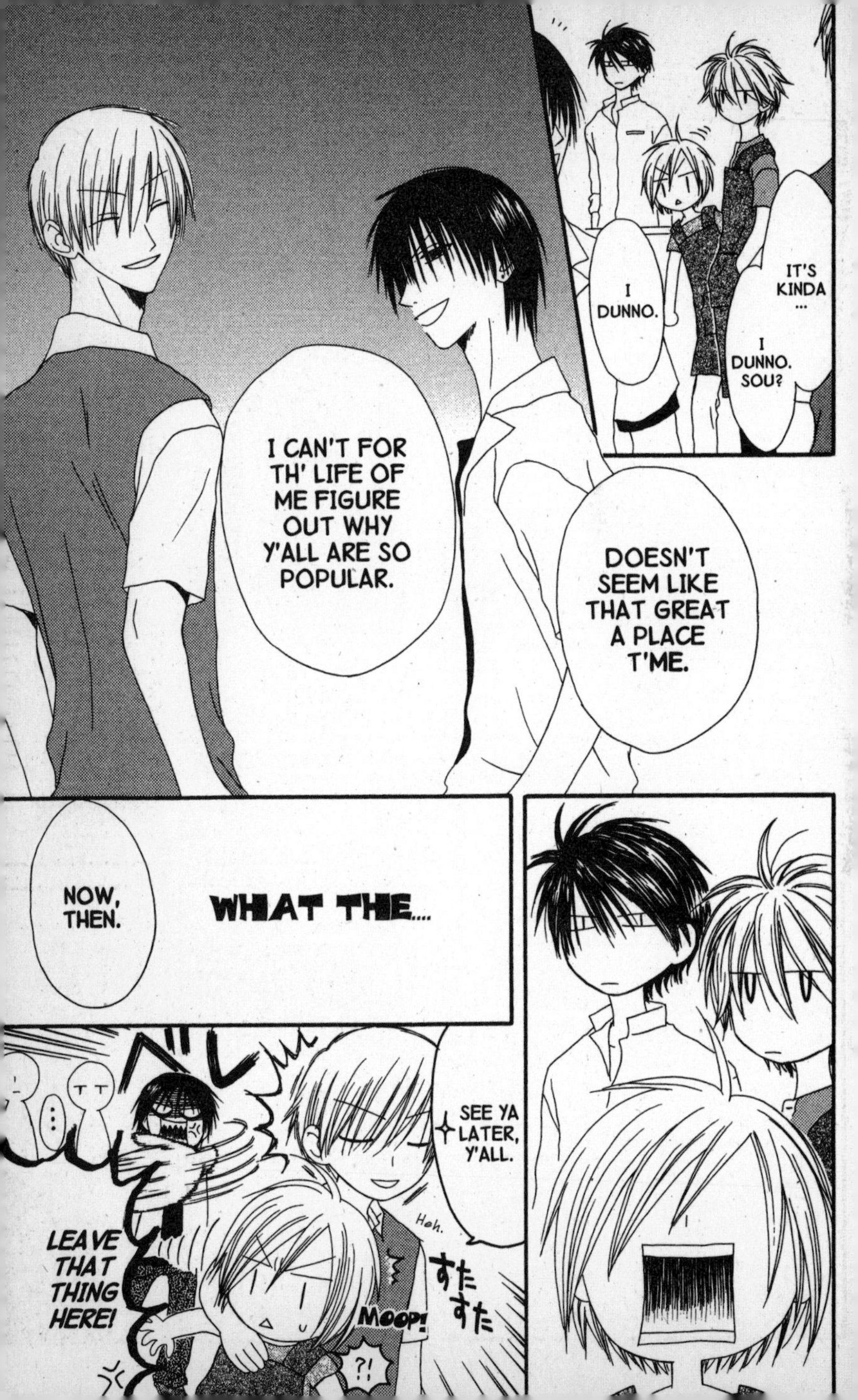
IT'S KINDA ...
I DUNNO. SOU?
I DUNNO.
I CAN'T FOR TH' LIFE OF ME FIGURE OUT WHY Y'ALL ARE SO POPULAR.
DOESN'T SEEM LIKE THAT GREAT A PLACE T'ME.
WHAT THE...
NOW, THEN.
SEE YA LATER, Y'ALL.
Heh.
すたすた
MOOP!
?!
LEAVE THAT THING HERE!

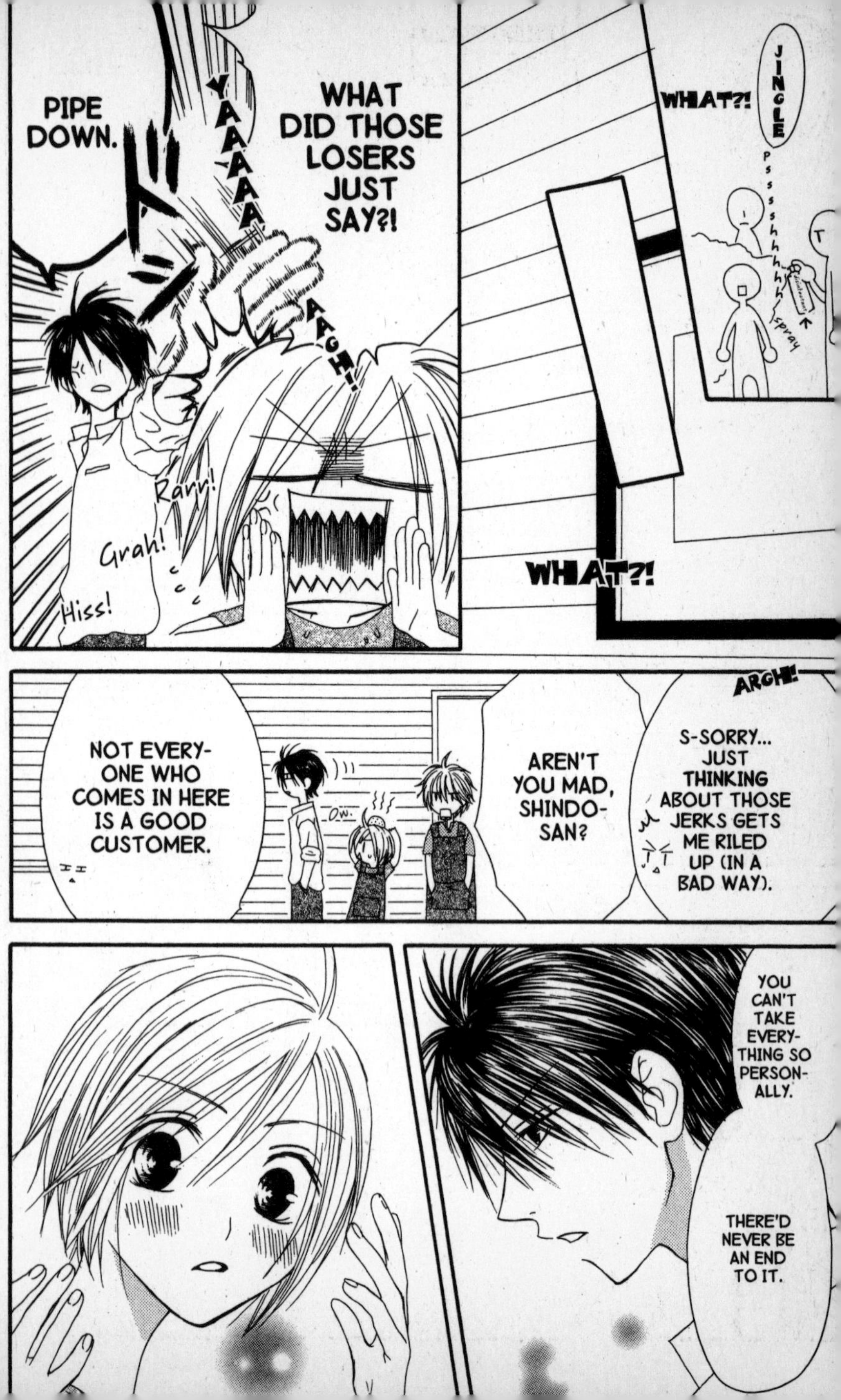
JINGLE
WHAT?!
Pssshhhhh
spray
WHAT?!
WHAT DID THOSE LOSERS JUST SAY?!
YAAAAA
PIPE DOWN.
AAGH!
Rarr!
Grah!
Hiss!
ARGH!
S-SORRY... JUST THINKING ABOUT THOSE JERKS GETS ME RILED UP (IN A BAD WAY).
AREN'T YOU MAD, SHINDO-SAN?
NOT EVERY-ONE WHO COMES IN HERE IS A GOOD CUSTOMER.
OW.
YOU CAN'T TAKE EVERY-THING SO PERSON-ALLY.
THERE'D NEVER BE AN END TO IT.

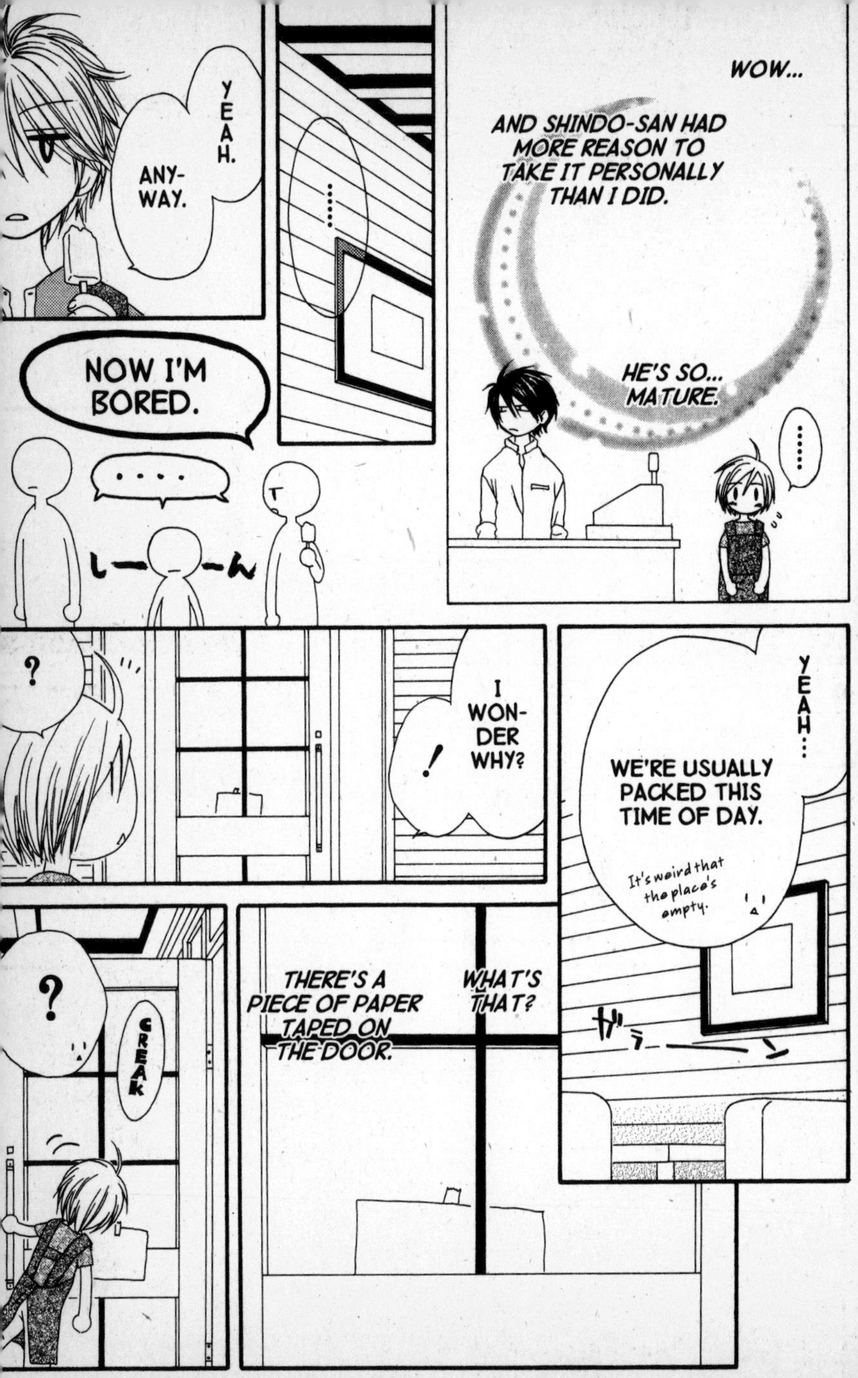
WOW...
AND SHINDO-SAN HAD MORE REASON TO TAKE IT PERSONALLY THAN I DID.
HE'S SO... MATURE.
......
......
YEAH.
ANY-WAY.
NOW I'M BORED.
....
しーーん
YEAH...
WE'RE USUALLY PACKED THIS TIME OF DAY.
It's weird that the place's empty.
ガラーッ
I WONDER WHY?
!
?
WHAT'S THAT?
THERE'S A PIECE OF PAPER TAPED ON THE DOOR.
?
CREAK

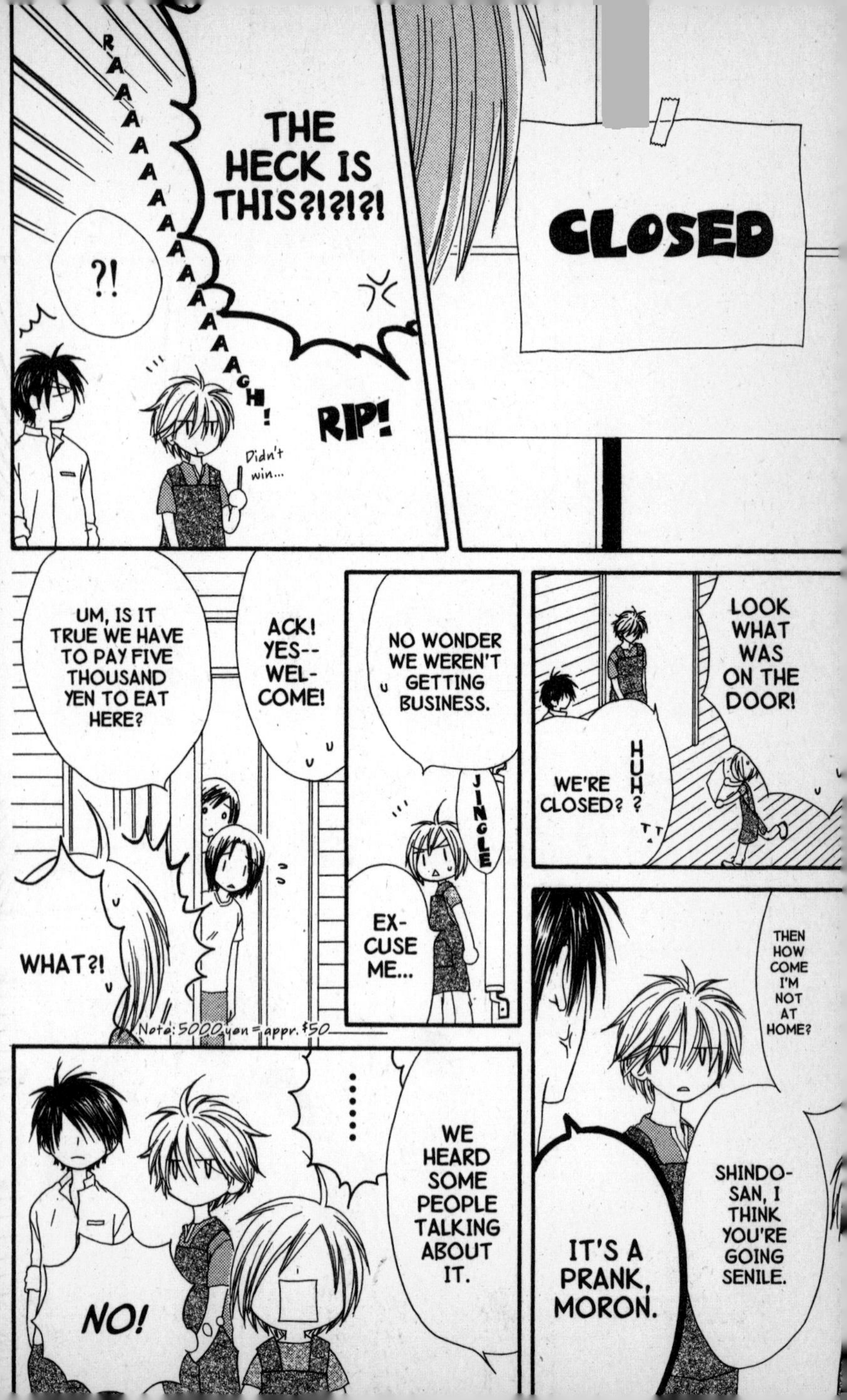
CLOSED
RAAAAAAAAAAAAAAGH!
THE HECK IS THIS?!?!?!
RIP!
?!
Didn't win...
LOOK WHAT WAS ON THE DOOR!
HUH?
WE'RE CLOSED?
THEN HOW COME I'M NOT AT HOME?
SHINDO-SAN, I THINK YOU'RE GOING SENILE.
IT'S A PRANK, MORON.
NO WONDER WE WEREN'T GETTING BUSINESS.
JINGLE
EX-CUSE ME...
ACK! YES-- WEL-COME!
UM, IS IT TRUE WE HAVE TO PAY FIVE THOUSAND YEN TO EAT HERE?
WHAT?!
Note: 5000 yen = appr. $50
......
WE HEARD SOME PEOPLE TALKING ABOUT IT.
NO!

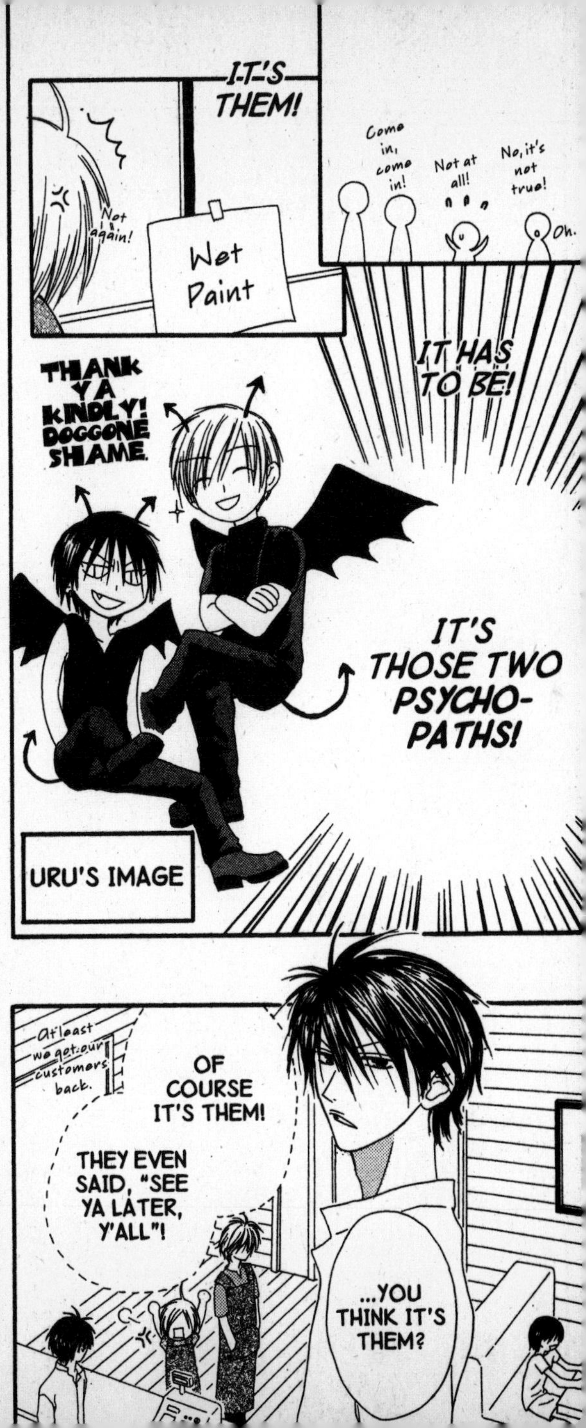
Come in, come in!
Not at all!
No, it's not true!
Oh.
IT'S THEM!
Not again!
Wet Paint
IT HAS TO BE!
IT'S THOSE TWO PSYCHOPATHS!
THANK YA KINDLY! DOGGONE SHAME.
URU'S IMAGE
...YOU THINK IT'S THEM?
OF COURSE IT'S THEM!
THEY EVEN SAID, "SEE YA LATER, Y'ALL"!
At least we got our customers back.

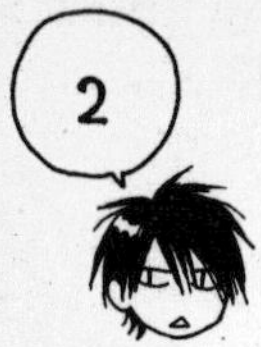
2

I haven't played any video games at all lately.

Shadow Hearts: From the New World.

I wanna play the sequel.

Johnnyyyyyy!

Well, it's my fault for working so slowly. I lose all time for games.

If I want to play, I need to work faster.

But when I'm working...

For some reason, I get really sleepy.

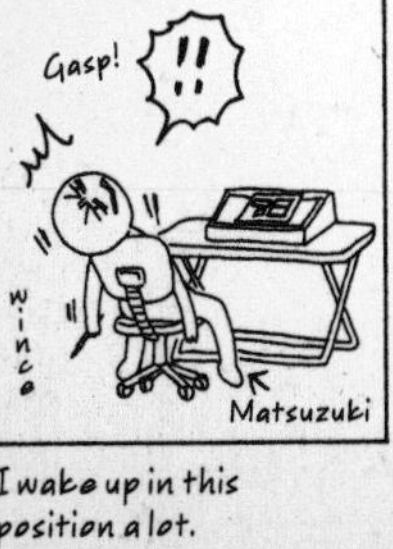
Gasp!
!!
wince
Matsuzuki

I wake up in this position a lot.

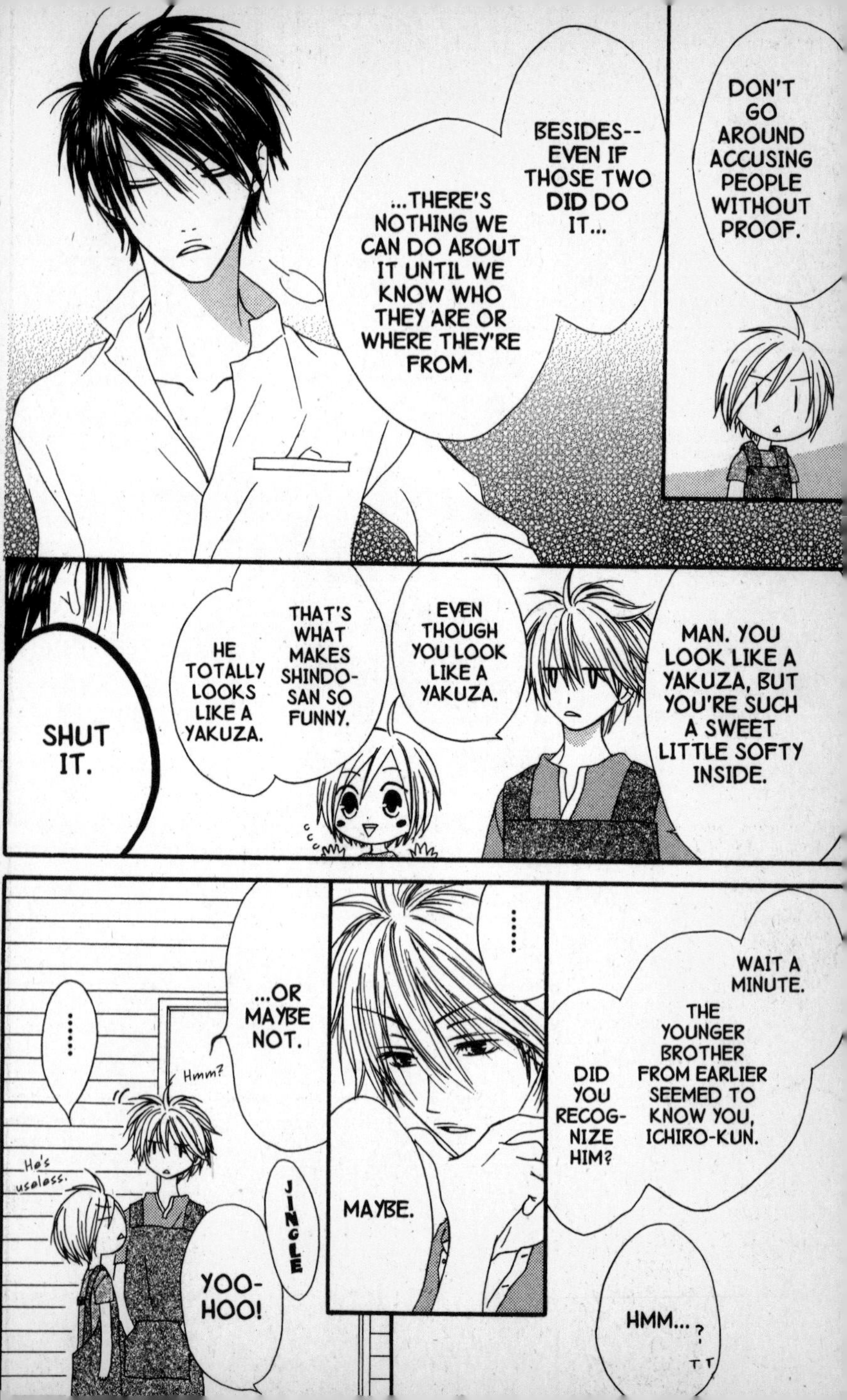

DON'T GO AROUND ACCUSING PEOPLE WITHOUT PROOF.
BESIDES-- EVEN IF THOSE TWO DID DO IT...
...THERE'S NOTHING WE CAN DO ABOUT IT UNTIL WE KNOW WHO THEY ARE OR WHERE THEY'RE FROM.
MAN. YOU LOOK LIKE A YAKUZA, BUT YOU'RE SUCH A SWEET LITTLE SOFTY INSIDE.
EVEN THOUGH YOU LOOK LIKE A YAKUZA.
THAT'S WHAT MAKES SHINDO-SAN SO FUNNY.
HE TOTALLY LOOKS LIKE A YAKUZA.
SHUT IT.
WAIT A MINUTE.
THE YOUNGER BROTHER FROM EARLIER SEEMED TO KNOW YOU, ICHIRO-KUN.
DID YOU RECOGNIZE HIM?
HMM...?
......
MAYBE.
...OR MAYBE NOT.
......
Hmm?
He's useless.
JINGLE
YOO-HOO!

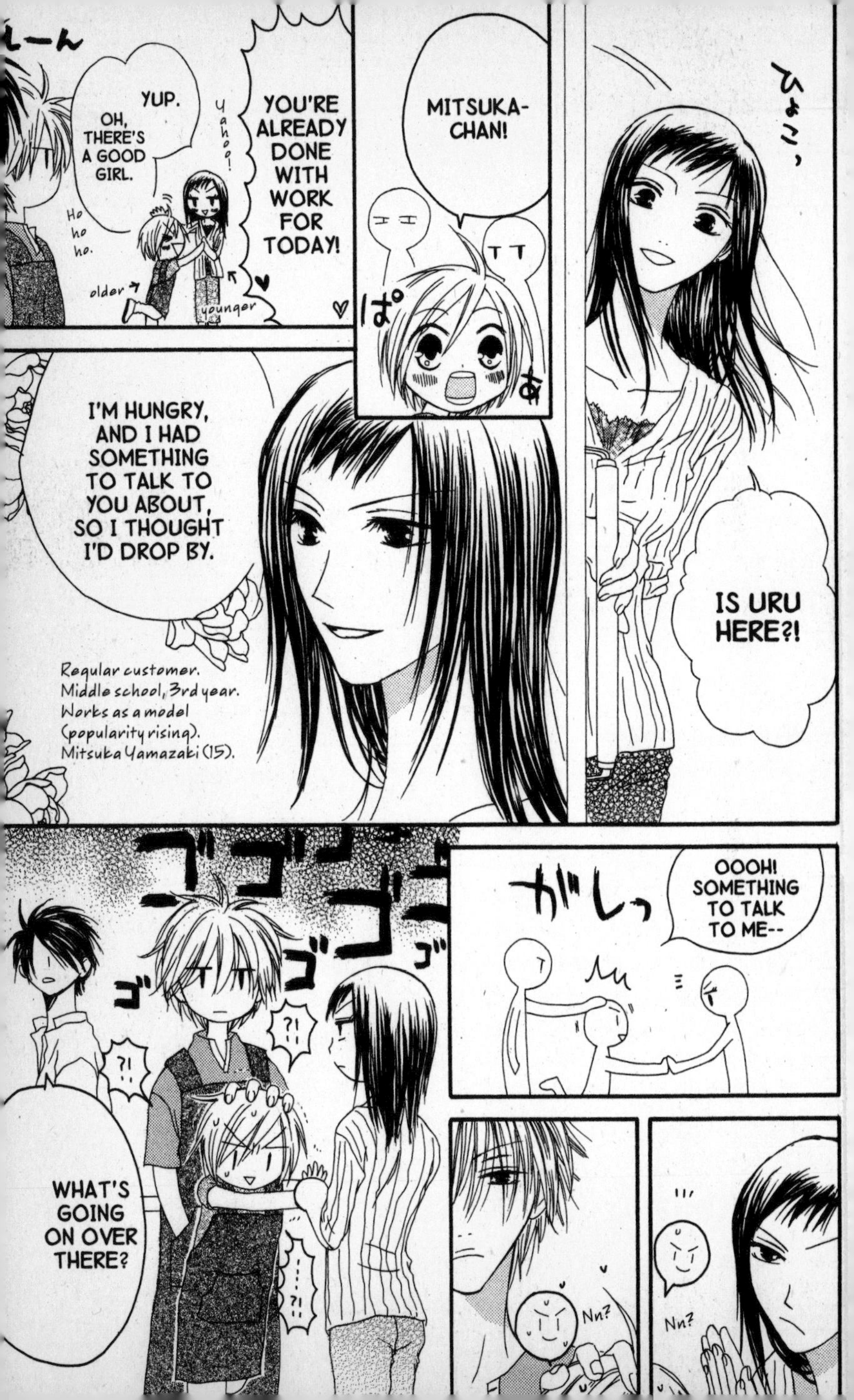

ひょこっ
IS URU HERE?!
MITSUKA-CHAN!
ぱ
あ
しーん
YOU'RE ALREADY DONE WITH WORK FOR TODAY!
YUP.
OH, THERE'S A GOOD GIRL.
Yahoo!
Ho ho ho.
older
younger
I'M HUNGRY, AND I HAD SOMETHING TO TALK TO YOU ABOUT, SO I THOUGHT I'D DROP BY.
Regular customer. Middle school, 3rd year. Works as a model (popularity rising). Mitsuka Yamazaki (15).
がしっ
OOOH! SOMETHING TO TALK TO ME--
Nn?
Nn?
ゴゴゴゴゴ
?!
?!
...?!
WHAT'S GOING ON OVER THERE?

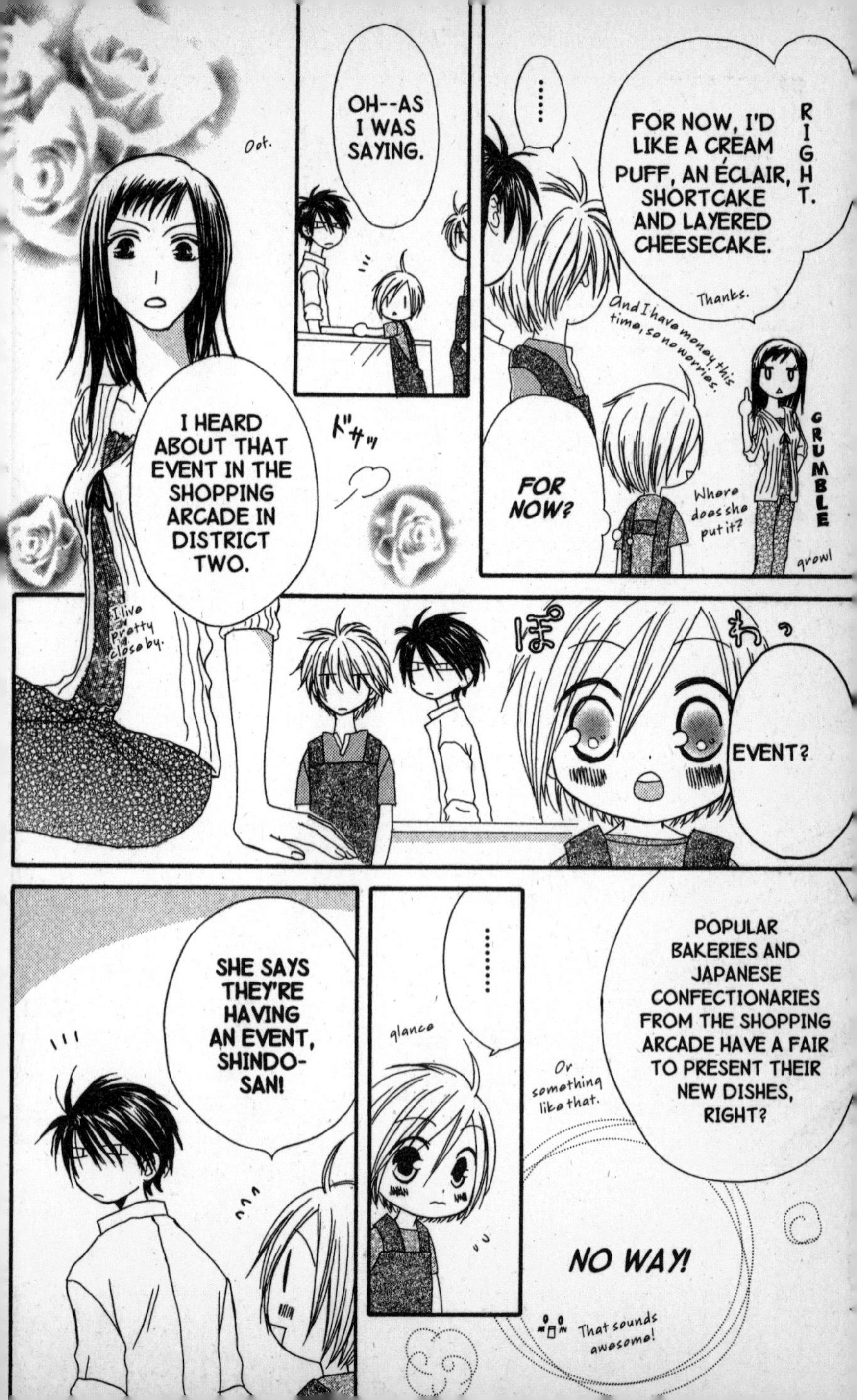

......
FOR NOW, I'D LIKE A CREAM PUFF, AN ÉCLAIR, SHORTCAKE AND LAYERED CHEESECAKE.
RIGHT.
Thanks.
And I have money this time, so no worries.
GRUMBLE
FOR NOW?
Where does she put it?
growl
OH--AS I WAS SAYING.
Oof.
ドサッ
I HEARD ABOUT THAT EVENT IN THE SHOPPING ARCADE IN DISTRICT TWO.
I live pretty close by.
ぽわっ
EVENT?
POPULAR BAKERIES AND JAPANESE CONFECTIONARIES FROM THE SHOPPING ARCADE HAVE A FAIR TO PRESENT THEIR NEW DISHES, RIGHT?
Or something like that.
NO WAY!
That sounds awesome!
....
glance
SHE SAYS THEY'RE HAVING AN EVENT, SHINDO-SAN!

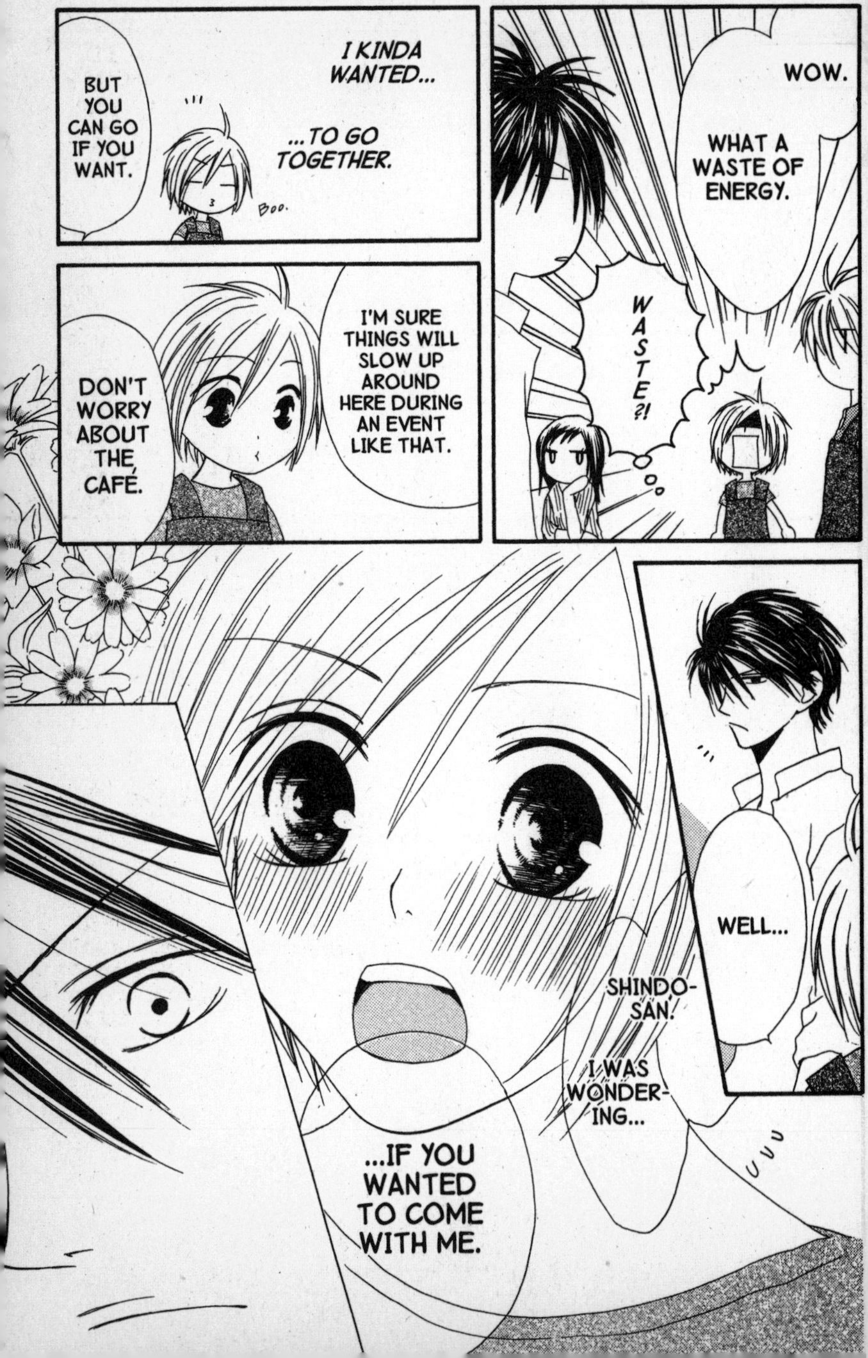
WOW.
WHAT A WASTE OF ENERGY.
WASTE?!
I KINDA WANTED...
...TO GO TOGETHER.
BUT YOU CAN GO IF YOU WANT.
BOO.
I'M SURE THINGS WILL SLOW UP AROUND HERE DURING AN EVENT LIKE THAT.
DON'T WORRY ABOUT THE CAFÉ.
WELL...
SHINDO-SAN!
I WAS WONDERING...
...IF YOU WANTED TO COME WITH ME.

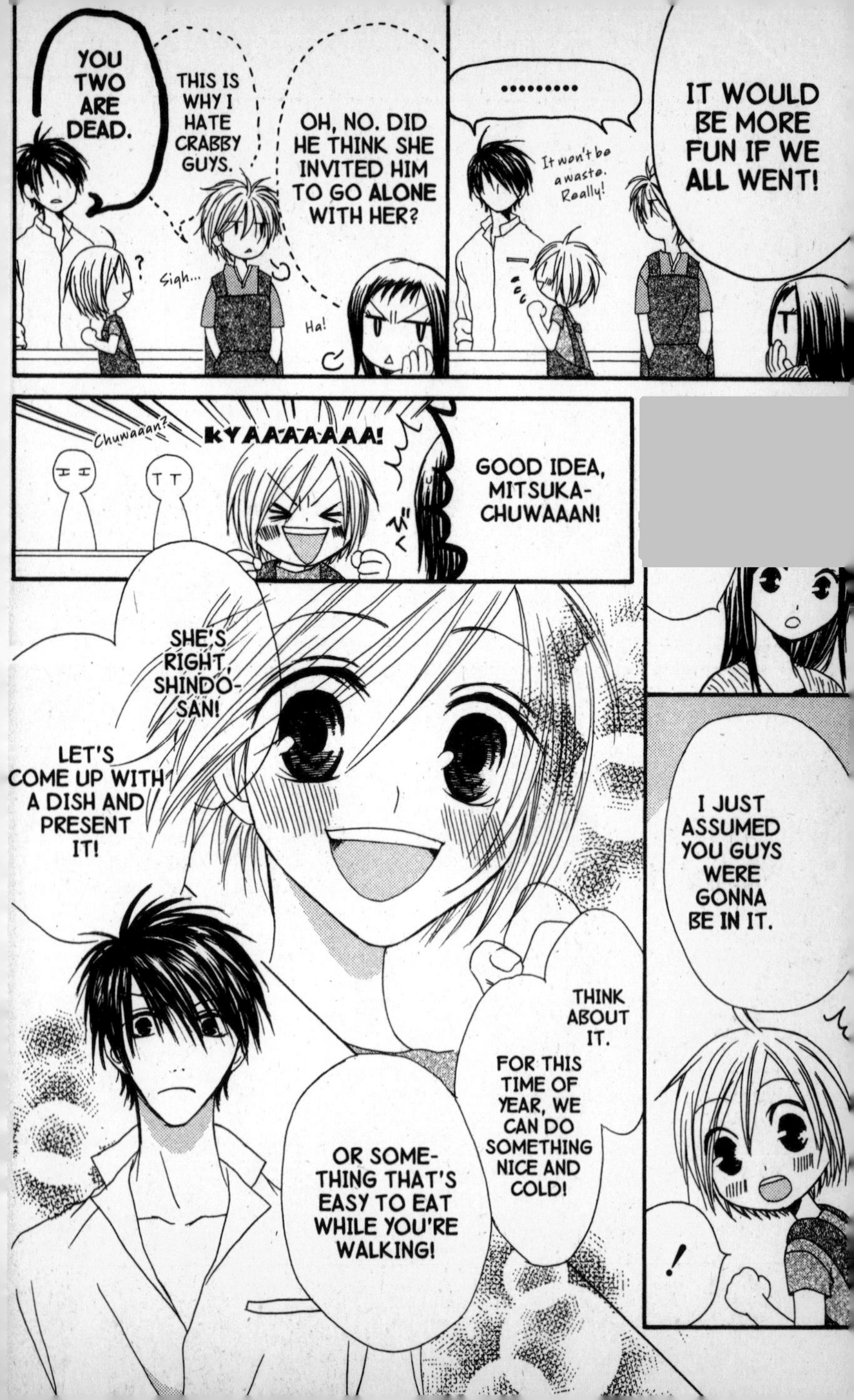
IT WOULD BE MORE FUN IF WE ALL WENT!
It won't be a waste. Really!
....
OH, NO. DID HE THINK SHE INVITED HIM TO GO ALONE WITH HER?
THIS IS WHY I HATE CRABBY GUYS.
YOU TWO ARE DEAD.
Sigh...
Ha!
GOOD IDEA, MITSUKA-CHUWAAAN!
KYAAAAAAAA!
Chuwaaan?
I JUST ASSUMED YOU GUYS WERE GONNA BE IN IT.
!
SHE'S RIGHT, SHINDO-SAN!
LET'S COME UP WITH A DISH AND PRESENT IT!
THINK ABOUT IT.
FOR THIS TIME OF YEAR, WE CAN DO SOMETHING NICE AND COLD!
OR SOMETHING THAT'S EASY TO EAT WHILE YOU'RE WALKING!

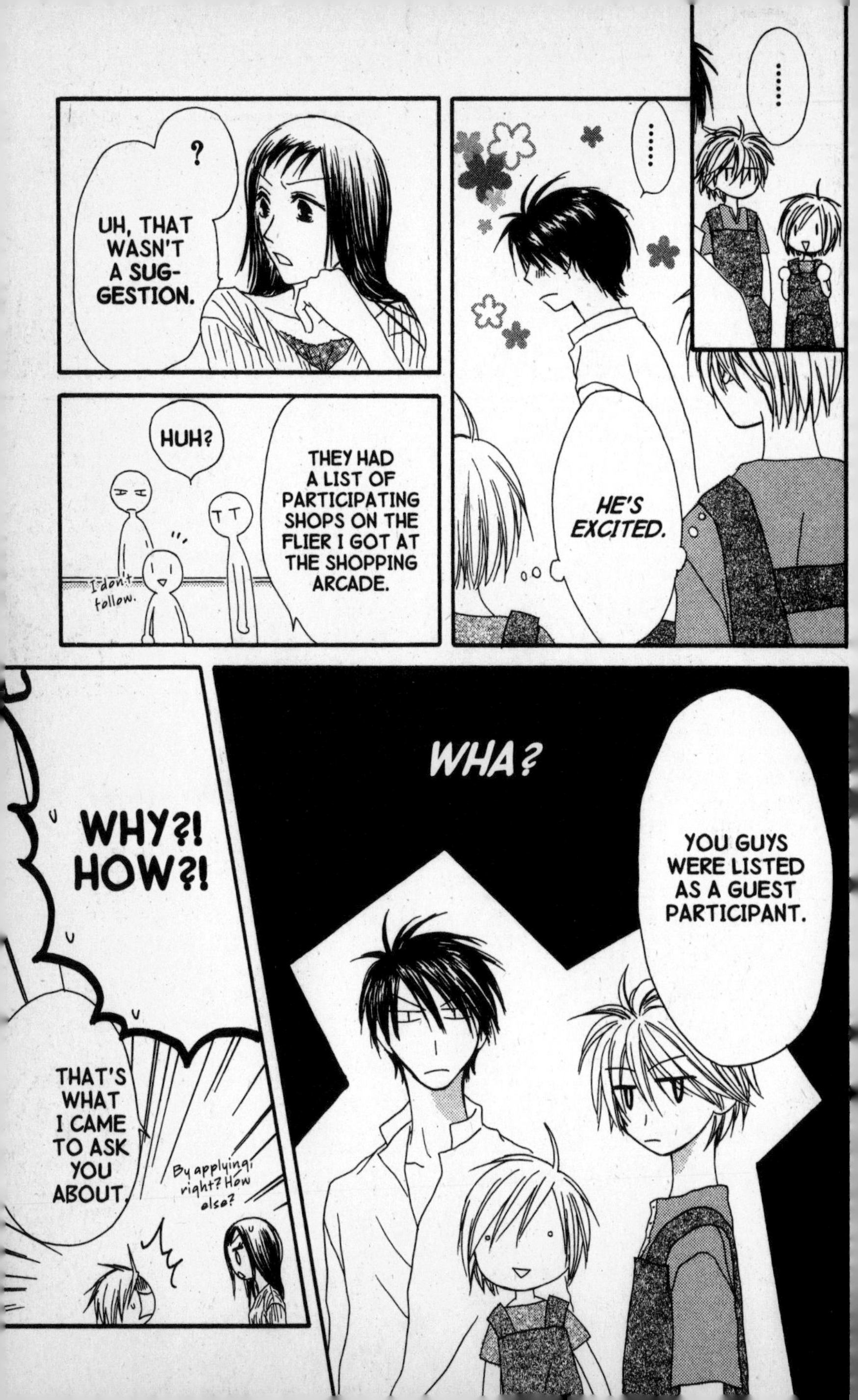
......
......
HE'S EXCITED.
?
UH, THAT WASN'T A SUG-GESTION.
THEY HAD A LIST OF PARTICIPATING SHOPS ON THE FLIER I GOT AT THE SHOPPING ARCADE.
HUH?
I don't follow.
WHA?
YOU GUYS WERE LISTED AS A GUEST PARTICIPANT.
WHY?! HOW?!
THAT'S WHAT I CAME TO ASK YOU ABOUT.
By applying, right? How else?

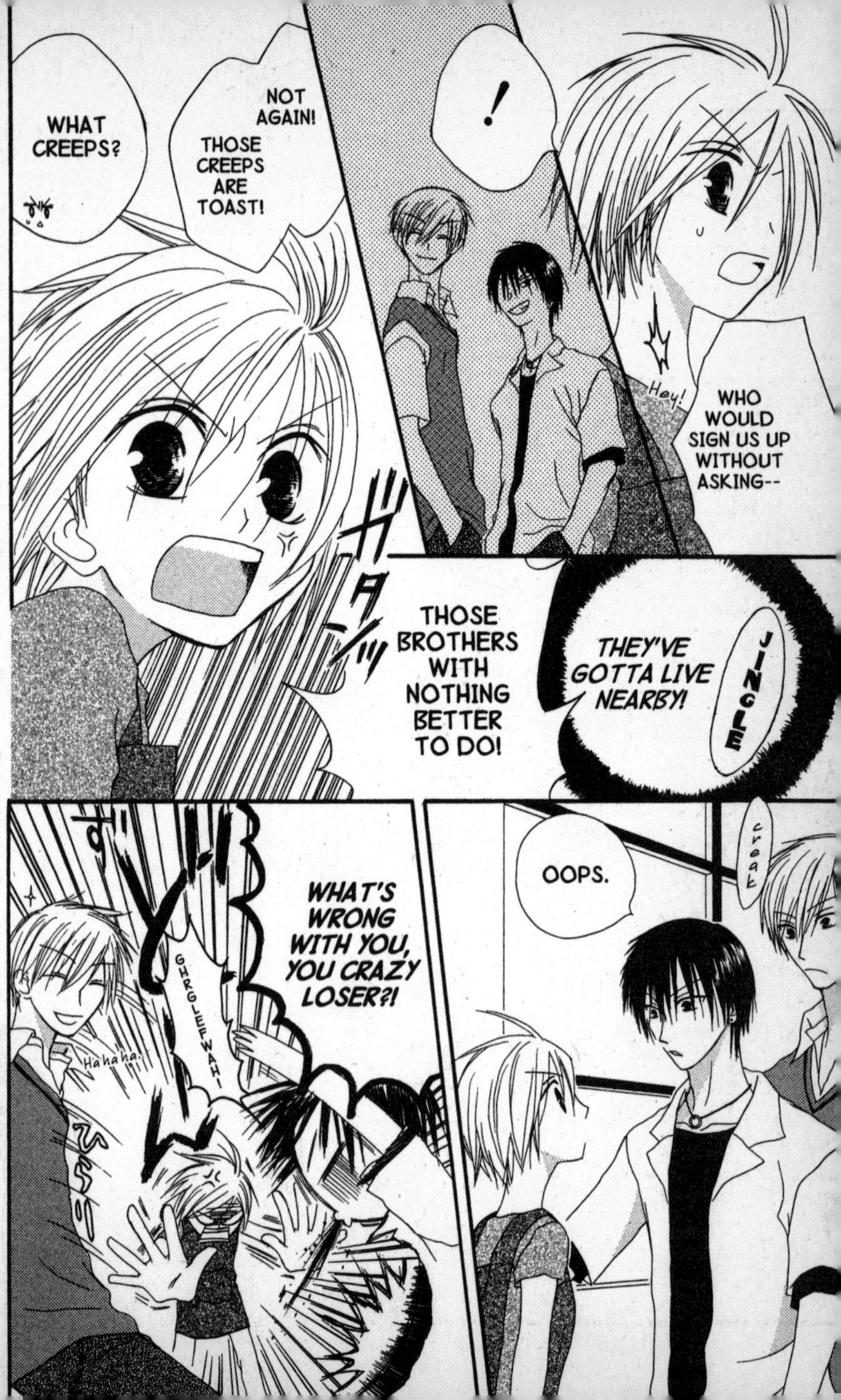
!
Hey!
WHO WOULD SIGN US UP WITHOUT ASKING--
JINGLE
THEY'VE GOTTA LIVE NEARBY!
THOSE BROTHERS WITH NOTHING BETTER TO DO!
NOT AGAIN! THOSE CREEPS ARE TOAST!
WHAT CREEPS?
creak
OOPS.
WHAT'S WRONG WITH YOU, YOU CRAZY LOSER?!
GHRGLEFWAH!
Ha ha ha.

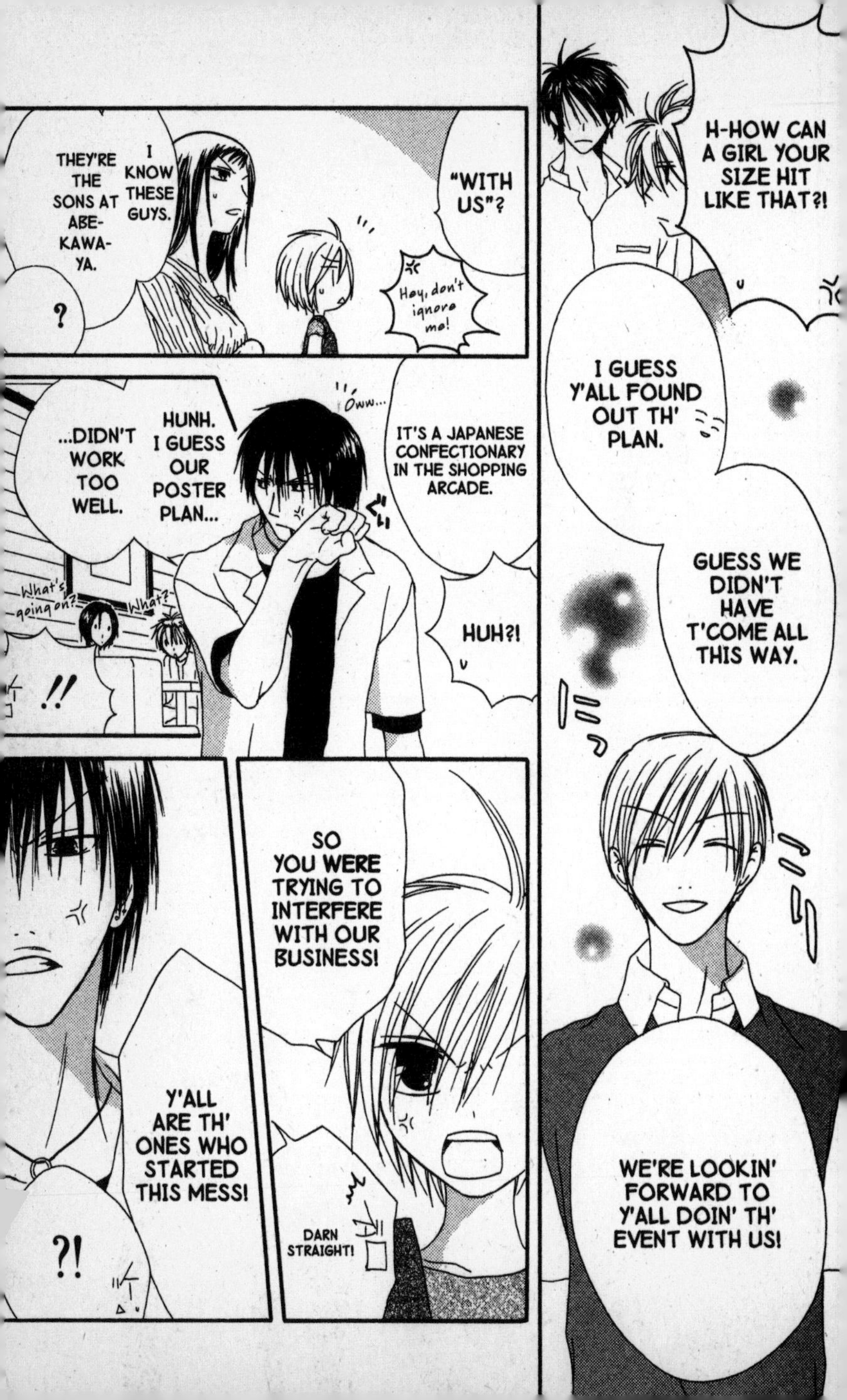
H-HOW CAN A GIRL YOUR SIZE HIT LIKE THAT?!
I GUESS Y'ALL FOUND OUT TH' PLAN.
GUESS WE DIDN'T HAVE T'COME ALL THIS WAY.
WE'RE LOOKIN' FORWARD TO Y'ALL DOIN' TH' EVENT WITH US!
"WITH US"?
Hey, don't ignore me!
I KNOW THESE GUYS.
THEY'RE THE SONS AT ABE-KAWA-YA.
?
IT'S A JAPANESE CONFECTIONARY IN THE SHOPPING ARCADE.
Oww...
HUNH. I GUESS OUR POSTER PLAN...
...DIDN'T WORK TOO WELL.
HUH?!
What?
What's going on?
!!
SO YOU WERE TRYING TO INTERFERE WITH OUR BUSINESS!
DARN STRAIGHT!
Y'ALL ARE TH' ONES WHO STARTED THIS MESS!
?!

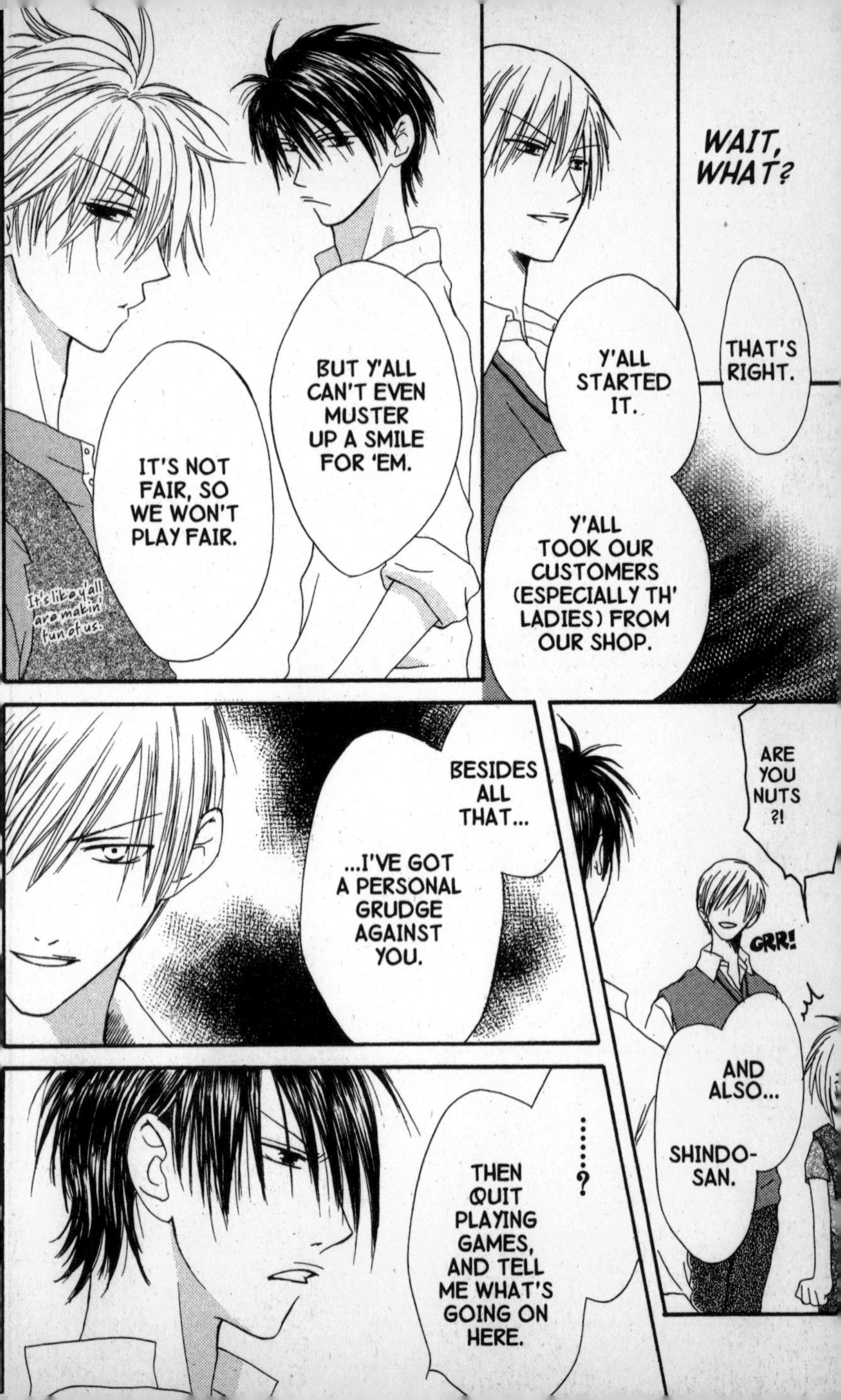

WAIT, WHAT?
THAT'S RIGHT.
Y'ALL STARTED IT.
Y'ALL TOOK OUR CUSTOMERS (ESPECIALLY TH' LADIES) FROM OUR SHOP.
BUT Y'ALL CAN'T EVEN MUSTER UP A SMILE FOR 'EM.
IT'S NOT FAIR, SO WE WON'T PLAY FAIR.
It's like y'all are makin' fun of us.
ARE YOU NUTS?!
GRR!
AND ALSO...
SHINDO-SAN.
BESIDES ALL THAT...
...I'VE GOT A PERSONAL GRUDGE AGAINST YOU.
......?
THEN QUIT PLAYING GAMES, AND TELL ME WHAT'S GOING ON HERE.

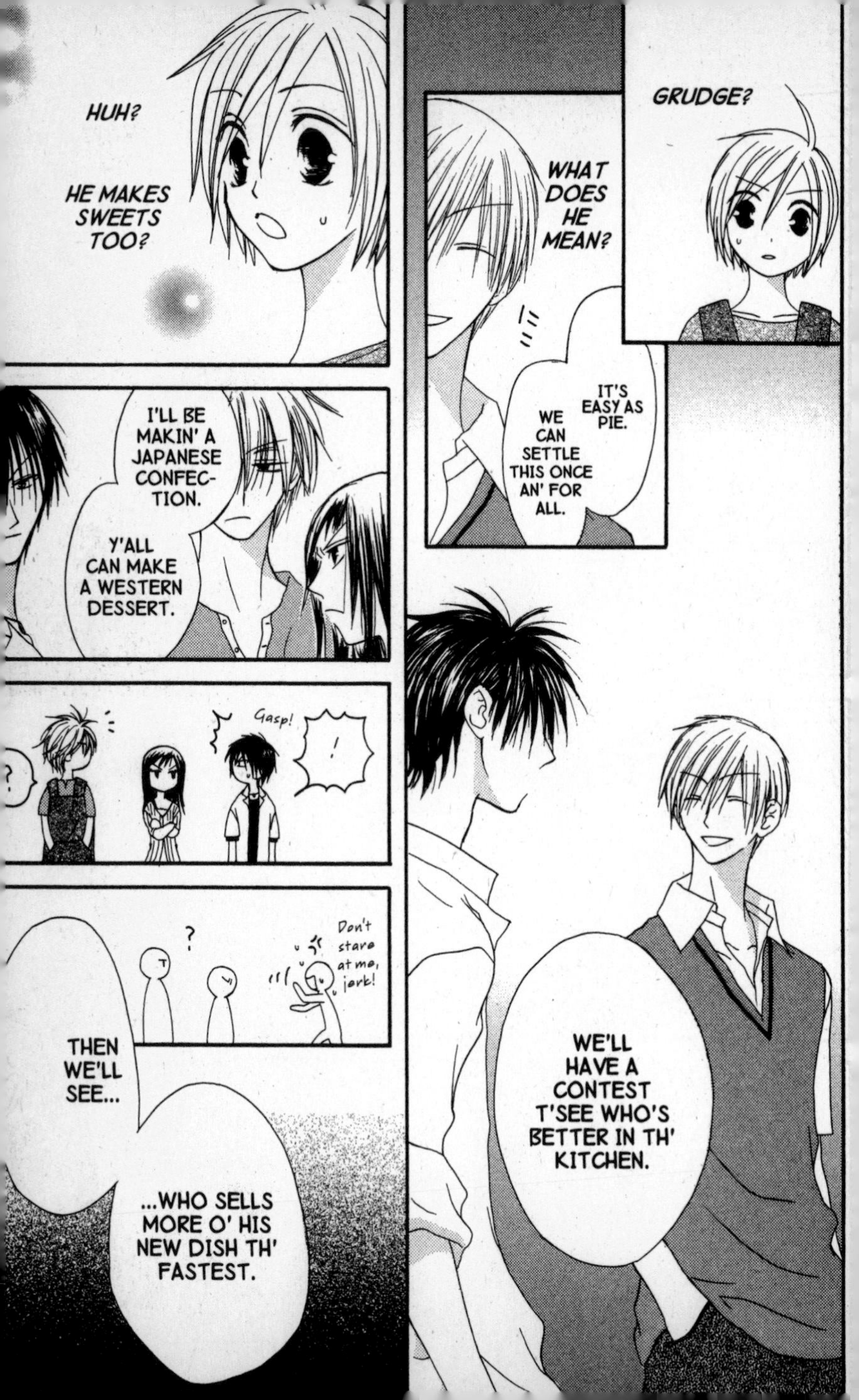
GRUDGE?
WHAT DOES HE MEAN?
IT'S EASY AS PIE.
WE CAN SETTLE THIS ONCE AN' FOR ALL.
WE'LL HAVE A CONTEST T'SEE WHO'S BETTER IN TH' KITCHEN.
HUH?
HE MAKES SWEETS TOO?
I'LL BE MAKIN' A JAPANESE CONFEC- TION.
Y'ALL CAN MAKE A WESTERN DESSERT.
Gasp!
!
?
Don't stare at me, jerk!
?
THEN WE'LL SEE...
...WHO SELLS MORE O' HIS NEW DISH TH' FASTEST.

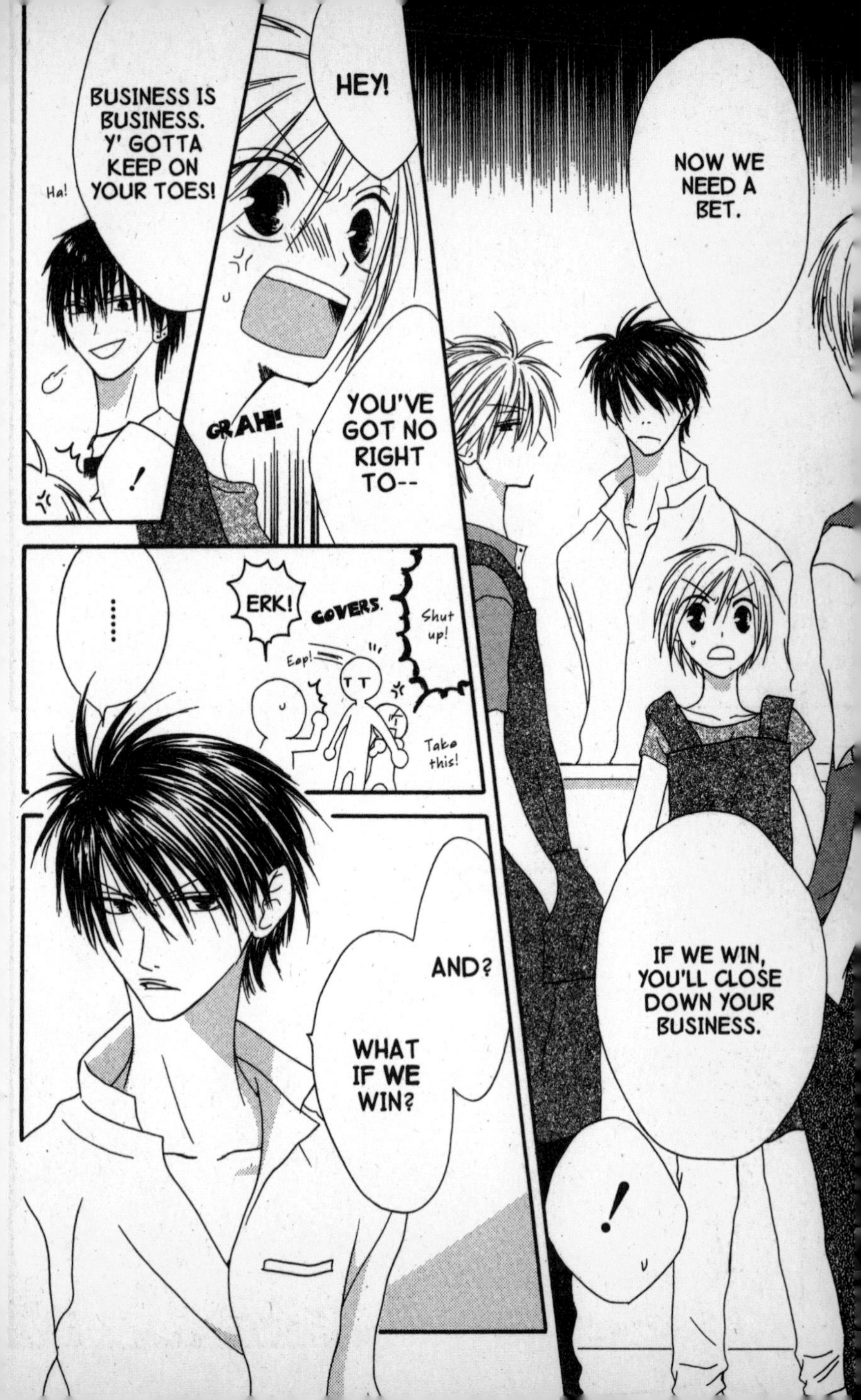
NOW WE NEED A BET.
IF WE WIN, YOU'LL CLOSE DOWN YOUR BUSINESS.
!
HEY!
YOU'VE GOT NO RIGHT TO--
GRAH!!
BUSINESS IS BUSINESS. Y' GOTTA KEEP ON YOUR TOES!
Ha!
!
ERK!
COVERS.
Shut up!
Take this!
Eep!
......
AND?
WHAT IF WE WIN?

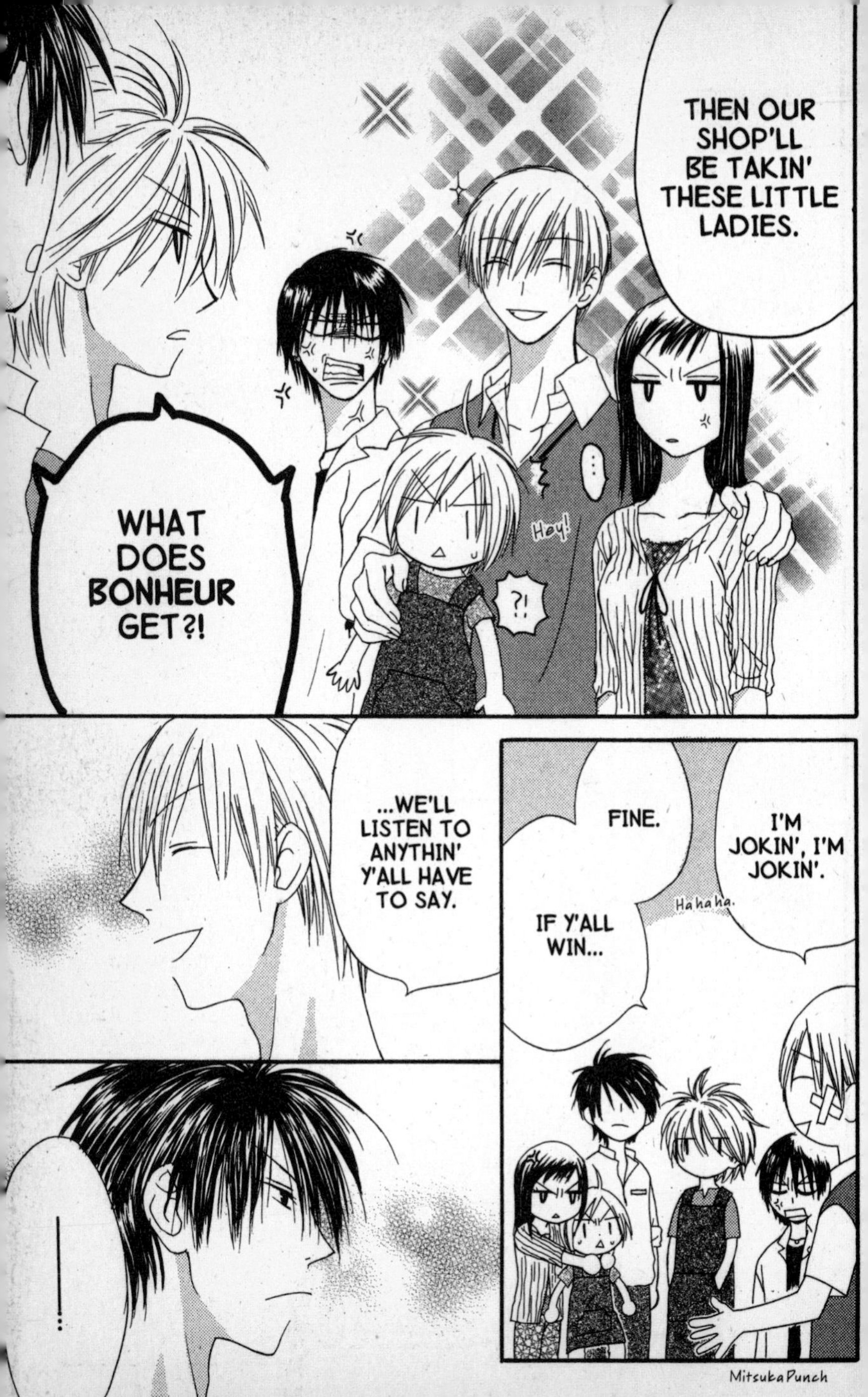
THEN OUR SHOP'LL BE TAKIN' THESE LITTLE LADIES.
Hey!
...
?!
WHAT DOES BONHEUR GET?!
I'M JOKIN', I'M JOKIN'.
Hahaha.
FINE.
IF Y'ALL WIN...
...WE'LL LISTEN TO ANYTHIN' Y'ALL HAVE TO SAY.
......!

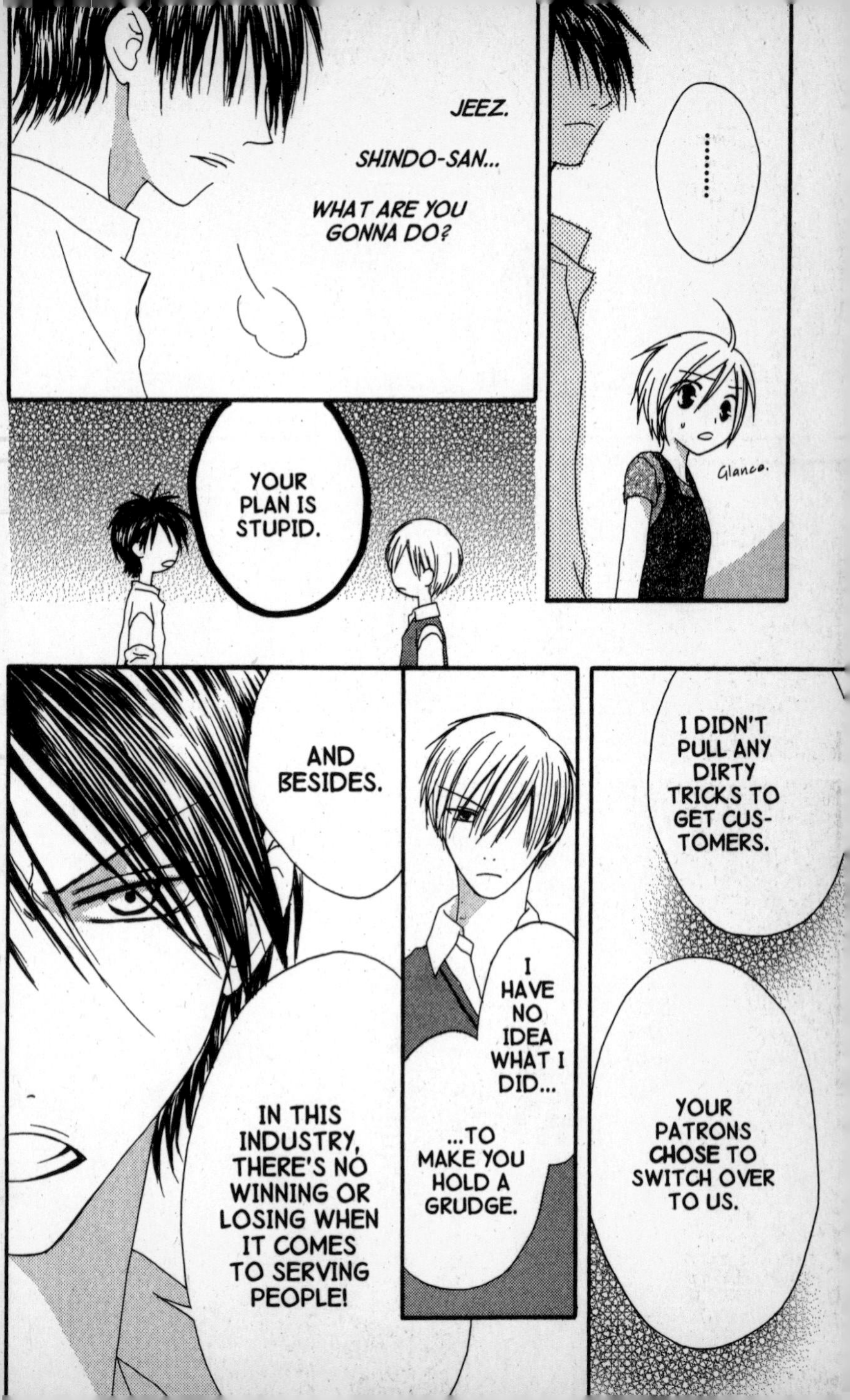
......
Glance.
JEEZ.
SHINDO-SAN...
WHAT ARE YOU GONNA DO?
YOUR PLAN IS STUPID.
I DIDN'T PULL ANY DIRTY TRICKS TO GET CUS-TOMERS.
YOUR PATRONS CHOSE TO SWITCH OVER TO US.
I HAVE NO IDEA WHAT I DID...
...TO MAKE YOU HOLD A GRUDGE.
AND BESIDES.
IN THIS INDUSTRY, THERE'S NO WINNING OR LOSING WHEN IT COMES TO SERVING PEOPLE!

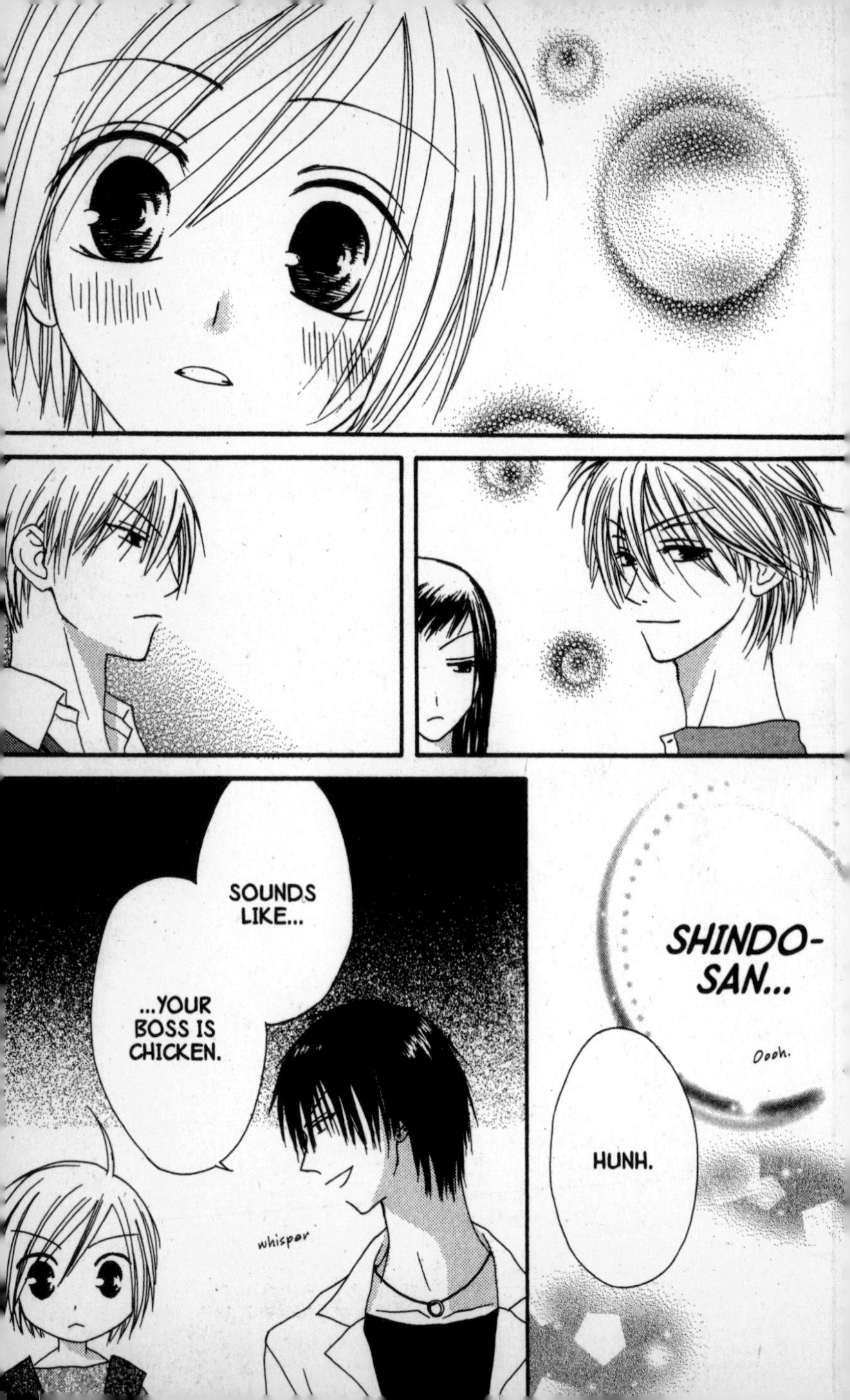
SHINDO-SAN...
Oooh.
HUNH.
SOUNDS LIKE... ...YOUR BOSS IS CHICKEN.
whisper

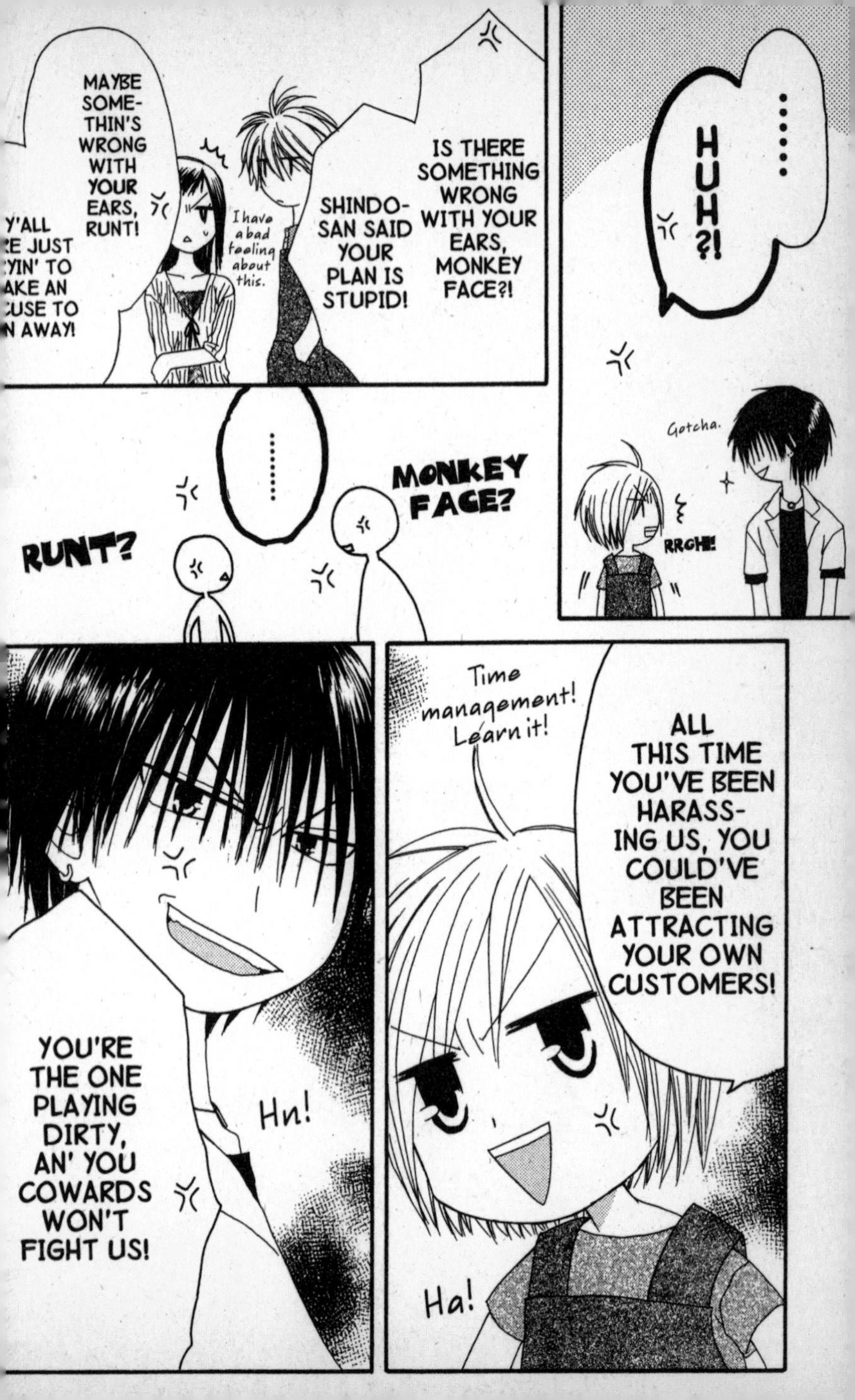
......
HUH?!
Gotcha.
RRGH!
IS THERE SOMETHING WRONG WITH YOUR EARS, MONKEY FACE?!
SHINDO-SAN SAID YOUR PLAN IS STUPID!
I have a bad feeling about this.
MAYBE SOME-THIN'S WRONG WITH YOUR EARS, RUNT!
Y'ALL E JUST YIN' TO AKE AN USE TO N AWAY!
......
MONKEY FACE?
RUNT?
ALL THIS TIME YOU'VE BEEN HARASS-ING US, YOU COULD'VE BEEN ATTRACTING YOUR OWN CUSTOMERS!
Time management! Learn it!
Ha!
YOU'RE THE ONE PLAYING DIRTY, AN' YOU COWARDS WON'T FIGHT US!
Hn!

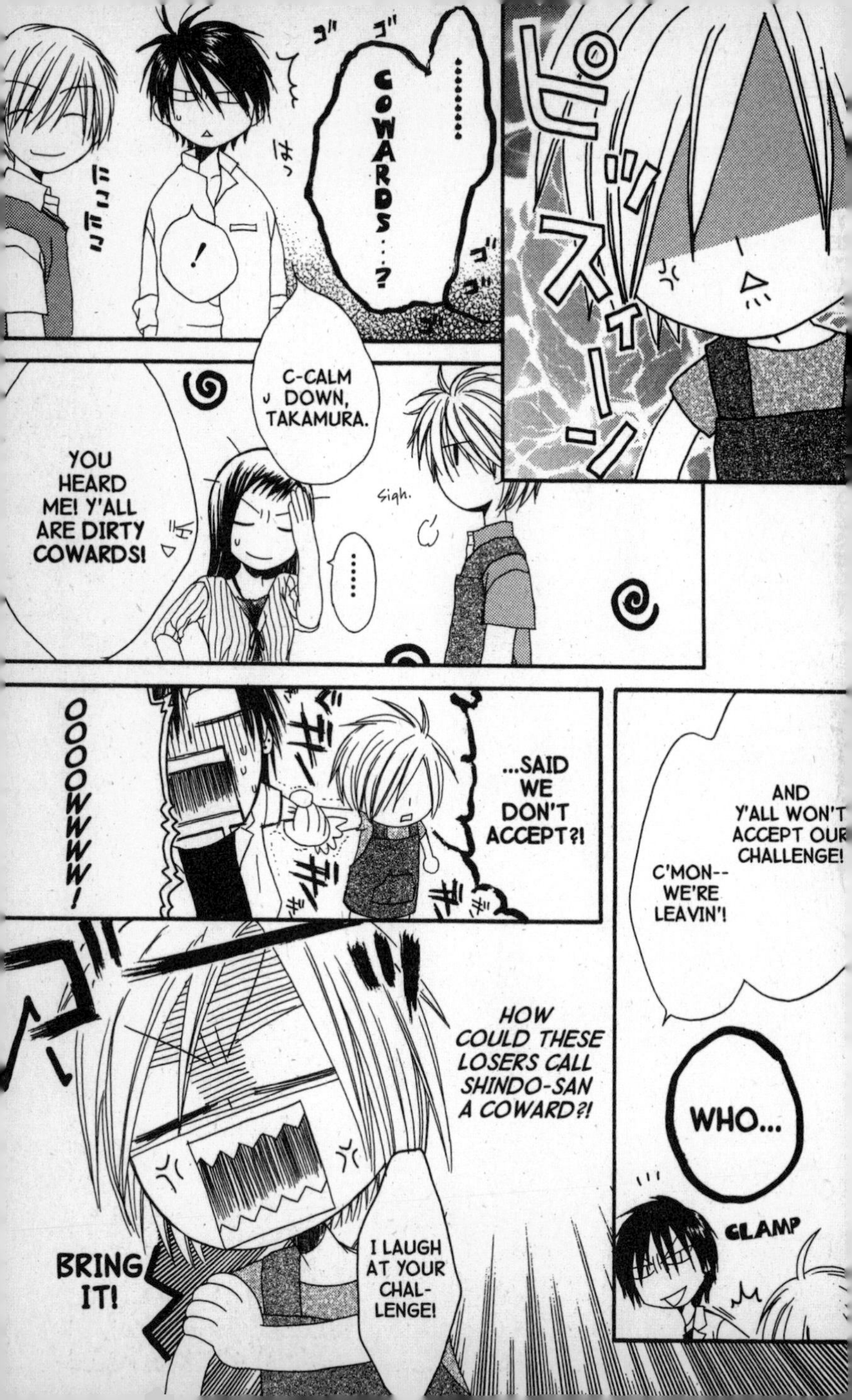

......
COWARDS...?
ゴゴゴ
はっ
!
C-CALM DOWN, TAKAMURA.
Sigh.
YOU HEARD ME! Y'ALL ARE DIRTY COWARDS!
......
AND Y'ALL WON'T ACCEPT OUR CHALLENGE!
C'MON-- WE'RE LEAVIN'!
WHO...
CLAMP
...SAID WE DON'T ACCEPT?!
OOOOOWWWW!
HOW COULD THESE LOSERS CALL SHINDO-SAN A COWARD?!
I LAUGH AT YOUR CHAL-LENGE!
BRING IT!

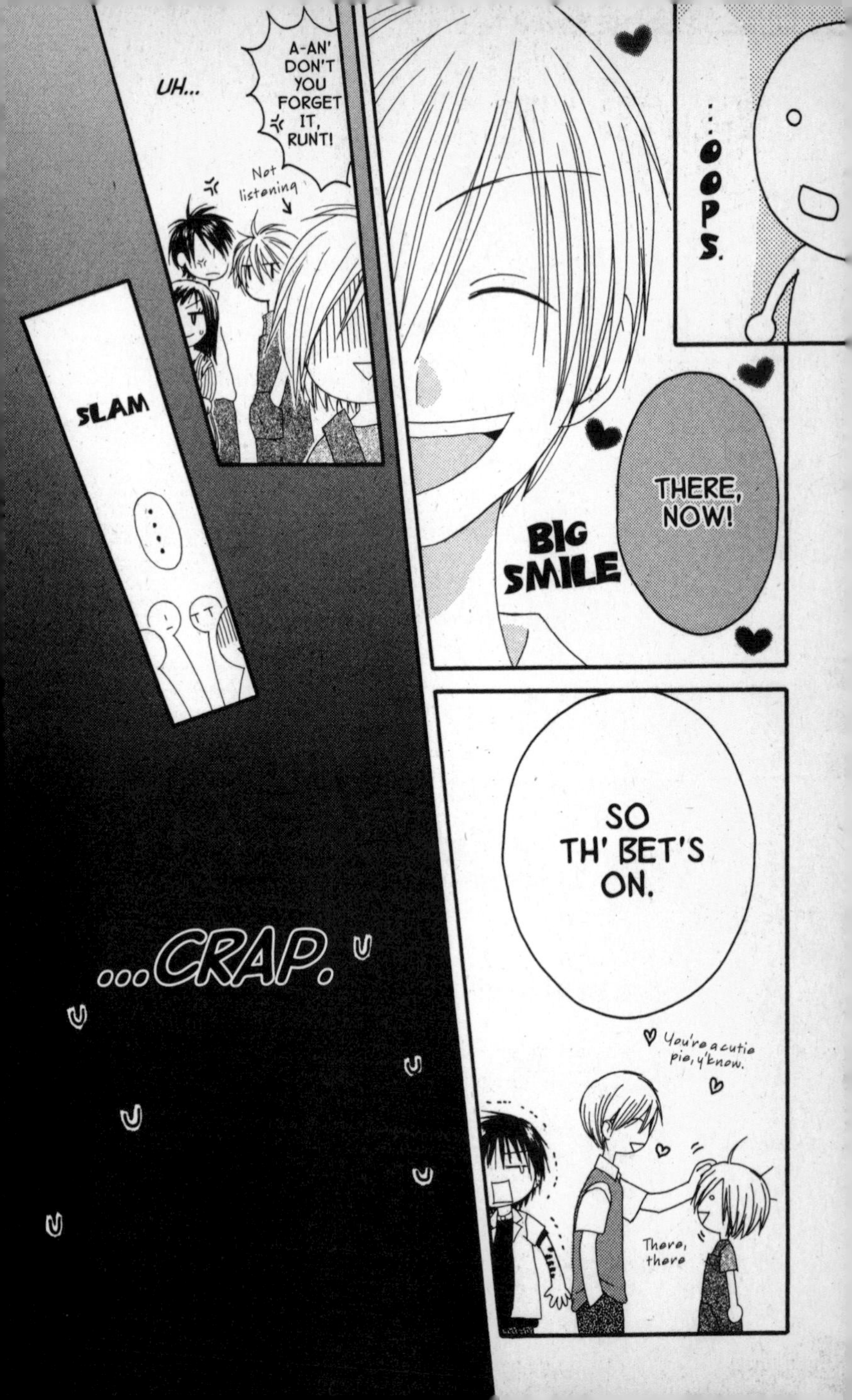
...OOPS.
THERE, NOW!
BIG SMILE
SO TH' BET'S ON.
You're a cutie pie, y'know.
There, there
A-AN' DON'T YOU FORGET IT, RUNT!
UH...
Not listening
SLAM
...
...CRAP.

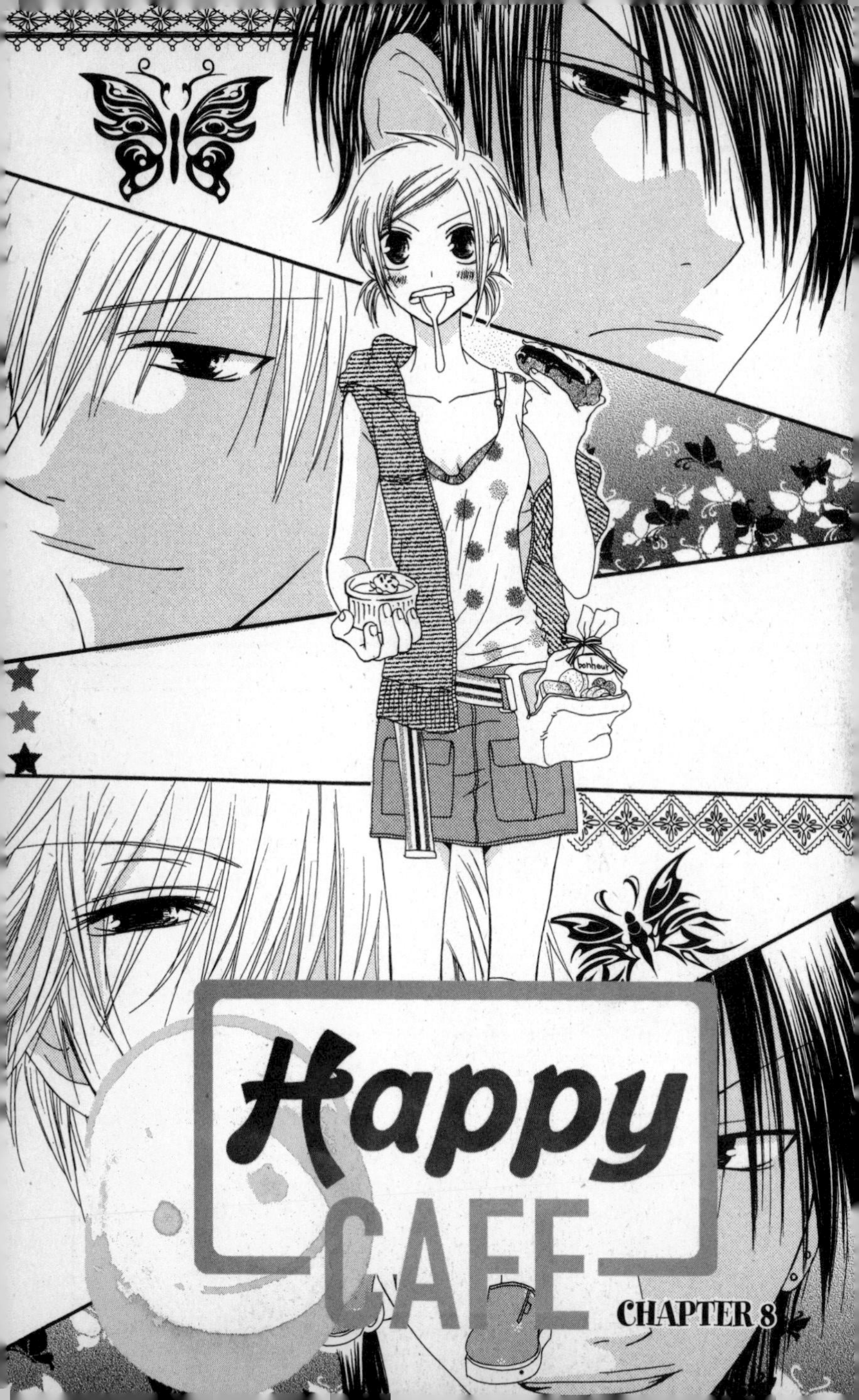
bonheur
Happy CAFE
CHAPTER 8

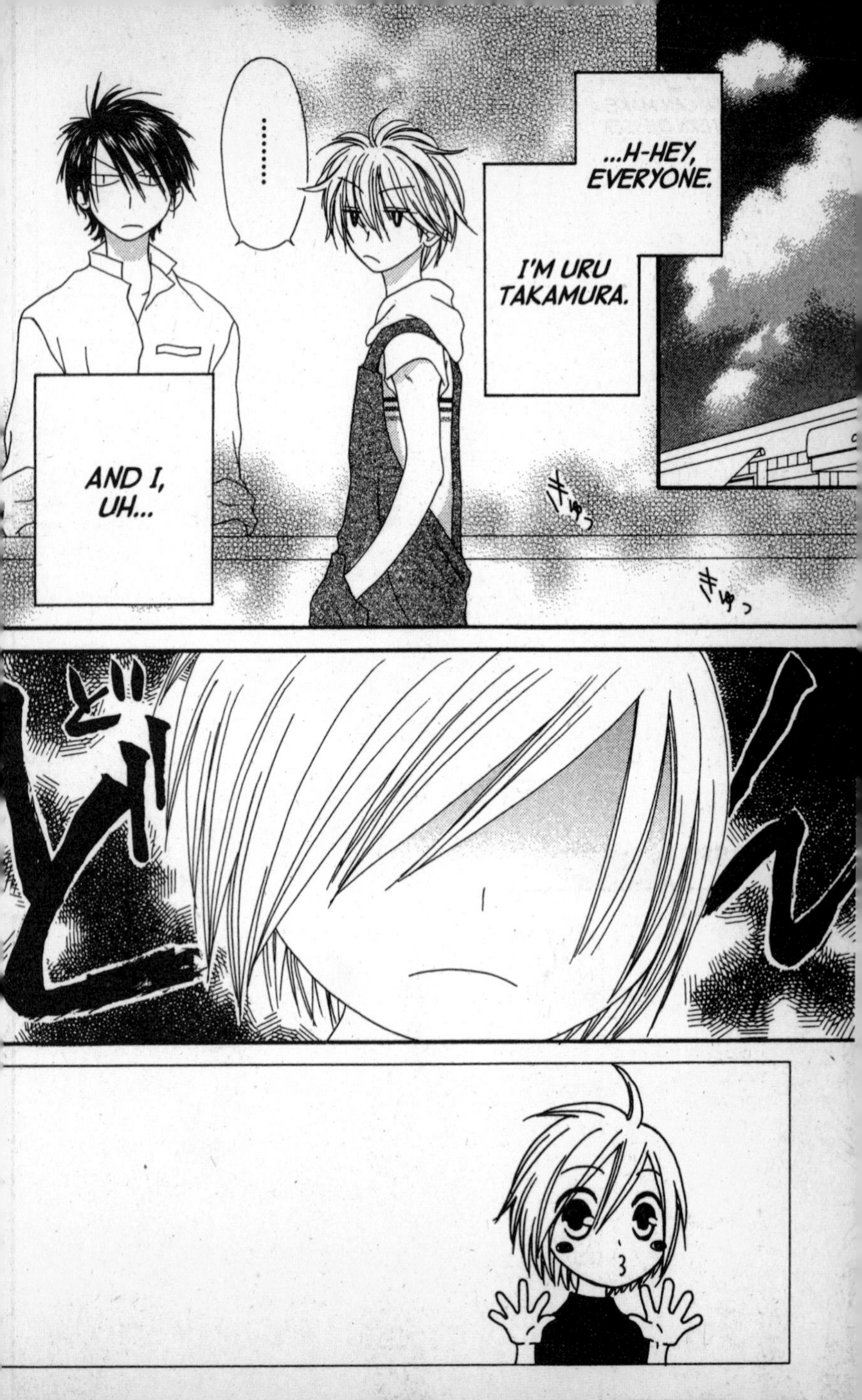
...H-HEY, EVERYONE.
I'M URU TAKAMURA.
......
AND I, UH...
きゅっ
きゅっ

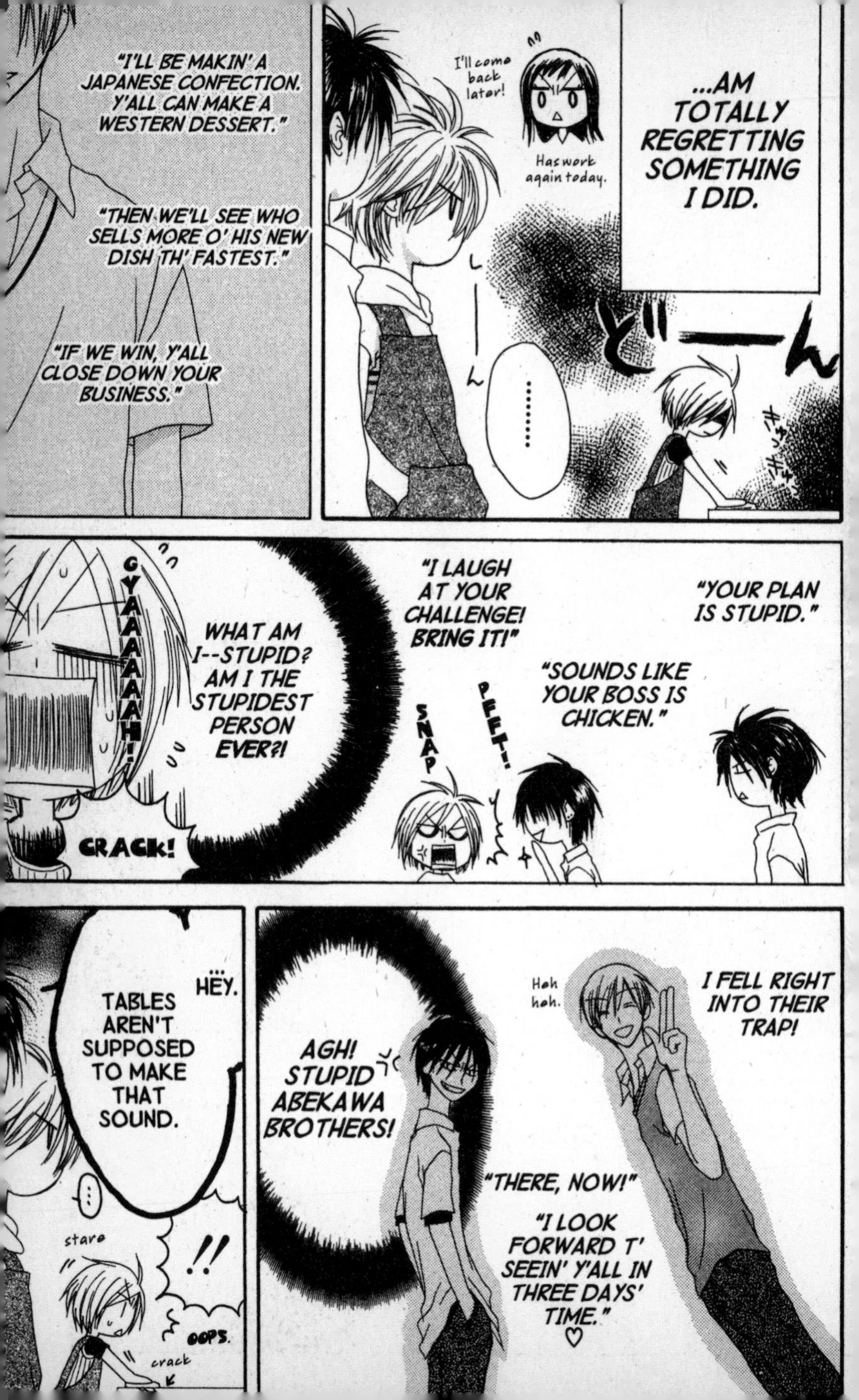
...AM TOTALLY REGRETTING SOMETHING I DID.
I'll come back later!
Has work again today.
....
どーーん
"I'LL BE MAKIN' A JAPANESE CONFECTION. Y'ALL CAN MAKE A WESTERN DESSERT."
"THEN WE'LL SEE WHO SELLS MORE O' HIS NEW DISH TH' FASTEST."
"IF WE WIN, Y'ALL CLOSE DOWN YOUR BUSINESS."
"YOUR PLAN IS STUPID."
"SOUNDS LIKE YOUR BOSS IS CHICKEN."
"I LAUGH AT YOUR CHALLENGE! BRING IT!"
PFFT!
SNAP
WHAT AM I--STUPID? AM I THE STUPIDEST PERSON EVER?!
GYAAAAAAAH!
CRACK!
I FELL RIGHT INTO THEIR TRAP!
Heh heh.
AGH! STUPID ABEKAWA BROTHERS!
"THERE, NOW!"
"I LOOK FORWARD T' SEEIN' Y'ALL IN THREE DAYS' TIME." ♡
...HEY.
TABLES AREN'T SUPPOSED TO MAKE THAT SOUND.
...
stare
!!
OOPS.
crack

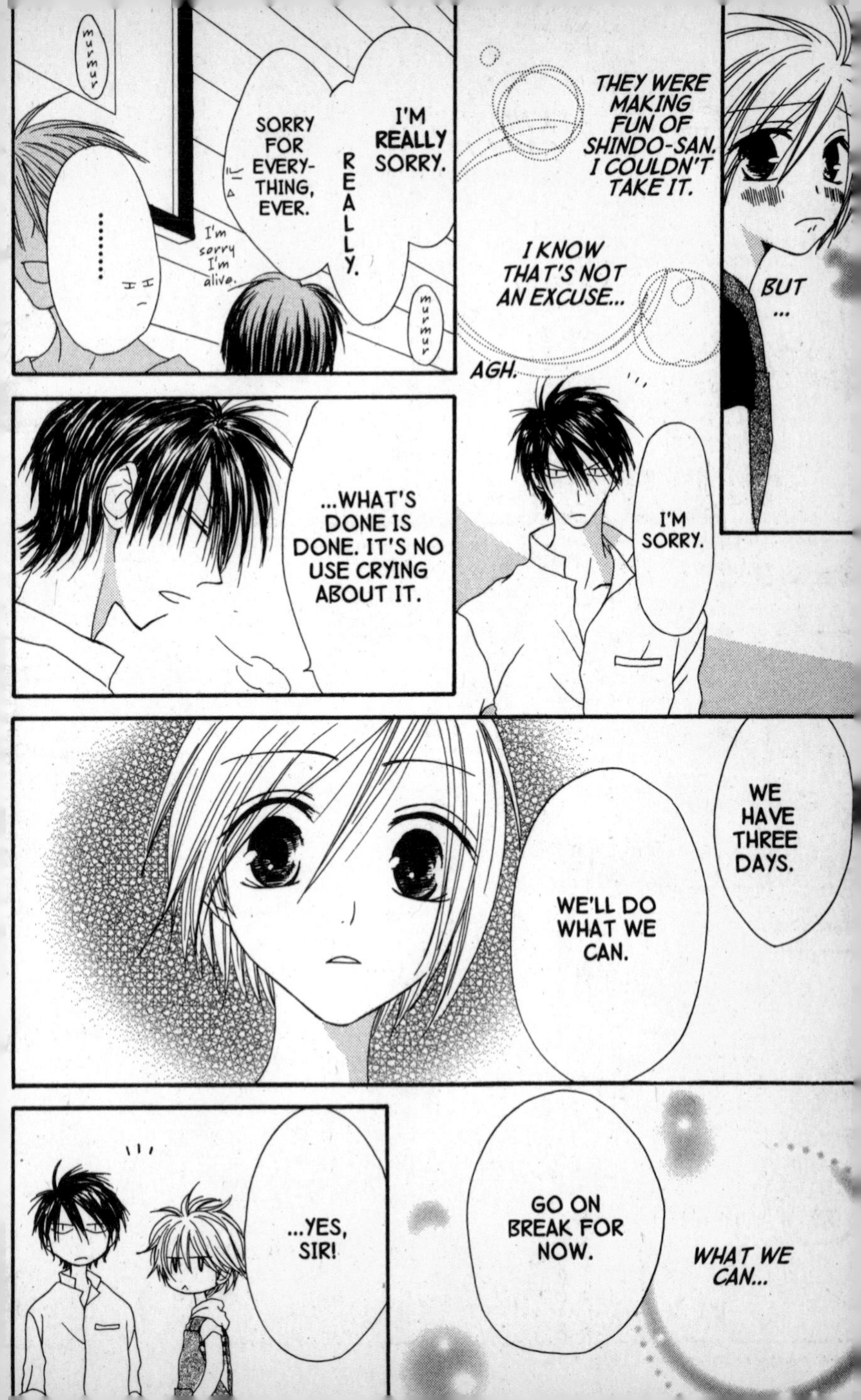
BUT ...
THEY WERE MAKING FUN OF SHINDO-SAN. I COULDN'T TAKE IT.
I KNOW THAT'S NOT AN EXCUSE...
AGH.
I'M SORRY.
I'M REALLY SORRY.
REALLY.
SORRY FOR EVERY-THING, EVER.
murmur
I'm sorry I'm alive.
murmur
......
...WHAT'S DONE IS DONE. IT'S NO USE CRYING ABOUT IT.
WE HAVE THREE DAYS.
WE'LL DO WHAT WE CAN.
WHAT WE CAN...
GO ON BREAK FOR NOW.
...YES, SIR!

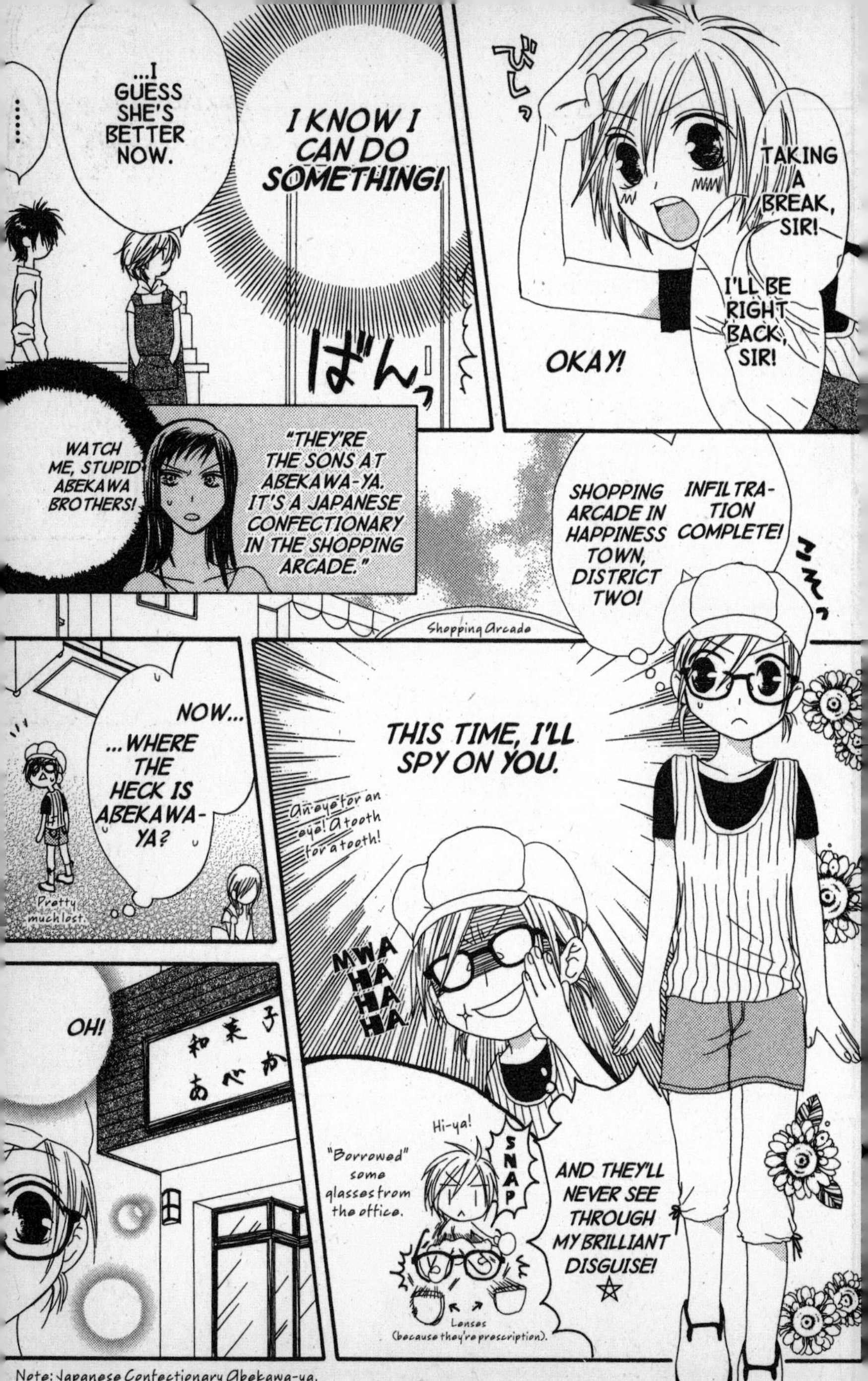
ぴしっ
TAKING A BREAK, SIR!
I'LL BE RIGHT BACK, SIR!
OKAY!
I KNOW I CAN DO SOMETHING!
...I GUESS SHE'S BETTER NOW.
......
ばんっ
"THEY'RE THE SONS AT ABEKAWA-YA. IT'S A JAPANESE CONFECTIONARY IN THE SHOPPING ARCADE."
WATCH ME, STUPID ABEKAWA BROTHERS!
INFILTRATION COMPLETE!
SHOPPING ARCADE IN HAPPINESS TOWN, DISTRICT TWO!
こそっ
Shopping Arcade
THIS TIME, I'LL SPY ON YOU.
An eye for an eye! A tooth for a tooth!
MWA HA HA HA HA
AND THEY'LL NEVER SEE THROUGH MY BRILLIANT DISGUISE! ☆
Hi-ya!
SNAP
"Borrowed" some glasses from the office.
Lenses (because they're prescription).
NOW... ...WHERE THE HECK IS ABEKAWA-YA?
Pretty much lost.
OH!
和菓子
あべか

Note: Japanese Confectionary Abekawa-ya.

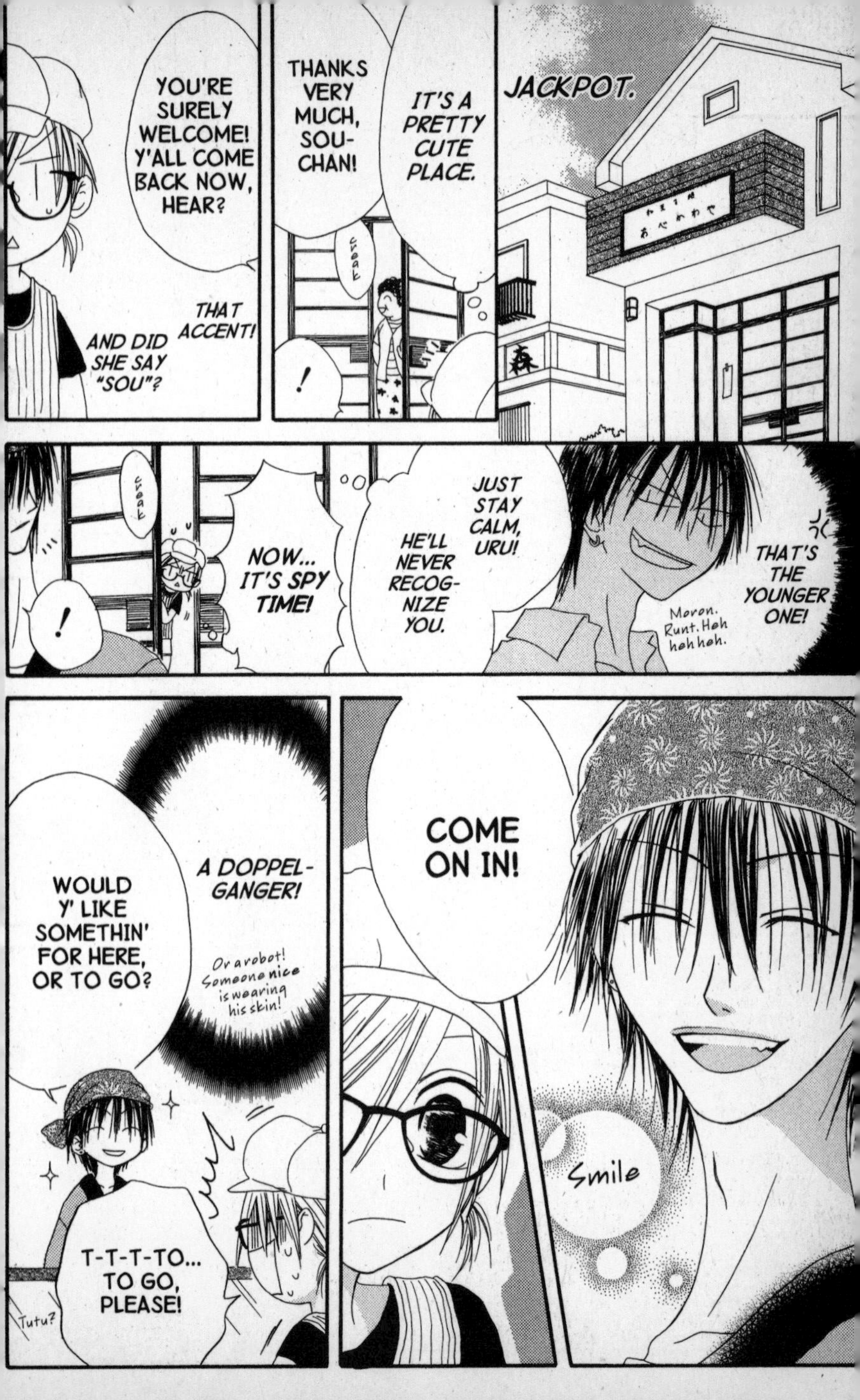
JACKPOT.
IT'S A PRETTY CUTE PLACE.
THANKS VERY MUCH, SOU-CHAN!
creak
!
YOU'RE SURELY WELCOME! Y'ALL COME BACK NOW, HEAR?
THAT ACCENT!
AND DID SHE SAY "SOU"?
THAT'S THE YOUNGER ONE!
Moron. Runt. Heh heh heh.
JUST STAY CALM, URU!
HE'LL NEVER RECOGNIZE YOU.
NOW... IT'S SPY TIME!
creak
!
COME ON IN!
Smile
A DOPPELGANGER!
Or a robot! Someone nice is wearing his skin!
WOULD Y' LIKE SOMETHIN' FOR HERE, OR TO GO?
T-T-T-TO... TO GO, PLEASE!
Tutu?

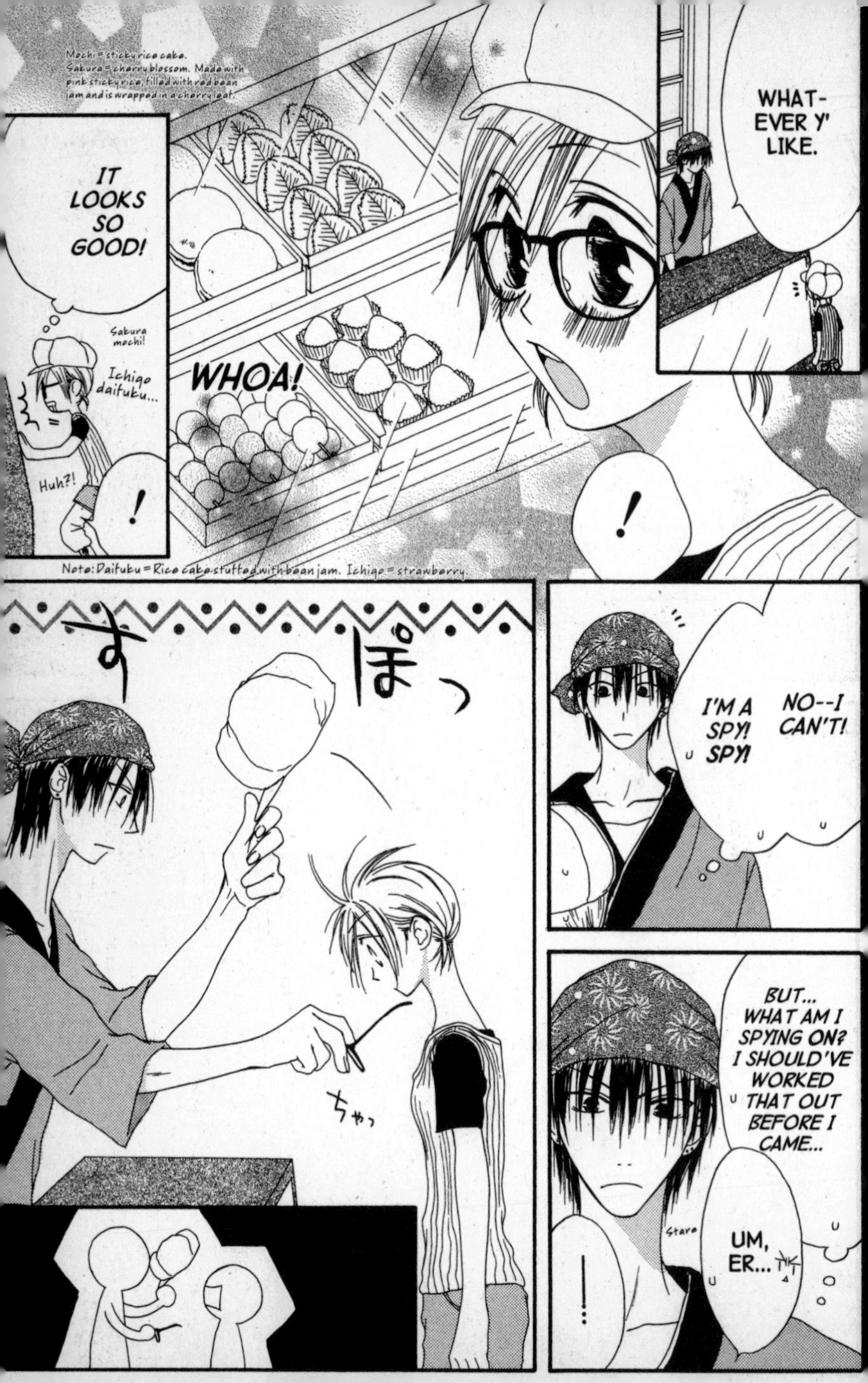
WHAT-EVER Y' LIKE.
Mochi = sticky rice cake. Sakura = cherry blossom. Made with pink sticky rice, filled with red bean jam and is wrapped in a cherry leaf.
WHOA!
!
IT LOOKS SO GOOD!
Sakura mochi!
Ichigo daifuku...
Huh?!
!
Note: Daifuku = Rice cake stuffed with bean jam. Ichigo = strawberry.
NO--I CAN'T!
I'M A SPY! SPY!
BUT... WHAT AM I SPYING ON? I SHOULD'VE WORKED THAT OUT BEFORE I CAME...
UM, ER...
Stare
!...
すぽっ
ちゃっ

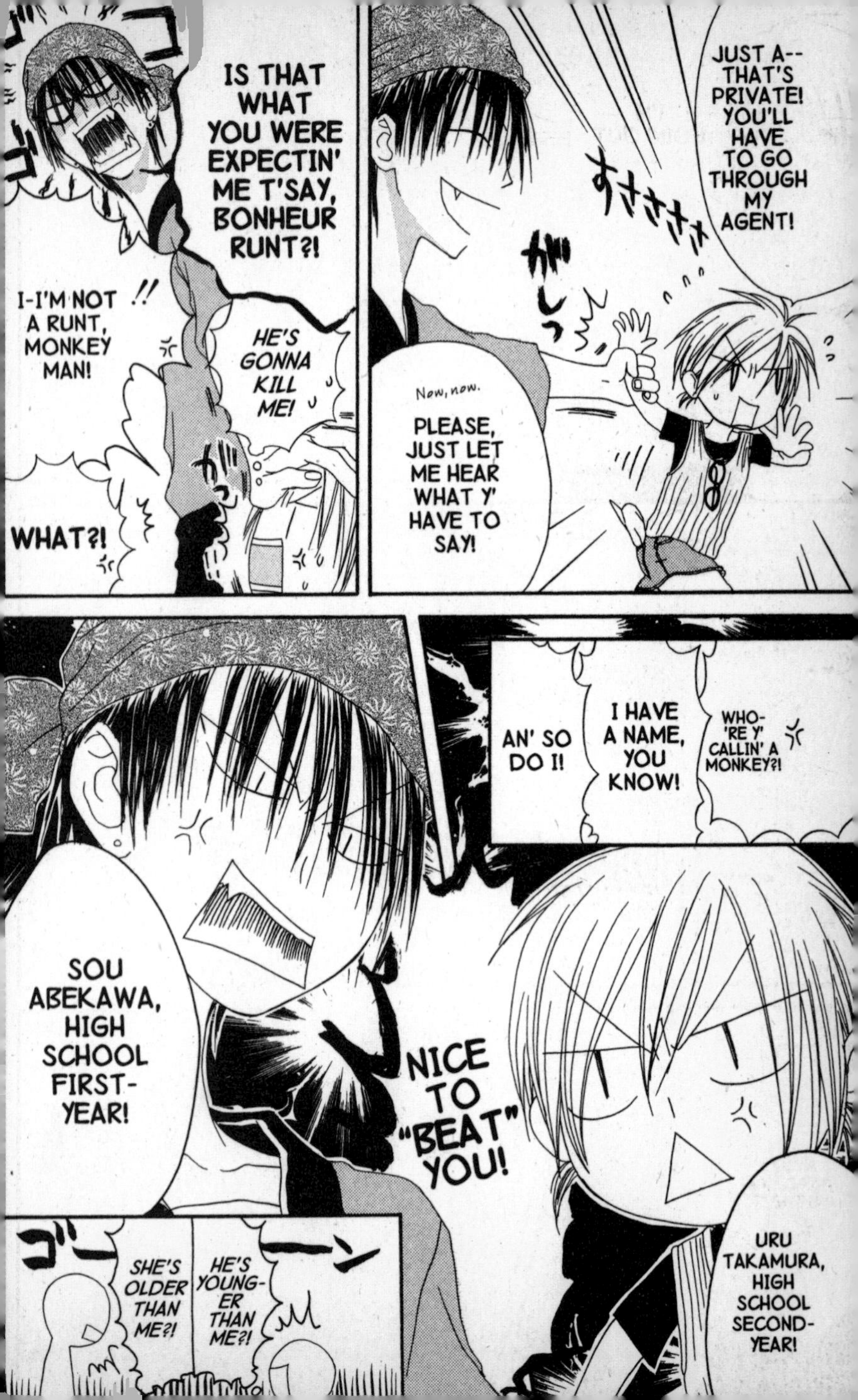
JUST A-- THAT'S PRIVATE! YOU'LL HAVE TO GO THROUGH MY AGENT!
すささささ
がしっ
Now, now.
PLEASE, JUST LET ME HEAR WHAT Y' HAVE TO SAY!
IS THAT WHAT YOU WERE EXPECTIN' ME T'SAY, BONHEUR RUNT?!
I-I'M NOT A RUNT, MONKEY MAN!
HE'S GONNA KILL ME!
WHAT?!
WHO-'RE Y' CALLIN' A MONKEY?!
I HAVE A NAME, YOU KNOW!
AN' SO DO I!
URU TAKAMURA, HIGH SCHOOL SECOND-YEAR!
SOU ABEKAWA, HIGH SCHOOL FIRST-YEAR!
NICE TO "BEAT" YOU!
HE'S YOUNG-ER THAN ME?!
SHE'S OLDER THAN ME?!

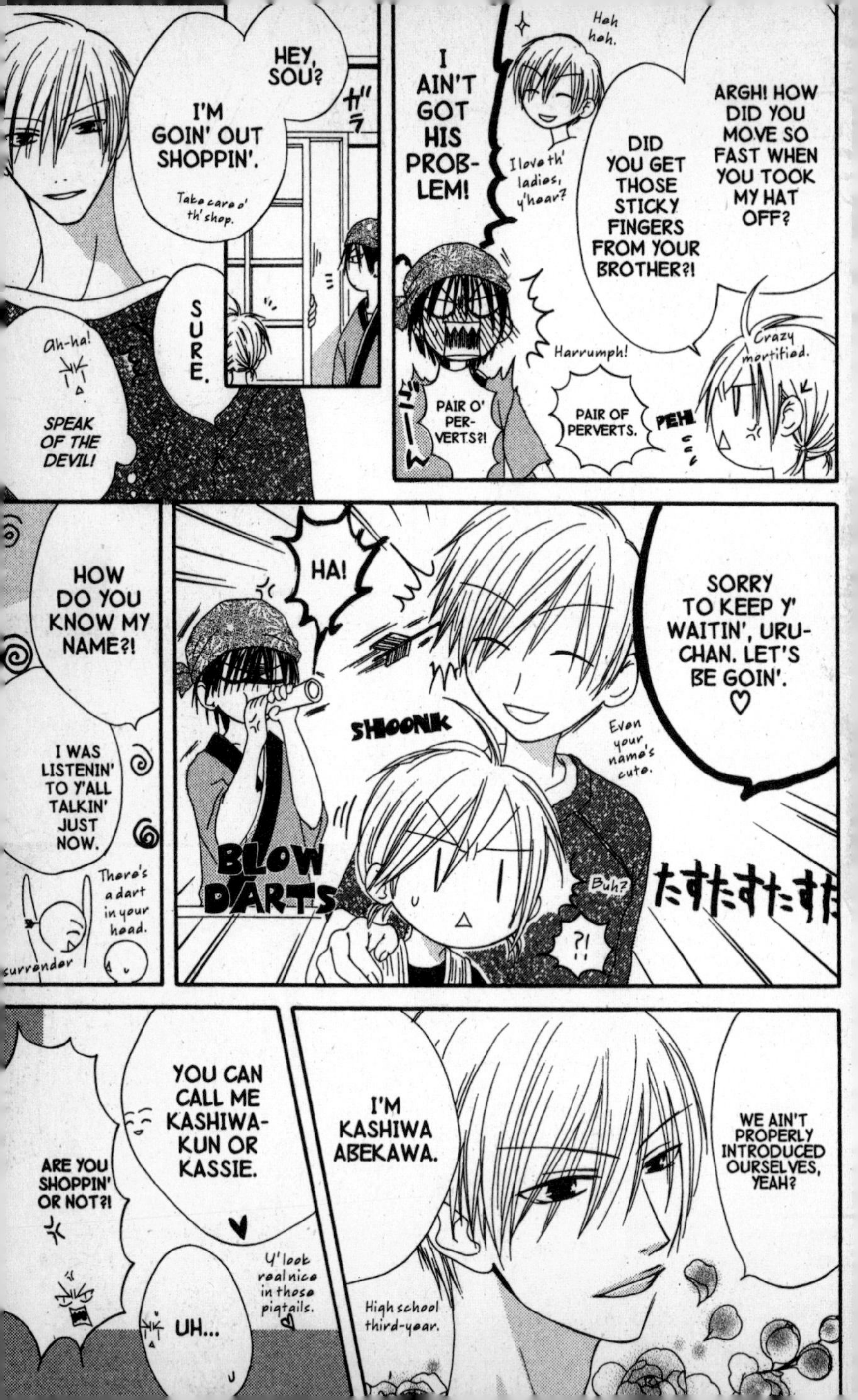
ARGH! HOW DID YOU MOVE SO FAST WHEN YOU TOOK MY HAT OFF?
Crazy mortified.
DID YOU GET THOSE STICKY FINGERS FROM YOUR BROTHER?!
Heh heh.
I love th' ladies, y'hear?
Harrumph!
PAIR OF PERVERTS.
PEH!
I AIN'T GOT HIS PROB-LEM!
PAIR O' PER-VERTS?!
HEY, SOU?
ガラ
I'M GOIN' OUT SHOPPIN'.
Take care o' th' shop.
SURE.
Ah-ha!
SPEAK OF THE DEVIL!
SORRY TO KEEP Y' WAITIN', URU-CHAN. LET'S BE GOIN'. ♡
Even your name's cute.
たすたすたすた
Buh?
?!
HA!
SHIOONK
BLOW DARTS
HOW DO YOU KNOW MY NAME?!
I WAS LISTENIN' TO Y'ALL TALKIN' JUST NOW.
There's a dart in your head.
surrender
WE AIN'T PROPERLY INTRODUCED OURSELVES, YEAH?
I'M KASHIWA ABEKAWA.
High school third-year.
YOU CAN CALL ME KASHIWA-KUN OR KASSIE. ♥
Y'look real nice in those pigtails.
UH...
ARE YOU SHOPPIN' OR NOT?!

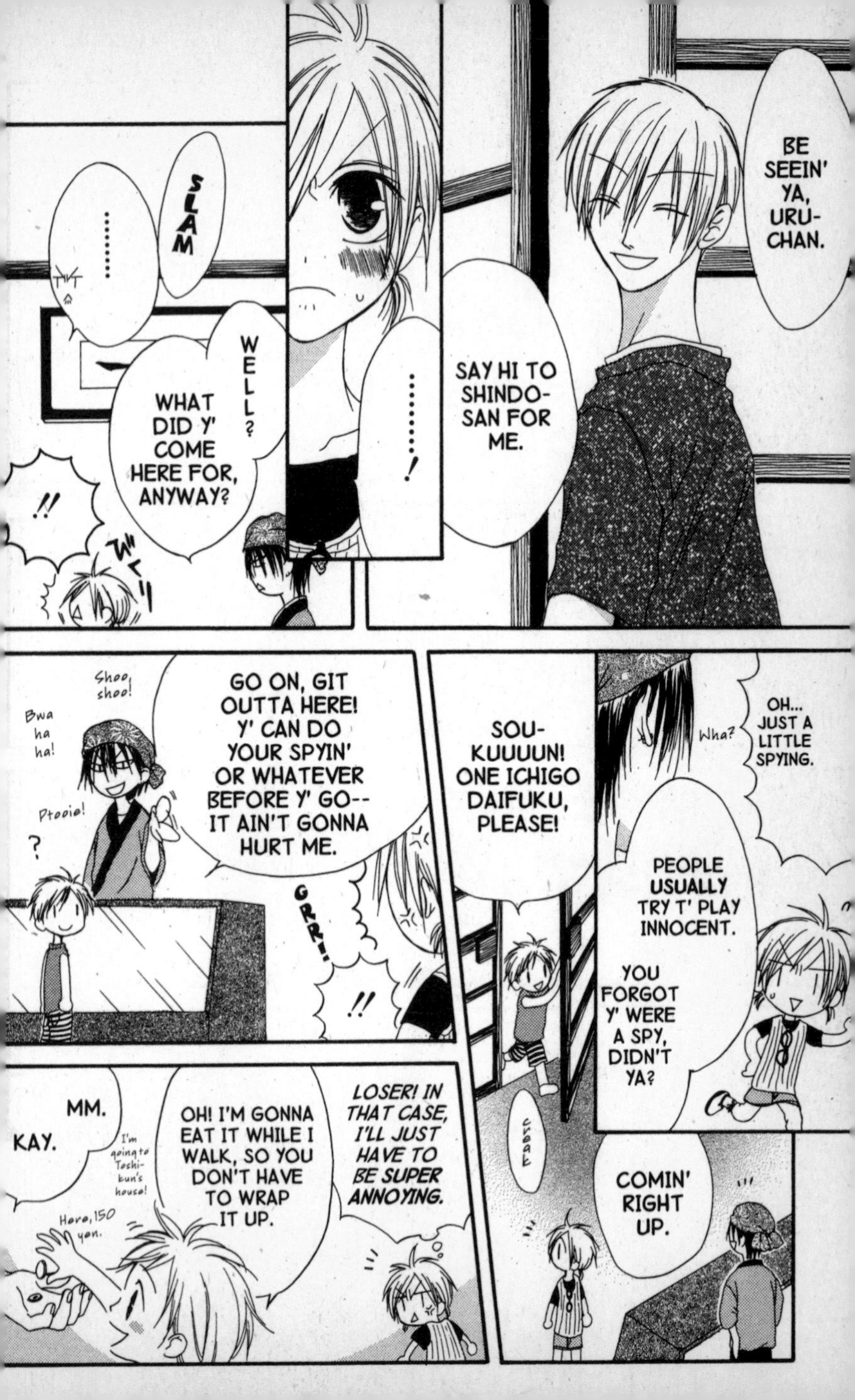

BE SEEIN' YA, URU-CHAN.
SAY HI TO SHINDO-SAN FOR ME.
......!
SLAM
......
WELL? WHAT DID Y' COME HERE FOR, ANYWAY?
!!
Wha?
OH... JUST A LITTLE SPYING.
PEOPLE USUALLY TRY T' PLAY INNOCENT.
YOU FORGOT Y' WERE A SPY, DIDN'T YA?
SOU-KUUUUN! ONE ICHIGO DAIFUKU, PLEASE!
creak
COMIN' RIGHT UP.
GO ON, GIT OUTTA HERE! Y' CAN DO YOUR SPYIN' OR WHATEVER BEFORE Y' GO-- IT AIN'T GONNA HURT ME.
Shoo shoo!
Bwa ha ha!
Ptooie!
?
GRR!!
!!
LOSER! IN THAT CASE, I'LL JUST HAVE TO BE SUPER ANNOYING.
OH! I'M GONNA EAT IT WHILE I WALK, SO YOU DON'T HAVE TO WRAP IT UP.
MM.
KAY.
I'm going to Toshi-kun's house!
Here, 150 yen.

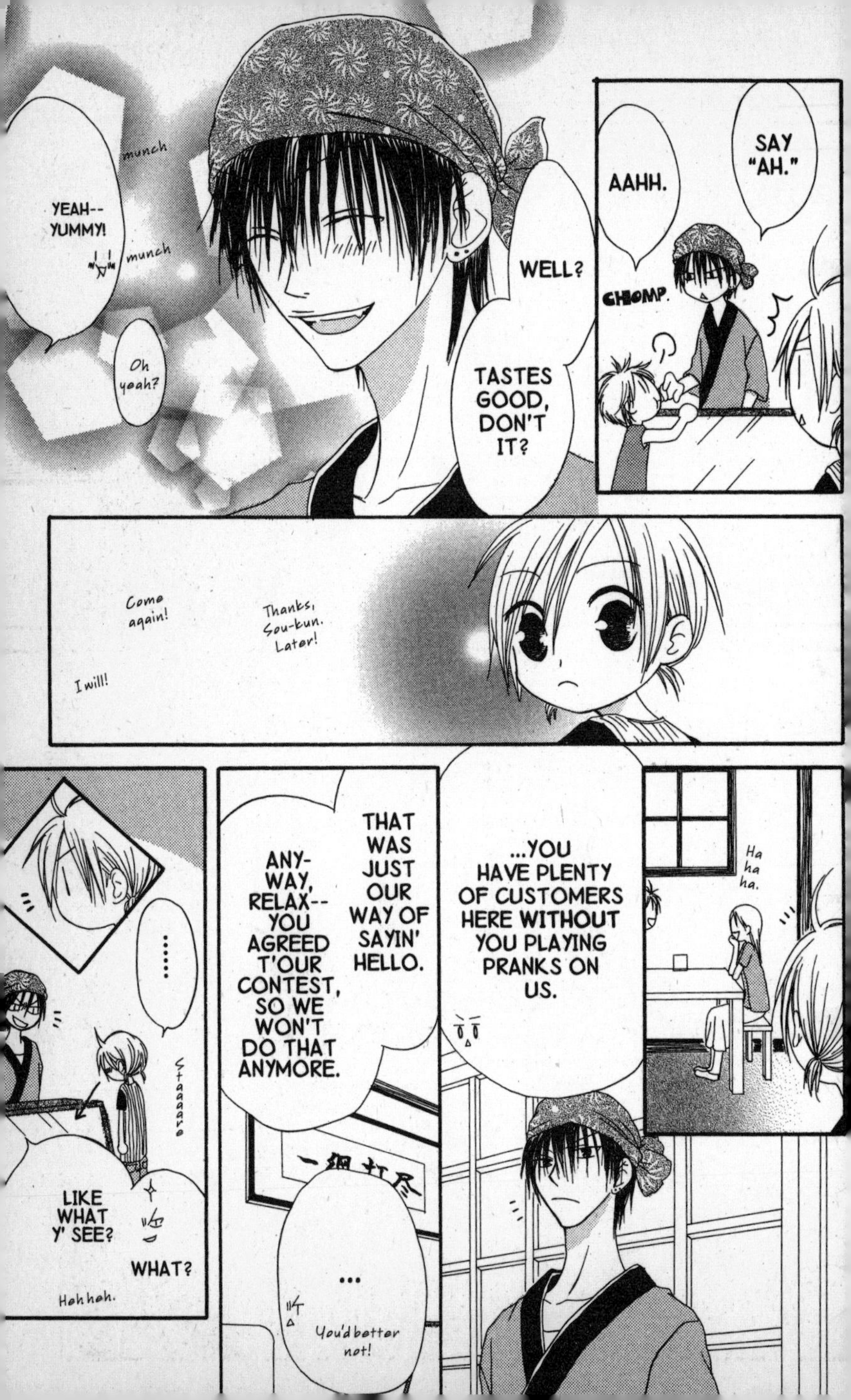
SAY "AH."
AAHH.
CHOMP.
WELL?
TASTES GOOD, DON'T IT?
munch
YEAH-- YUMMY!
munch
Oh yeah?
Thanks, Sou-kun. Later!
Come again!
I will!
Ha ha ha.
...YOU HAVE PLENTY OF CUSTOMERS HERE WITHOUT YOU PLAYING PRANKS ON US.
THAT WAS JUST OUR WAY OF SAYIN' HELLO.
ANY-WAY, RELAX-- YOU AGREED T'OUR CONTEST, SO WE WON'T DO THAT ANYMORE.
...
You'd better not!
......
Staaaare
LIKE WHAT Y' SEE?
WHAT?
Heh heh.

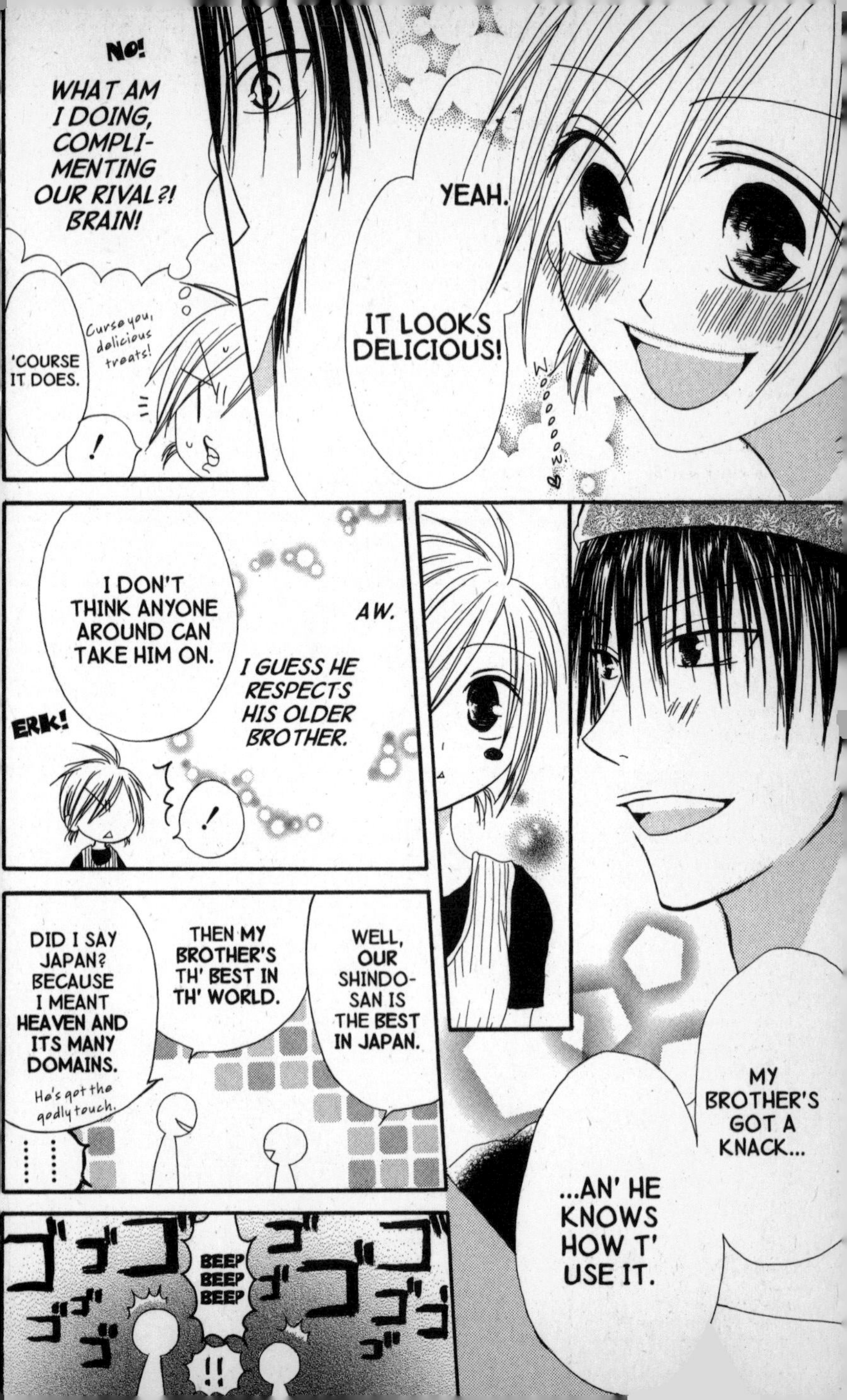
YEAH.
IT LOOKS DELICIOUS!
WOOOOOOOW♥
NO!
WHAT AM I DOING, COMPLIMENTING OUR RIVAL?! BRAIN!
Curse you, delicious treats!
'COURSE IT DOES.
!
MY BROTHER'S GOT A KNACK...
...AN' HE KNOWS HOW T' USE IT.
AW.
I GUESS HE RESPECTS HIS OLDER BROTHER.
I DON'T THINK ANYONE AROUND CAN TAKE HIM ON.
ERK!
!
WELL, OUR SHINDO-SAN IS THE BEST IN JAPAN.
THEN MY BROTHER'S TH' BEST IN TH' WORLD.
DID I SAY JAPAN? BECAUSE I MEANT HEAVEN AND ITS MANY DOMAINS.
He's got the godly touch.
......
ゴゴゴ
BEEP BEEP BEEP
!!

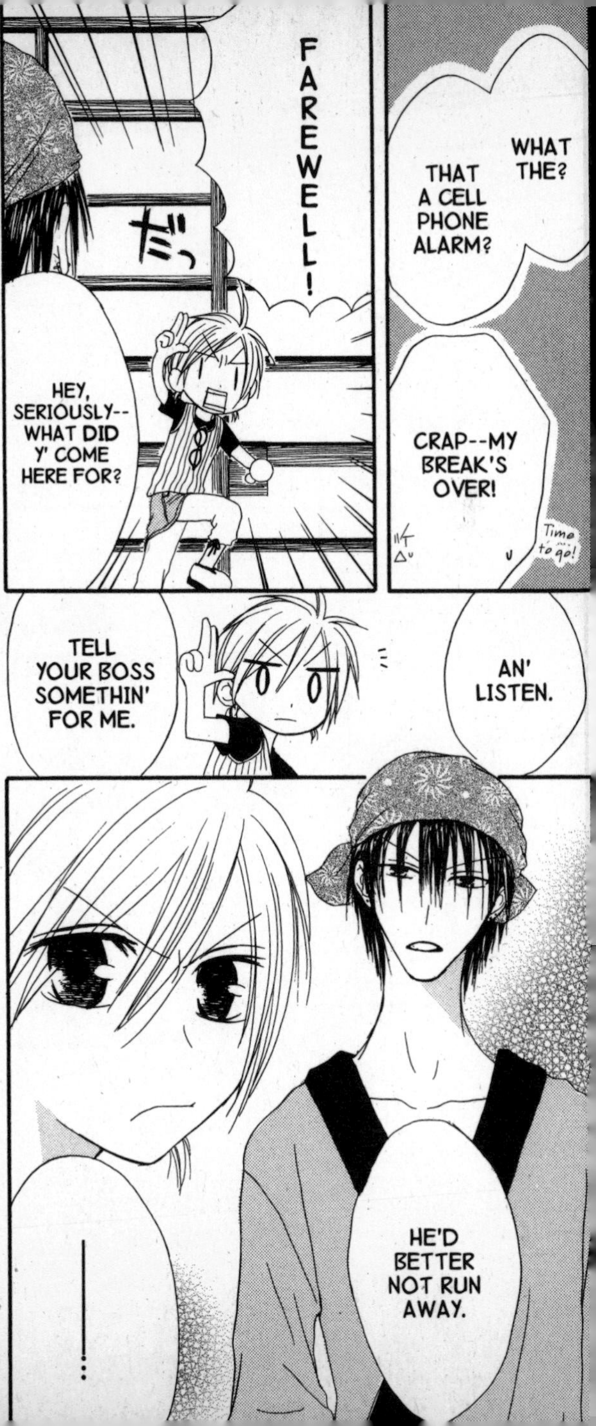
WHAT THE?
THAT A CELL PHONE ALARM?
CRAP--MY BREAK'S OVER!
Time to go!
FAREWELL!
HEY, SERIOUSLY-- WHAT DID Y' COME HERE FOR?
AN' LISTEN.
TELL YOUR BOSS SOMETHIN' FOR ME.
HE'D BETTER NOT RUN AWAY.

3

When Volume 1 went on sale, I got flowers from my old editor and a necklace from my current editor!

Like, whoa.

Thank you so much!

I was so happy that I equipped Uru with them on the cover of this volume.

(The flowers and the necklace are both more gorgeous in real life.)

And I'm really grateful for the letters and presents congratulating me from readers!

Are you all plotting to make me cry?!

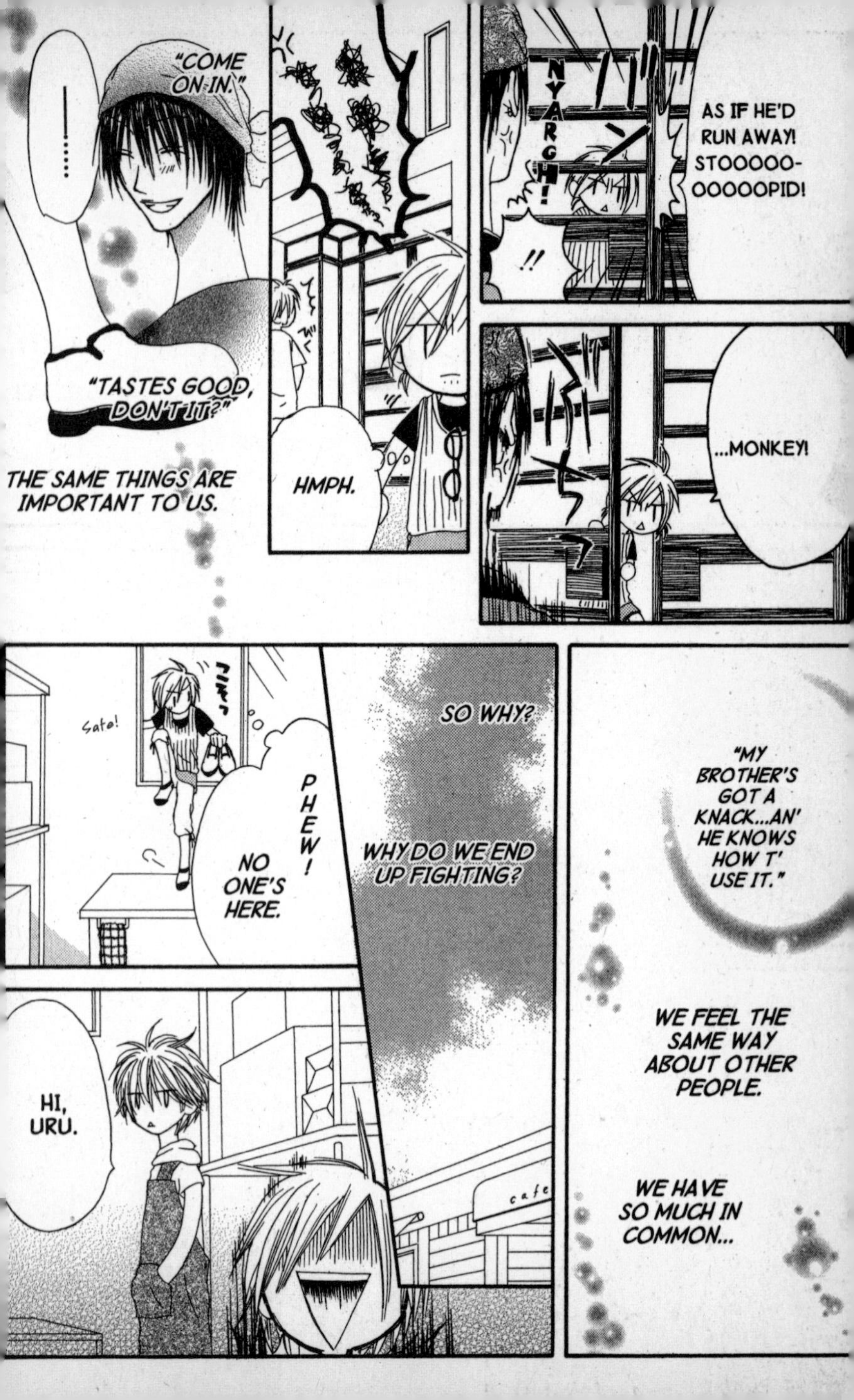

NYARGH!
AS IF HE'D RUN AWAY! STOOOOO-OOOOOPID!
!!
...MONKEY!
HMPH.
"COME ON IN."
!......
"TASTES GOOD, DON'T IT?"
THE SAME THINGS ARE IMPORTANT TO US.
"MY BROTHER'S GOT A KNACK...AN' HE KNOWS HOW T' USE IT."
WE FEEL THE SAME WAY ABOUT OTHER PEOPLE.
WE HAVE SO MUCH IN COMMON...
SO WHY?
WHY DO WE END UP FIGHTING?
PHEW!
NO ONE'S HERE.
Safe!
HI, URU.
cafe

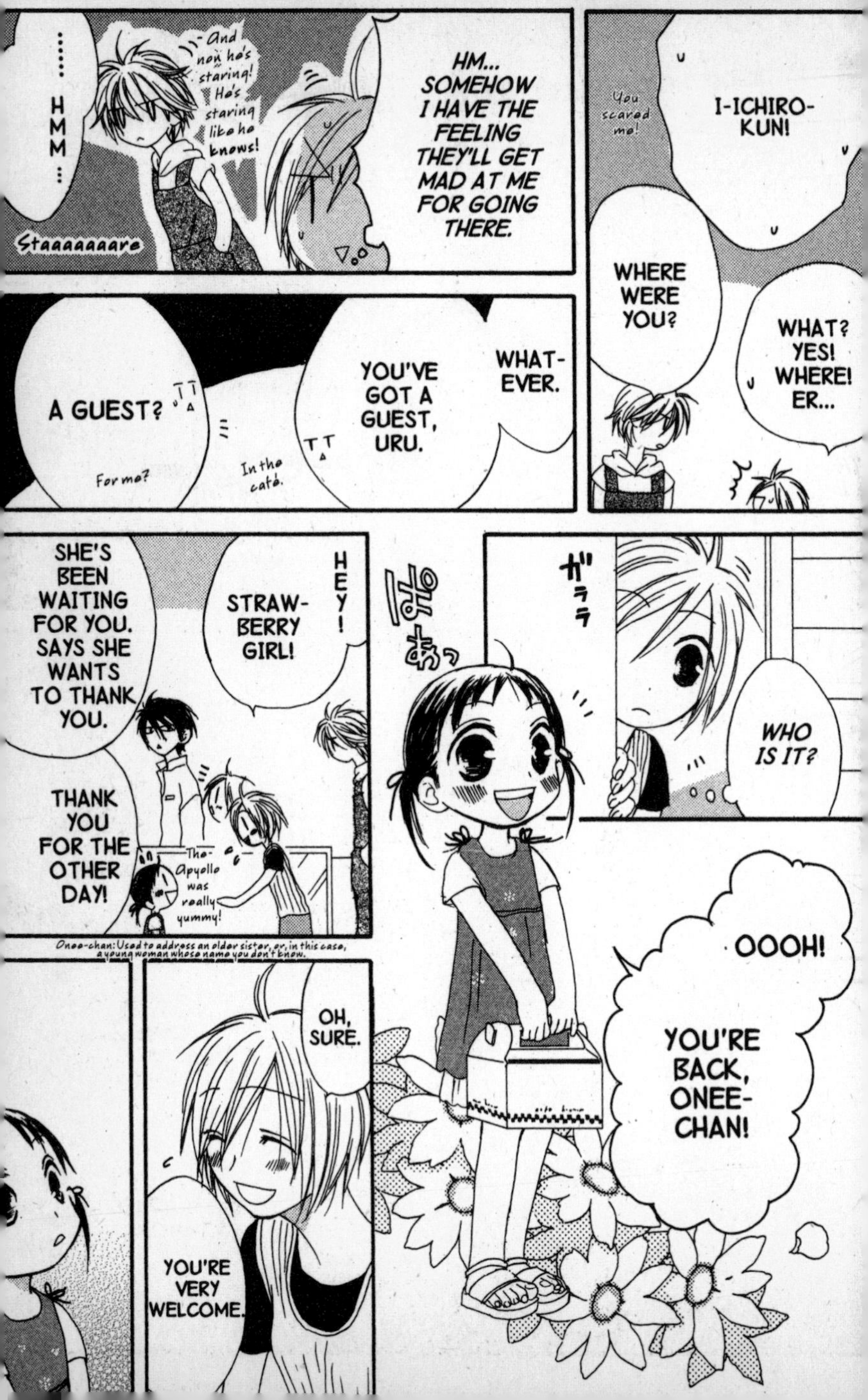
You scared me!
I-ICHIRO-KUN!
WHERE WERE YOU?
WHAT? YES! WHERE! ER...
HM... SOMEHOW I HAVE THE FEELING THEY'LL GET MAD AT ME FOR GOING THERE.
And now he's staring! He's staring like he knows!
...... HMM ...
Staaaaaaare
WHAT-EVER.
YOU'VE GOT A GUEST, URU.
In the café.
A GUEST?
For me?
ガララ
WHO IS IT?
ぱあっ
OOOH!
YOU'RE BACK, ONEE-CHAN!
HEY!
STRAW-BERRY GIRL!
SHE'S BEEN WAITING FOR YOU. SAYS SHE WANTS TO THANK YOU.
THANK YOU FOR THE OTHER DAY!
The Apyollo was really yummy!
Onee-chan: Used to address an older sister, or, in this case, a young woman whose name you don't know.
OH, SURE.
YOU'RE VERY WELCOME.

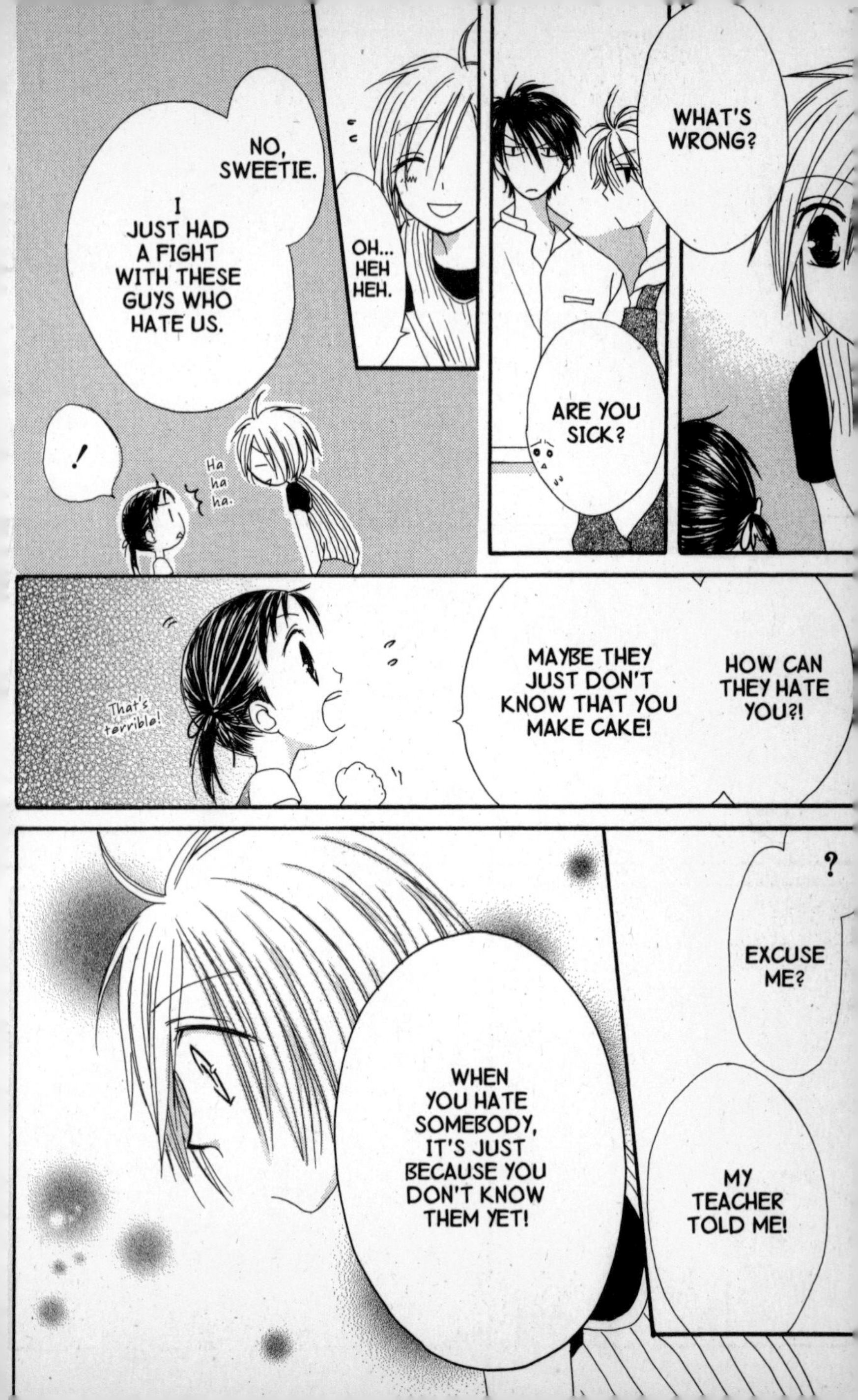
WHAT'S WRONG?
ARE YOU SICK?
OH... HEH HEH.
NO, SWEETIE.
I JUST HAD A FIGHT WITH THESE GUYS WHO HATE US.
Ha ha ha.
!
HOW CAN THEY HATE YOU?!
MAYBE THEY JUST DON'T KNOW THAT YOU MAKE CAKE!
That's terrible!
?
EXCUSE ME?
MY TEACHER TOLD ME!
WHEN YOU HATE SOMEBODY, IT'S JUST BECAUSE YOU DON'T KNOW THEM YET!

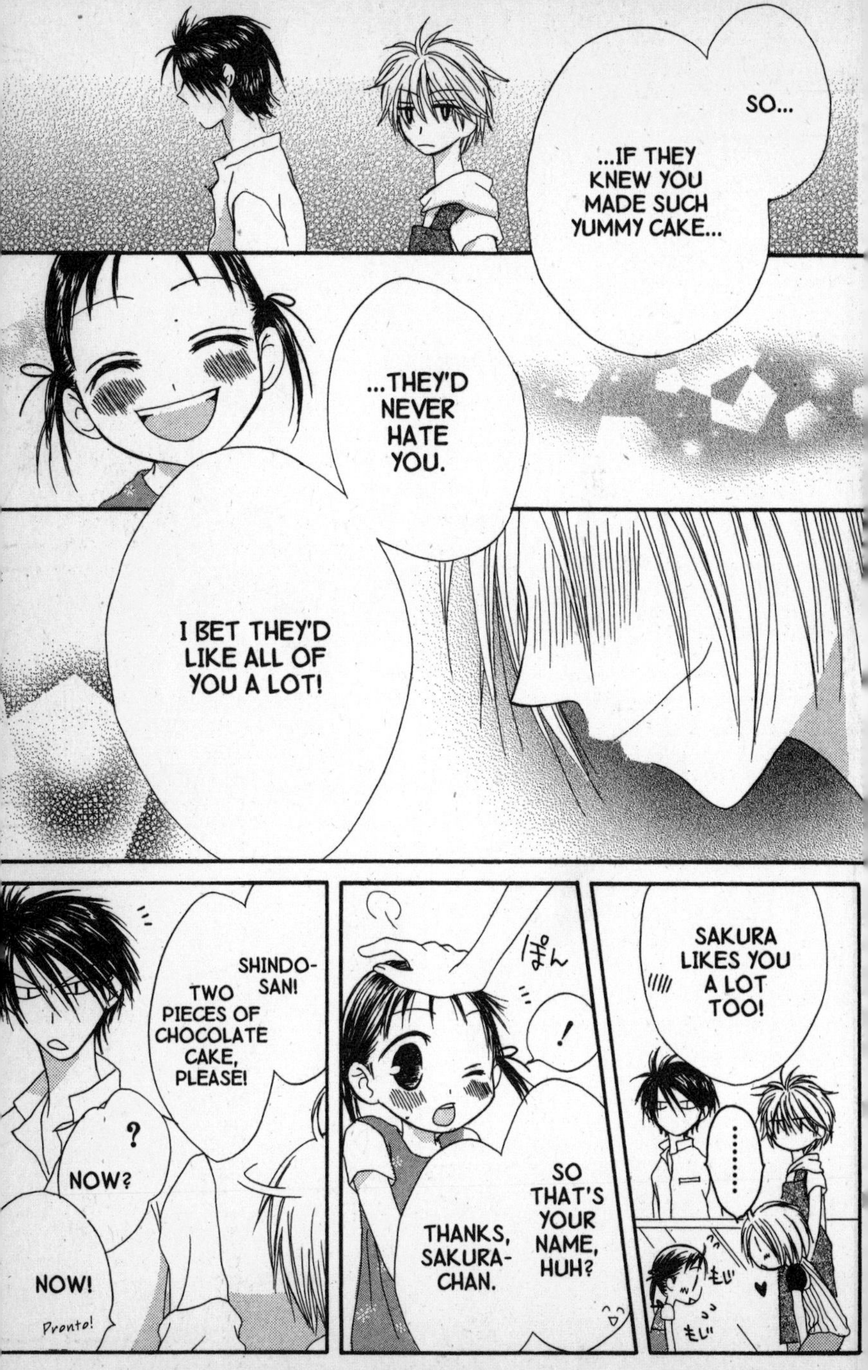
SO...
...IF THEY KNEW YOU MADE SUCH YUMMY CAKE...
...THEY'D NEVER HATE YOU.
I BET THEY'D LIKE ALL OF YOU A LOT!
SAKURA LIKES YOU A LOT TOO!
....
もじ
もじ
ぽん
!
SO THAT'S YOUR NAME, HUH?
THANKS, SAKURA-CHAN.
SHINDO-SAN! TWO PIECES OF CHOCOLATE CAKE, PLEASE!
?
NOW?
NOW!
Pronto!

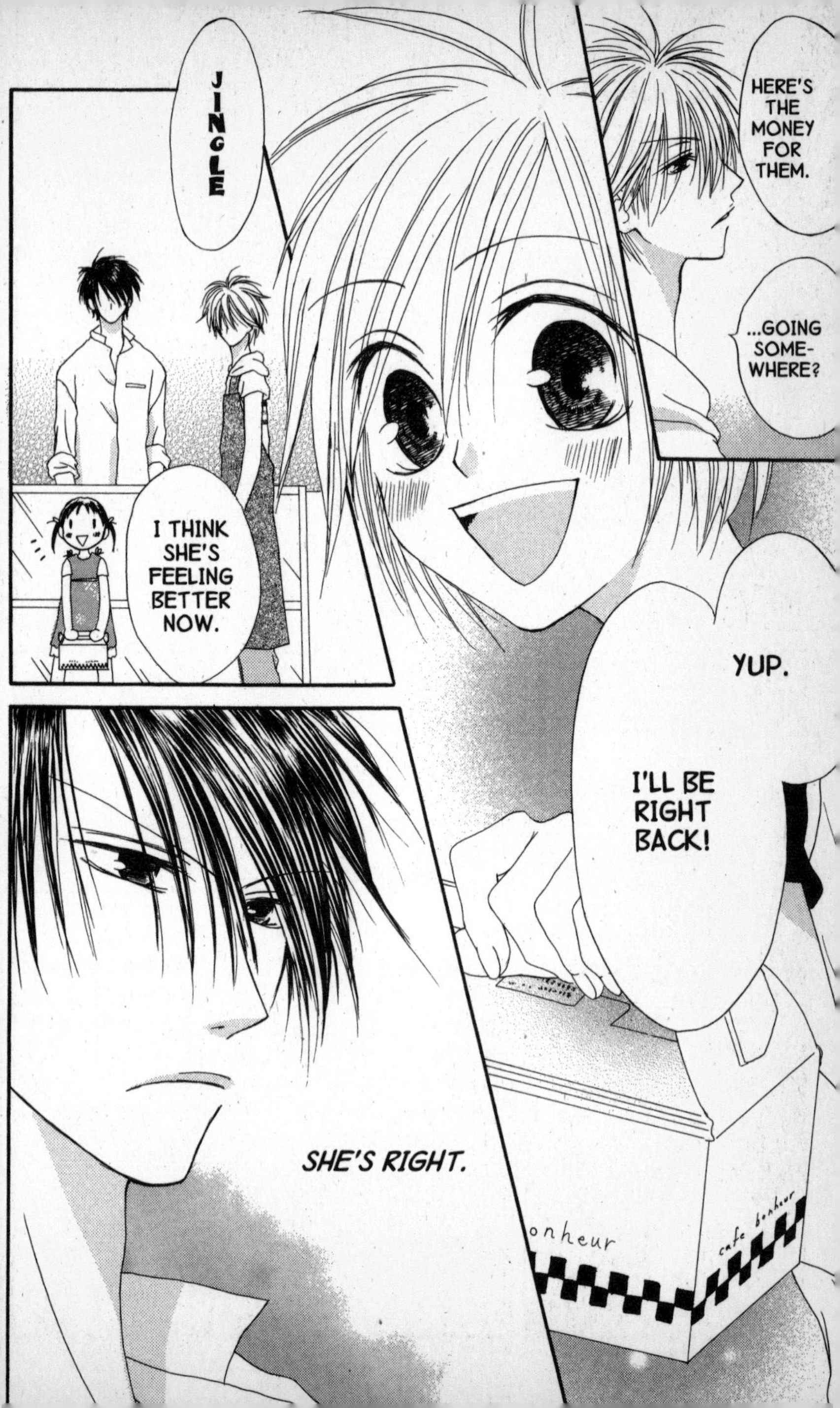
HERE'S THE MONEY FOR THEM.
...GOING SOMEWHERE?
YUP.
I'LL BE RIGHT BACK!
cafe bonheur
JINGLE
I THINK SHE'S FEELING BETTER NOW.
SHE'S RIGHT.

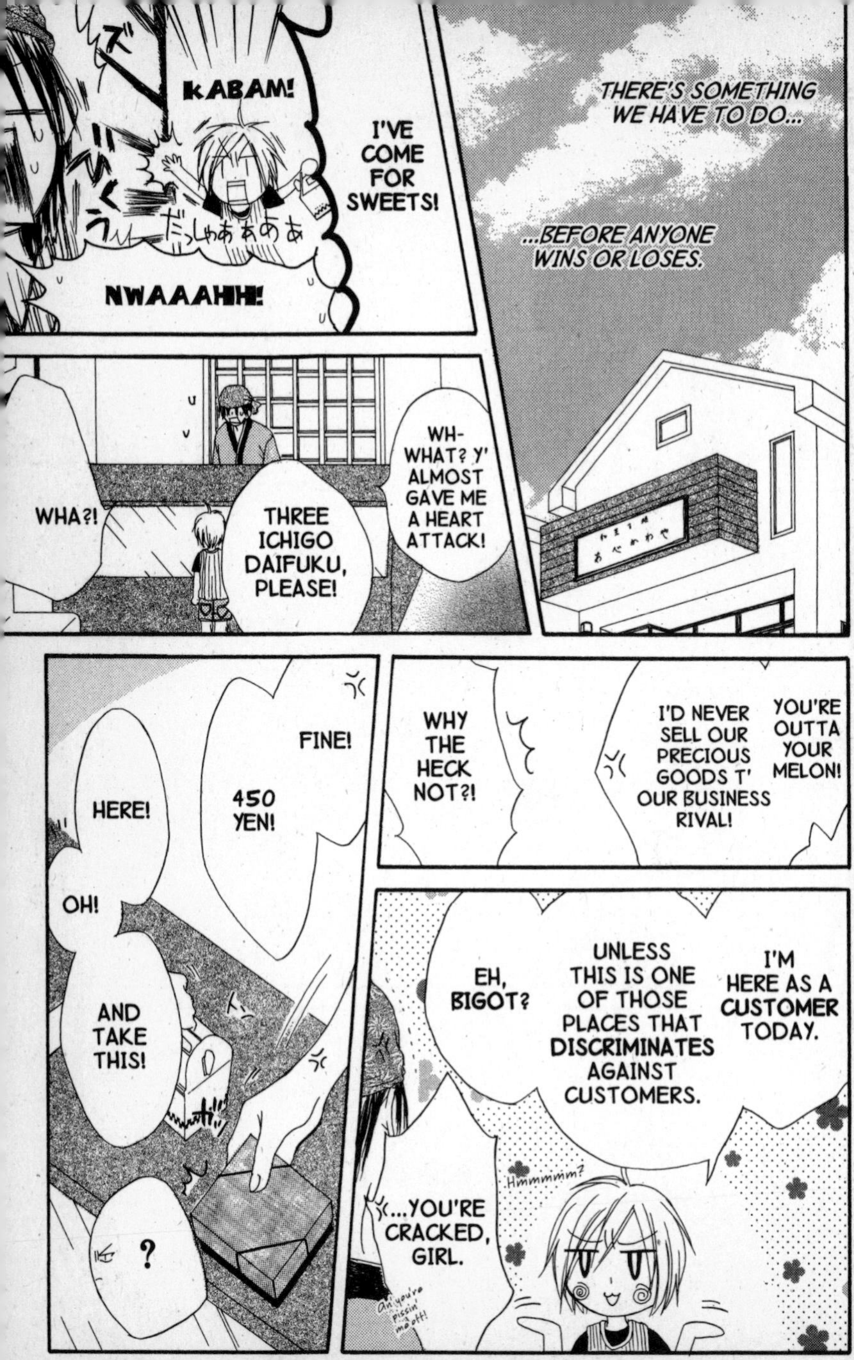
THERE'S SOMETHING WE HAVE TO DO...
...BEFORE ANYONE WINS OR LOSES.
I'VE COME FOR SWEETS!
KABAM!
ズ
びくぅ
だっしゃあああああ
NWAAAHH!
WH-WHAT? Y' ALMOST GAVE ME A HEART ATTACK!
THREE ICHIGO DAIFUKU, PLEASE!
WHA?!
YOU'RE OUTTA YOUR MELON!
I'D NEVER SELL OUR PRECIOUS GOODS T' OUR BUSINESS RIVAL!
WHY THE HECK NOT?!
I'M HERE AS A CUSTOMER TODAY.
UNLESS THIS IS ONE OF THOSE PLACES THAT DISCRIMINATES AGAINST CUSTOMERS.
EH, BIGOT?
Hmmmmm?
...YOU'RE CRACKED, GIRL.
An' you're pissin' me off!
FINE!
450 YEN!
HERE!
OH!
AND TAKE THIS!
?

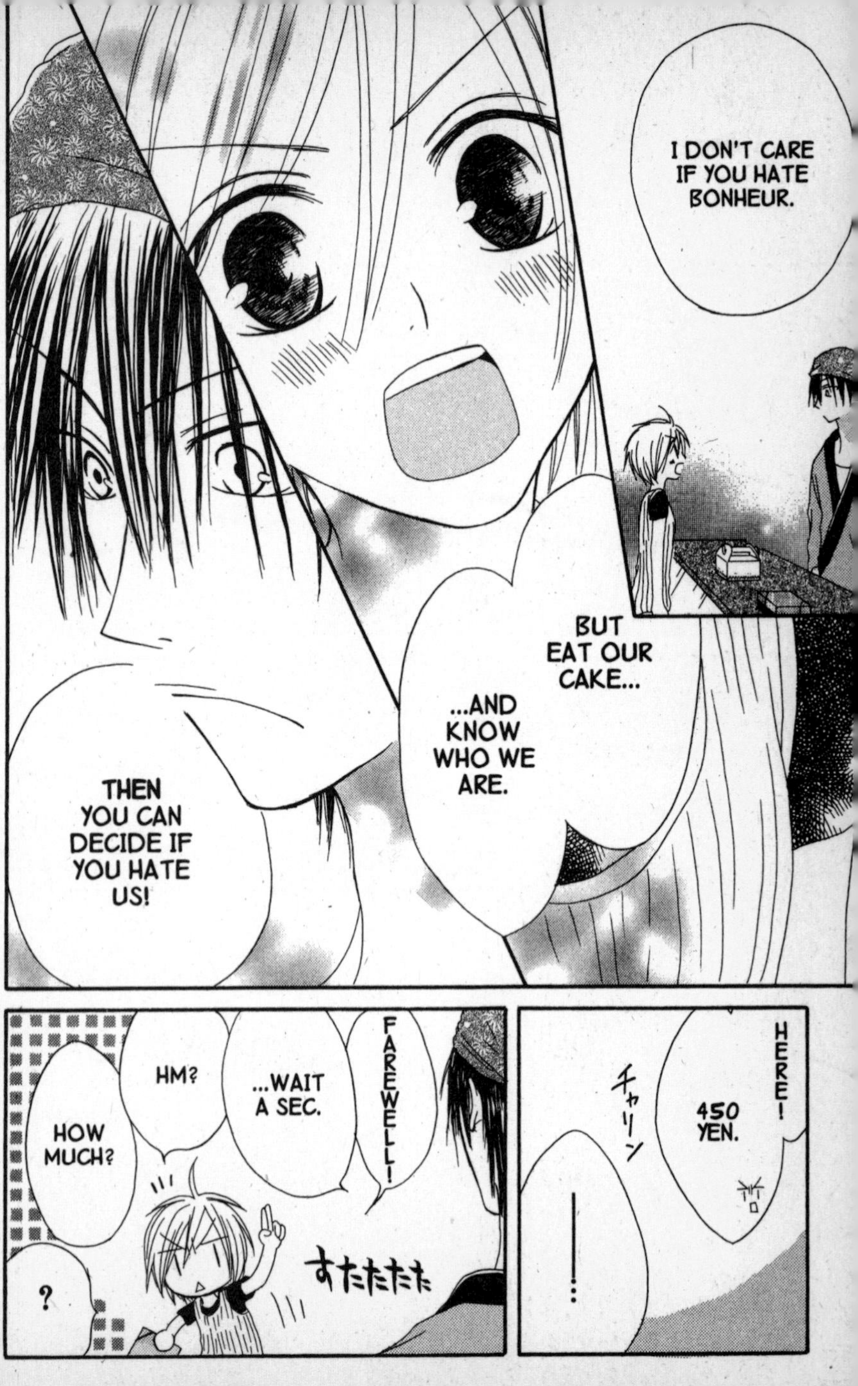
I DON'T CARE IF YOU HATE BONHEUR.
BUT EAT OUR CAKE...
...AND KNOW WHO WE ARE.
THEN YOU CAN DECIDE IF YOU HATE US!
HERE!
450 YEN.
チャリーン
—!..
FAREWELL!
...WAIT A SEC.
HM?
HOW MUCH?
?
すたたたた

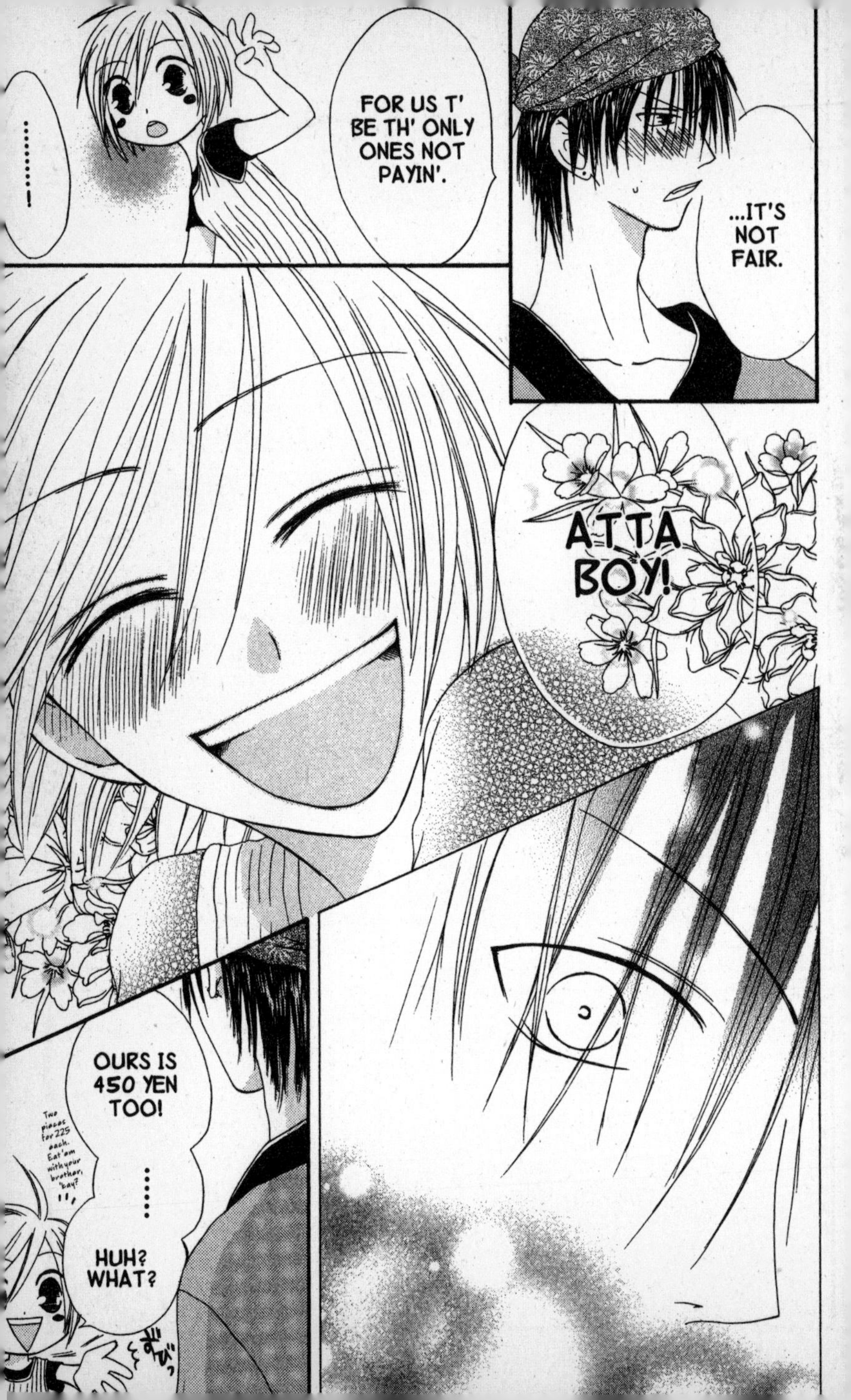
...IT'S NOT FAIR.
FOR US T' BE TH' ONLY ONES NOT PAYIN'.
......!
ATTA BOY!
OURS IS 450 YEN TOO!
Two pieces for 225 each. Eat'em with your brother, 'kay?
......
HUH? WHAT?

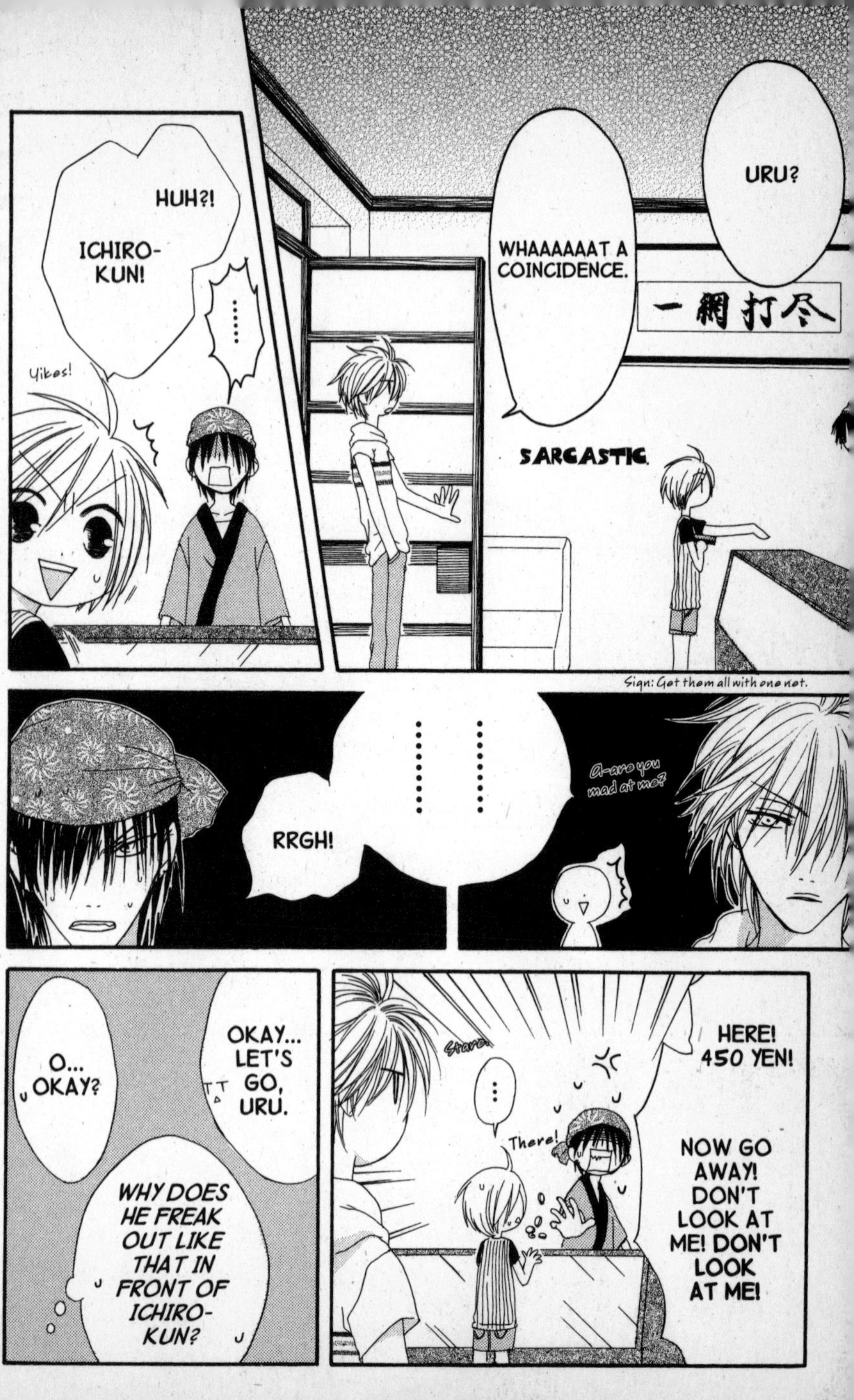
URU?
WHAAAAAAT A COINCIDENCE.
一網打尽
SARCASTIC.
HUH?!
ICHIRO-KUN!
......
Yikes!
Sign: Get them all with one net.
A-are you mad at me?
......
......
RRGH!
HERE! 450 YEN!
NOW GO AWAY! DON'T LOOK AT ME! DON'T LOOK AT ME!
Stare...
...
There!
OKAY... LET'S GO, URU.
O... OKAY?
WHY DOES HE FREAK OUT LIKE THAT IN FRONT OF ICHIRO-KUN?

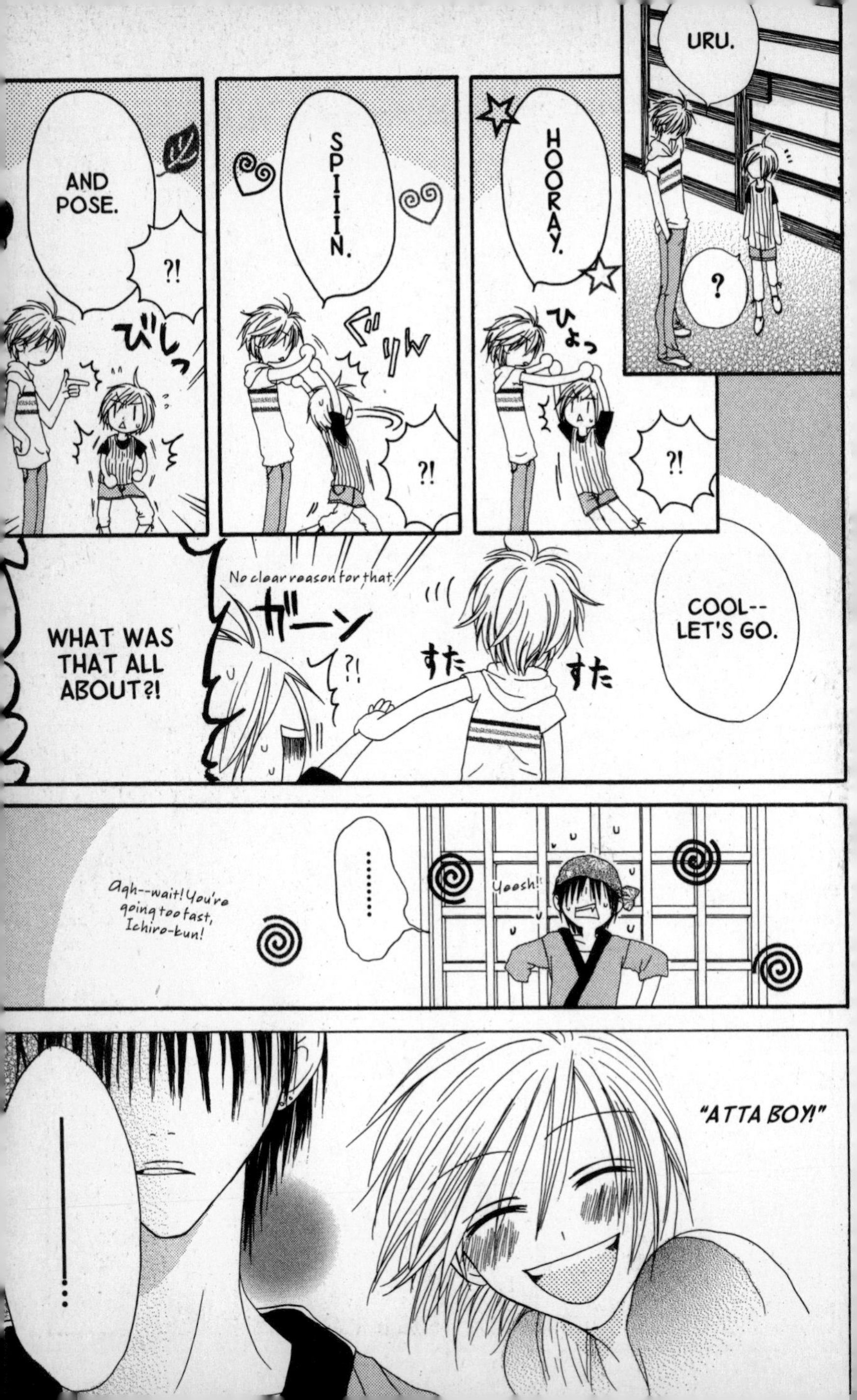
URU.
?
HOORAY.
ひょっ
?!
SPIIIN.
ぐりん
?!
AND POSE.
?!
びしっ
COOL--LET'S GO.
すた すた
No clear reason for that.
ガーン
?!
WHAT WAS THAT ALL ABOUT?!
Yeosh!
....
Agh--wait! You're going too fast, Ichiro-kun!
"ATTA BOY!"
......

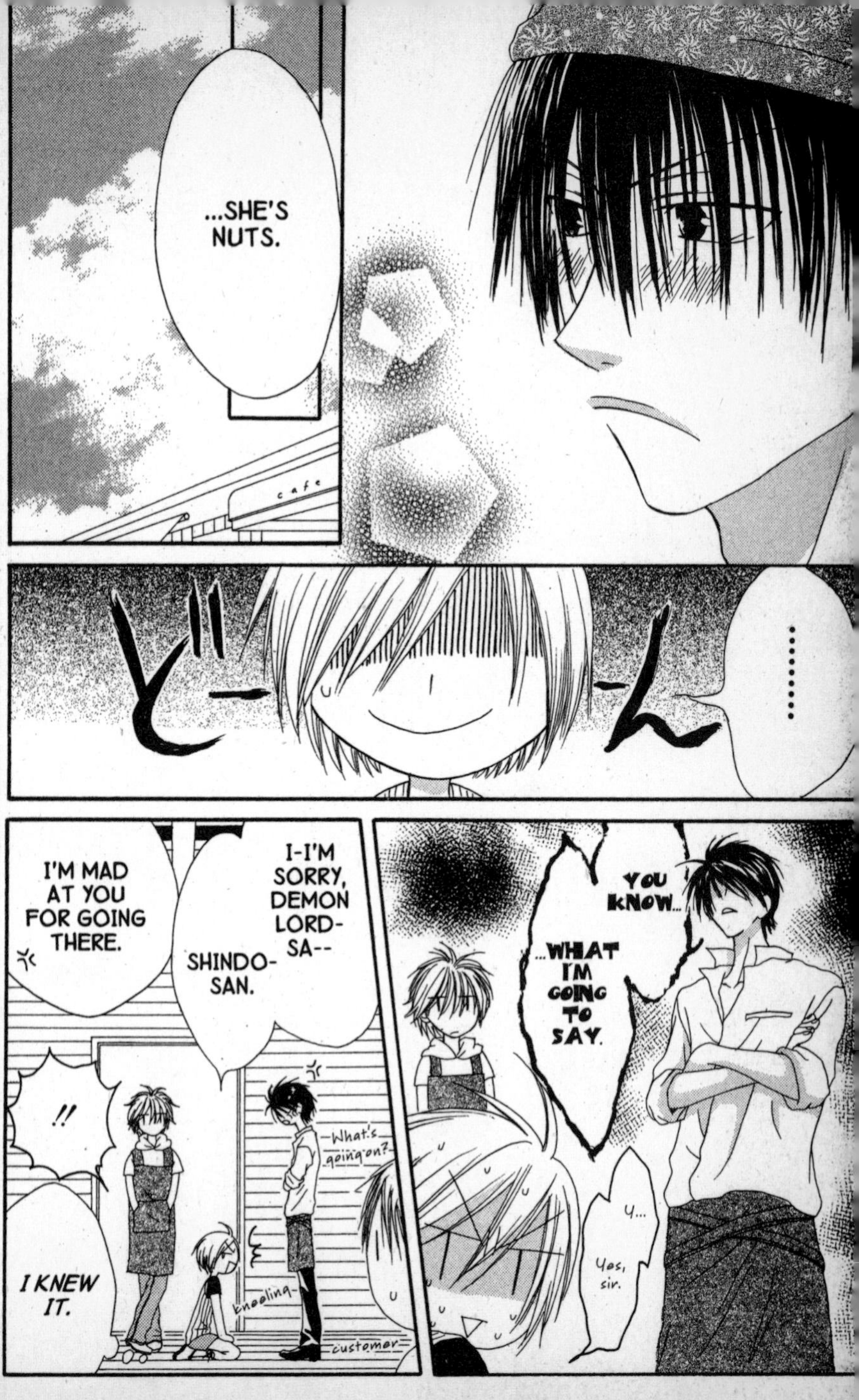

...SHE'S NUTS.
cafe
......
どーん
YOU KNOW...
...WHAT I'M GOING TO SAY.
Y...
Yes, sir.
I-I'M SORRY, DEMON LORD-SA--
SHINDO-SAN.
I'M MAD AT YOU FOR GOING THERE.
!!
What's going on?
kneeling
customer
I KNEW IT.

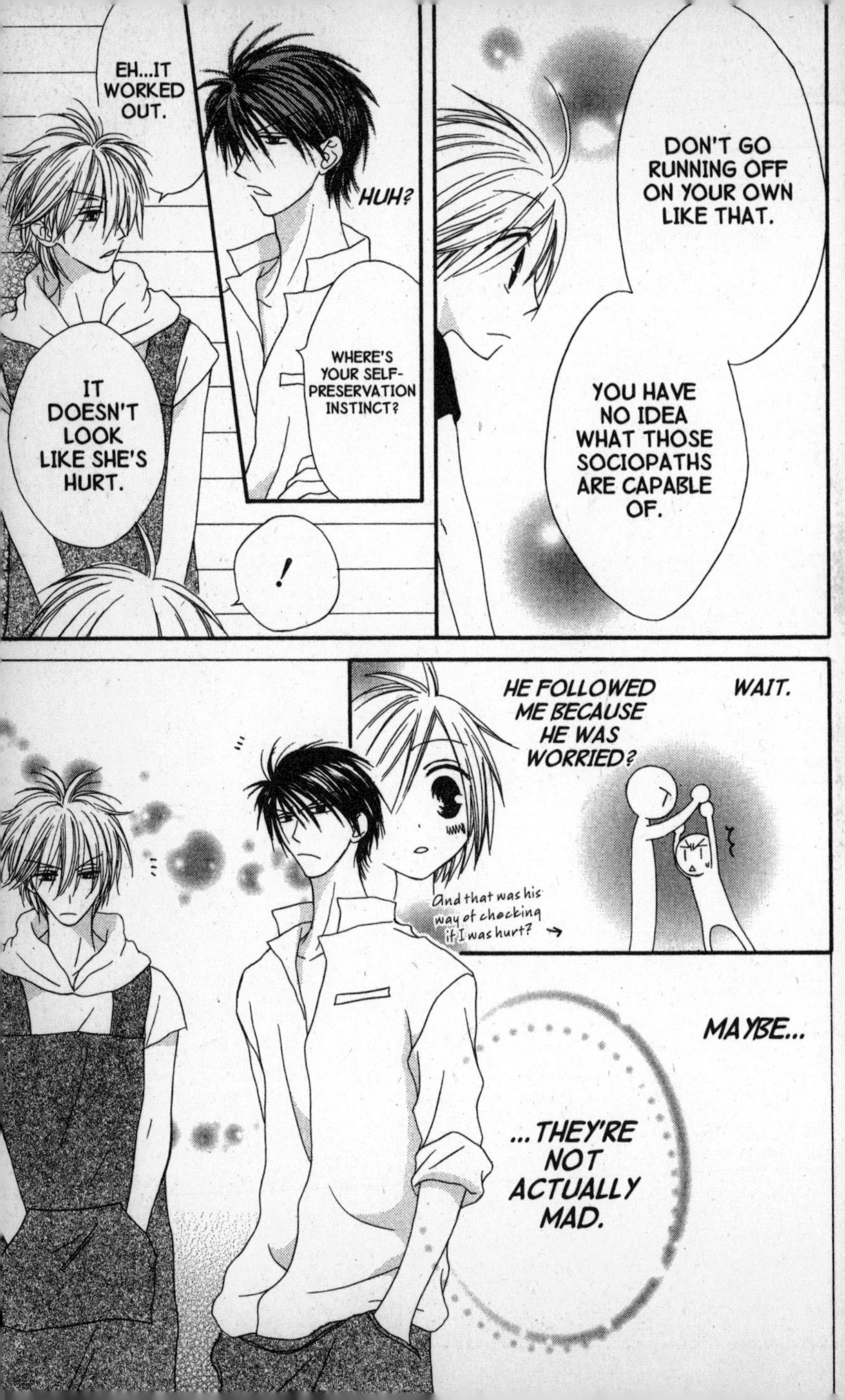
DON'T GO RUNNING OFF ON YOUR OWN LIKE THAT.
YOU HAVE NO IDEA WHAT THOSE SOCIOPATHS ARE CAPABLE OF.
HUH?
WHERE'S YOUR SELF-PRESERVATION INSTINCT?
EH...IT WORKED OUT.
IT DOESN'T LOOK LIKE SHE'S HURT.
!
WAIT.
HE FOLLOWED ME BECAUSE HE WAS WORRIED?
And that was his way of checking if I was hurt?
MAYBE...
...THEY'RE NOT ACTUALLY MAD.

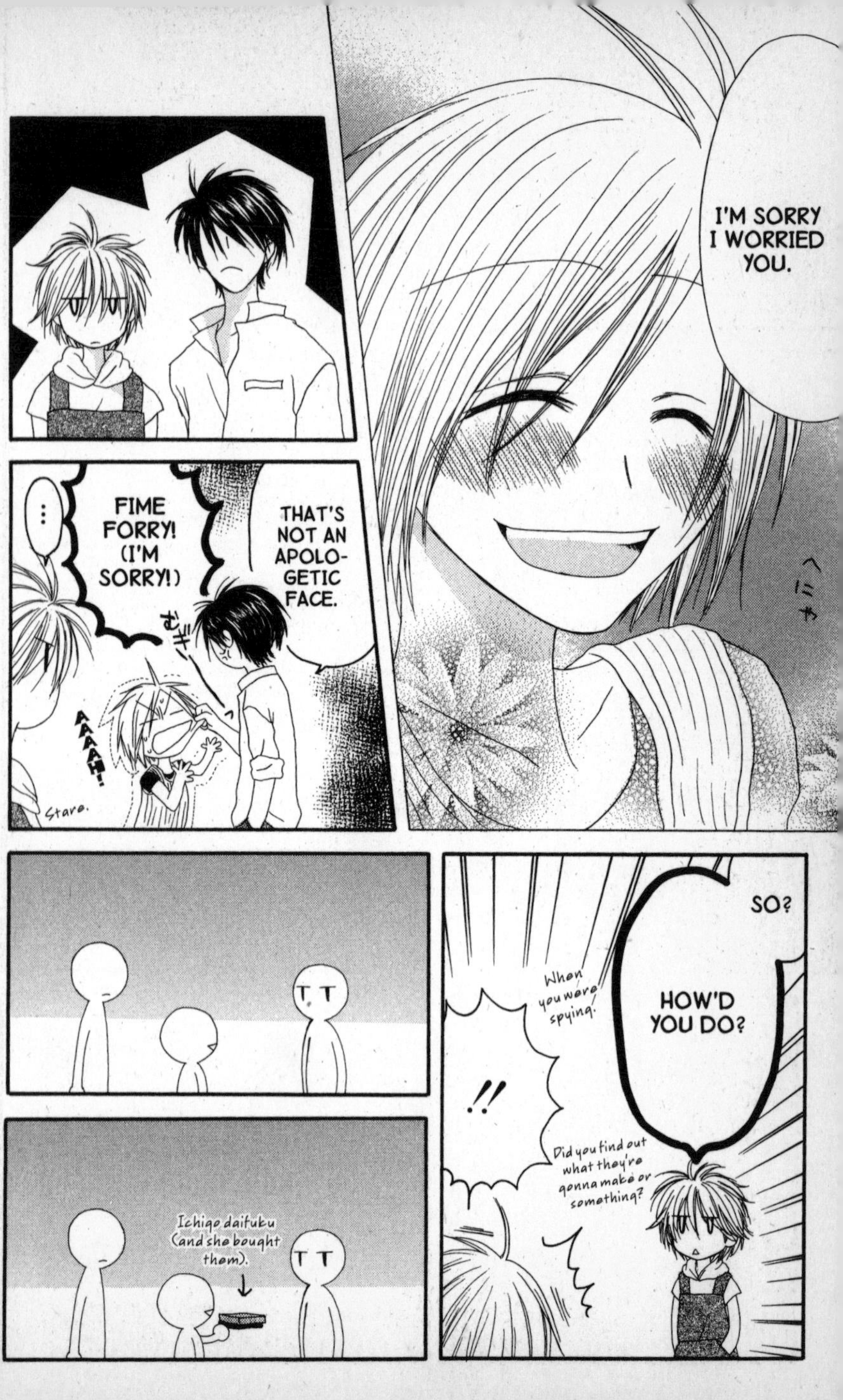
I'M SORRY I WORRIED YOU.
へにゃ
THAT'S NOT AN APOLOGETIC FACE.
FIME FORRY! (I'M SORRY!)
...
むぎ
AAAAH!
Stare.
SO?
HOW'D YOU DO?
When you were spying.
!!
Did you find out what they're gonna make or something?
Ichigo daifuku (and she bought them).

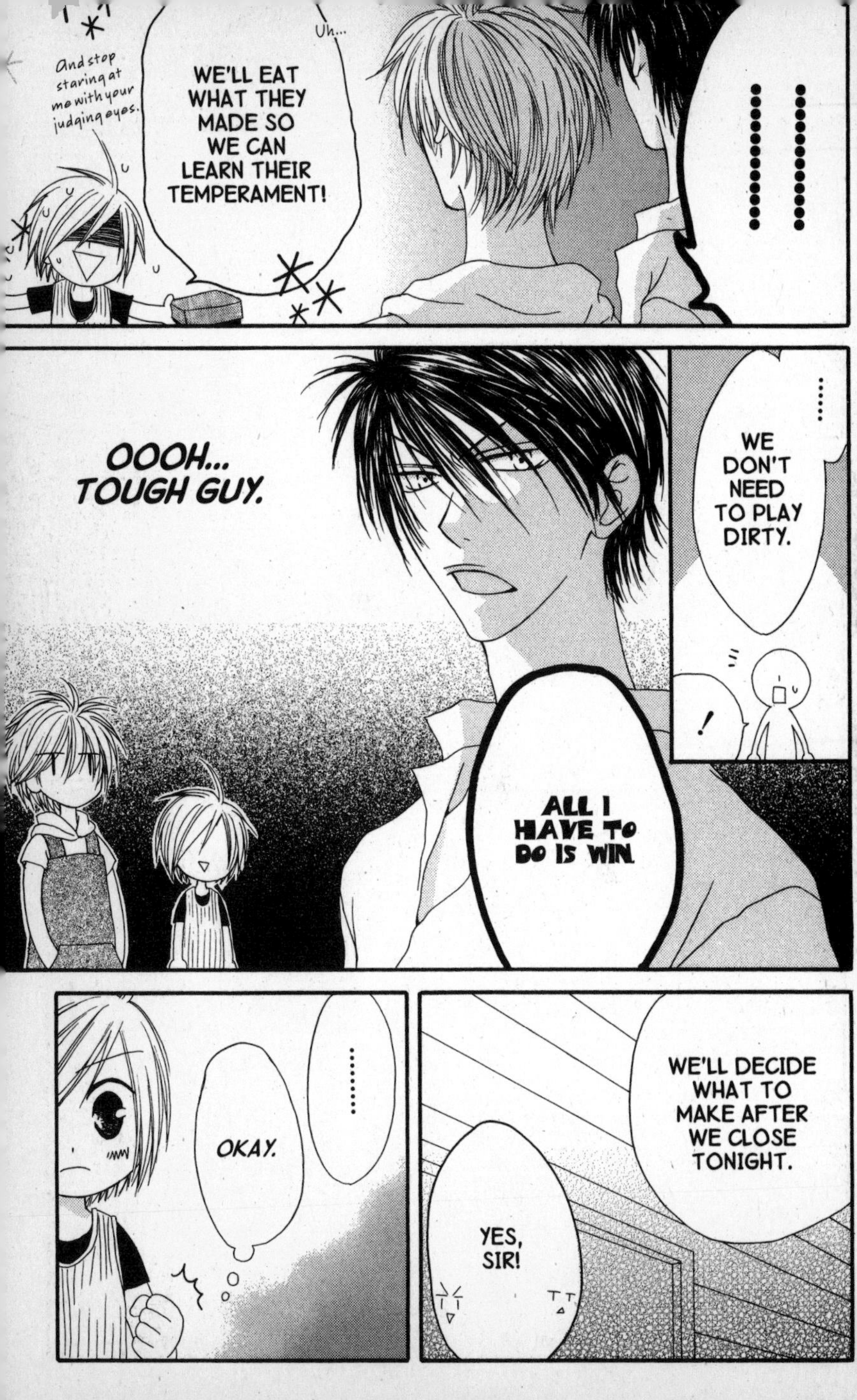
......
Uh...
WE'LL EAT WHAT THEY MADE SO WE CAN LEARN THEIR TEMPERAMENT!
And stop staring at me with your judging eyes.
......
WE DON'T NEED TO PLAY DIRTY.
!
ALL I HAVE TO DO IS WIN.
OOOH... TOUGH GUY.
WE'LL DECIDE WHAT TO MAKE AFTER WE CLOSE TONIGHT.
YES, SIR!
......
OKAY.

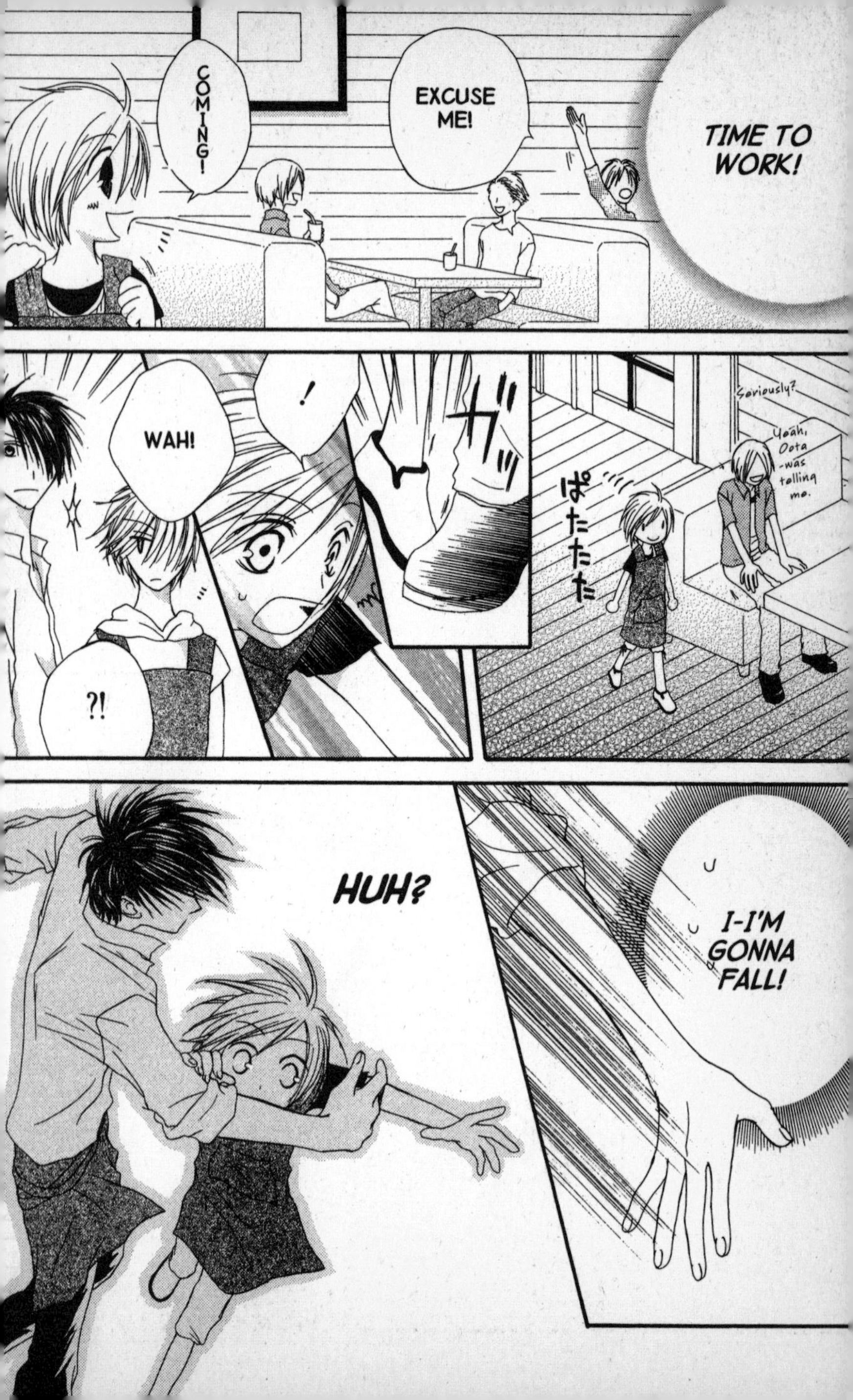

TIME TO WORK!
EXCUSE ME!
COMING!
Seriously?
Yeah, Oota was telling me.
ぱたたた
ガッ
!
WAH!
?!
I-I'M GONNA FALL!
HUH?

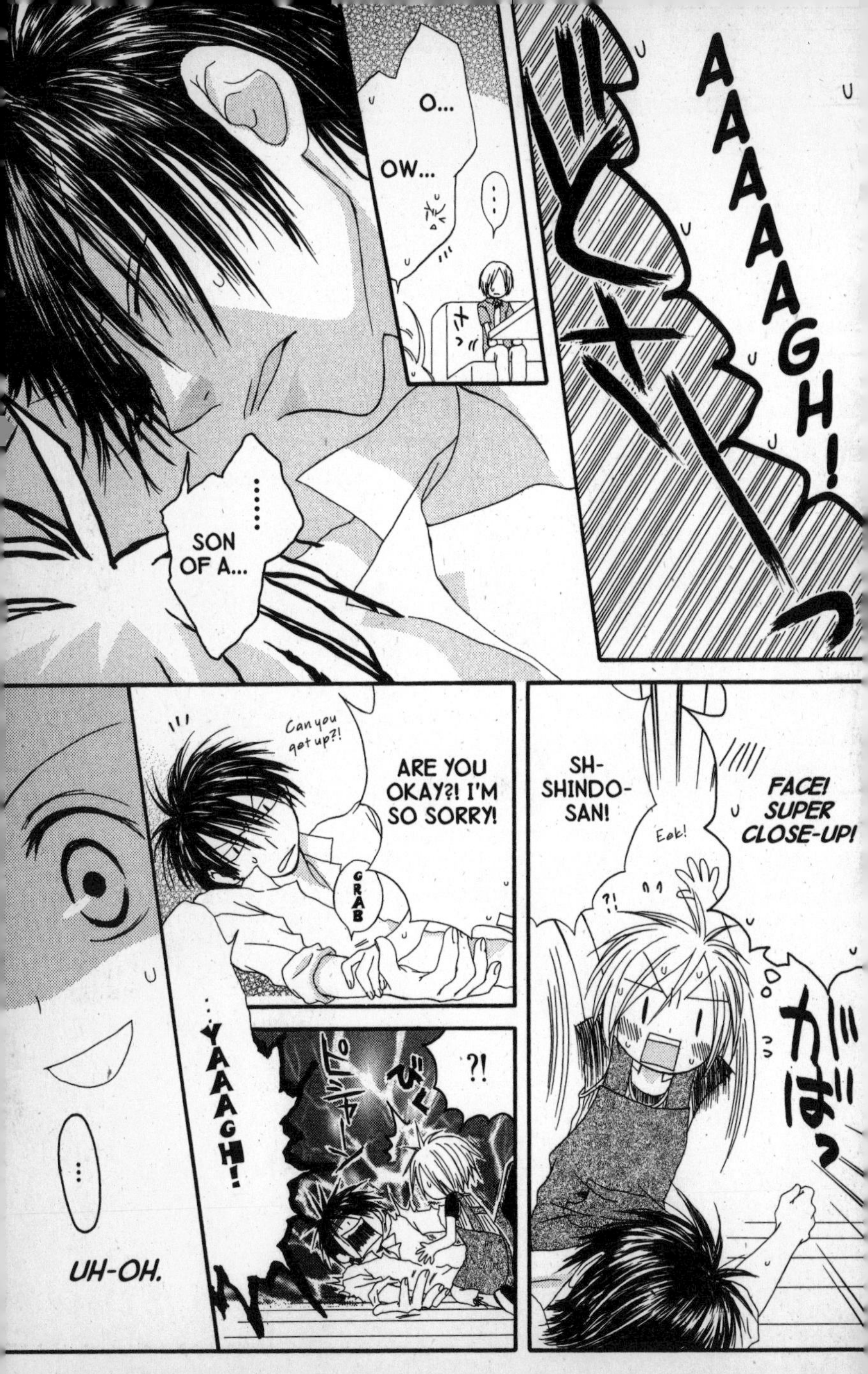
AAAAAAGH!
O...
OW...
...
......
SON OF A...
FACE! SUPER CLOSE-UP!
がばっ
SH- SHINDO-SAN!
Eek!
?!
ARE YOU OKAY?! I'M SO SORRY!
Can you get up?!
GRAB
?!
...YAAAAGH!
...
UH-OH.

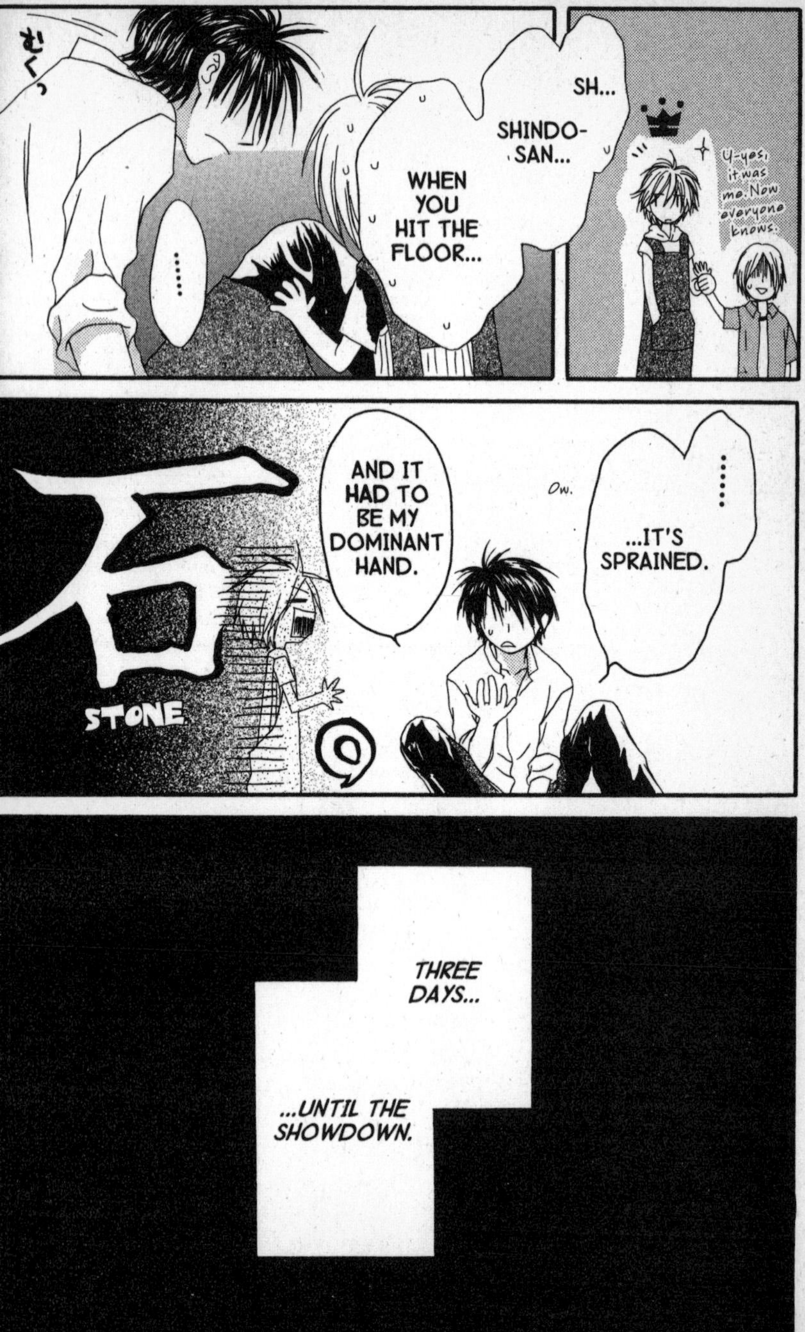
U-yes, it was me. Now everyone knows.
SH... SHINDO-SAN... WHEN YOU HIT THE FLOOR...
むくっ
......
......
...IT'S SPRAINED.
Ow.
AND IT HAD TO BE MY DOMINANT HAND.
石
STONE
THREE DAYS...
...UNTIL THE SHOWDOWN.

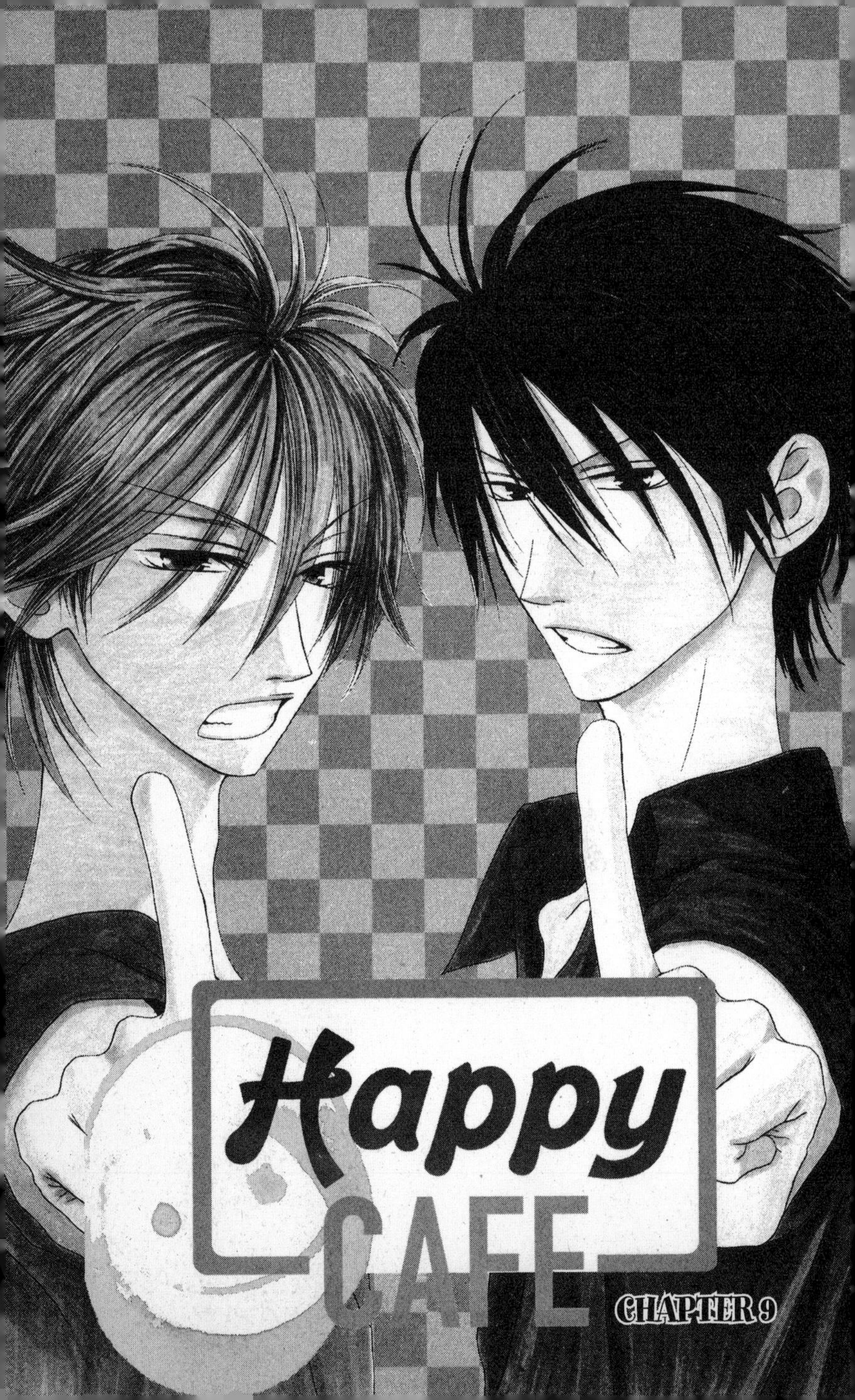
Happy
CAFE
CHAPTER 9

★Illustration for Bookstore POP Ad★

I had a lot of fun drawing it...
but coloring is really hard.

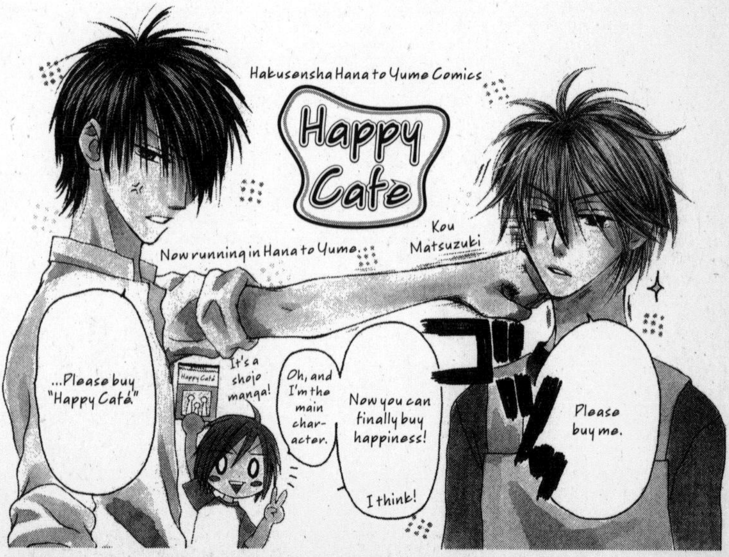
Hakusensha Hana to Yume Comics
Happy Cafe
Kou Matsuzuki
Now running in Hana to Yume...
Please buy me.
Now you can finally buy happiness!
I think!
Oh, and I'm the main char-acter.
It's a shojo manga!
...Please buy "Happy Café."

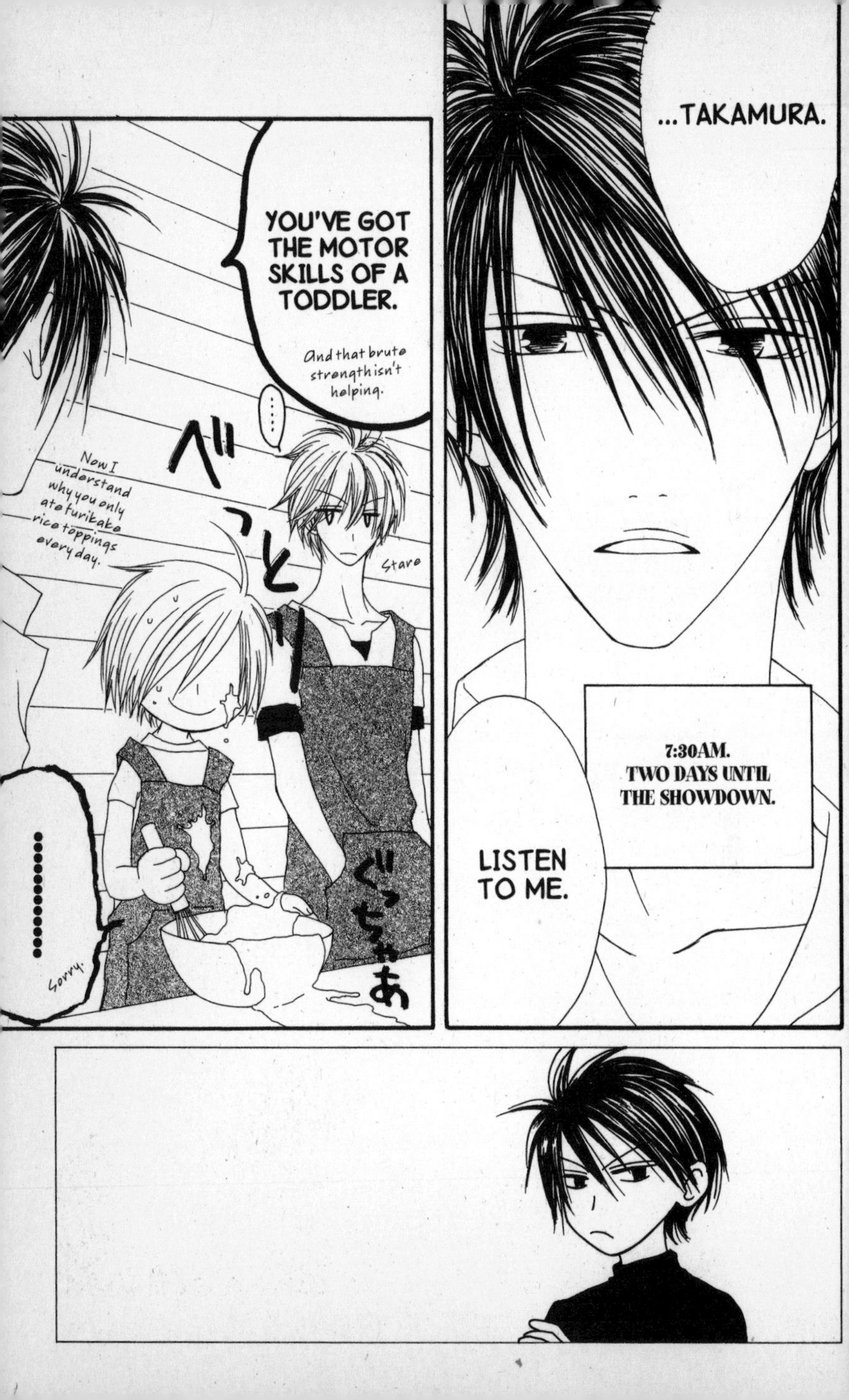
...TAKAMURA.
LISTEN TO ME.
7:30AM. TWO DAYS UNTIL THE SHOWDOWN.
YOU'VE GOT THE MOTOR SKILLS OF A TODDLER.
And that brute strength isn't helping.
......
べっとり
Stare
Now I understand why you only ate furikake rice toppings every day.
ぐっちゃあ
....
Sorry.

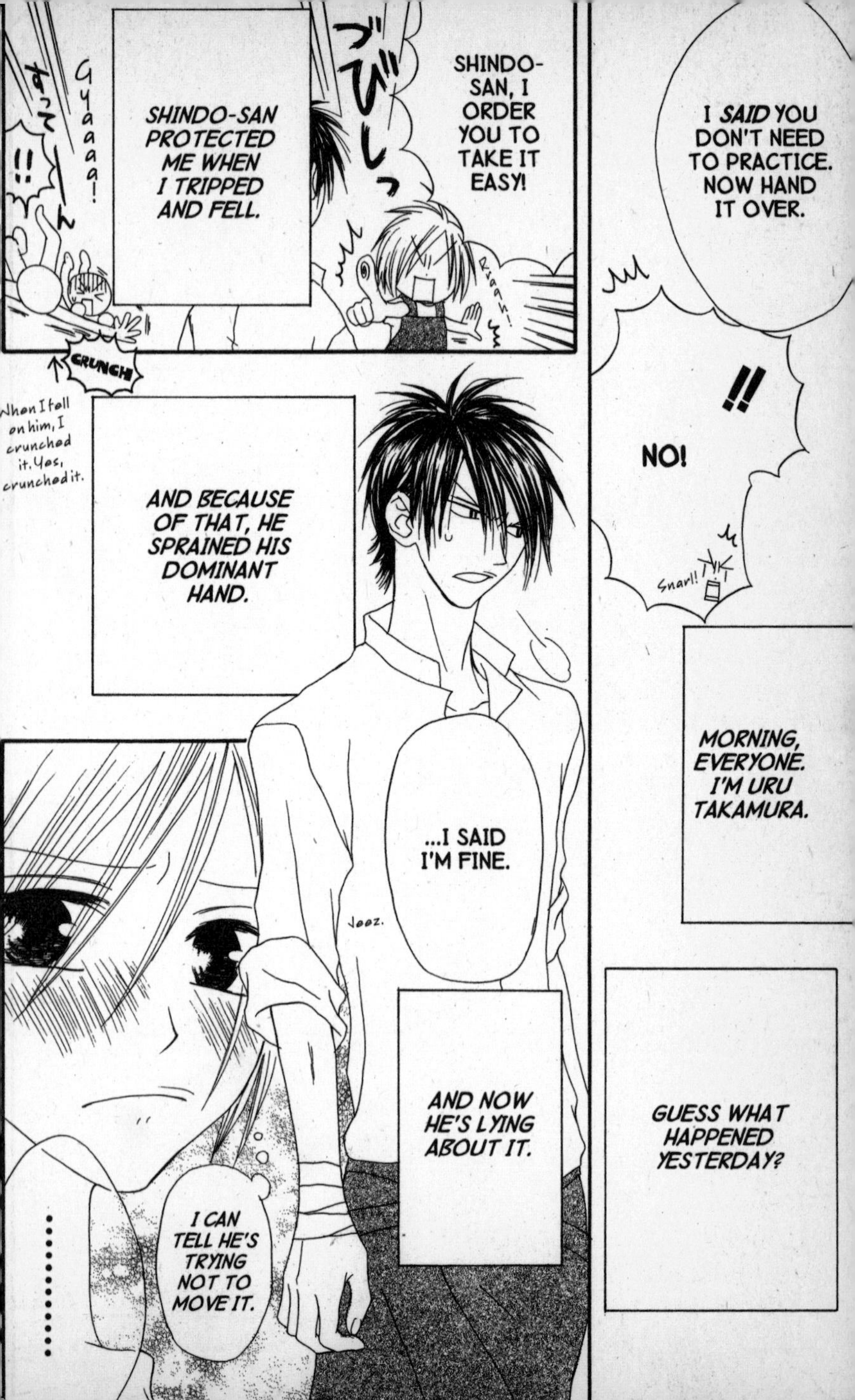
I SAID YOU DON'T NEED TO PRACTICE. NOW HAND IT OVER.
!!
NO!
Snarl!
MORNING, EVERYONE. I'M URU TAKAMURA.
GUESS WHAT HAPPENED YESTERDAY?
SHINDO-SAN, I ORDER YOU TO TAKE IT EASY!
ずびしっ
Rraagh!
SHINDO-SAN PROTECTED ME WHEN I TRIPPED AND FELL.
Gyaaaaa!
すってーん
!!
CRUNCH
When I fell on him, I crunched it. Yes, crunched it.
AND BECAUSE OF THAT, HE SPRAINED HIS DOMINANT HAND.
...I SAID I'M FINE.
Jeez.
AND NOW HE'S LYING ABOUT IT.
I CAN TELL HE'S TRYING NOT TO MOVE IT.
....

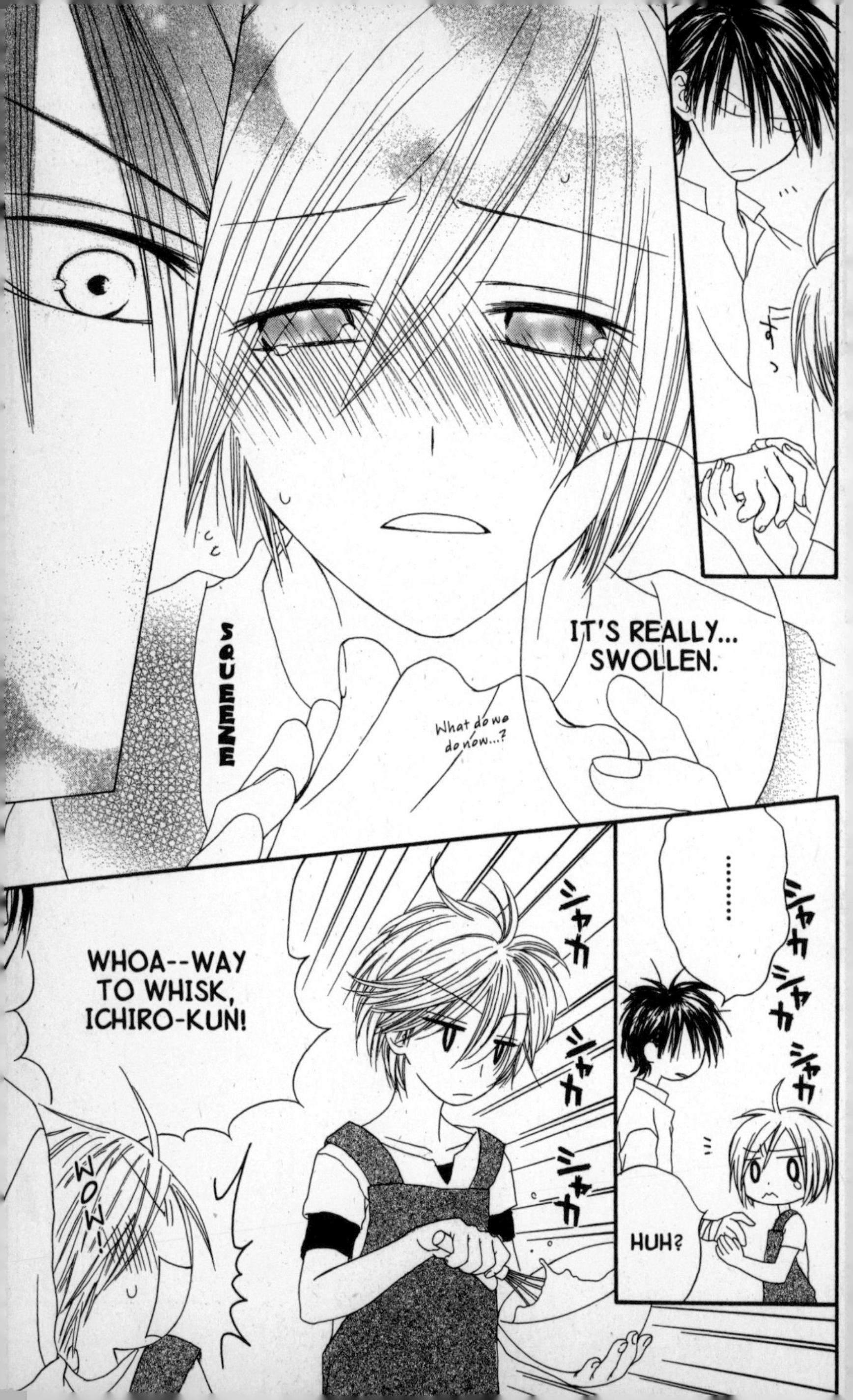

すっ
IT'S REALLY... SWOLLEN.
What do we do now...?
SQUEEZE
......
シャカ
シャカ
シャカ
HUH?
シャカ
シャカ
シャカ
WHOA--WAY TO WHISK, ICHIRO-KUN!
WOW!

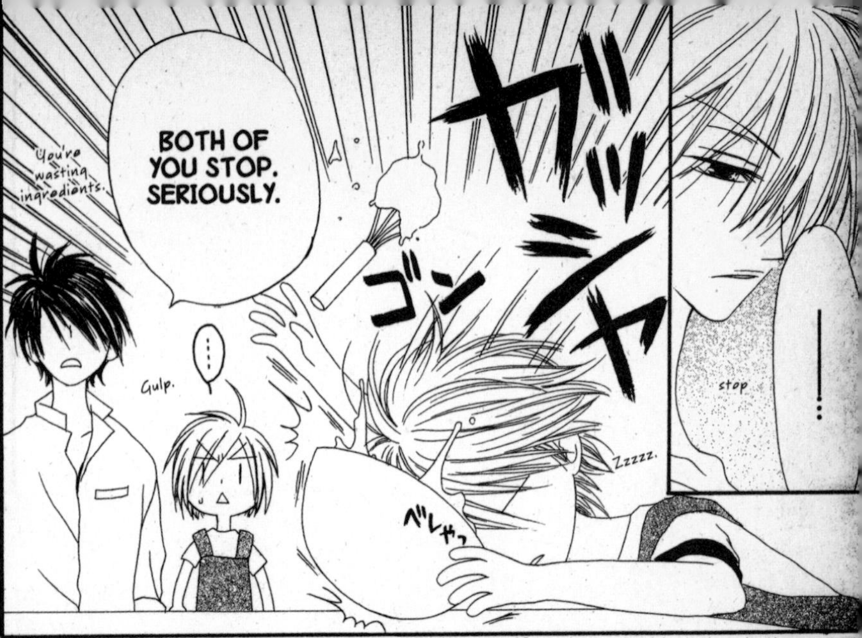
stop
...!
Zzzzz.
BOTH OF YOU STOP. SERIOUSLY.
You're wasting ingredients.
...
Gulp.

Takenoko no Mori: Forest of Bamboo Shoots. The parody name of "takenoko no sato (bamboo shoot village)," the bamboo shoot shaped chocolate covered cookies.

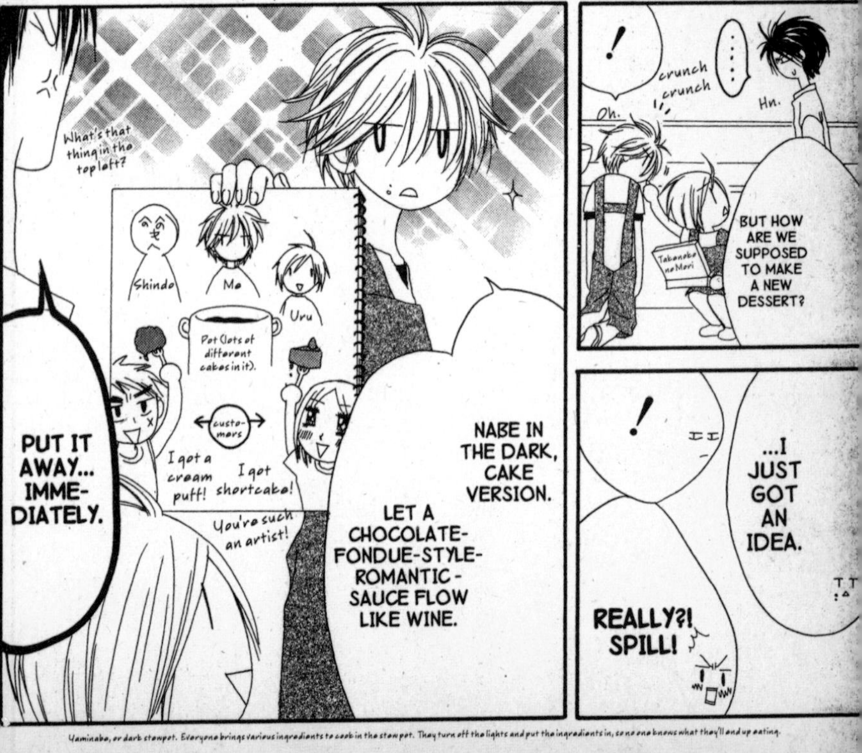
....
Hn.
!
crunch crunch
Oh.
Takenoko no Mori
BUT HOW ARE WE SUPPOSED TO MAKE A NEW DESSERT?
...I JUST GOT AN IDEA.
!
REALLY?! SPILL!
NABE IN THE DARK, CAKE VERSION.
LET A CHOCOLATE-FONDUE-STYLE-ROMANTIC-SAUCE FLOW LIKE WINE.
Shindo
Me
Uru
Pot (lots of different cakes in it).
custo-mers
I got a cream puff!
I got shortcake!
You're such an artist!
What's that thing in the top left?
PUT IT AWAY... IMME-DIATELY.

Yaminabe, or dark stewpot. Everyone brings various ingredients to cook in the stew pot. They turn off the lights and put the ingredients in, so no one knows what they'll end up eating.

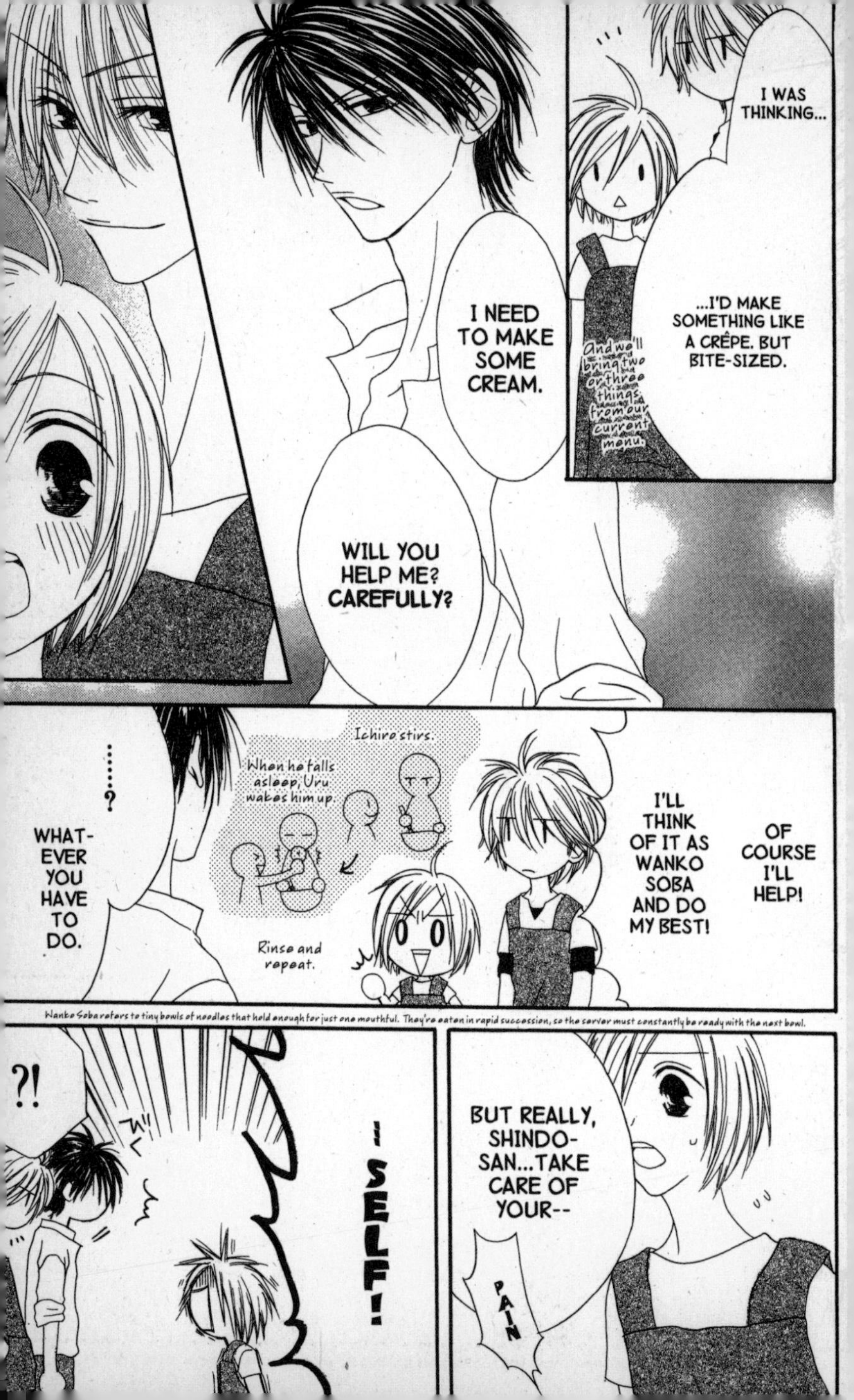
I WAS THINKING...
...I'D MAKE SOMETHING LIKE A CRÊPE. BUT BITE-SIZED.
And we'll bring two or three things from our current menu.
I NEED TO MAKE SOME CREAM.
WILL YOU HELP ME? CAREFULLY?
OF COURSE I'LL HELP!
I'LL THINK OF IT AS WANKO SOBA AND DO MY BEST!
Ichiro stirs.
When he falls asleep, Uru wakes him up.
Rinse and repeat.
......?
WHATEVER YOU HAVE TO DO.
Wanko Soba refers to tiny bowls of noodles that hold enough for just one mouthful. They're eaten in rapid succession, so the server must constantly be ready with the next bowl.
BUT REALLY, SHINDO-SAN...TAKE CARE OF YOUR--
PAIN
SELF!!
?!

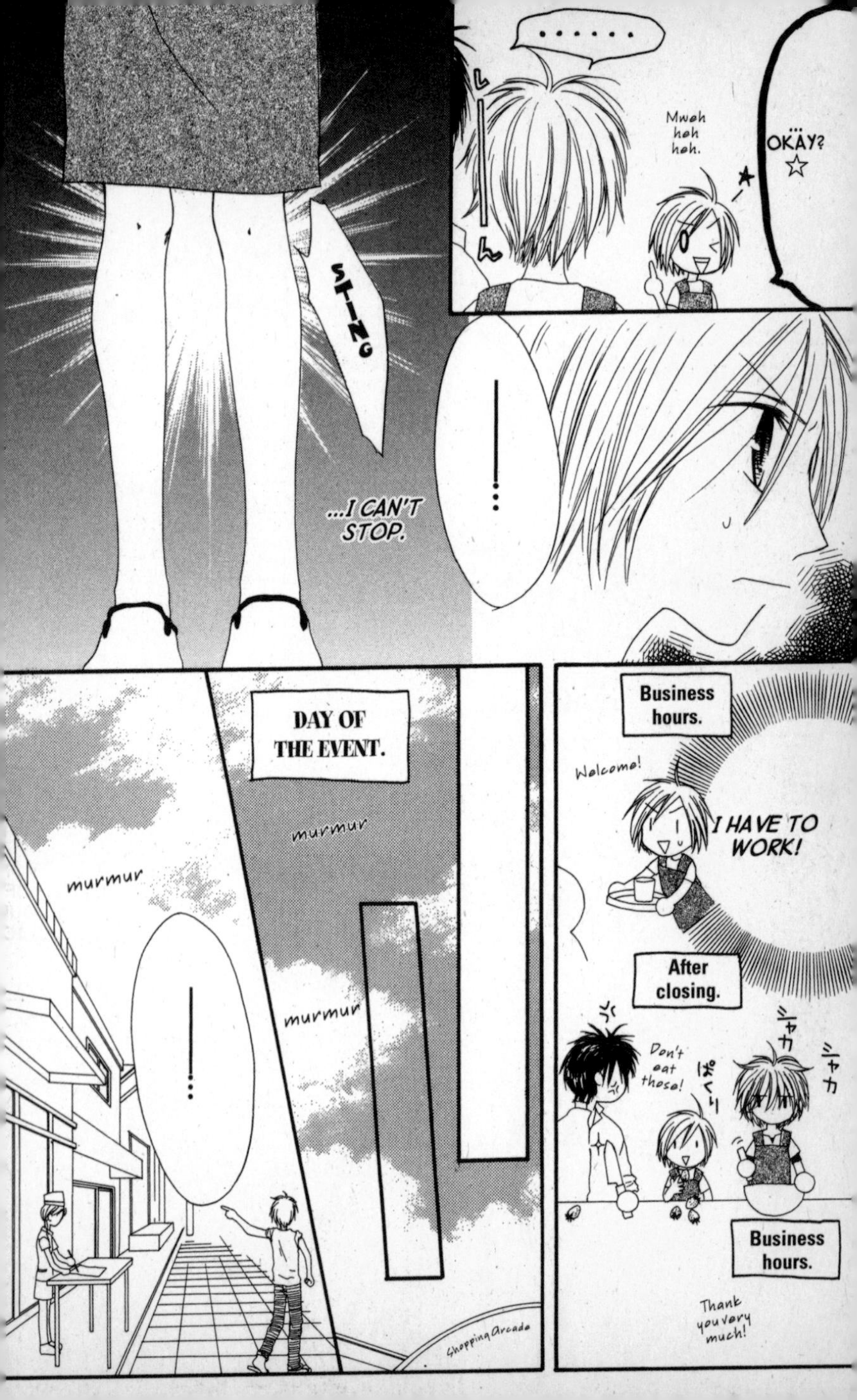

OKÄY? ☆
Mweh heh heh.
....
—...
STING
...I CAN'T STOP.
Business hours.
Welcome!
I HAVE TO WORK!
After closing.
シャカ
シャカ
ぱくり
Don't eat these!
Business hours.
Thank you very much!
DAY OF THE EVENT.
murmur
murmur
—...
murmur
Shopping Arcade

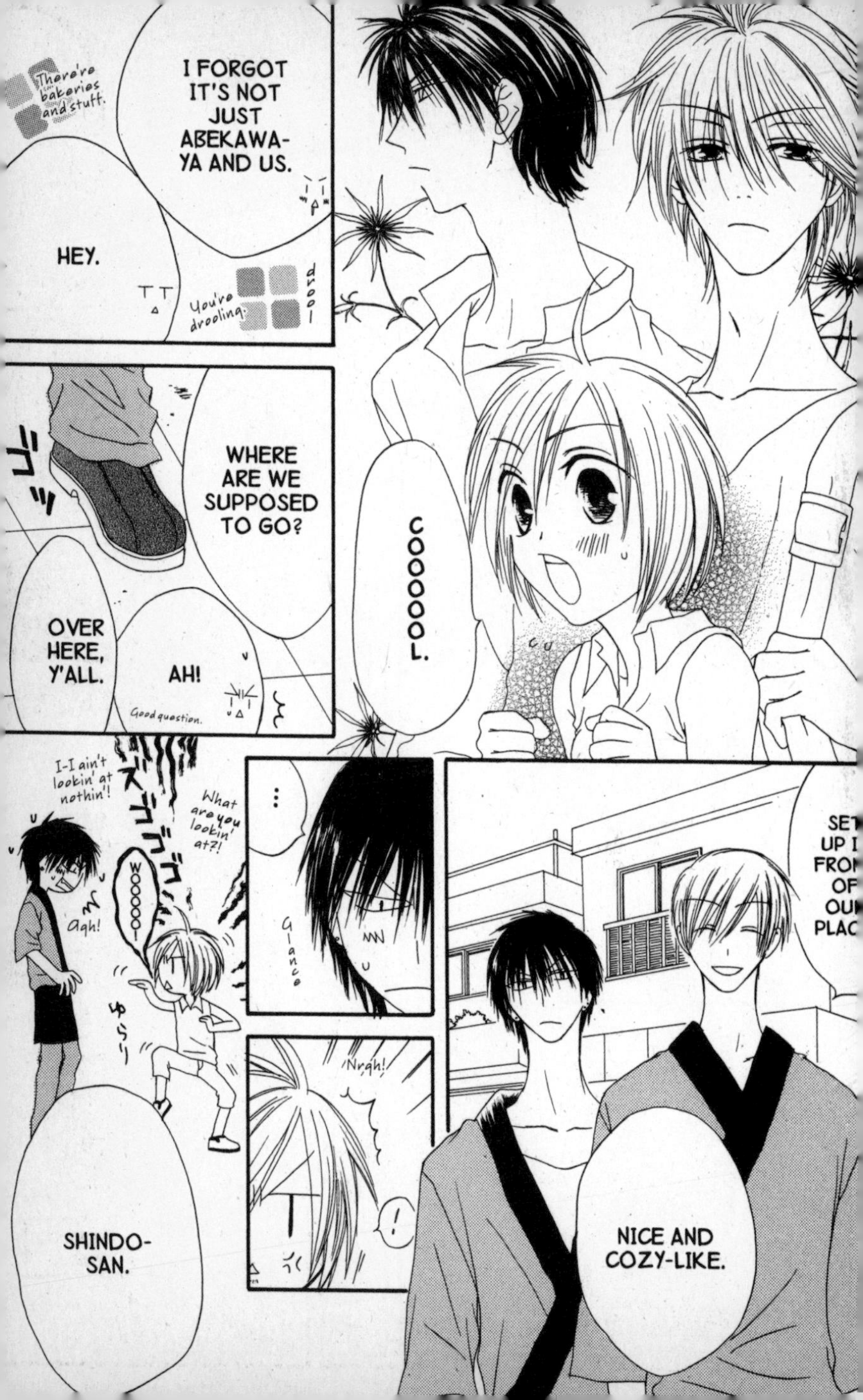
COOOOOOL.
I FORGOT IT'S NOT JUST ABEKAWA-YA AND US.
There're bakeries and stuff.
HEY.
You're drooling.
drool
WHERE ARE WE SUPPOSED TO GO?
AH!
Good question.
OVER HERE, Y'ALL.
SET UP I FRON OF OU PLAC
NICE AND COZY-LIKE.
...
Glance
Nrgh!
!
WOOOOO!
What are you lookin' at?!
I-I ain't lookin' at nothin'!
Agh!
ゆらり
SHINDO-SAN.

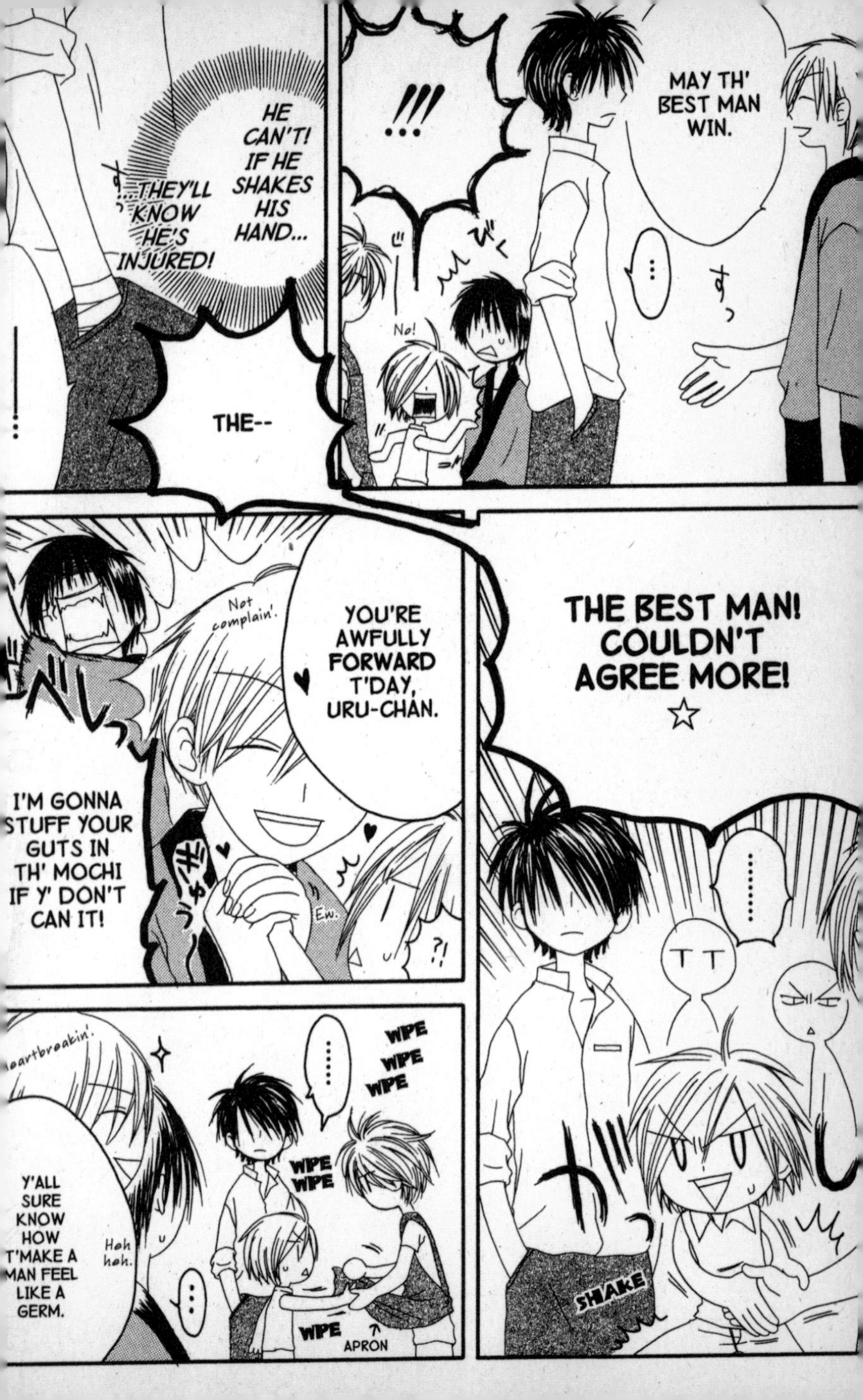
MAY TH' BEST MAN WIN.
...
!!!
...
No!
HE CAN'T! IF HE SHAKES HIS HAND...
...THEY'LL KNOW HE'S INJURED!
THE--
...
THE BEST MAN! COULDN'T AGREE MORE! ☆
......
SHAKE
YOU'RE AWFULLY FORWARD T'DAY, URU-CHAN.
Not complain'.
I'M GONNA STUFF YOUR GUTS IN TH' MOCHI IF Y' DON'T CAN IT!
Ew.
?!
......
WIPE WIPE WIPE
WIPE WIPE
WIPE
APRON
Y'ALL SURE KNOW HOW T'MAKE A MAN FEEL LIKE A GERM.
Heh heh.
...

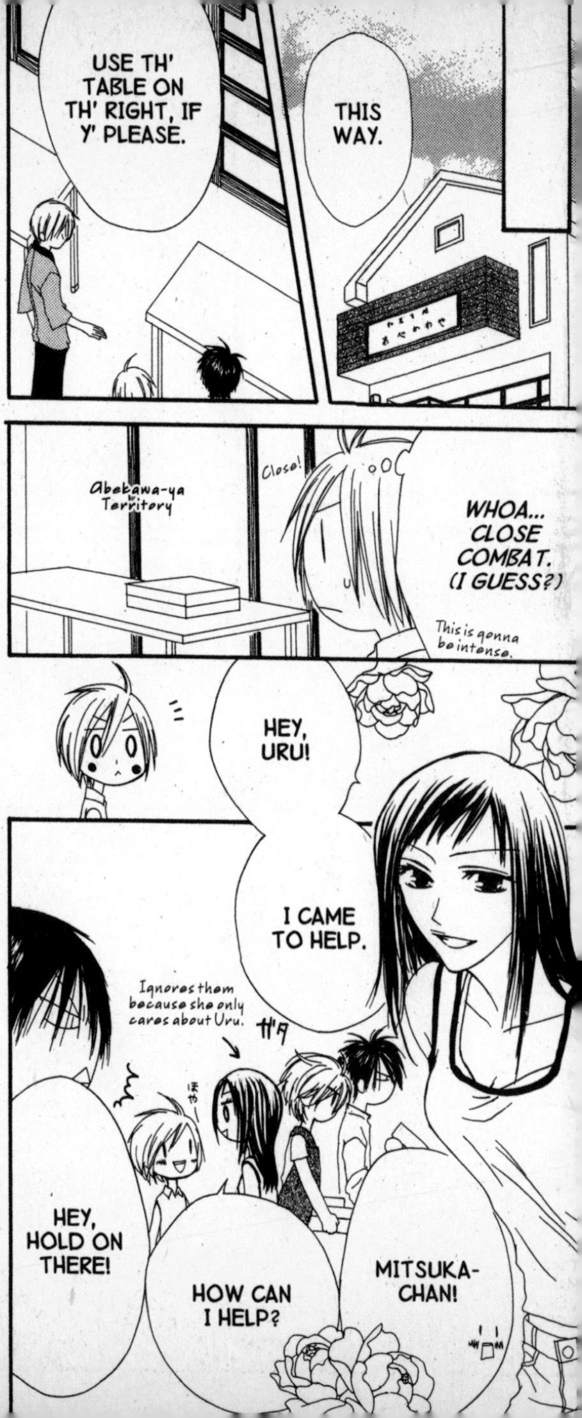
THIS WAY.
USE TH' TABLE ON TH' RIGHT, IF Y' PLEASE.
WHOA... CLOSE COMBAT. (I GUESS?)
This is gonna be intense.
Close!
Abekawa-ya Territory
HEY, URU!
I CAME TO HELP.
MITSUKA-CHAN!
HOW CAN I HELP?
Ignores them because she only cares about Uru.
ガタ
HEY, HOLD ON THERE!

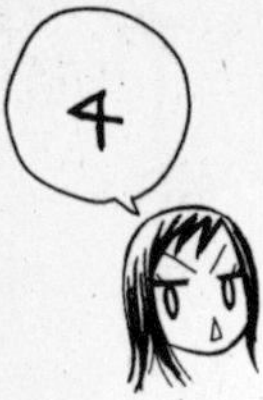
4

You may already know this, but Matsuzuki is very bad at coloring pictures.

I've hated coloring since elementary school.

Maybe the way I colored pictures during art time was really crude, because they always made me do it over.

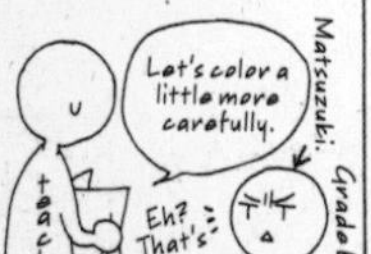
Let's color a little more carefully.
teacher
Matsuzuki, Grade 6.
Eh? That's too much work.
....

Actually, I had to redraw the colored picture for the cover of chapter nine, too.

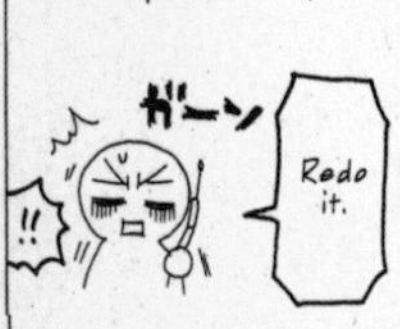
ガーン
!!
Redo it.

...I guess I should practice more.

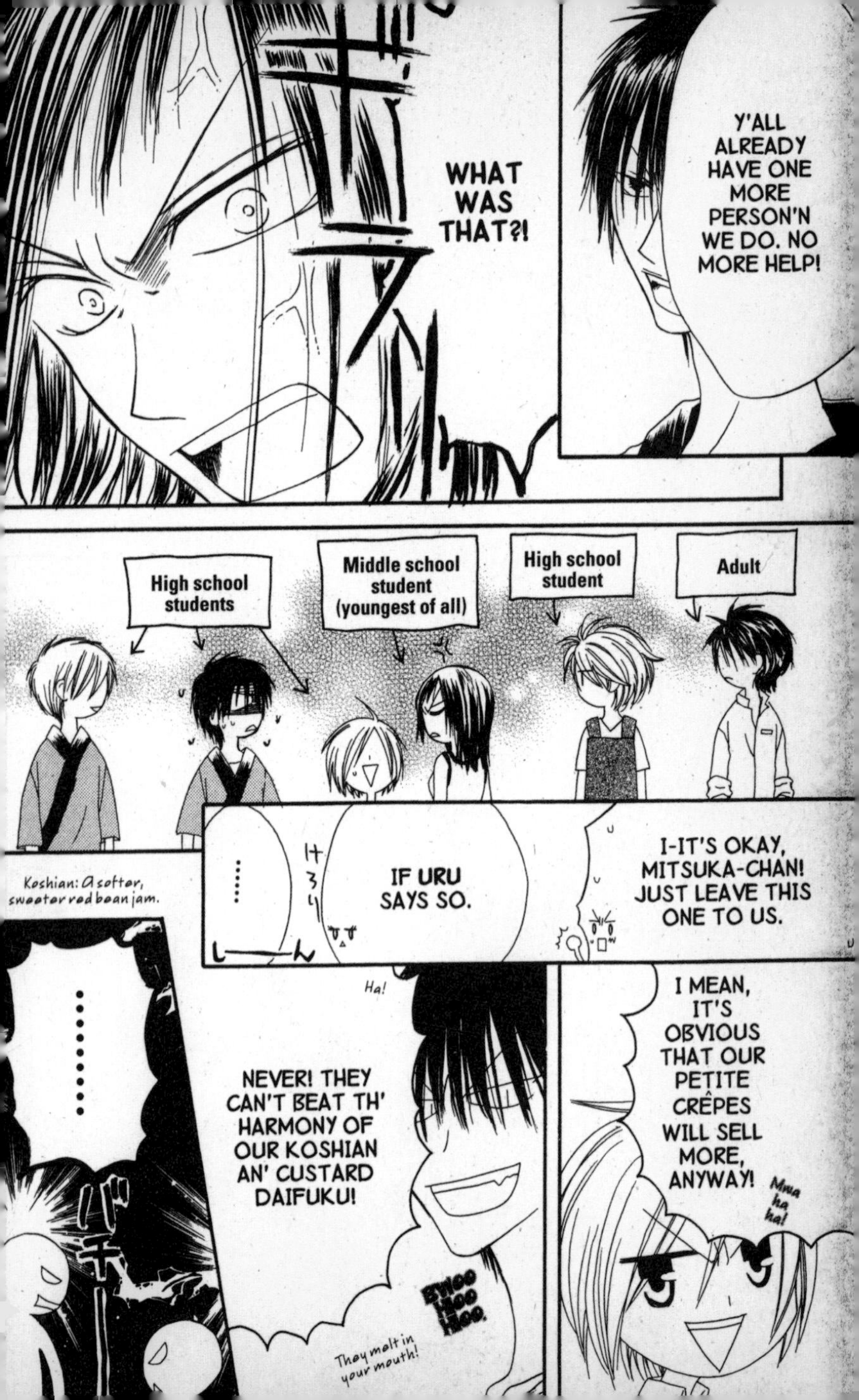
Y'ALL ALREADY HAVE ONE MORE PERSON'N WE DO. NO MORE HELP!
WHAT WAS THAT?!
Adult
High school student
Middle school student (youngest of all)
High school students
I-IT'S OKAY, MITSUKA-CHAN! JUST LEAVE THIS ONE TO US.
IF URU SAYS SO.
......
Koshian: A softer, sweeter red bean jam.
I MEAN, IT'S OBVIOUS THAT OUR PETITE CRÊPES WILL SELL MORE, ANYWAY!
Mwa ha ha!
Ha!
NEVER! THEY CAN'T BEAT TH' HARMONY OF OUR KOSHIAN AN' CUSTARD DAIFUKU!
They melt in your mouth!
....

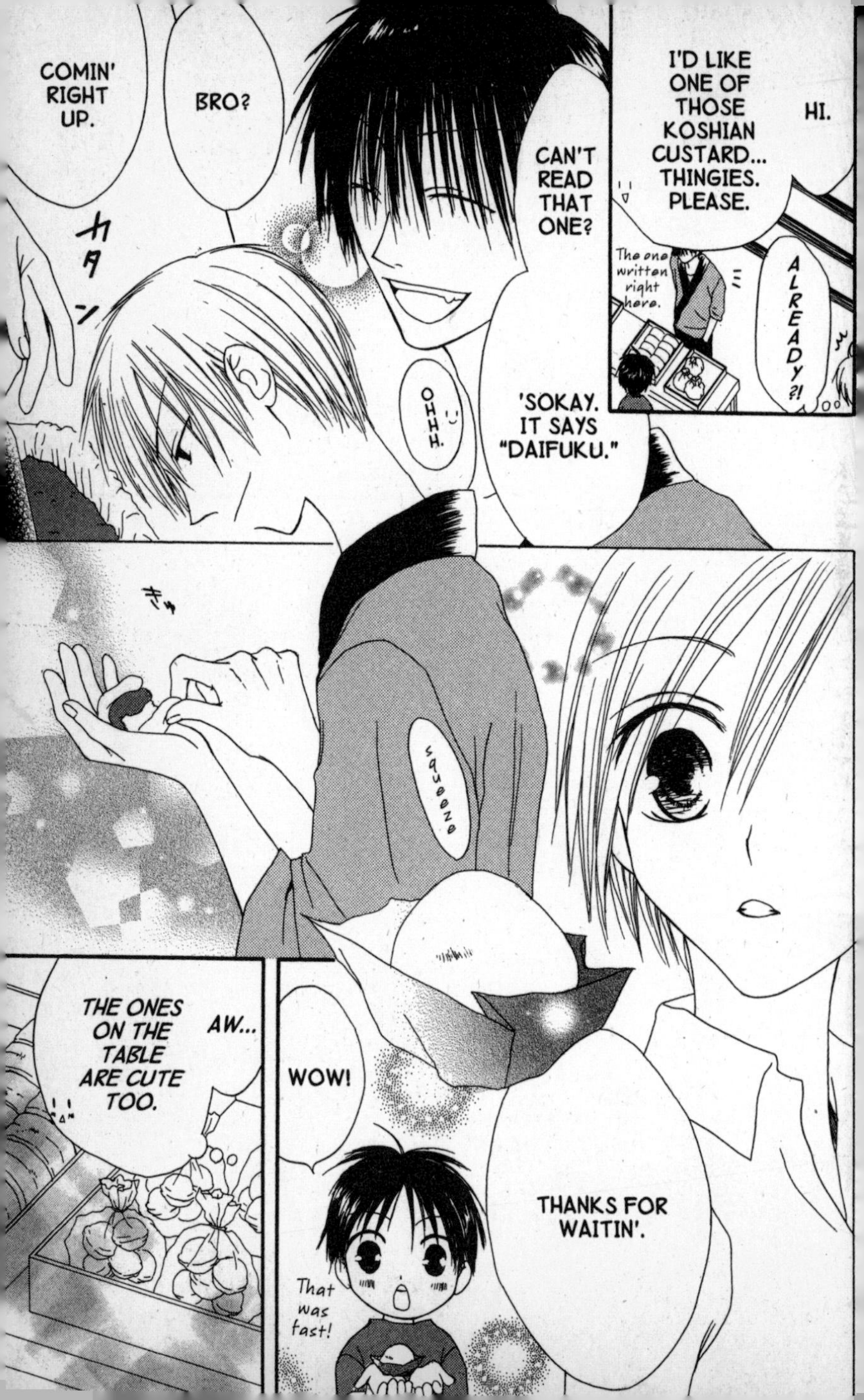
HI.
I'D LIKE ONE OF THOSE KOSHIAN CUSTARD... THINGIES. PLEASE.
ALREADY?!
The one written right here.
CAN'T READ THAT ONE?
'SOKAY. IT SAYS "DAIFUKU."
OHHH.
BRO?
COMIN' RIGHT UP.
カタン
squeeze
きゅ
THANKS FOR WAITIN'.
WOW!
That was fast!
AW...
THE ONES ON THE TABLE ARE CUTE TOO.

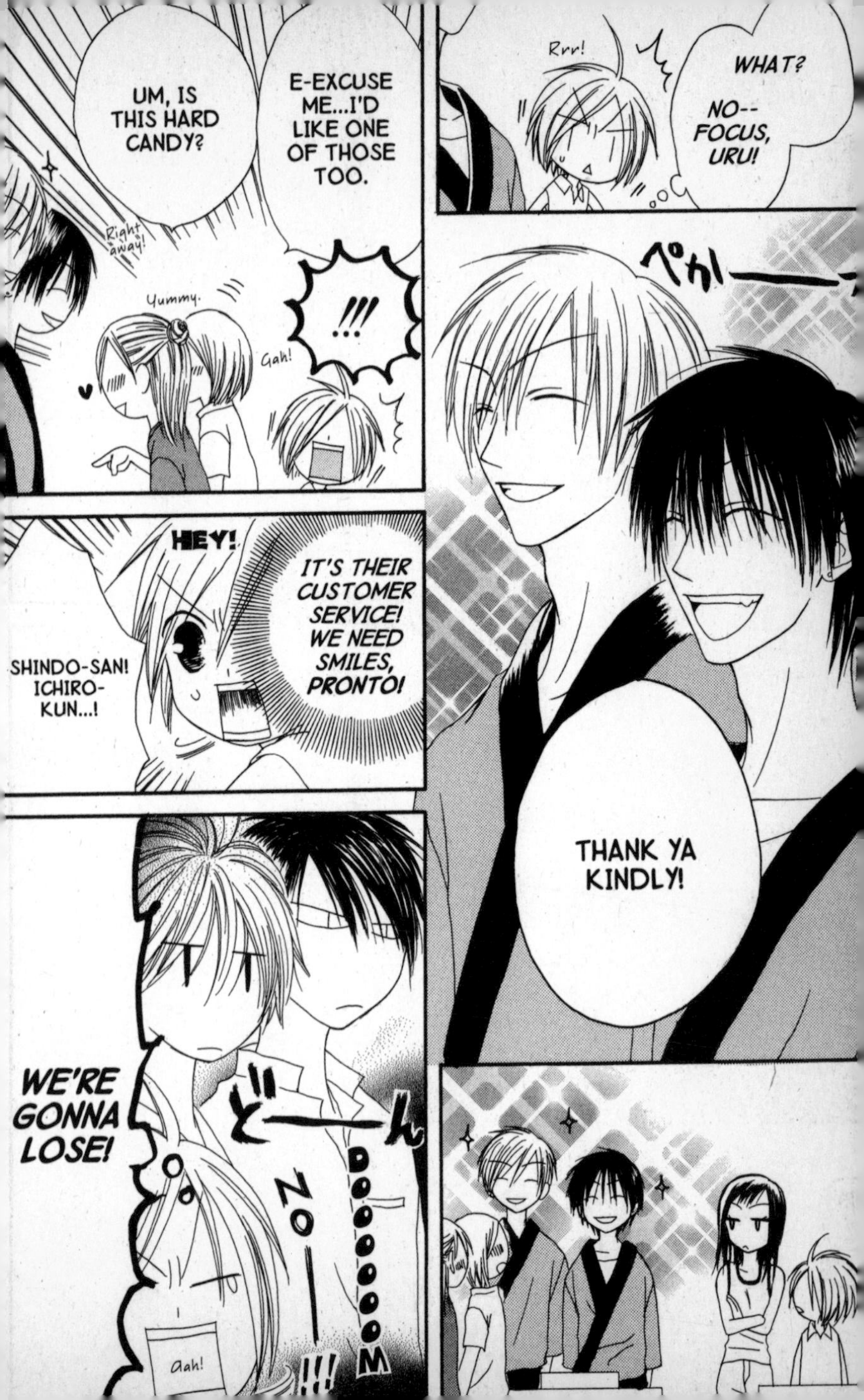
Rrr!
WHAT?
NO-- FOCUS, URU!
E-EXCUSE ME...I'D LIKE ONE OF THOSE TOO.
UM, IS THIS HARD CANDY?
Right away!
Yummy.
!!!
Gah!
ぺか———
THANK YA KINDLY!
HEY!
IT'S THEIR CUSTOMER SERVICE! WE NEED SMILES, PRONTO!
SHINDO-SAN! ICHIRO-KUN...!
ど——ん
DOOOOOOOOM
NO—!!!
WE'RE GONNA LOSE!
aah!

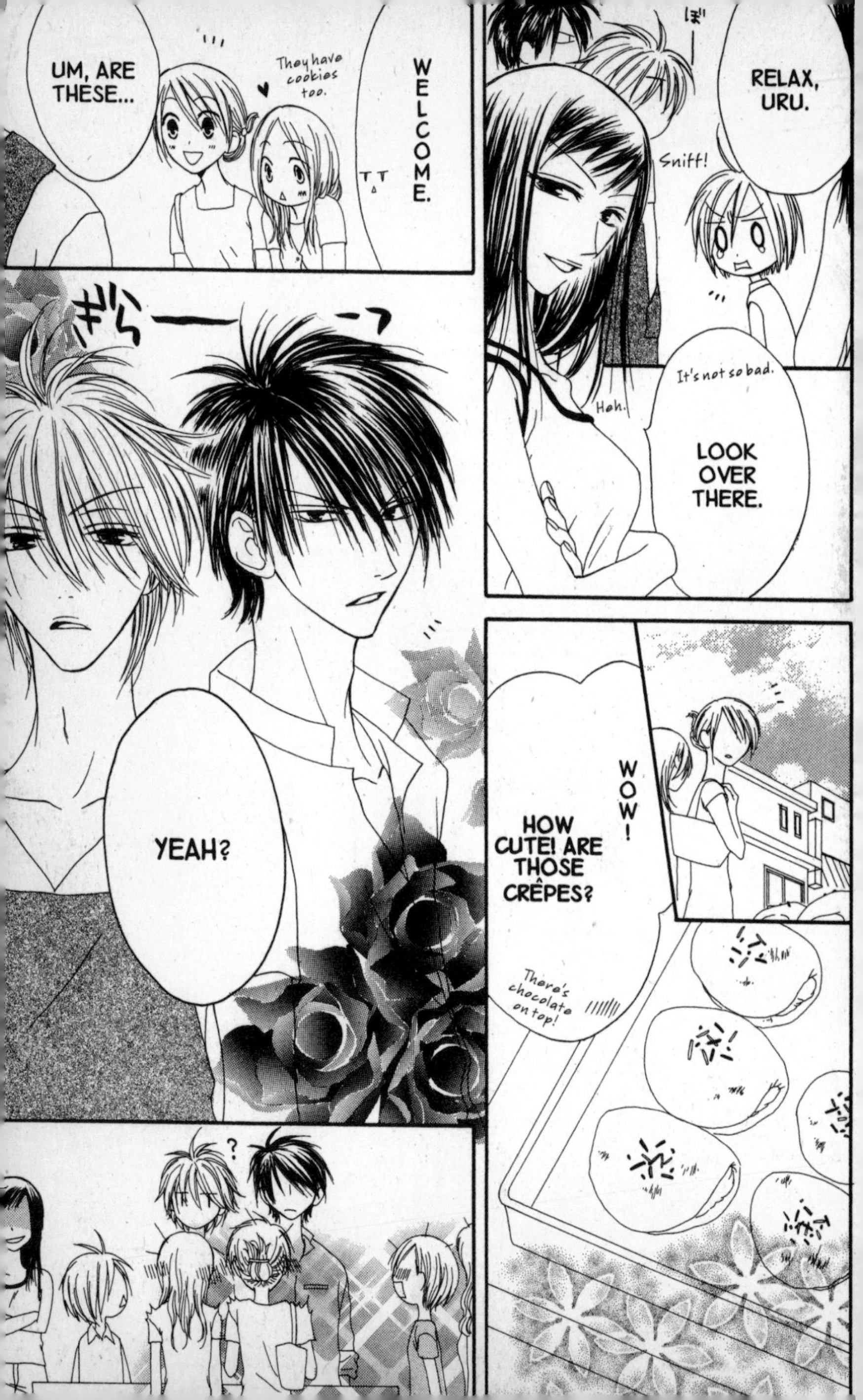
RELAX, URU.
Sniff!
WELCOME.
They have cookies too.
UM, ARE THESE...
It's not so bad.
LOOK OVER THERE.
Heh.
YEAH?
WOW!
HOW CUTE! ARE THOSE CRÊPES?
There's chocolate on top!
?

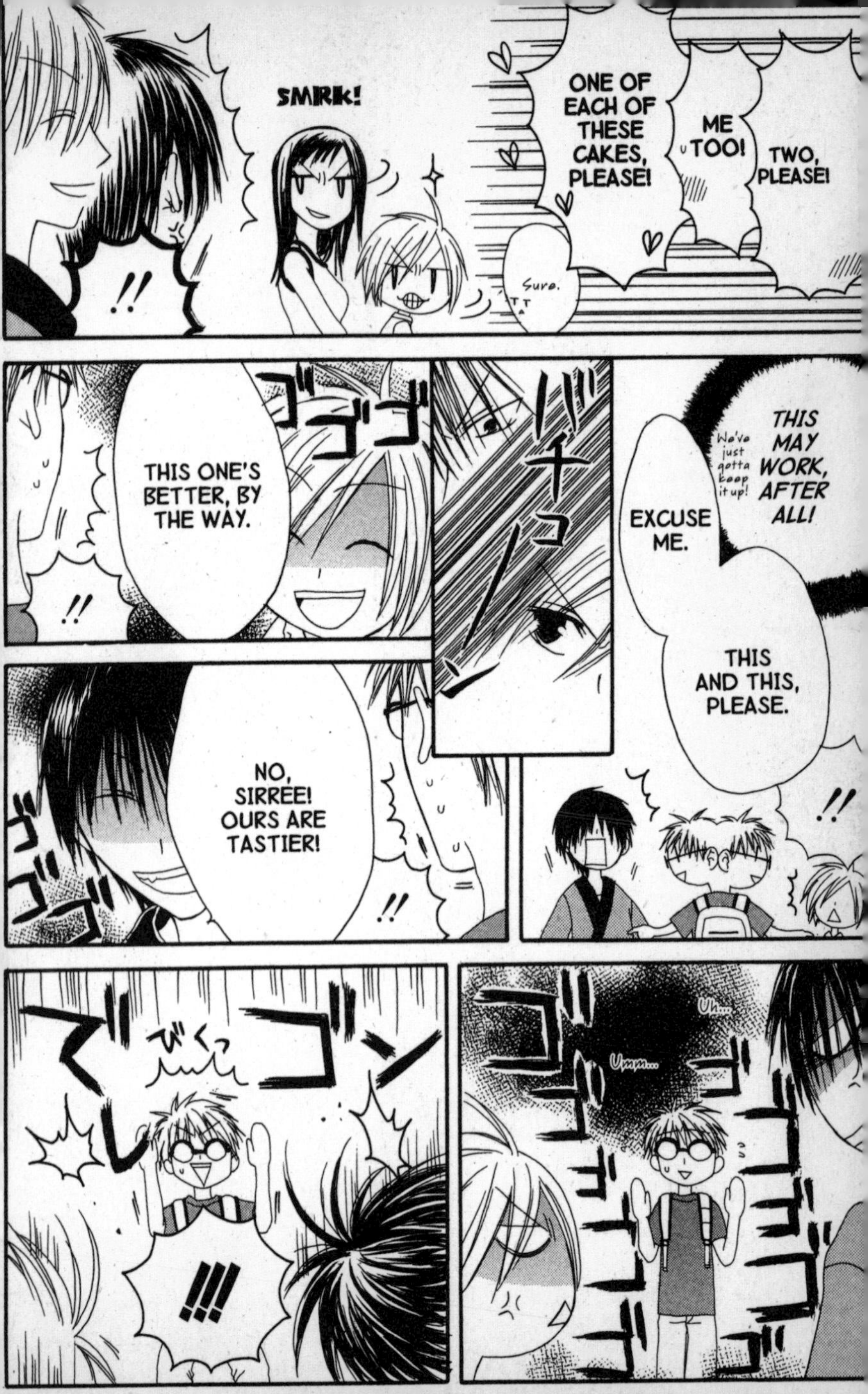
TWO, PLEASE!
ME TOO!
ONE OF EACH OF THESE CAKES, PLEASE!
Sure.
SMRK!
!!
THIS MAY WORK, AFTER ALL!
We've just gotta keep it up!
EXCUSE ME.
THIS AND THIS, PLEASE.
!!
ゴゴゴ
THIS ONE'S BETTER, BY THE WAY.
!!
NO, SIRREE! OURS ARE TASTIER!
ゴゴゴ
!!
Uh...
Umm...
ゴゴゴ
ゴン
びくっ
!!!

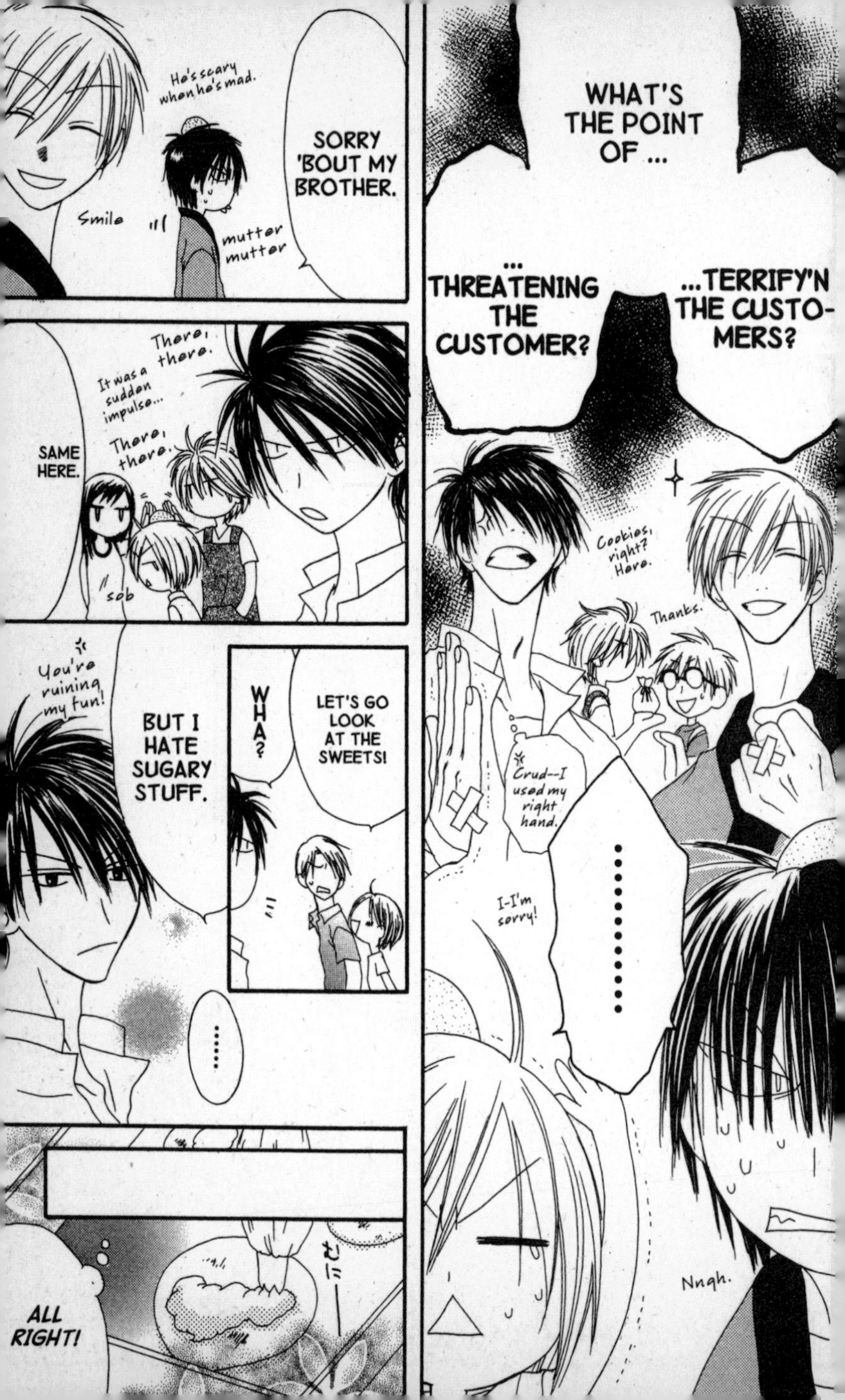
WHAT'S THE POINT OF ...
...TERRIFY'N THE CUSTOMERS?
... THREATENING THE CUSTOMER?
Cookies, right? Here.
Thanks.
Crud--I used my right hand.
....
I-I'm sorry!
Nngh.
SORRY 'BOUT MY BROTHER.
He's scary when he's mad.
mutter mutter
Smile
There, there.
It was a sudden impulse...
There, there.
SAME HERE.
sob
LET'S GO LOOK AT THE SWEETS!
WHA?
You're ruining my fun!
BUT I HATE SUGARY STUFF.
......
むにー
ALL RIGHT!

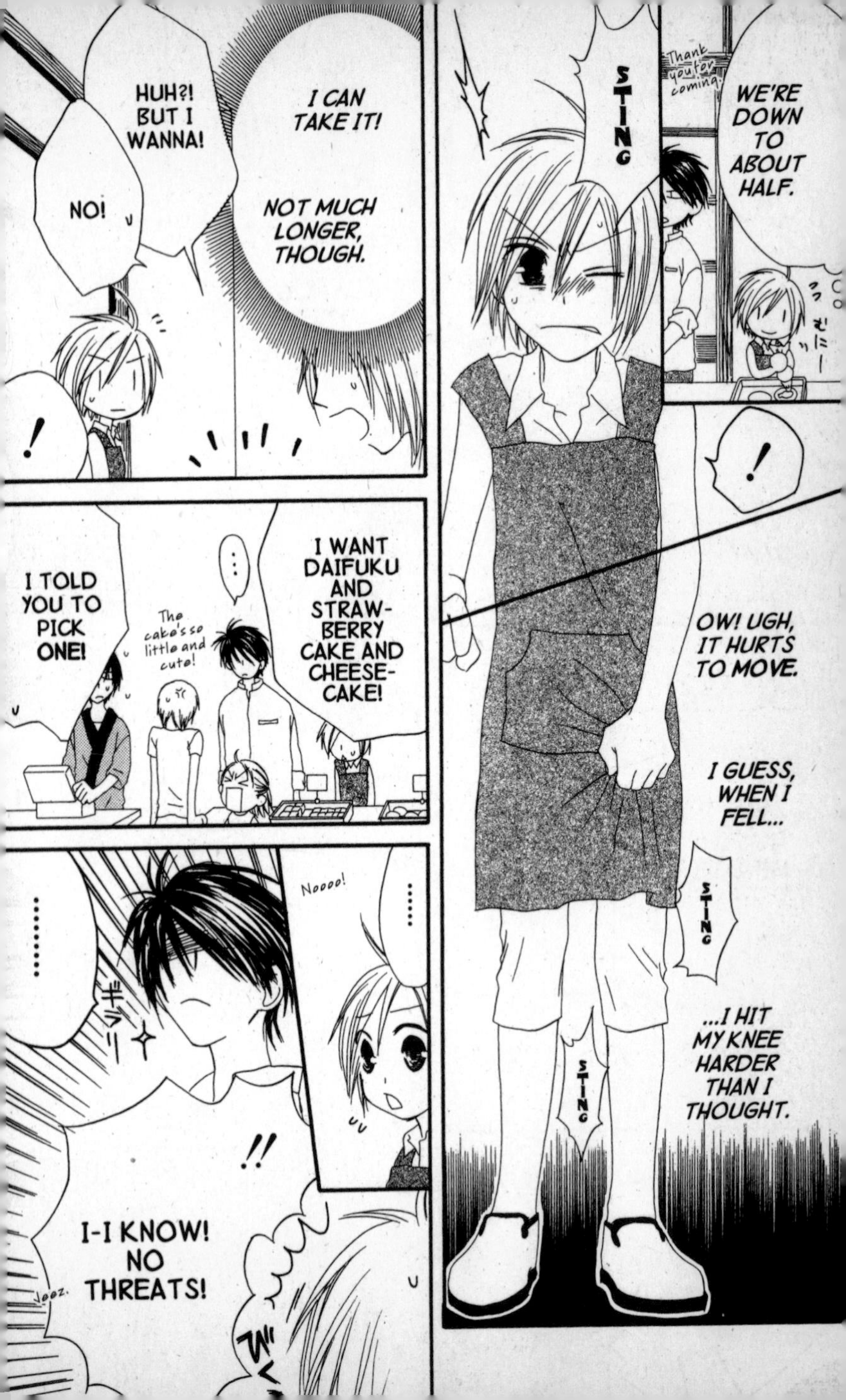
Thank you for coming.
WE'RE DOWN TO ABOUT HALF.
STING
!
OW! UGH, IT HURTS TO MOVE.
I GUESS, WHEN I FELL...
STING
...I HIT MY KNEE HARDER THAN I THOUGHT.
STING
I CAN TAKE IT!
NOT MUCH LONGER, THOUGH.
HUH?! BUT I WANNA!
NO!
!
I WANT DAIFUKU AND STRAWBERRY CAKE AND CHEESECAKE!
...
The cake's so little and cute!
I TOLD YOU TO PICK ONE!
Noooo!
......
....
!!
I-I KNOW! NO THREATS!
Jeez.

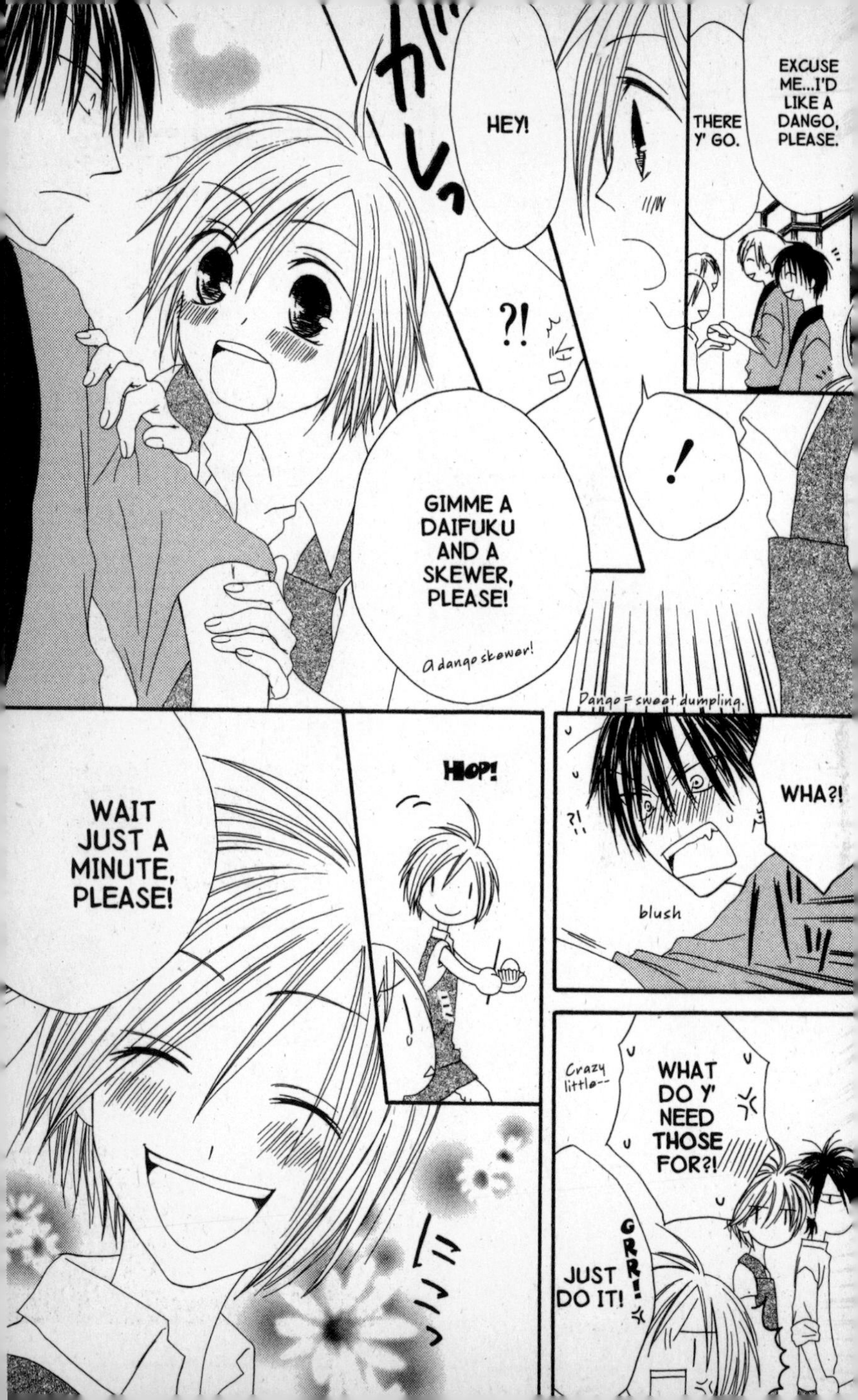
EXCUSE ME...I'D LIKE A DANGO, PLEASE.
THERE Y' GO.
HEY!
?!
!
GIMME A DAIFUKU AND A SKEWER, PLEASE!
A dango skewer!
Dango = sweet dumpling.
WHA?!
?!
blush
WHAT DO Y' NEED THOSE FOR?!
Crazy little--
GRR!!
JUST DO IT!
HOP!
WAIT JUST A MINUTE, PLEASE!

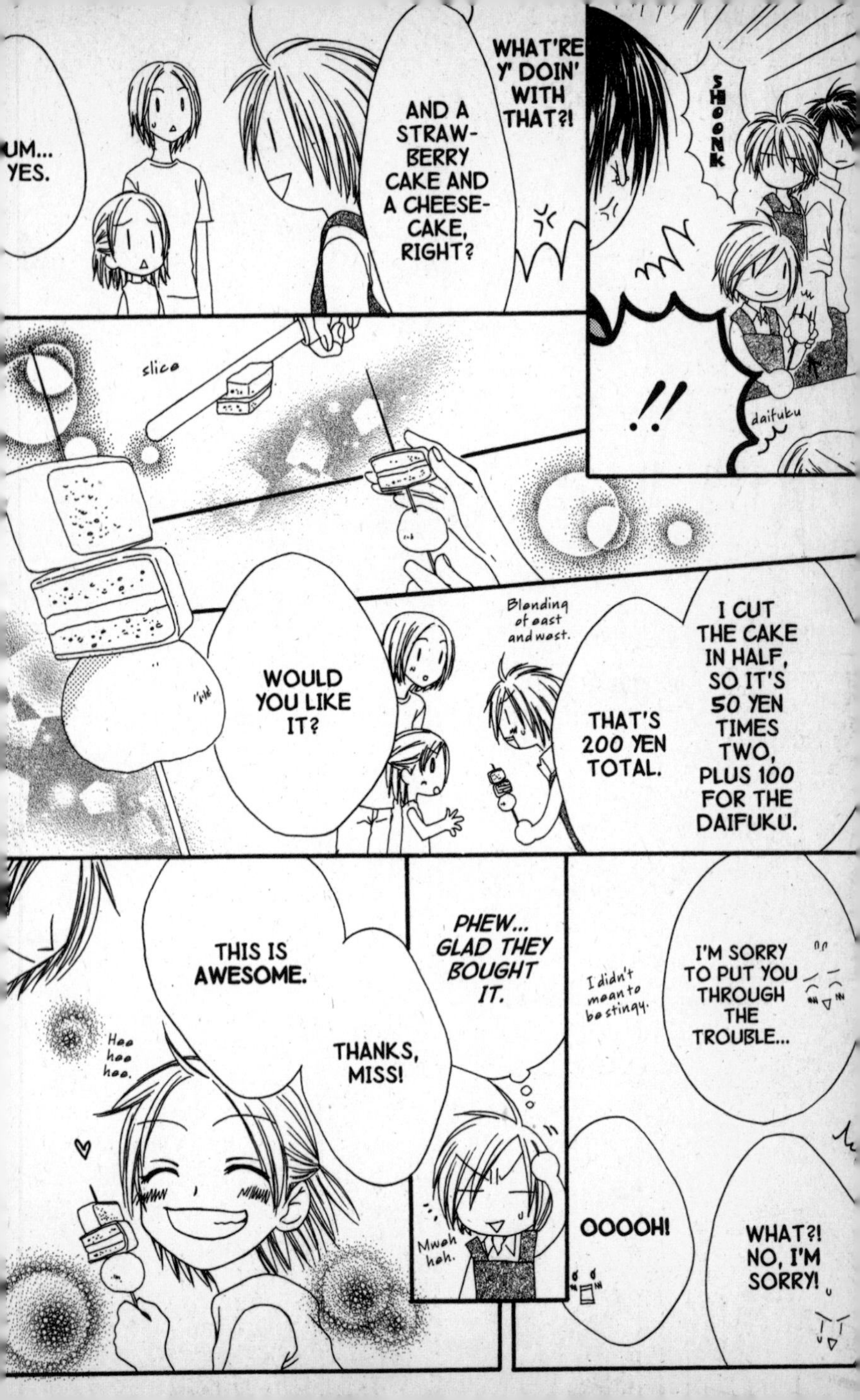
SHOOONK
!!
daifuku
WHAT'RE Y' DOIN' WITH THAT?!
AND A STRAWBERRY CAKE AND A CHEESECAKE, RIGHT?
UM... YES.
slice
I CUT THE CAKE IN HALF, SO IT'S 50 YEN TIMES TWO, PLUS 100 FOR THE DAIFUKU.
THAT'S 200 YEN TOTAL.
Blending of east and west.
WOULD YOU LIKE IT?
I'M SORRY TO PUT YOU THROUGH THE TROUBLE...
I didn't mean to be stingy.
WHAT?! NO, I'M SORRY!
OOOOH!
PHEW... GLAD THEY BOUGHT IT.
Mwah heh.
THIS IS AWESOME.
THANKS, MISS!
Hee hee hee.

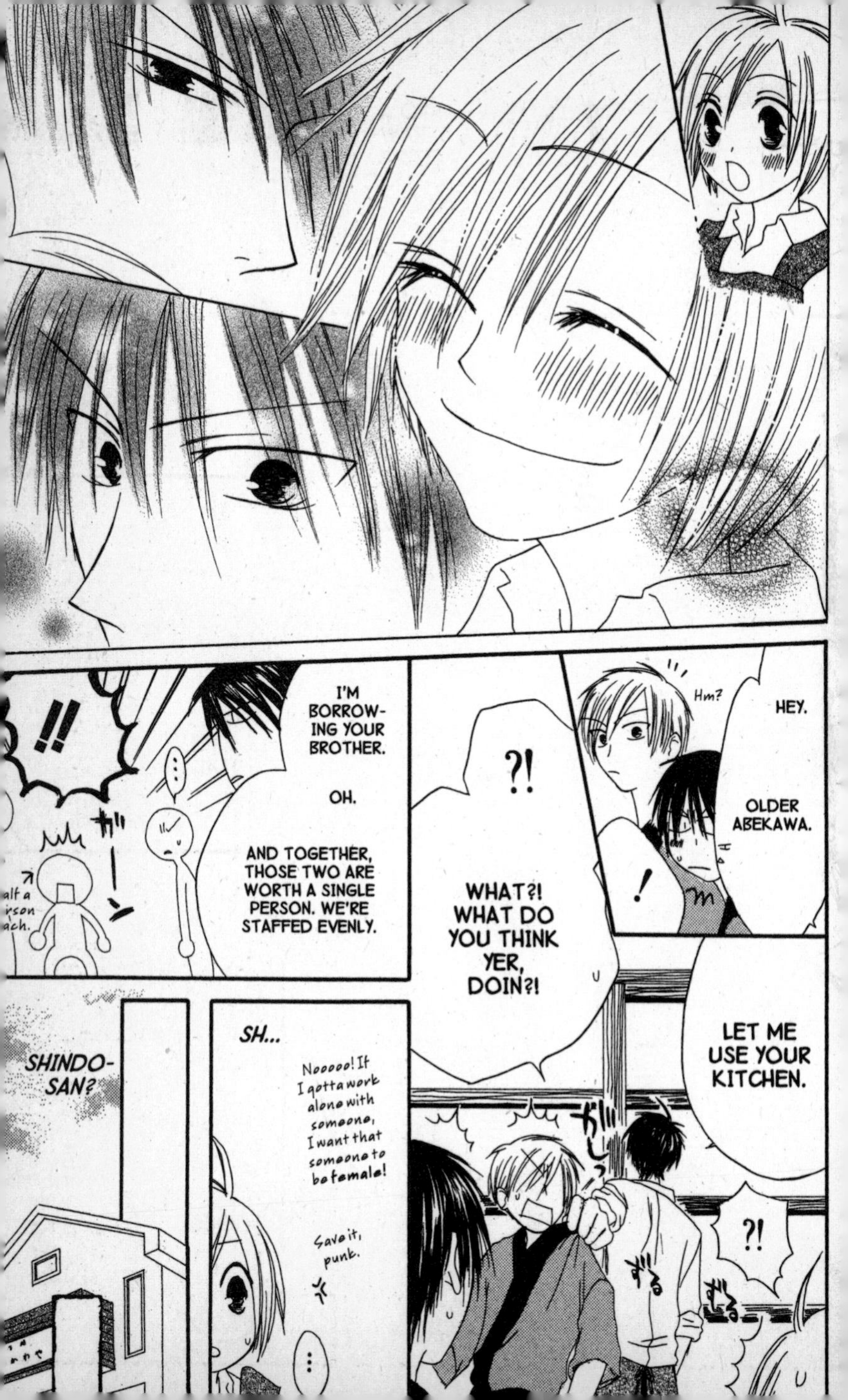

Hm?
HEY.
OLDER ABEKAWA.
!
?!
LET ME USE YOUR KITCHEN.
?!
WHAT?! WHAT DO YOU THINK YER, DOIN?!
I'M BORROWING YOUR BROTHER.
OH.
AND TOGETHER, THOSE TWO ARE WORTH A SINGLE PERSON. WE'RE STAFFED EVENLY.
!!
alf a rson ach.
SH...
Noooooo! If I gotta work alone with someone, I want that someone to be female!
Save it, punk.
...
SHINDO-SAN?

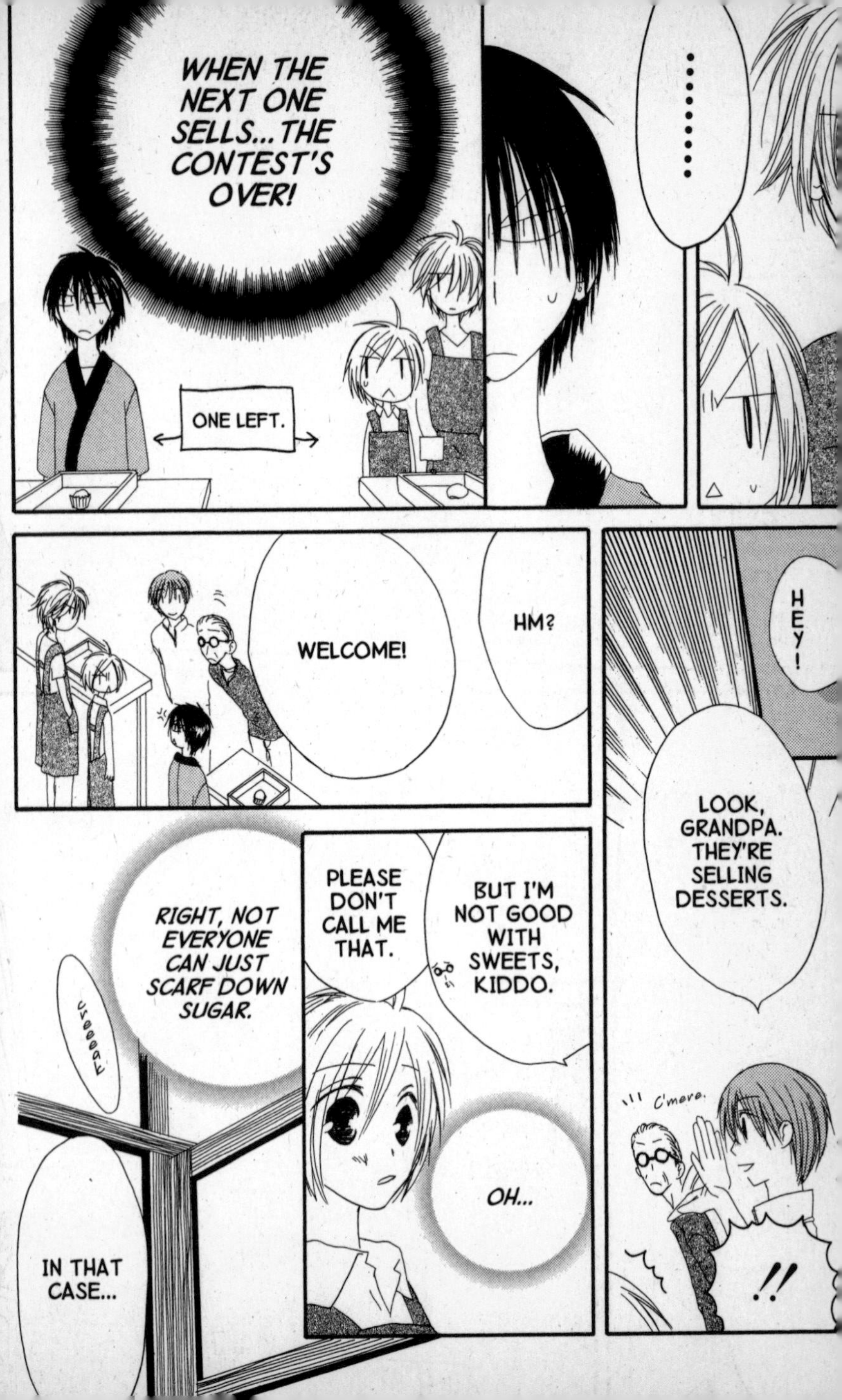

....
WHEN THE NEXT ONE SELLS...THE CONTEST'S OVER!
ONE LEFT.
HEY!
LOOK, GRANDPA. THEY'RE SELLING DESSERTS.
C'mere.
!!
HM?
WELCOME!
BUT I'M NOT GOOD WITH SWEETS, KIDDO.
PLEASE DON'T CALL ME THAT.
OH...
RIGHT, NOT EVERYONE CAN JUST SCARF DOWN SUGAR.
creeeak
IN THAT CASE...

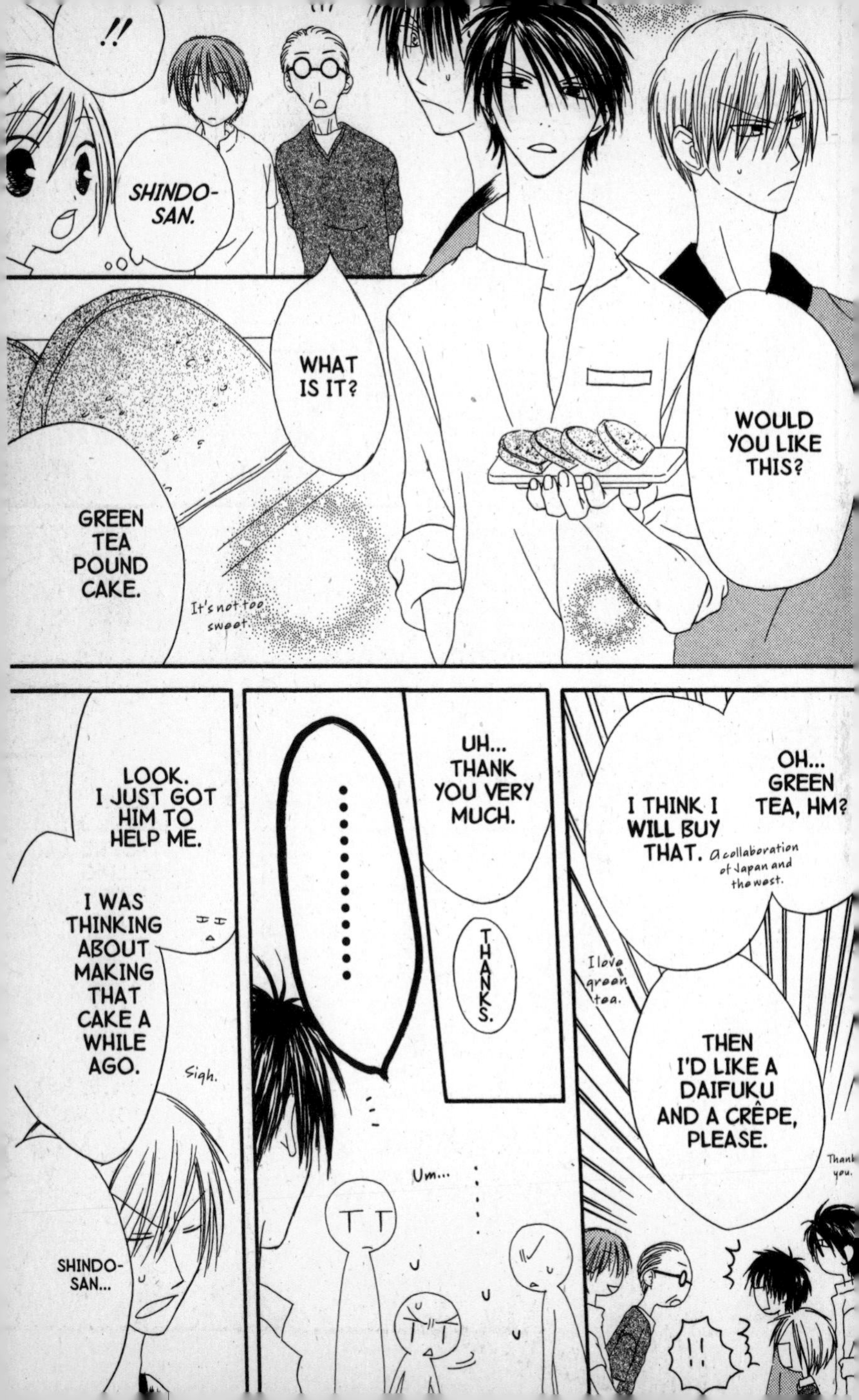
!!
SHINDO-SAN.
WHAT IS IT?
WOULD YOU LIKE THIS?
GREEN TEA POUND CAKE.
It's not too sweet.
OH... GREEN TEA, HM?
I THINK I WILL BUY THAT.
A collaboration of Japan and the west.
I love green tea.
THEN I'D LIKE A DAIFUKU AND A CRÊPE, PLEASE.
Thank you.
!!
UH... THANK YOU VERY MUCH.
THANKS.
....
Um...
LOOK. I JUST GOT HIM TO HELP ME.
I WAS THINKING ABOUT MAKING THAT CAKE A WHILE AGO.
Sigh.
SHINDO-SAN...

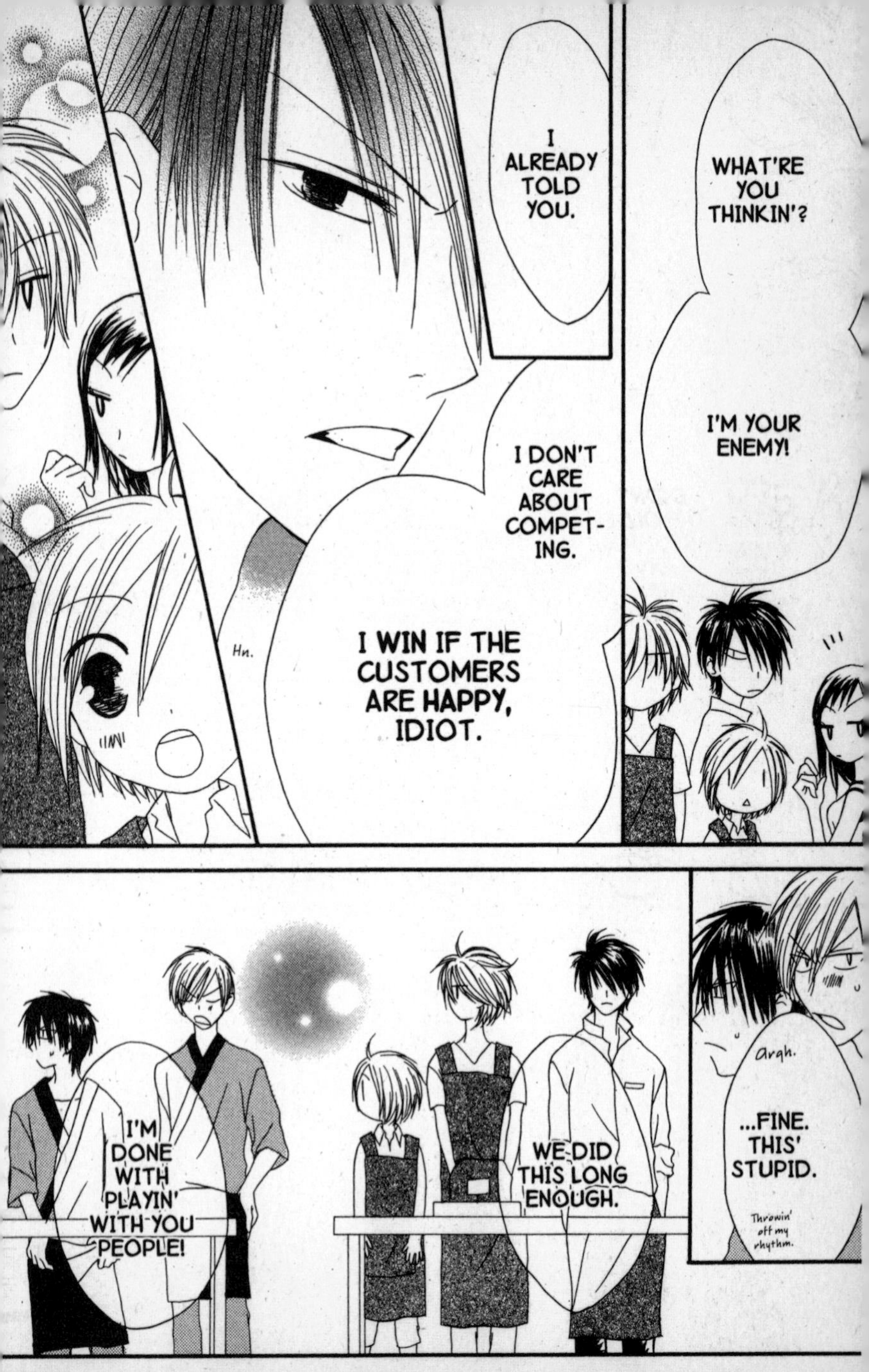
WHAT'RE YOU THINKIN'?
I'M YOUR ENEMY!
I ALREADY TOLD YOU.
I DON'T CARE ABOUT COMPET-ING.
Hn.
I WIN IF THE CUSTOMERS ARE HAPPY, IDIOT.
Argh.
...FINE. THIS' STUPID.
Throwin' off my rhythm.
WE DID THIS LONG ENOUGH.
I'M DONE WITH PLAYIN' WITH YOU PEOPLE!

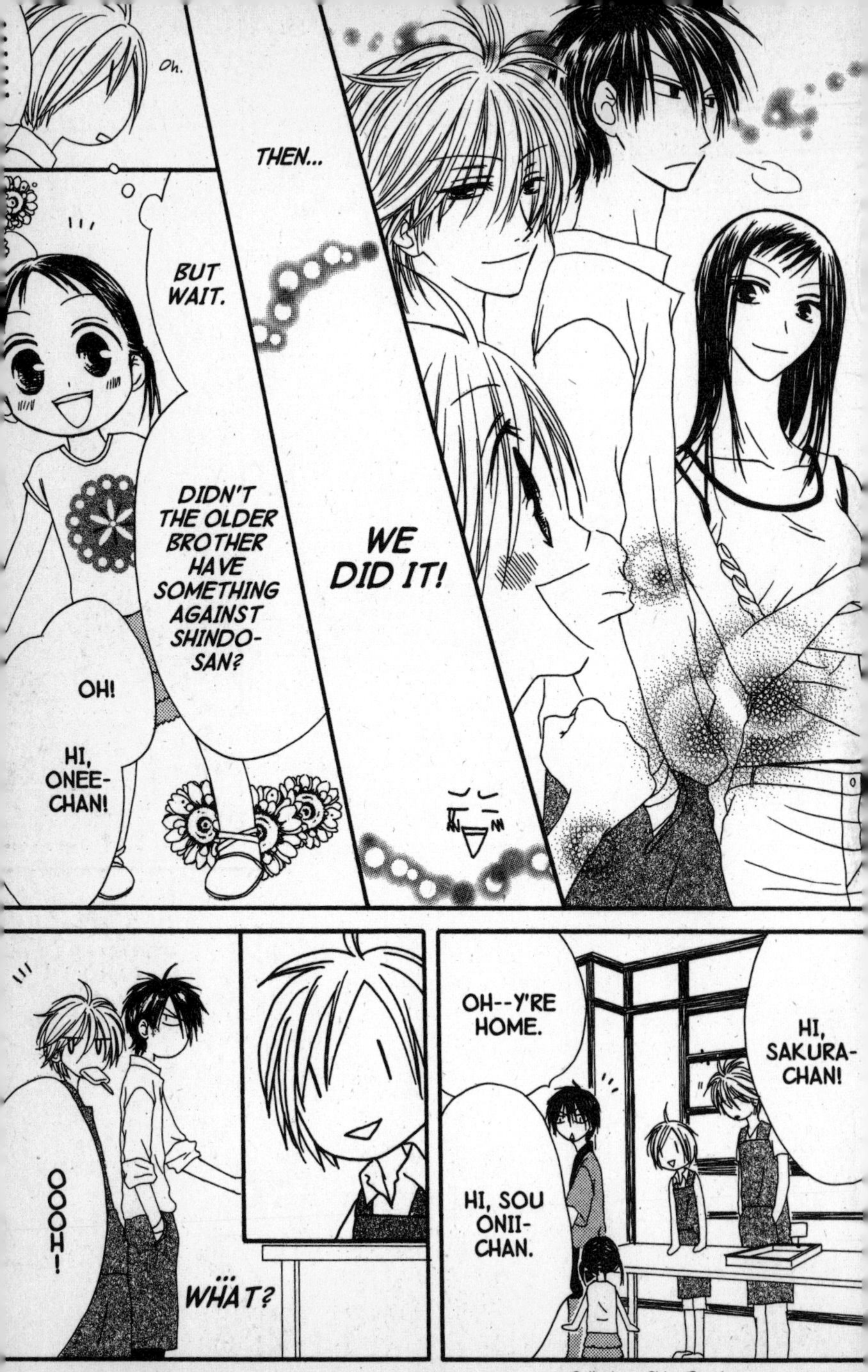
THEN...
WE DID IT!
Oh.
BUT WAIT.
DIDN'T THE OLDER BROTHER HAVE SOMETHING AGAINST SHINDO-SAN?
OH!
HI, ONEE-CHAN!
HI, SAKURA-CHAN!
OH--Y'RE HOME.
HI, SOU ONII-CHAN.
...WHAT?
OOOH!

Onii-chan: Older Brother.

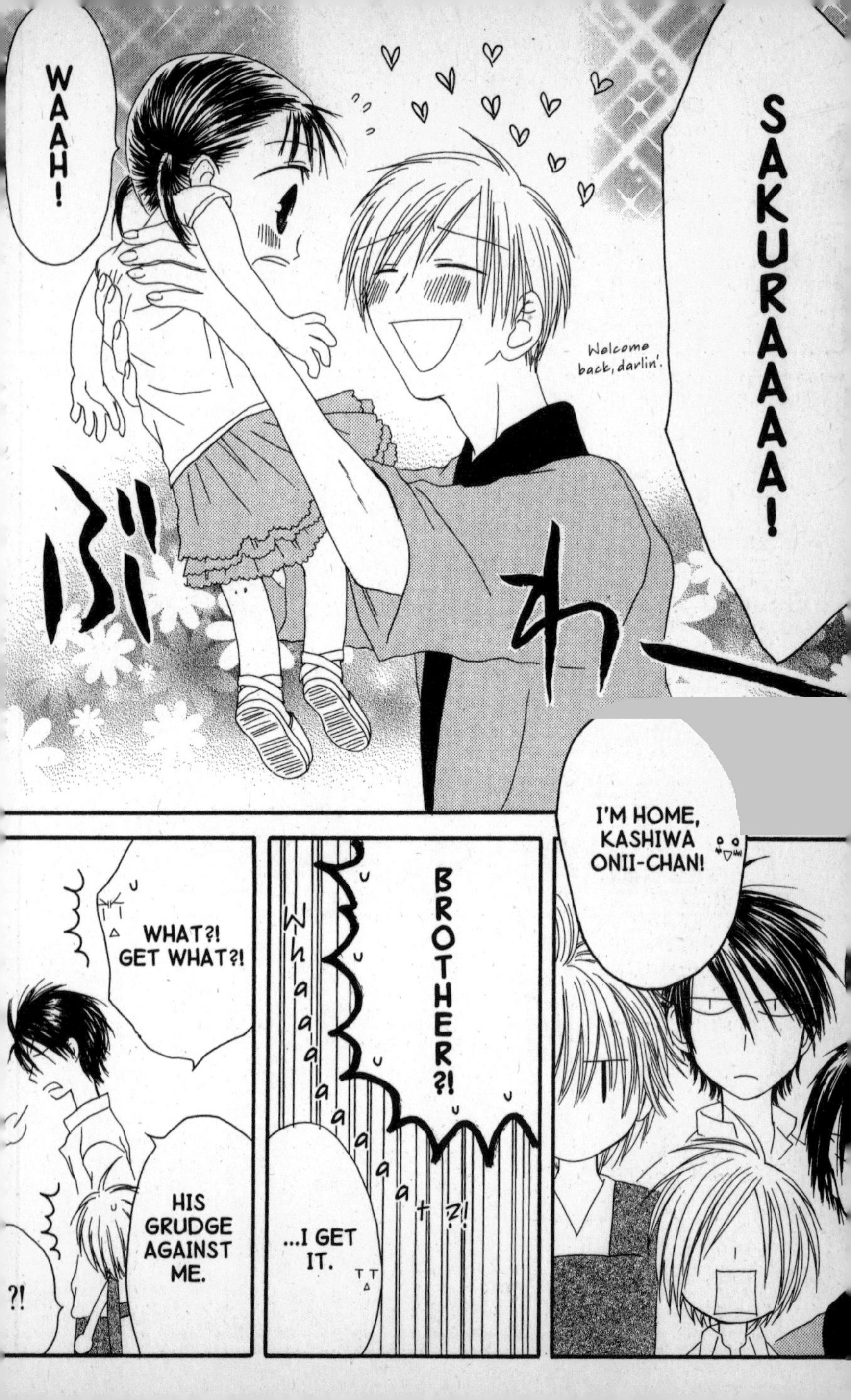
SAKURAAAAA!
Welcome back, darlin'.
わー
ぶ
WAAH!
I'M HOME, KASHIWA ONII-CHAN!
BROTHER?!
Whaaaaaaaaaat?!
...I GET IT.
WHAT?! GET WHAT?!
HIS GRUDGE AGAINST ME.
?!

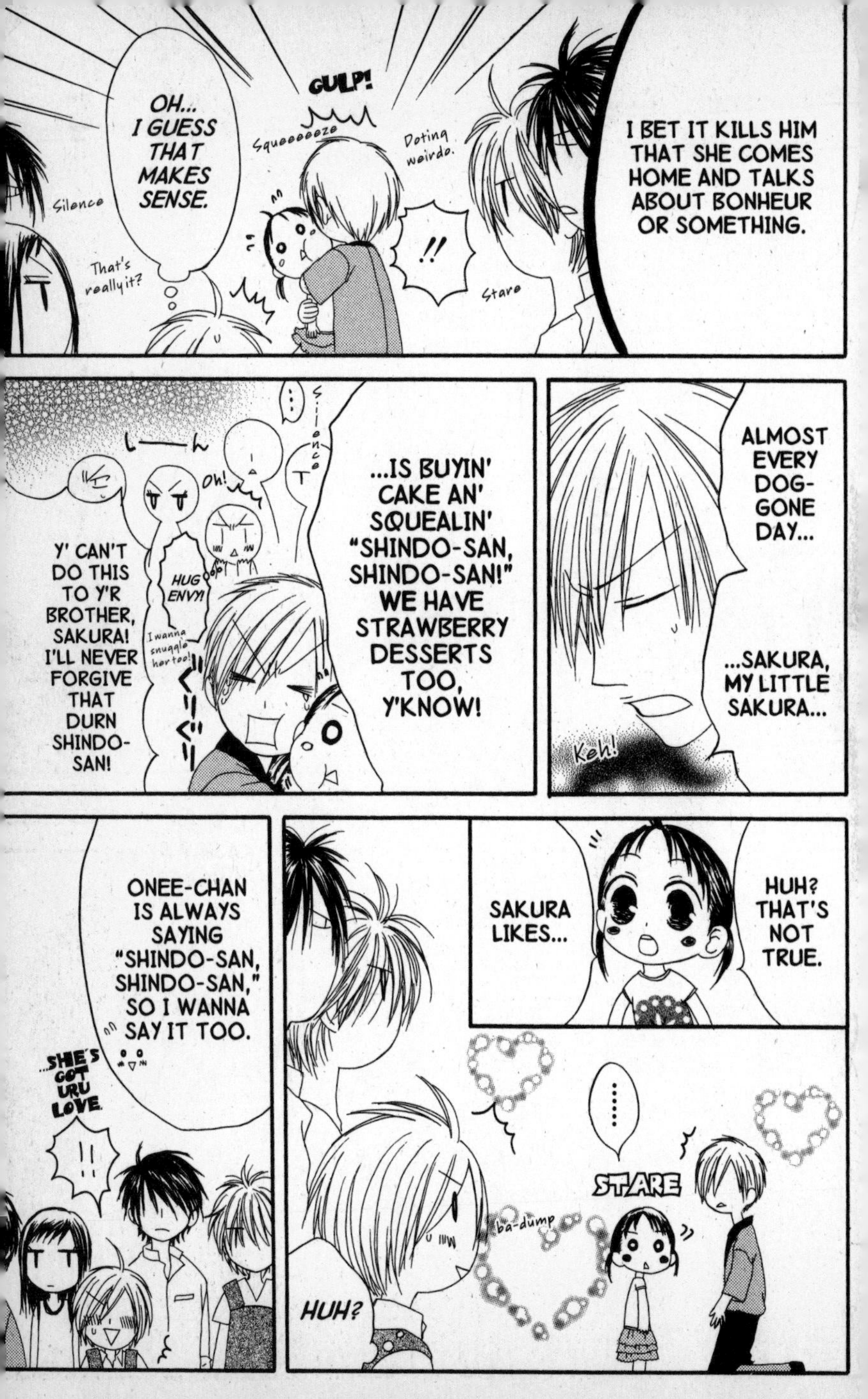

I BET IT KILLS HIM THAT SHE COMES HOME AND TALKS ABOUT BONHEUR OR SOMETHING.
Stare
!!
Doting weirdo.
GULP!
Squeeeeeze
OH... I GUESS THAT MAKES SENSE.
That's really it?
Silence
ALMOST EVERY DOG-GONE DAY...
...SAKURA, MY LITTLE SAKURA...
Keh!
...IS BUYIN' CAKE AN' SQUEALIN' "SHINDO-SAN, SHINDO-SAN!" WE HAVE STRAWBERRY DESSERTS TOO, Y'KNOW!
Silence
...
Oh!
HUG ENVY!
I wanna snuggle her too!
Y' CAN'T DO THIS TO Y'R BROTHER, SAKURA! I'LL NEVER FORGIVE THAT DURN SHINDO-SAN!
HUH? THAT'S NOT TRUE.
SAKURA LIKES...
......
STARE
ba-dump
HUH?
ONEE-CHAN IS ALWAYS SAYING "SHINDO-SAN, SHINDO-SAN," SO I WANNA SAY IT TOO.
...SHE'S GOT URU LOVE.
!!

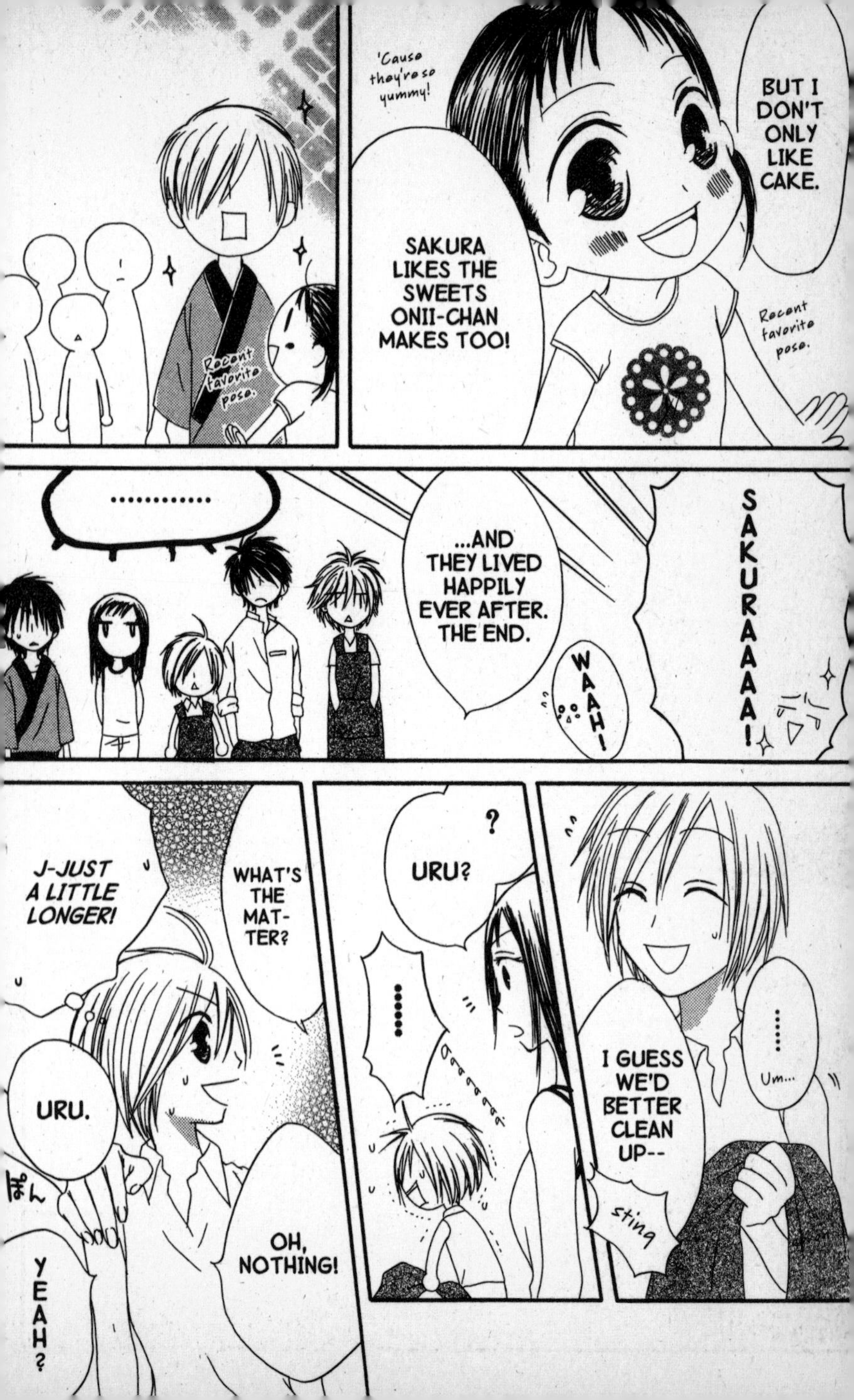
BUT I DON'T ONLY LIKE CAKE.
SAKURA LIKES THE SWEETS ONII-CHAN MAKES TOO!
'Cause they're so yummy!
Recent favorite pose.
Recent favorite pose.
SAKURAAAAA!
WAAH!
...AND THEY LIVED HAPPILY EVER AFTER. THE END.
....
Um...
......
I GUESS WE'D BETTER CLEAN UP--
sting
?
URU?
......
WHAT'S THE MAT-TER?
J-JUST A LITTLE LONGER!
URU.
ぽん
OH, NOTHING!
YEAH?

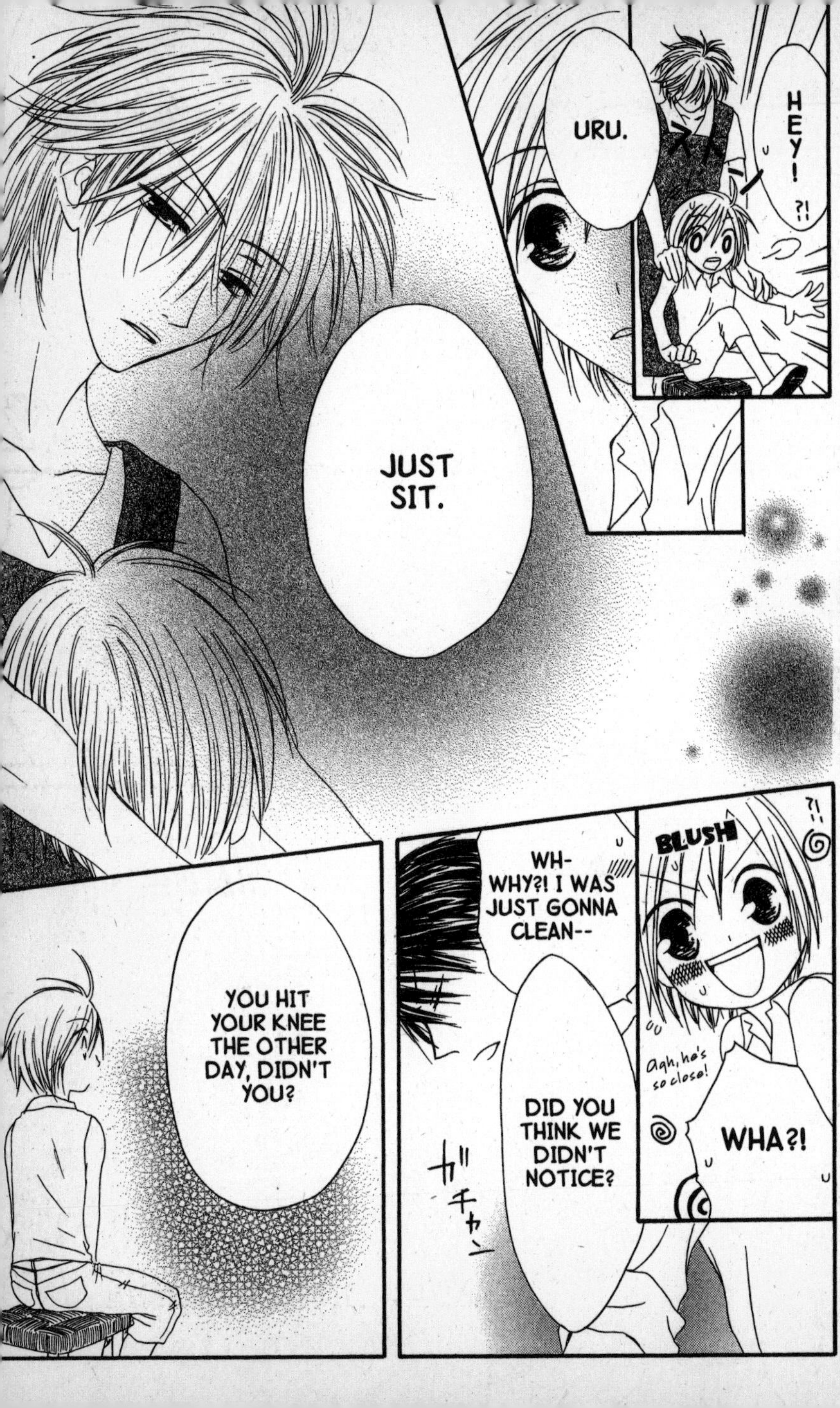
HEY! ?!
URU.
JUST SIT.
BLUSH
?!
Agh, he's so close!
WHA?!
WH- WHY?! I WAS JUST GONNA CLEAN--
DID YOU THINK WE DIDN'T NOTICE?
YOU HIT YOUR KNEE THE OTHER DAY, DIDN'T YOU?

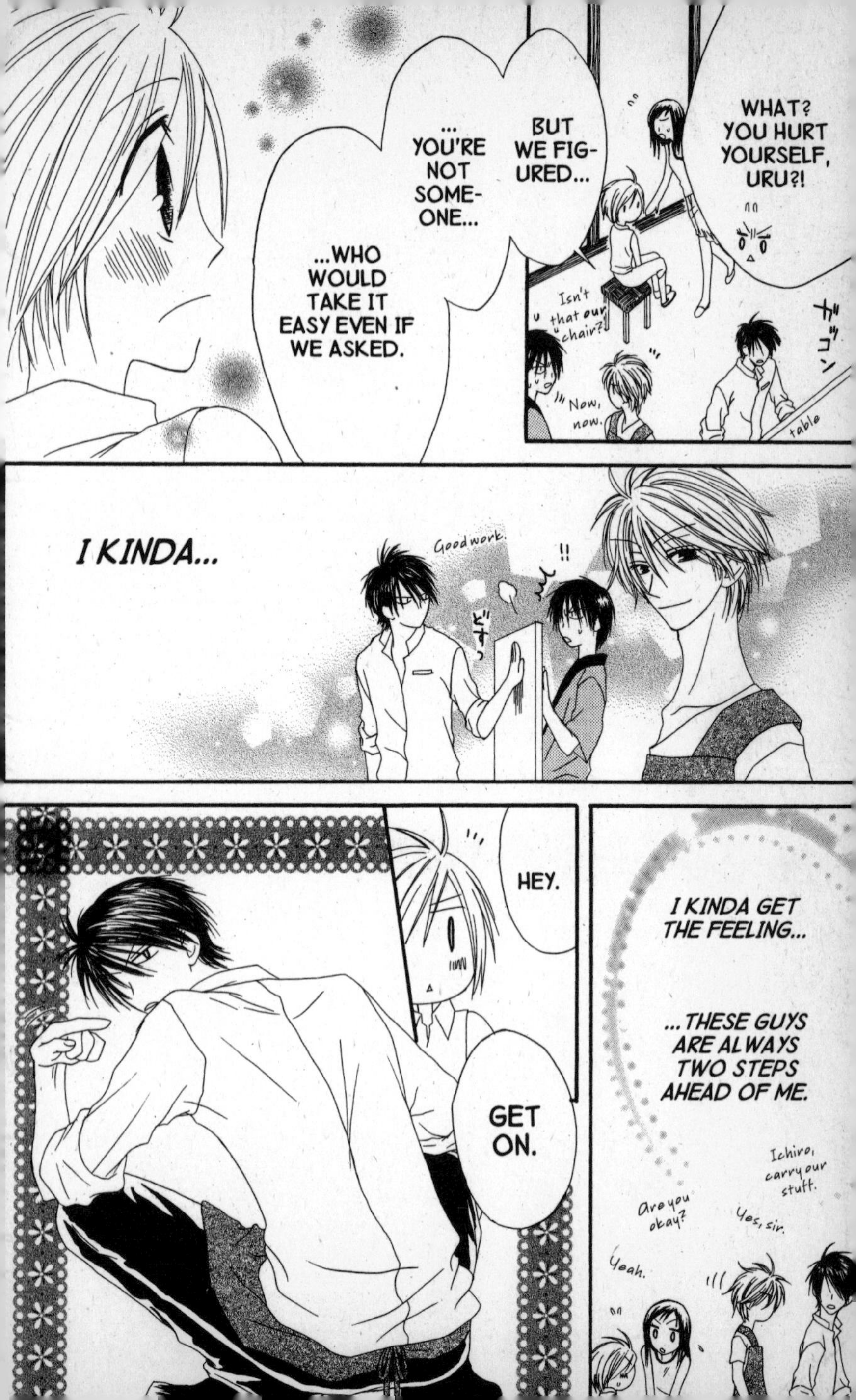
WHAT? YOU HURT YOURSELF, URU?!
Isn't that our chair?!
Now, now.
table
BUT WE FIGURED...
...YOU'RE NOT SOMEONE...
...WHO WOULD TAKE IT EASY EVEN IF WE ASKED.
!!
Good work.
どすっ
I KINDA...
I KINDA GET THE FEELING...
...THESE GUYS ARE ALWAYS TWO STEPS AHEAD OF ME.
Ichiro, carry our stuff.
Yes, sir.
Are you okay?
Yeah.
HEY.
GET ON.

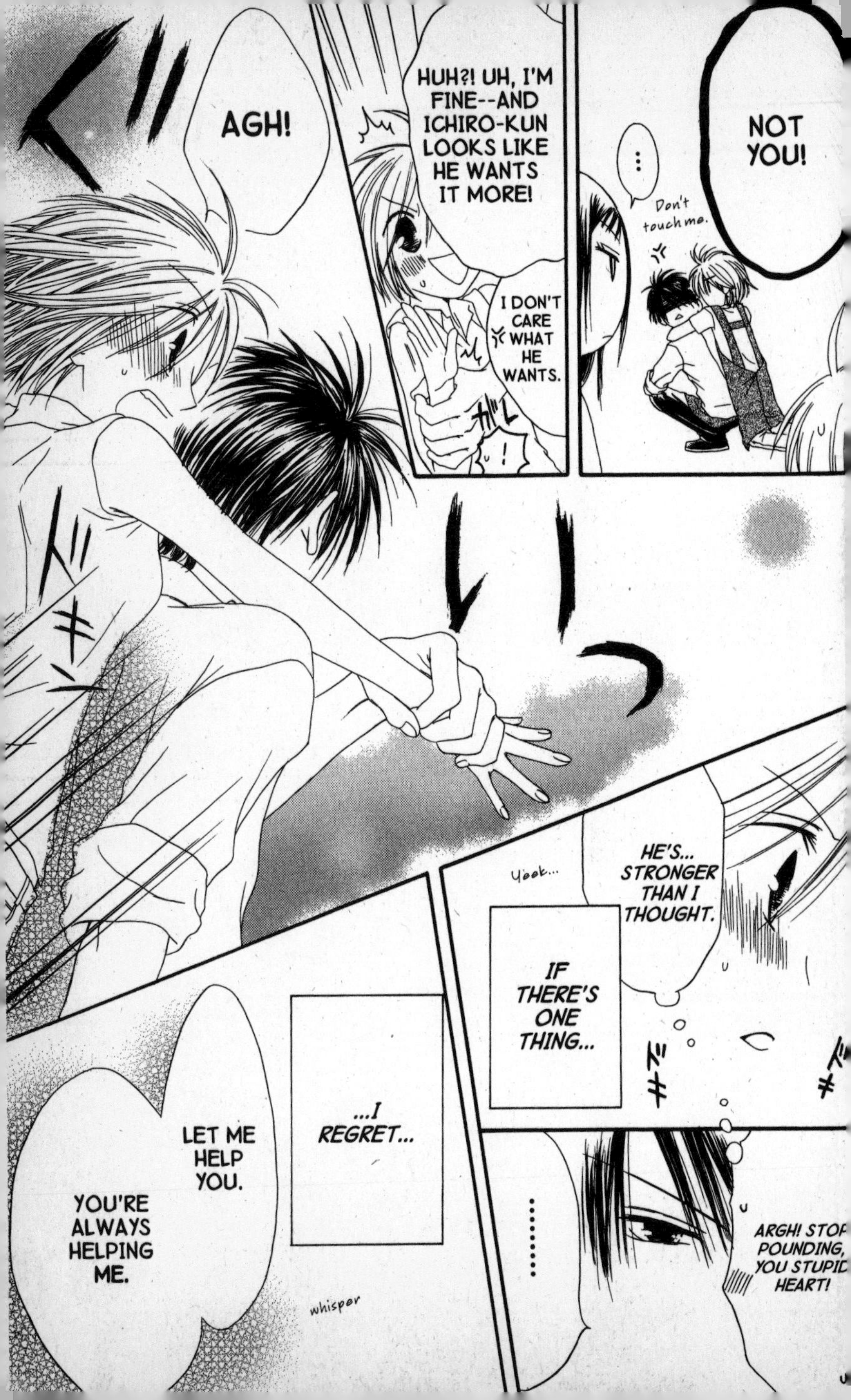
NOT YOU!
...
Don't touch me.
HUH?! UH, I'M FINE--AND ICHIRO-KUN LOOKS LIKE HE WANTS IT MORE!
I DON'T CARE WHAT HE WANTS.
AGH!
HE'S... STRONGER THAN I THOUGHT.
Yeek...
IF THERE'S ONE THING...
ARGH! STOP POUNDING, YOU STUPID HEART!
....
...I REGRET...
LET ME HELP YOU.
YOU'RE ALWAYS HELPING ME.
whisper

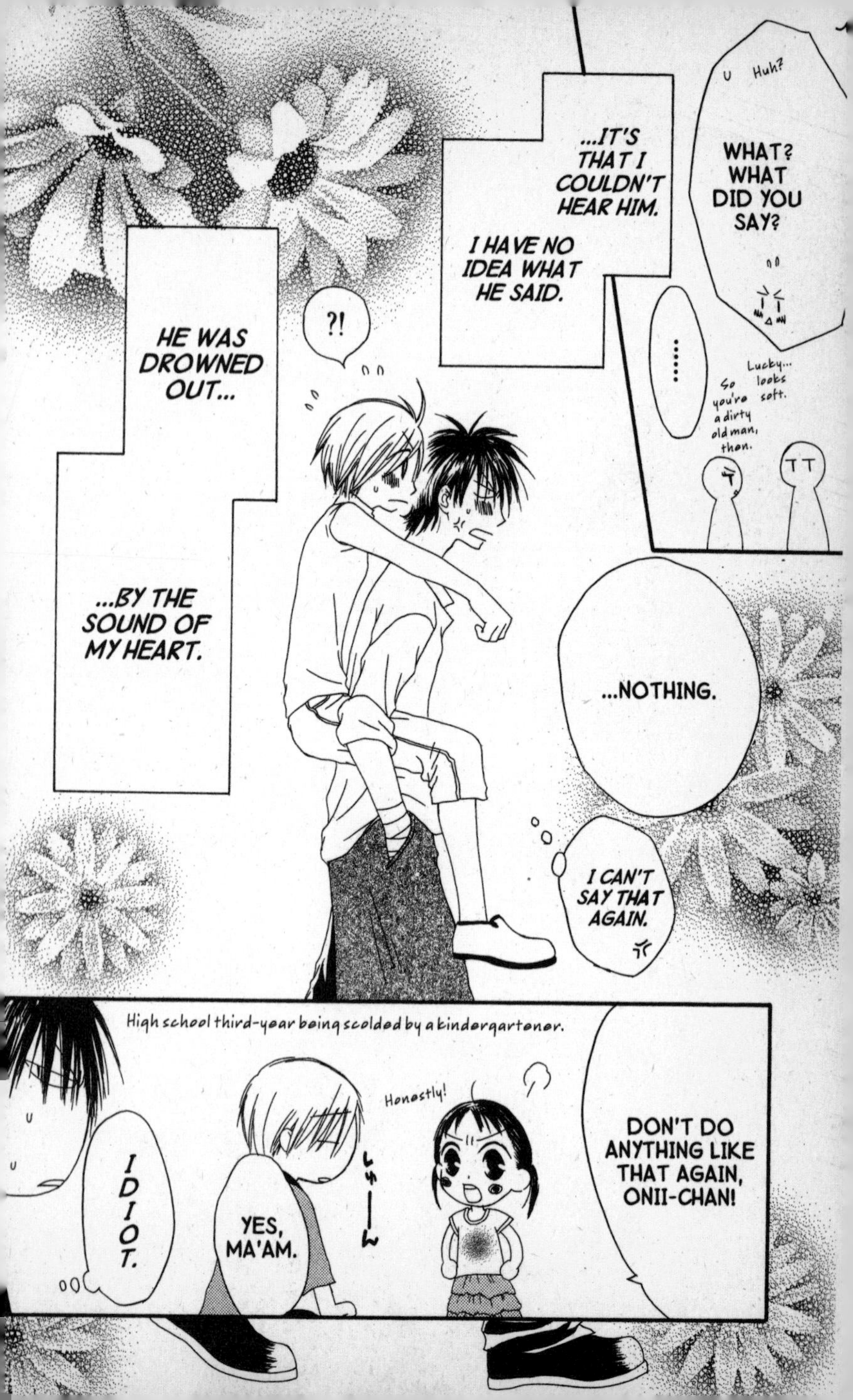
Huh?
WHAT? WHAT DID YOU SAY?
......
Lucky... looks soft.
So you're a dirty old man, then.
...IT'S THAT I COULDN'T HEAR HIM.
I HAVE NO IDEA WHAT HE SAID.
?!
...NOTHING.
I CAN'T SAY THAT AGAIN.
HE WAS DROWNED OUT...
...BY THE SOUND OF MY HEART.
High school third-year being scolded by a kindergartener.
DON'T DO ANYTHING LIKE THAT AGAIN, ONII-CHAN!
Honestly!
しゅーん
YES, MA'AM.
IDIOT.

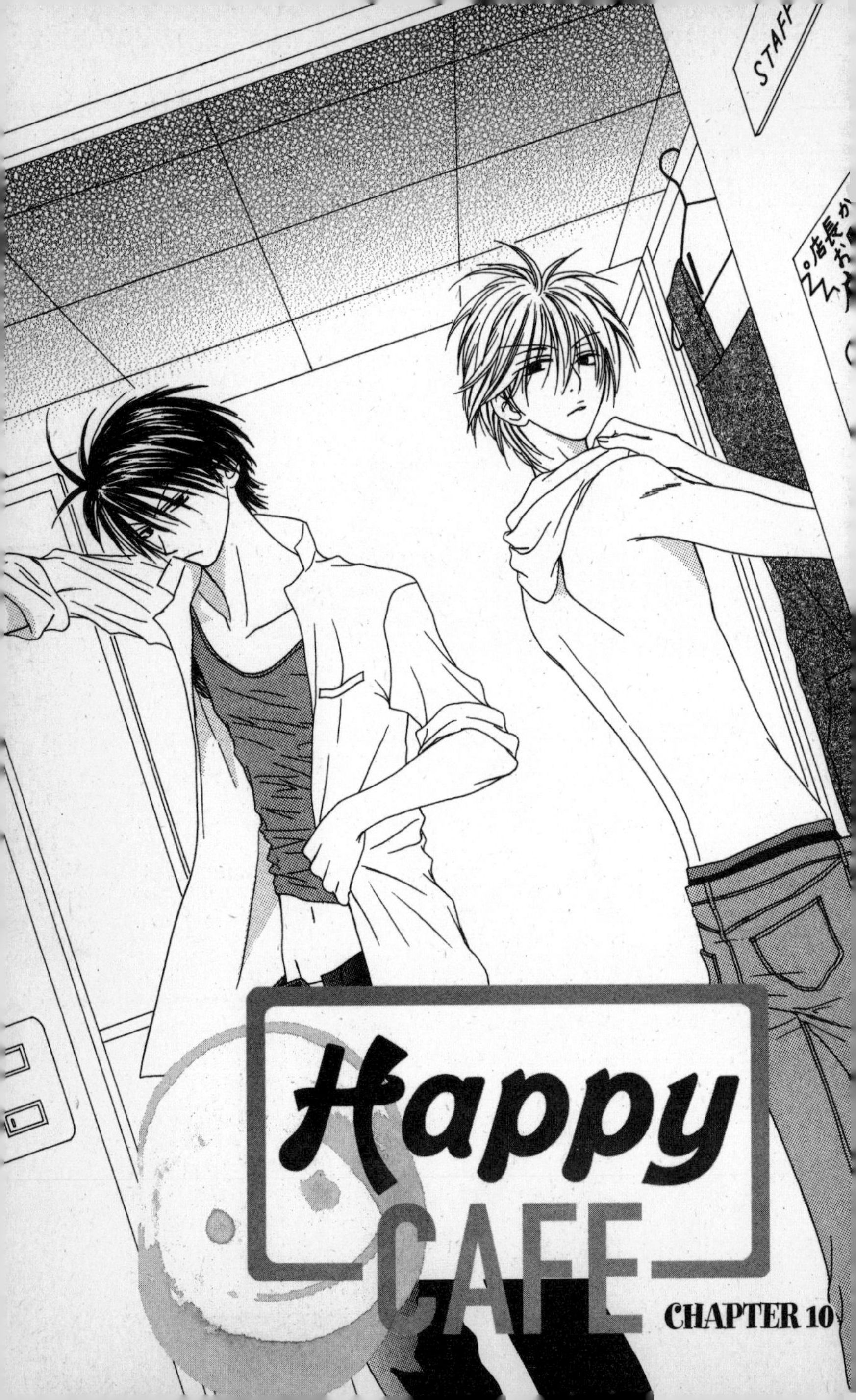
Happy
CAFE
CHAPTER 10

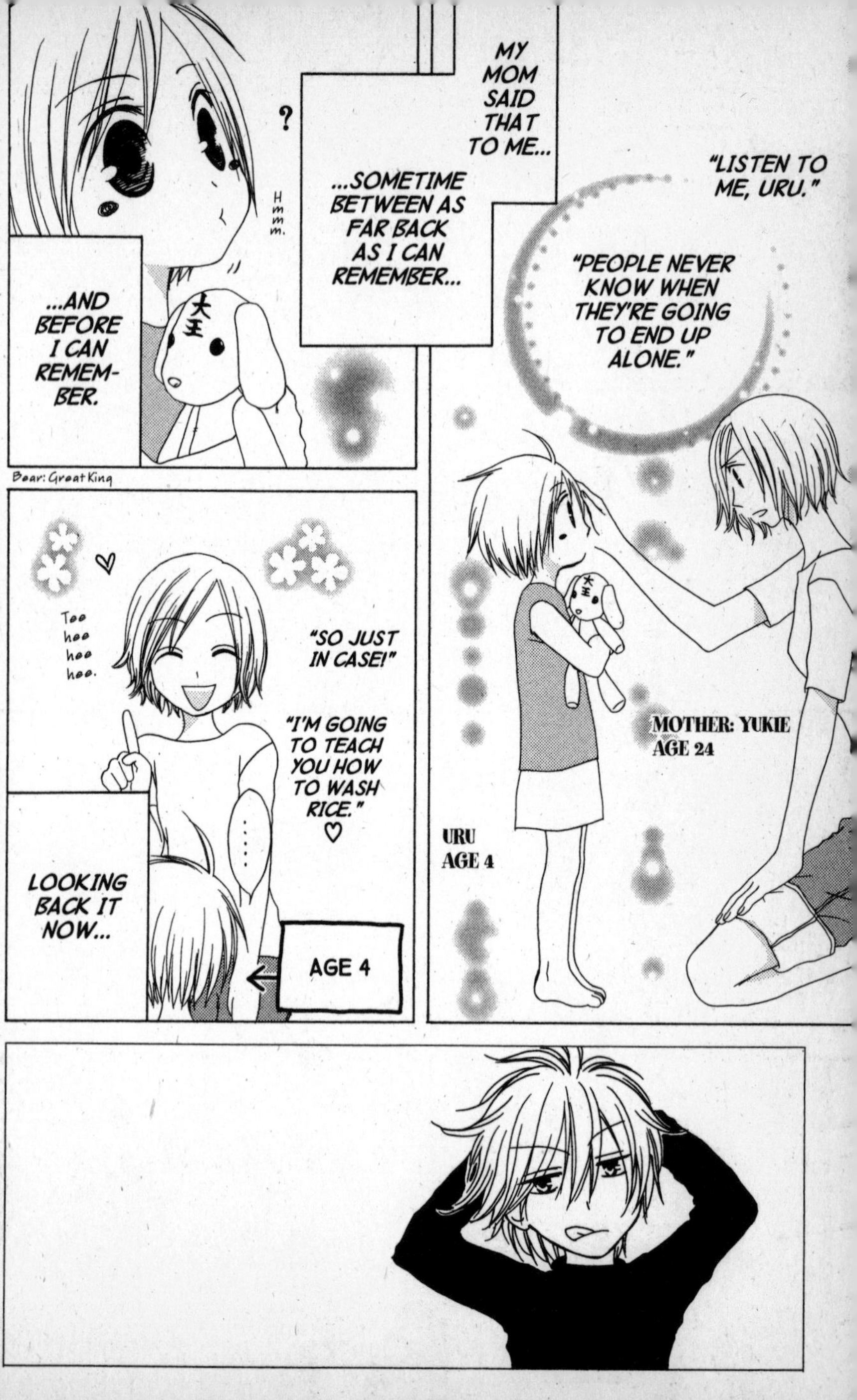
"LISTEN TO ME, URU."
"PEOPLE NEVER KNOW WHEN THEY'RE GOING TO END UP ALONE."
MOTHER: YUKIE AGE 24
URU AGE 4
MY MOM SAID THAT TO ME...
...SOMETIME BETWEEN AS FAR BACK AS I CAN REMEMBER...
?
Hmmm.
...AND BEFORE I CAN REMEMBER.
Bear: Great King
"SO JUST IN CASE!"
"I'M GOING TO TEACH YOU HOW TO WASH RICE." ♡
Tee hee hee hee.
.....
LOOKING BACK IT NOW...
AGE 4

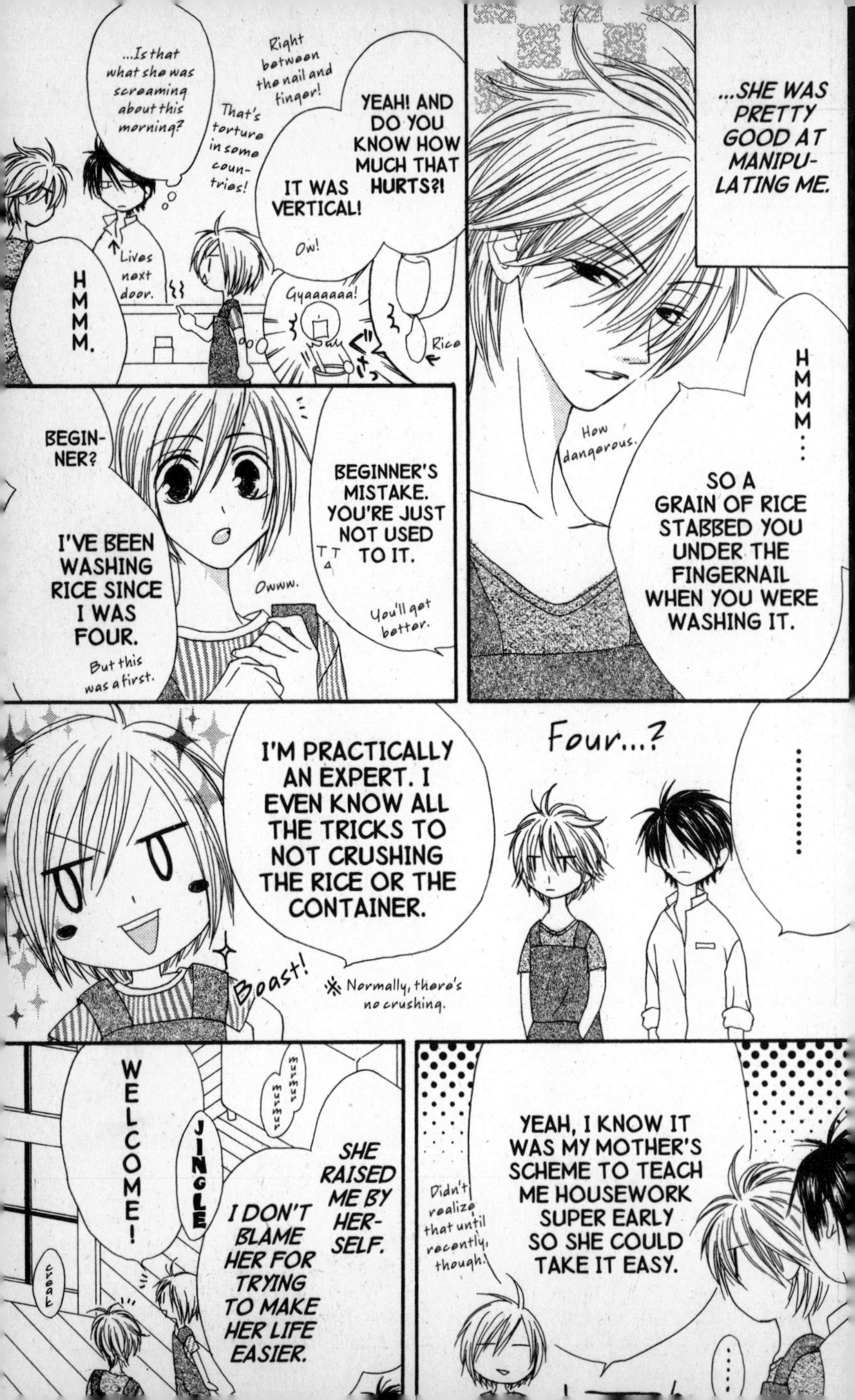
...SHE WAS PRETTY GOOD AT MANIPULATING ME.
HMMM...
SO A GRAIN OF RICE STABBED YOU UNDER THE FINGERNAIL WHEN YOU WERE WASHING IT.
How dangerous.
YEAH! AND DO YOU KNOW HOW MUCH THAT HURTS?!
IT WAS VERTICAL!
Right between the nail and finger!
That's torture in some countries!
...Is that what she was screaming about this morning?
Lives next door.
HMMM.
Ow!
Gyaaaaaa!
Rice
BEGINNER'S MISTAKE. YOU'RE JUST NOT USED TO IT.
You'll get better.
Owww.
BEGINNER?
I'VE BEEN WASHING RICE SINCE I WAS FOUR.
But this was a first.
....
Four...?
I'M PRACTICALLY AN EXPERT. I EVEN KNOW ALL THE TRICKS TO NOT CRUSHING THE RICE OR THE CONTAINER.
Boast!
※ Normally, there's no crushing.
YEAH, I KNOW IT WAS MY MOTHER'S SCHEME TO TEACH ME HOUSEWORK SUPER EARLY SO SHE COULD TAKE IT EASY.
Didn't realize that until recently, though!
...
SHE RAISED ME BY HERSELF.
I DON'T BLAME HER FOR TRYING TO MAKE HER LIFE EASIER.
murmur murmur
JINGLE
WELCOME!
creak

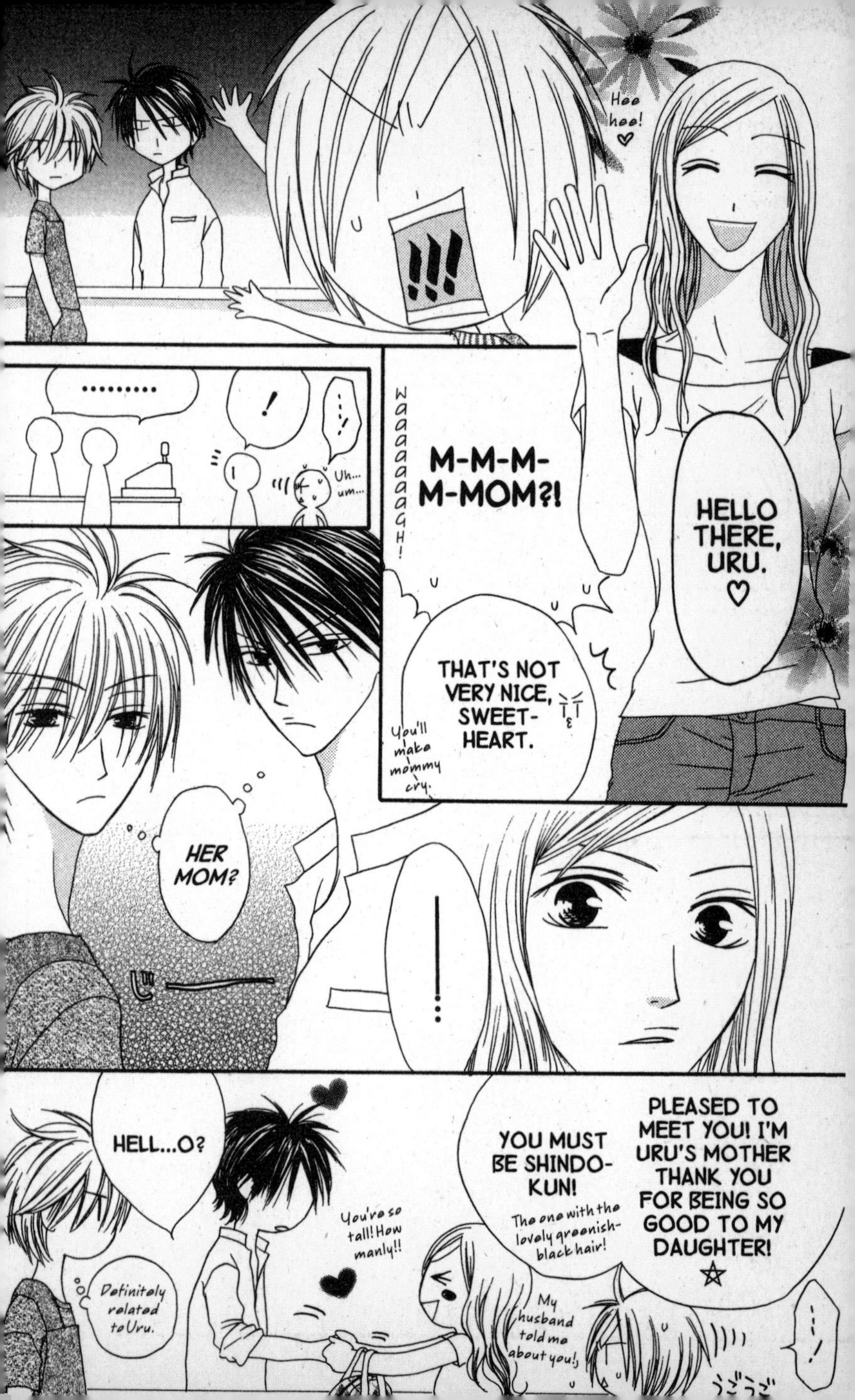
Hee hee! ♥
!!!
HELLO THERE, URU. ♡
M-M-M-M-MOM?!
Waaaaaaaaagh!
THAT'S NOT VERY NICE, SWEET-HEART.
You'll make mommy cry.
....
!
Uh... um...
...!
HER MOM?
PLEASED TO MEET YOU! I'M URU'S MOTHER THANK YOU FOR BEING SO GOOD TO MY DAUGHTER! ☆
YOU MUST BE SHINDO-KUN!
The one with the lovely greenish-black hair!
...!
My husband told me about you!
You're so tall! How manly!!
HELL...O?
Definitely related to Uru.

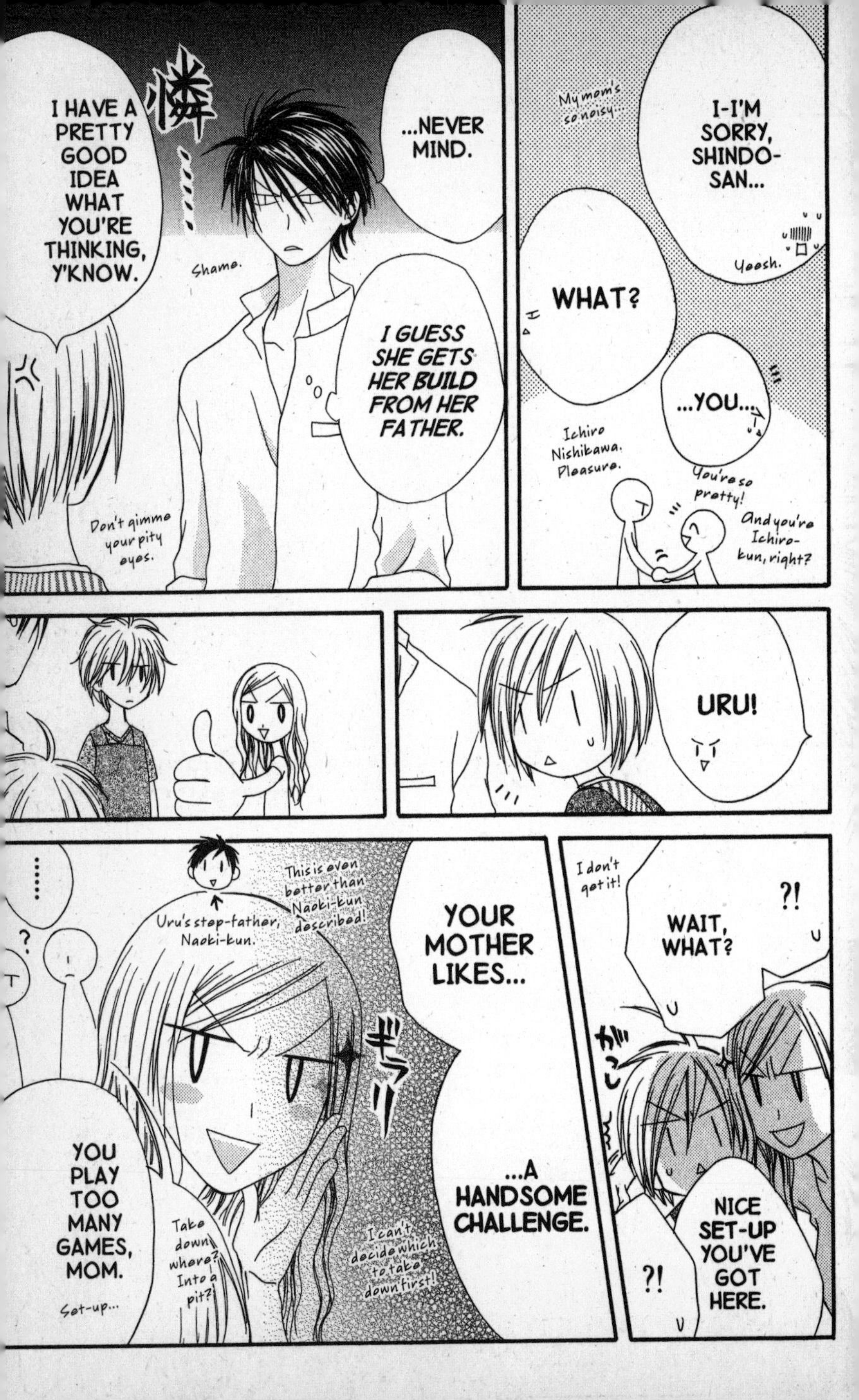
I-I'M SORRY, SHINDO-SAN...
My mom's so noisy...
Yeesh.
WHAT?
...YOU...
Ichiro Nishikawa. Pleasure.
You're so pretty!
And you're Ichiro-kun, right?
...NEVER MIND.
I HAVE A PRETTY GOOD IDEA WHAT YOU'RE THINKING, Y'KNOW.
I GUESS SHE GETS HER BUILD FROM HER FATHER.
Shame.
Don't gimme your pity eyes.
URU!
?!
WAIT, WHAT?
I don't get it!
NICE SET-UP YOU'VE GOT HERE.
?!
YOUR MOTHER LIKES...
...A HANDSOME CHALLENGE.
This is even better than Naoki-kun described!
I can't decide which to take down first!
Uru's step-father, Naoki-kun.
......
?
YOU PLAY TOO MANY GAMES, MOM.
Take down where? Into a pit?
Set-up...

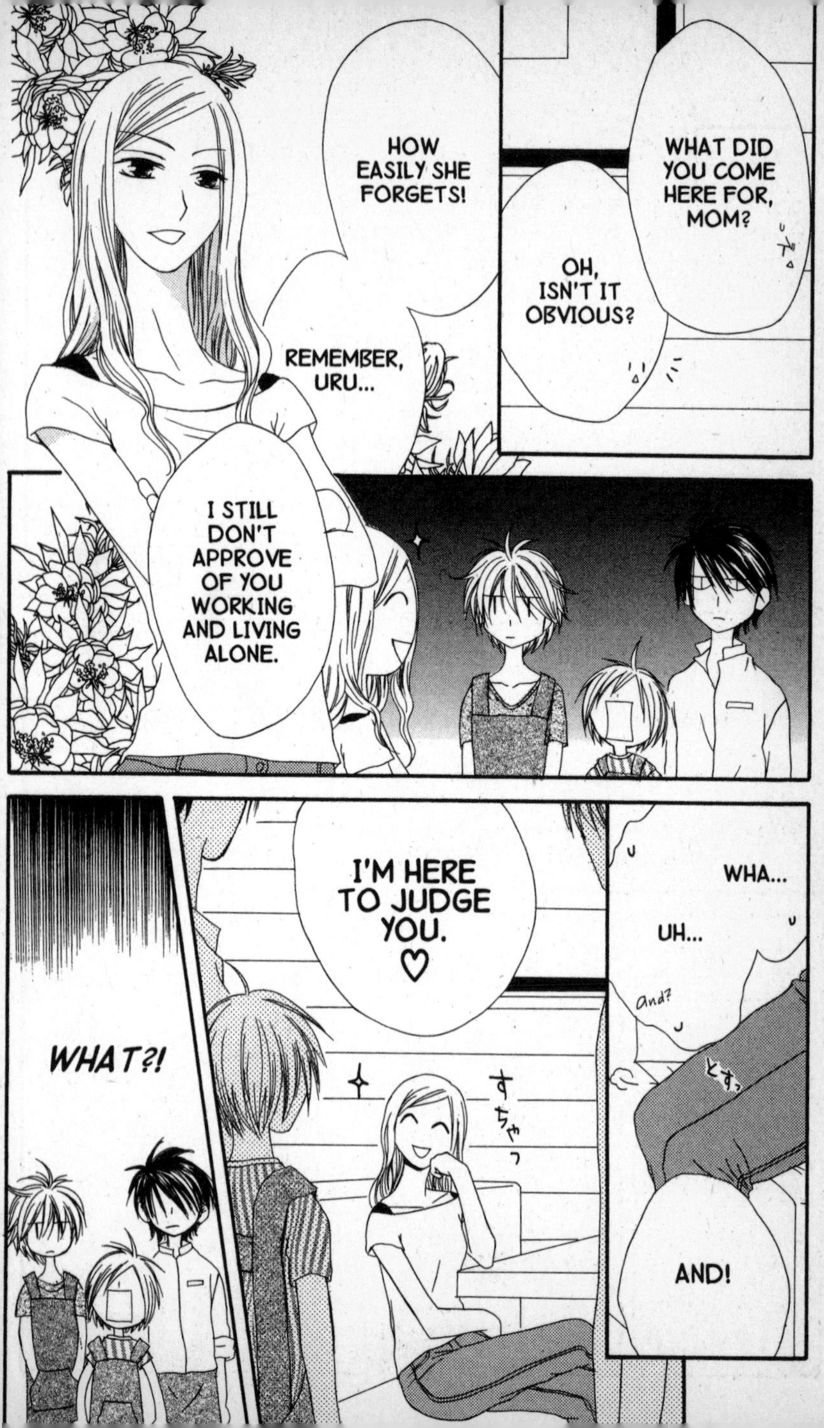
WHAT DID YOU COME HERE FOR, MOM?
OH, ISN'T IT OBVIOUS?
HOW EASILY SHE FORGETS!
REMEMBER, URU...
I STILL DON'T APPROVE OF YOU WORKING AND LIVING ALONE.
WHA...
UH...
and?
とすっ
AND!
I'M HERE TO JUDGE YOU. ♡
すちゃっ
WHAT?!

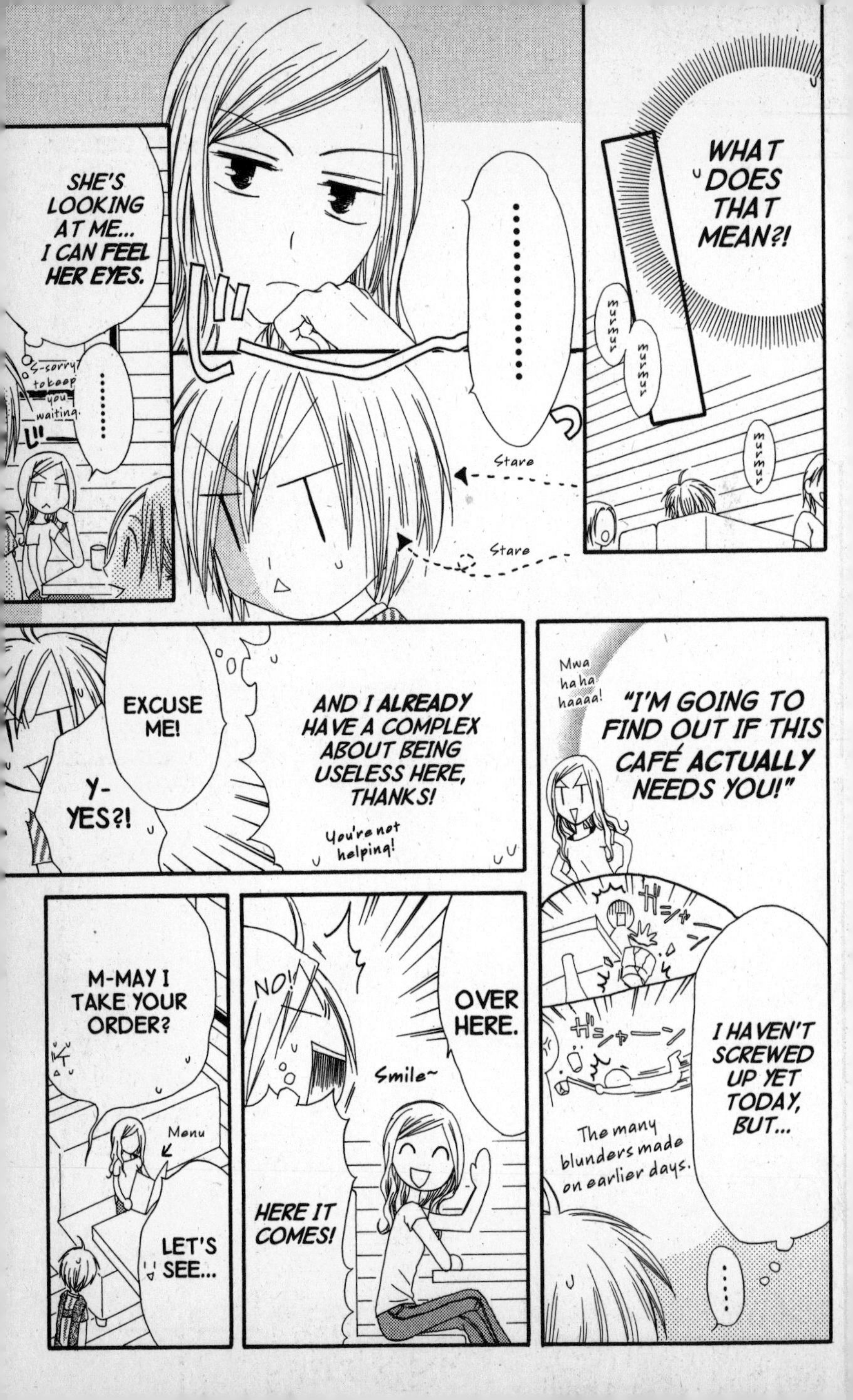
WHAT DOES THAT MEAN?!
murmur
murmur
murmur
......
Stare
Stare
じー
SHE'S LOOKING AT ME... I CAN FEEL HER EYES.
S-sorry to keep you waiting.
......
"I'M GOING TO FIND OUT IF THIS CAFÉ ACTUALLY NEEDS YOU!"
Mwa ha ha haaaa!
The many blunders made on earlier days.
I HAVEN'T SCREWED UP YET TODAY, BUT...
......
AND I ALREADY HAVE A COMPLEX ABOUT BEING USELESS HERE, THANKS!
You're not helping!
EXCUSE ME!
Y- YES?!
OVER HERE.
NO!
Smile~
HERE IT COMES!
M-MAY I TAKE YOUR ORDER?
Menu
LET'S SEE...

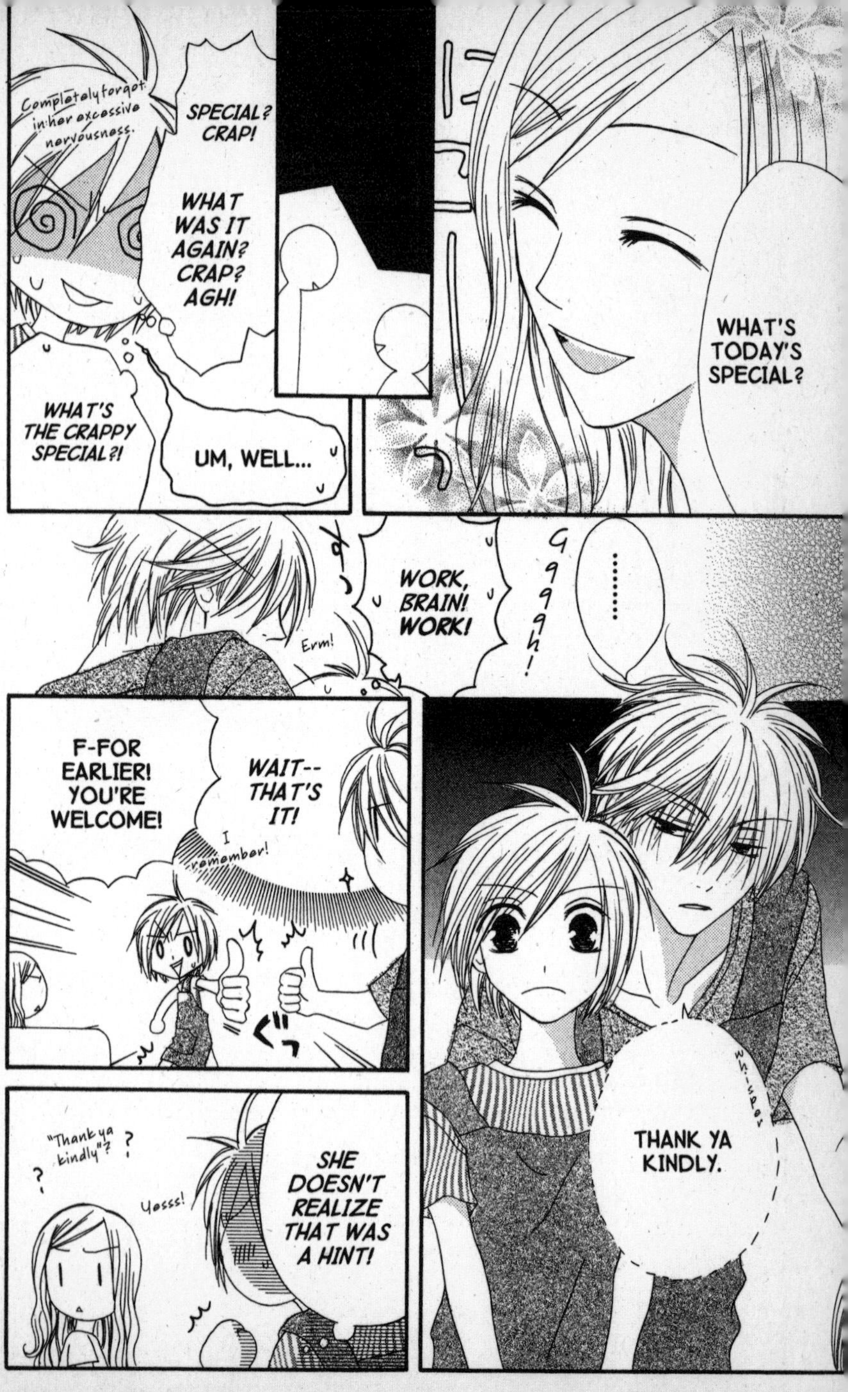
WHAT'S TODAY'S SPECIAL?
SPECIAL? CRAP!
WHAT WAS IT AGAIN? CRAP? AGH!
Completely forgot in her excessive nervousness.
UM, WELL...
WHAT'S THE CRAPPY SPECIAL?!
......
Gggggh!
WORK, BRAIN! WORK!
Erm!
whisper
THANK YA KINDLY.
WAIT-- THAT'S IT!
I remember!
F-FOR EARLIER! YOU'RE WELCOME!
SHE DOESN'T REALIZE THAT WAS A HINT!
Yesss!
"Thank ya kindly"? ?
?

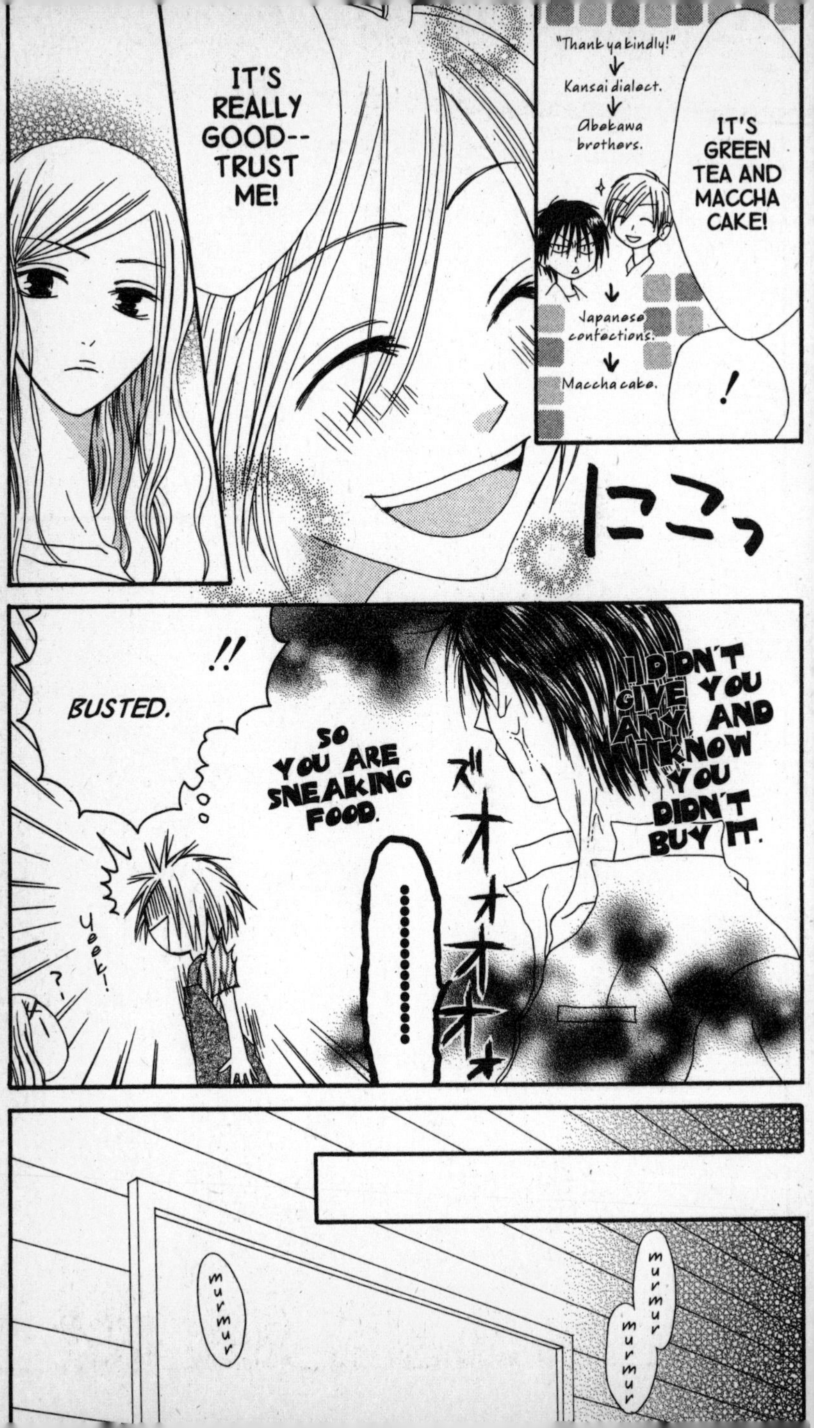
IT'S GREEN TEA AND MACCHA CAKE!
"Thank ya kindly!"
Kansai dialect.
Abekawa brothers.
Japanese confections.
Maccha cake.
!
にこっ
IT'S REALLY GOOD-- TRUST ME!
I DIDN'T GIVE YOU ANY AND I KNOW YOU DIDN'T BUY IT.
ズオオオオ
....
SO YOU ARE SNEAKING FOOD.
!!
BUSTED.
Yeek!
murmur
murmur
murmur

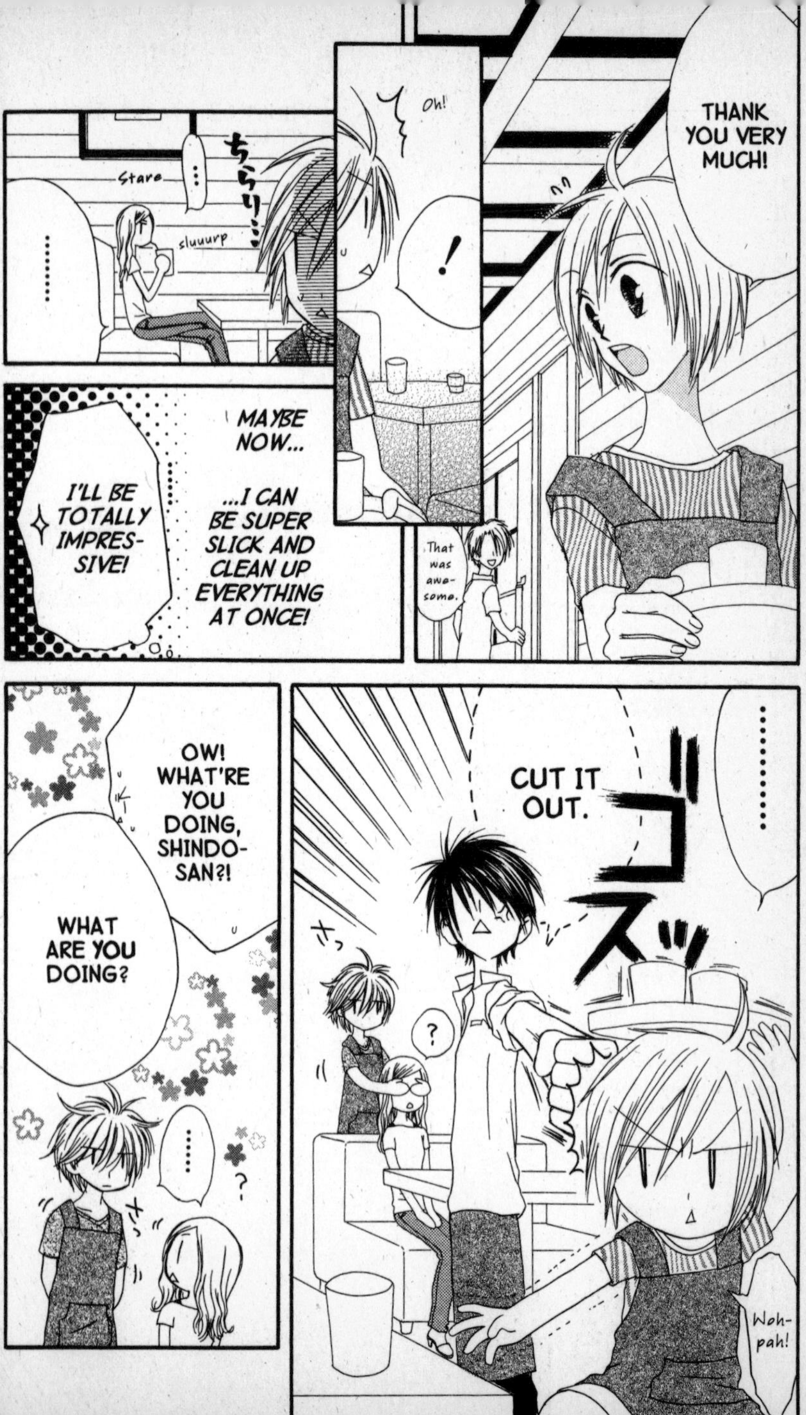
THANK YOU VERY MUCH!
That was awesome.
Oh!
!
Stare
...
ちらり
sluuurp
......
MAYBE NOW...
...I CAN BE SUPER SLICK AND CLEAN UP EVERYTHING AT ONCE!
I'LL BE TOTALLY IMPRES-SIVE!
......
CUT IT OUT.
ゴスッ
?
Woh-pah!
OW! WHAT'RE YOU DOING, SHINDO-SAN?!
WHAT ARE YOU DOING?
......
?

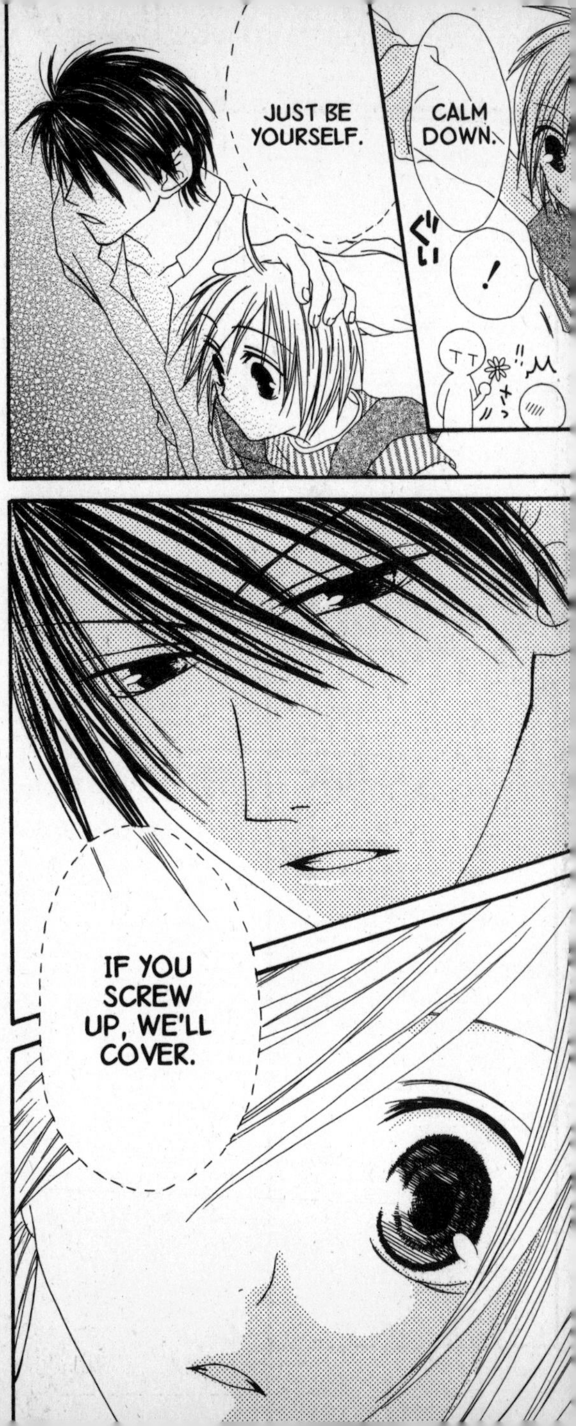
CALM DOWN.
!
JUST BE YOURSELF.
IF YOU SCREW UP, WE'LL COVER.

5

Seriously, thanks for always sending letters.

Whenever I get them, I ditch my manuscript to read them!

When I'm discouraged, I read them again and think, "Wow...I have to work hard for everyone."

I mean...

Letters are my favorite. I love them so much, I could fall in love with the people who send them.

Ah, I'm sorry! Don't run away from meeee!

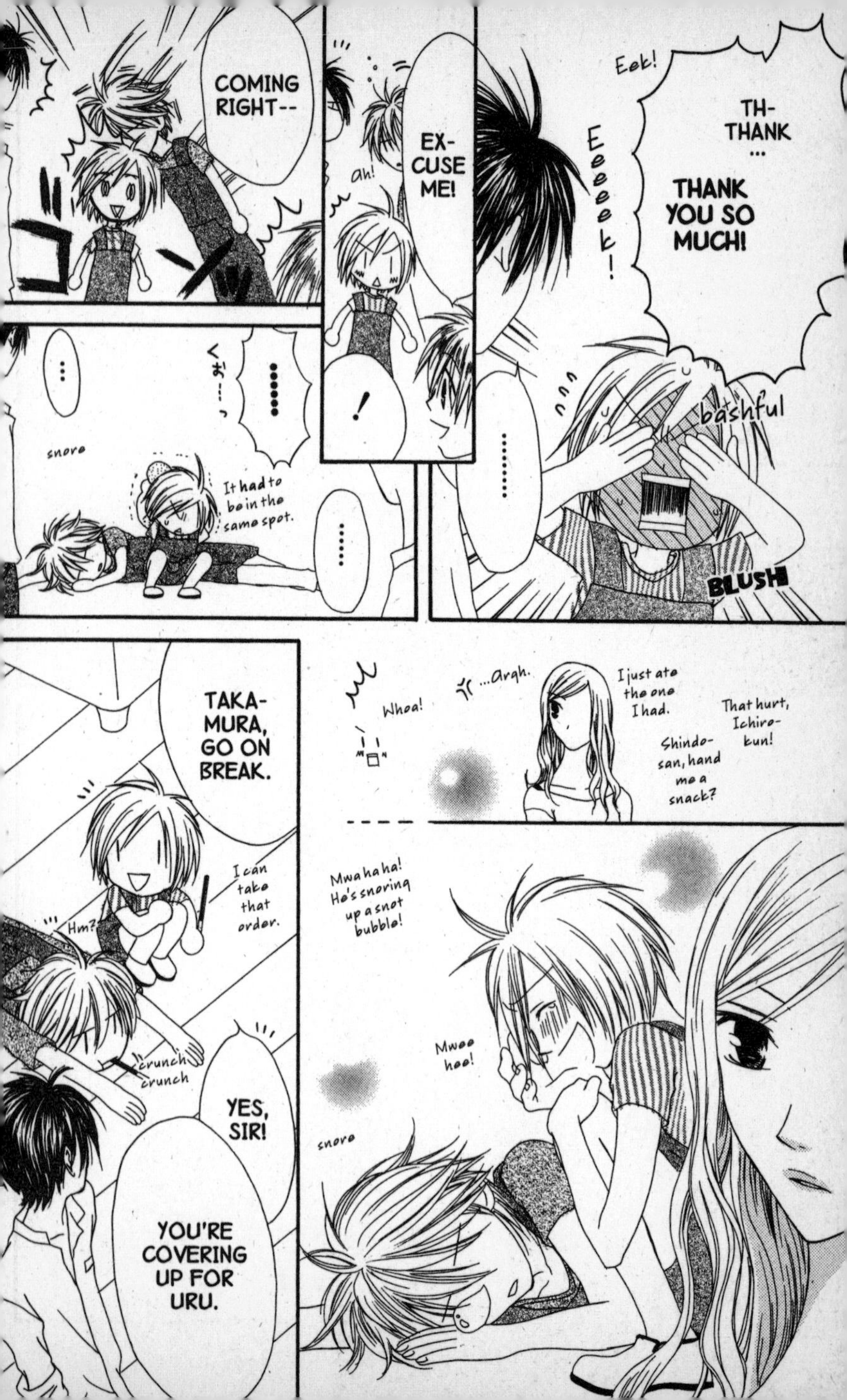
Eek!
Eeeeek!
TH-THANK...
THANK YOU SO MUCH!
bashful
......
BLUSH
EX-CUSE ME!
ah!
!
COMING RIGHT--
......
くお…っ
...
snore
It had to be in the same spot.
......
...Argh.
Whoa!
I just ate the one I had.
That hurt, Ichiro-kun!
Shindo-san, hand me a snack?
Mwahaha! He's snoring up a snot bubble!
Mwee hee!
snore
TAKAMURA, GO ON BREAK.
I can take that order.
Hm?
crunch crunch
YES, SIR!
YOU'RE COVERING UP FOR URU.

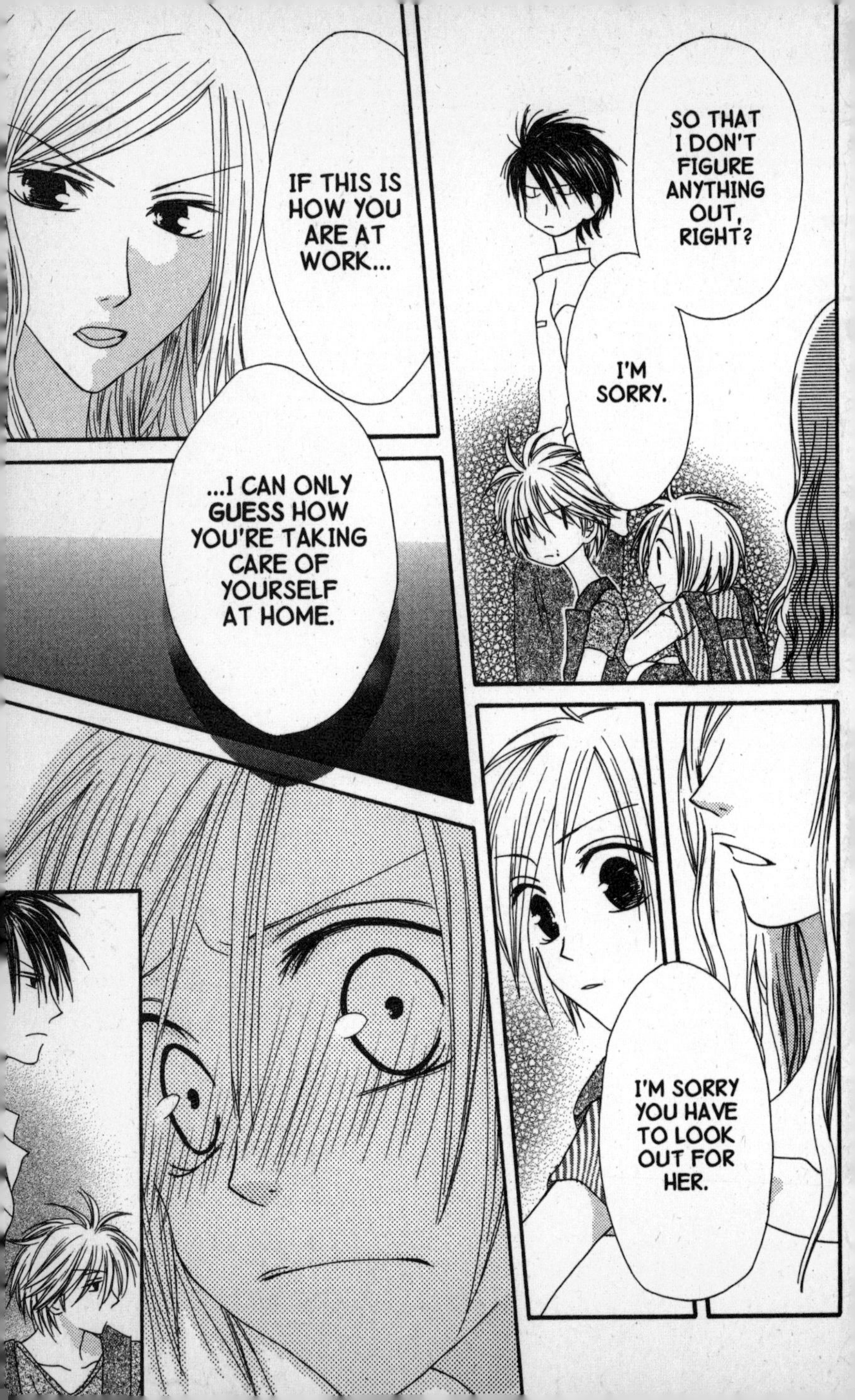
SO THAT I DON'T FIGURE ANYTHING OUT, RIGHT?
I'M SORRY.
IF THIS IS HOW YOU ARE AT WORK...
...I CAN ONLY GUESS HOW YOU'RE TAKING CARE OF YOURSELF AT HOME.
I'M SORRY YOU HAVE TO LOOK OUT FOR HER.

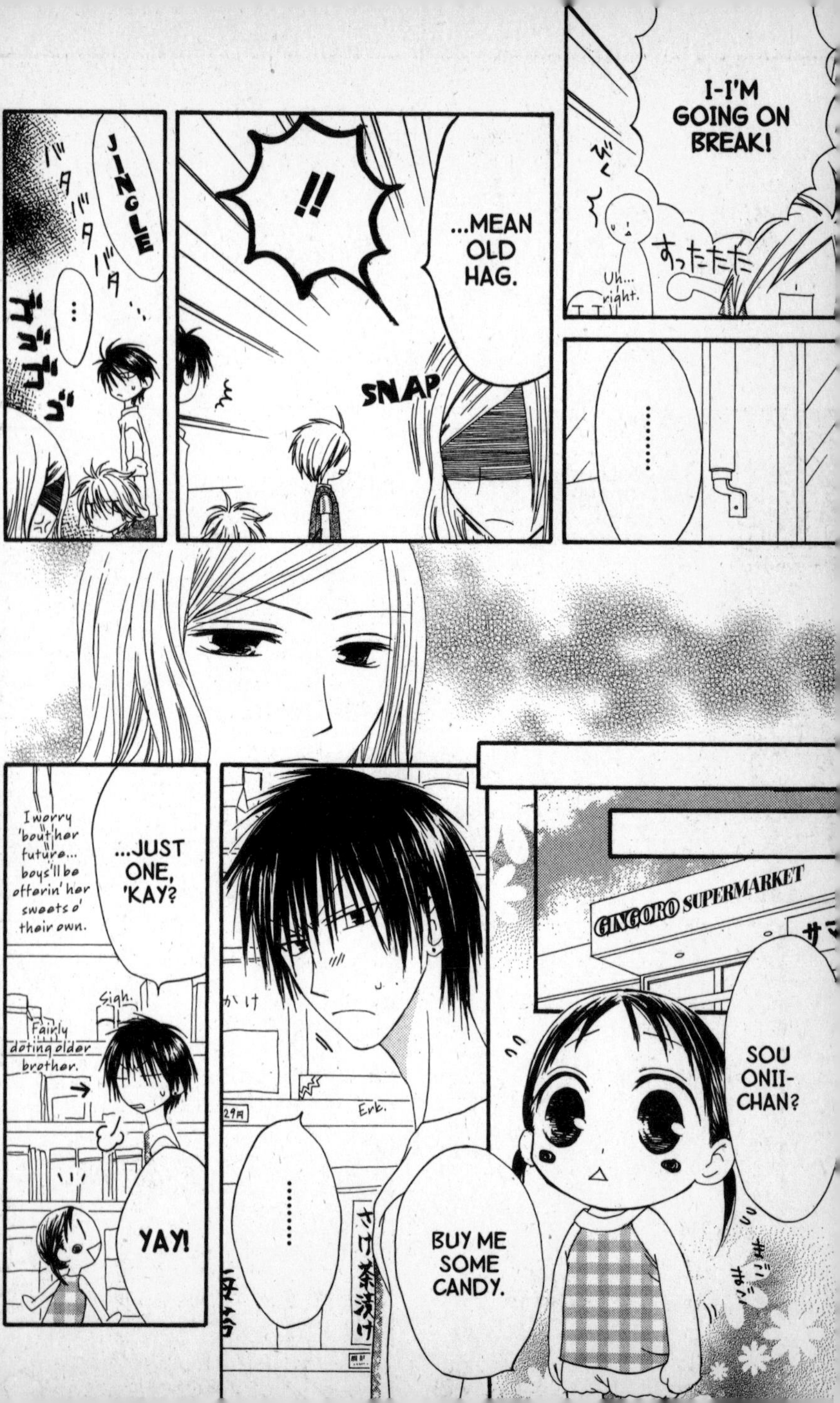
I-I'M GOING ON BREAK!
びく
すったたた
Uh... right.
......
!!
...MEAN OLD HAG.
SNAP
JINGLE
バタバタバタバタ...
...
ゴゴゴ
GINGORO SUPERMARKET
SOU ONII-CHAN?
BUY ME SOME CANDY.
まごまご
......
かけ
Erk.
さけ茶漬け
...JUST ONE, 'KAY?
I worry 'bout her future... boys'll be offerin' her sweets o' their own.
Sigh.
Fairly doting older brother.
YAY!

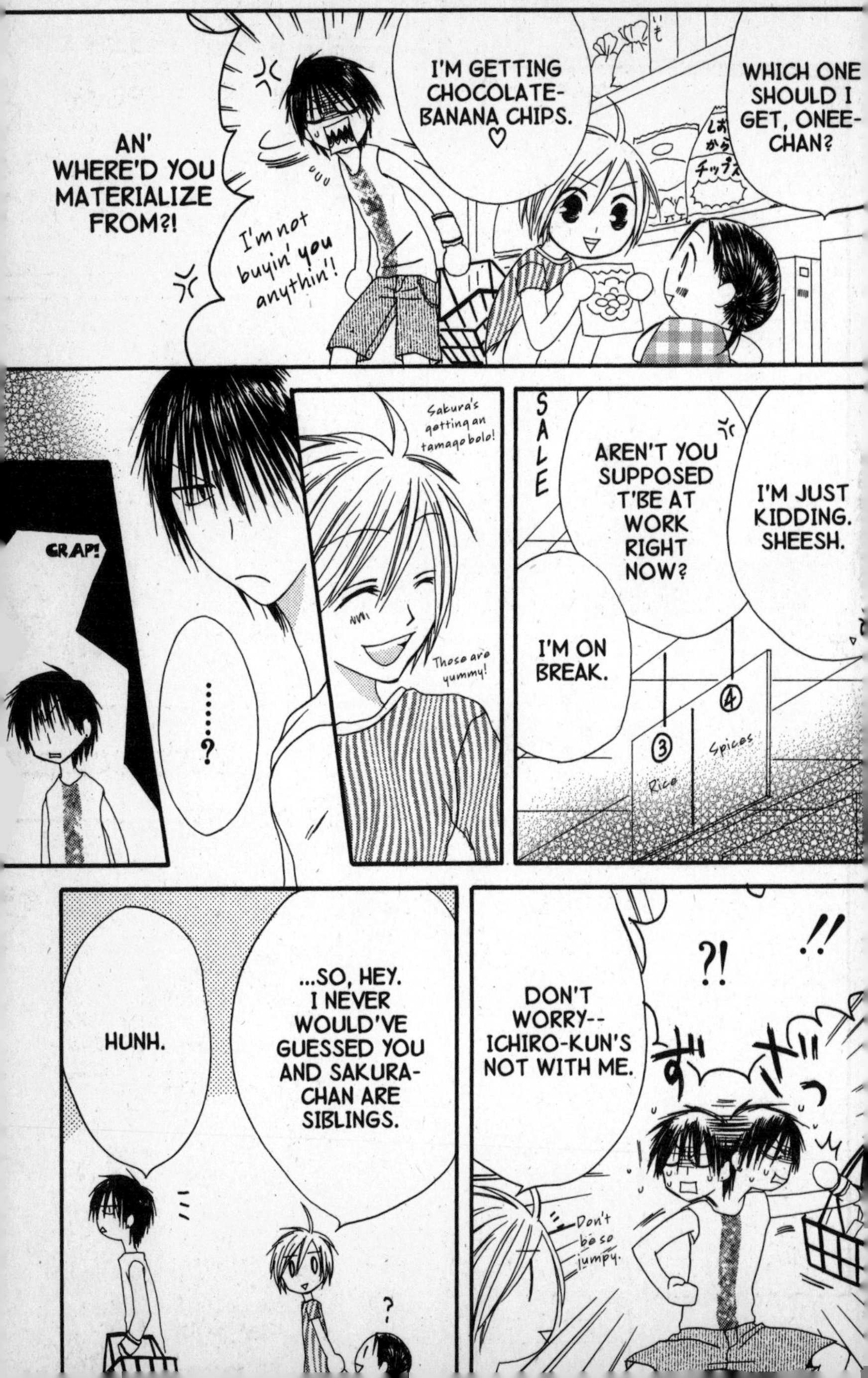
WHICH ONE SHOULD I GET, ONEE-CHAN?
I'M GETTING CHOCOLATE-BANANA CHIPS. ♡
AN' WHERE'D YOU MATERIALIZE FROM?!
I'm not buyin' you anythin'!
SALE
I'M JUST KIDDING. SHEESH.
AREN'T YOU SUPPOSED T'BE AT WORK RIGHT NOW?
I'M ON BREAK.
④ Spices
③ Rice
Sakura's getting an tamago bolo!
Those are yummy!
......?
CRAP!
!!
?!
DON'T WORRY-- ICHIRO-KUN'S NOT WITH ME.
Don't be so jumpy.
...SO, HEY. I NEVER WOULD'VE GUESSED YOU AND SAKURA-CHAN ARE SIBLINGS.
HUNH.
?

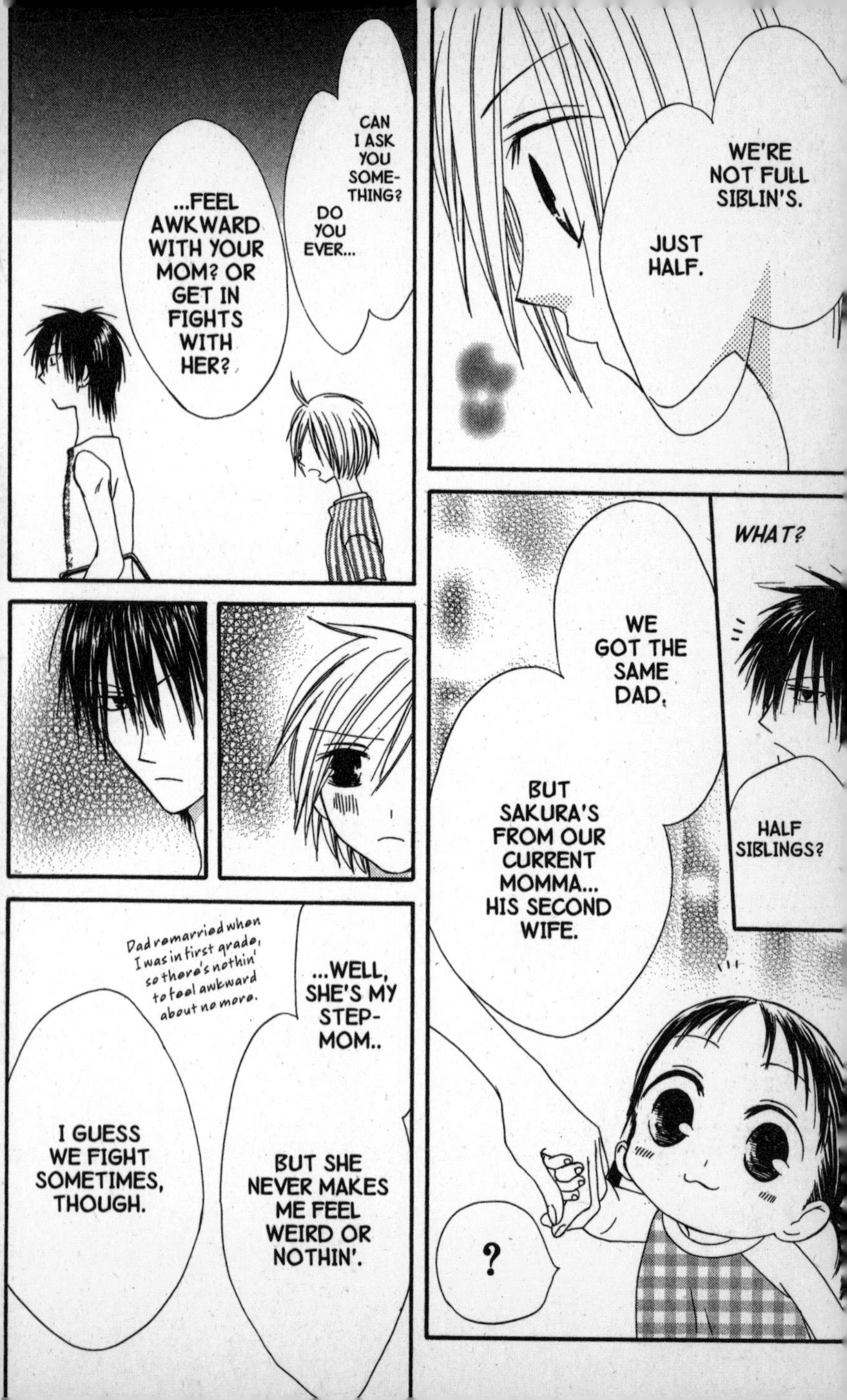
WE'RE NOT FULL SIBLIN'S.
JUST HALF.
WHAT?
HALF SIBLINGS?
WE GOT THE SAME DAD.
BUT SAKURA'S FROM OUR CURRENT MOMMA... HIS SECOND WIFE.
?
CAN I ASK YOU SOME-THING?
DO YOU EVER...
...FEEL AWKWARD WITH YOUR MOM? OR GET IN FIGHTS WITH HER?
...WELL, SHE'S MY STEP-MOM..
Dad remarried when I was in first grade, so there's nothin' to feel awkward about no more.
BUT SHE NEVER MAKES ME FEEL WEIRD OR NOTHIN'.
I GUESS WE FIGHT SOMETIMES, THOUGH.

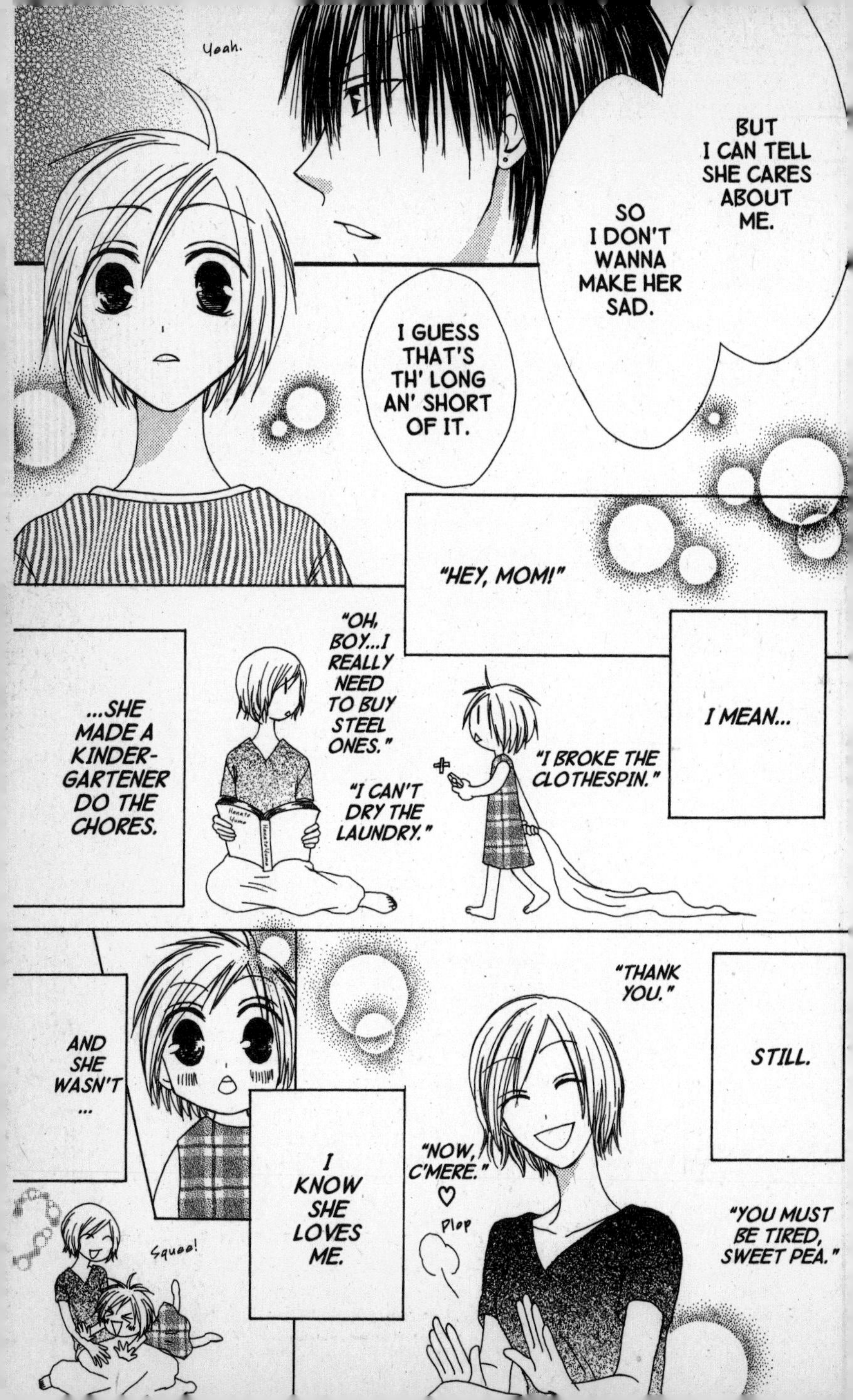
BUT I CAN TELL SHE CARES ABOUT ME.
SO I DON'T WANNA MAKE HER SAD.
I GUESS THAT'S TH' LONG AN' SHORT OF IT.
Yeah.
"HEY, MOM!"
I MEAN...
"I BROKE THE CLOTHESPIN."
"I CAN'T DRY THE LAUNDRY."
"OH, BOY...I REALLY NEED TO BUY STEEL ONES."
Hana to Yume
...SHE MADE A KINDER-GARTENER DO THE CHORES.
STILL.
"THANK YOU."
"YOU MUST BE TIRED, SWEET PEA."
"NOW, C'MERE." ♡
Plop
I KNOW SHE LOVES ME.
AND SHE WASN'T ...
Squee!

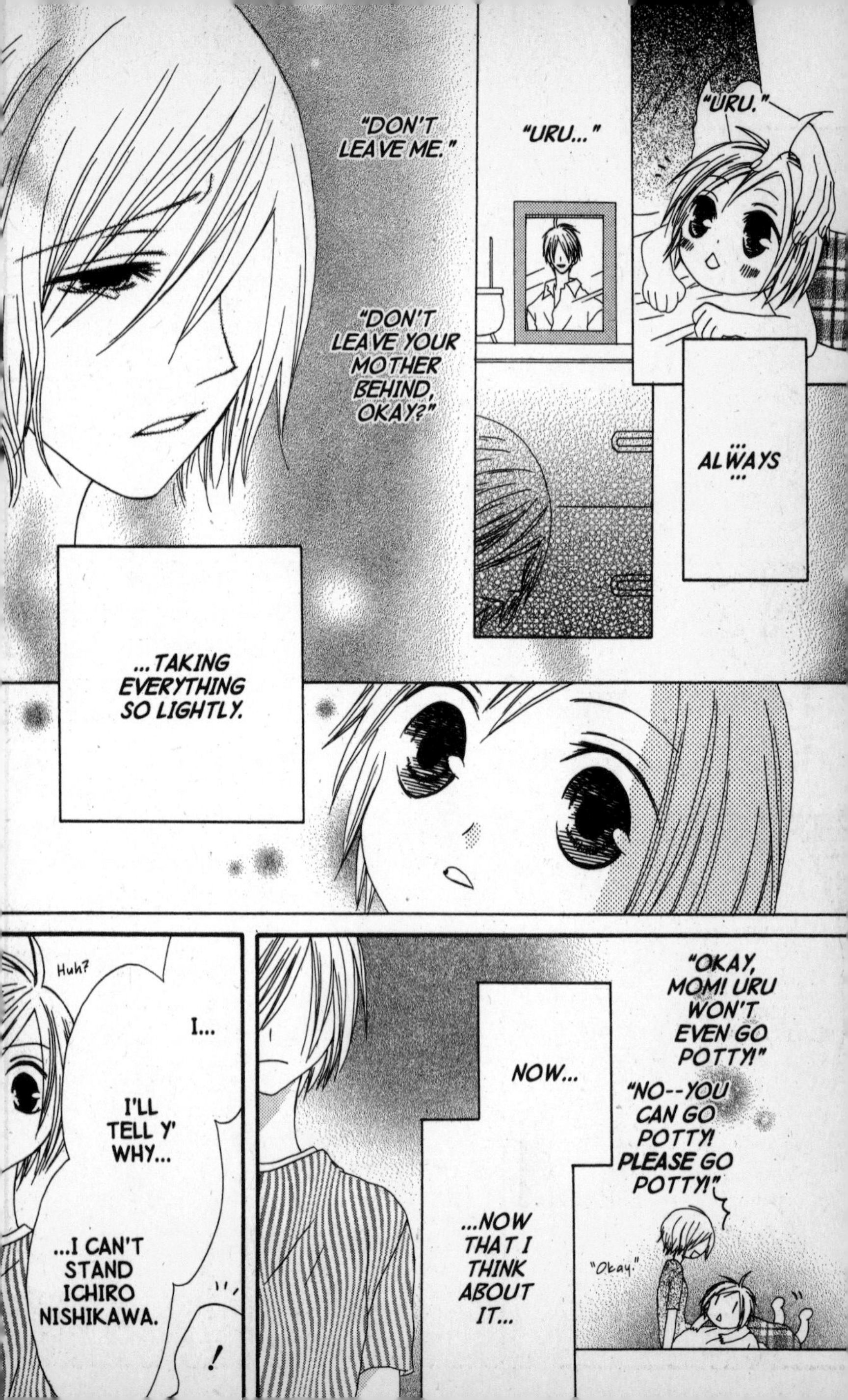
"URU."
"URU..."
...ALWAYS...
"DON'T LEAVE ME."
"DON'T LEAVE YOUR MOTHER BEHIND, OKAY?"
...TAKING EVERYTHING SO LIGHTLY.
"OKAY, MOM! URU WON'T EVEN GO POTTY!"
"NO--YOU CAN GO POTTY! PLEASE GO POTTY!"
"Okay."
NOW...
...NOW THAT I THINK ABOUT IT...
Huh?
I...
I'LL TELL Y' WHY...
...I CAN'T STAND ICHIRO NISHIKAWA.
!

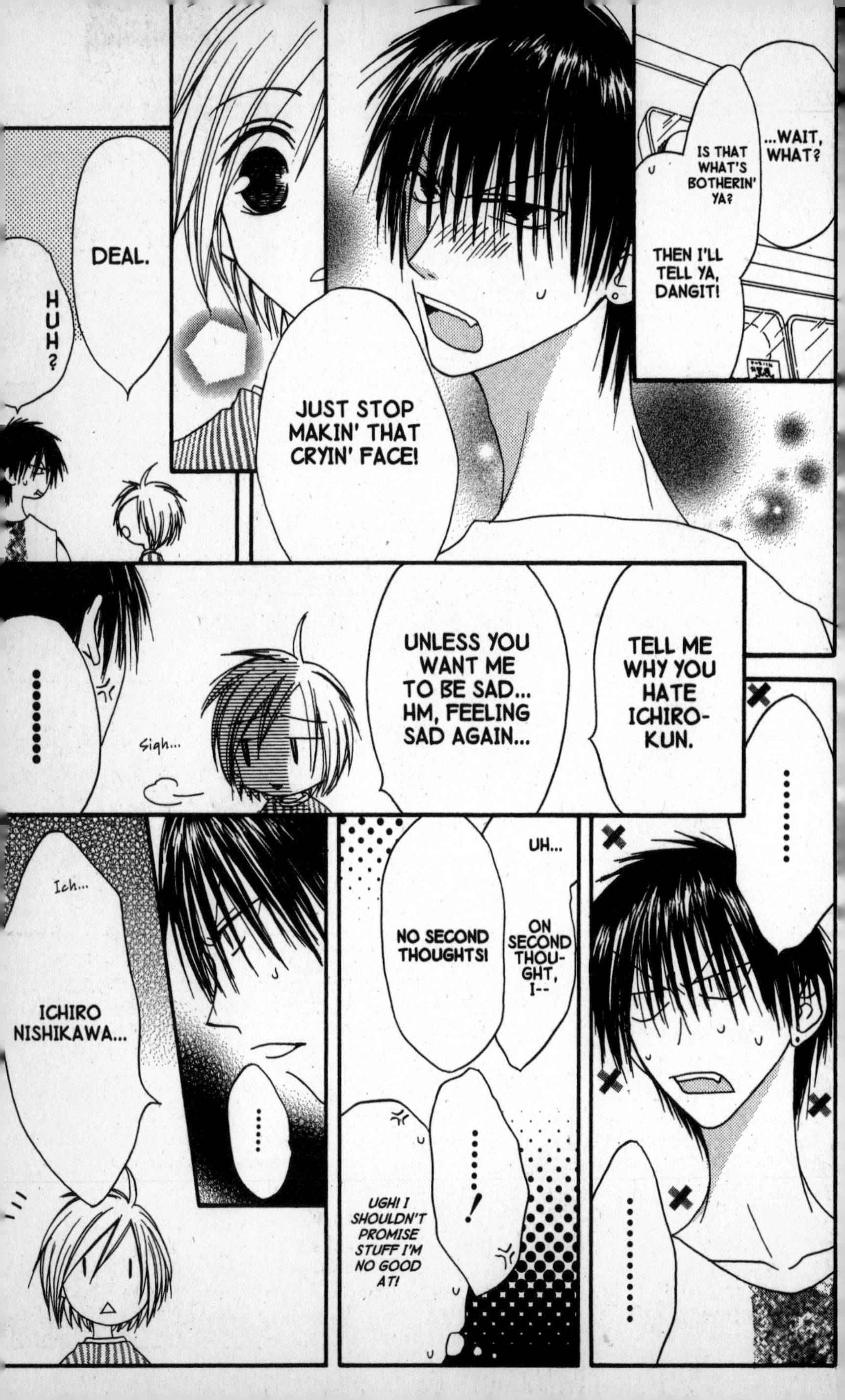
...WAIT, WHAT?
IS THAT WHAT'S BOTHERIN' YA?
THEN I'LL TELL YA, DANGIT!
JUST STOP MAKIN' THAT CRYIN' FACE!
DEAL.
HUH?
TELL ME WHY YOU HATE ICHIRO-KUN.
UNLESS YOU WANT ME TO BE SAD... HM, FEELING SAD AGAIN...
Sigh...
....
....
....
UH...
ON SECOND THOUGHT, I--
NO SECOND THOUGHTS!
......!
UGH! I SHOULDN'T PROMISE STUFF I'M NO GOOD AT!
Ich...
ICHIRO NISHIKAWA...
......

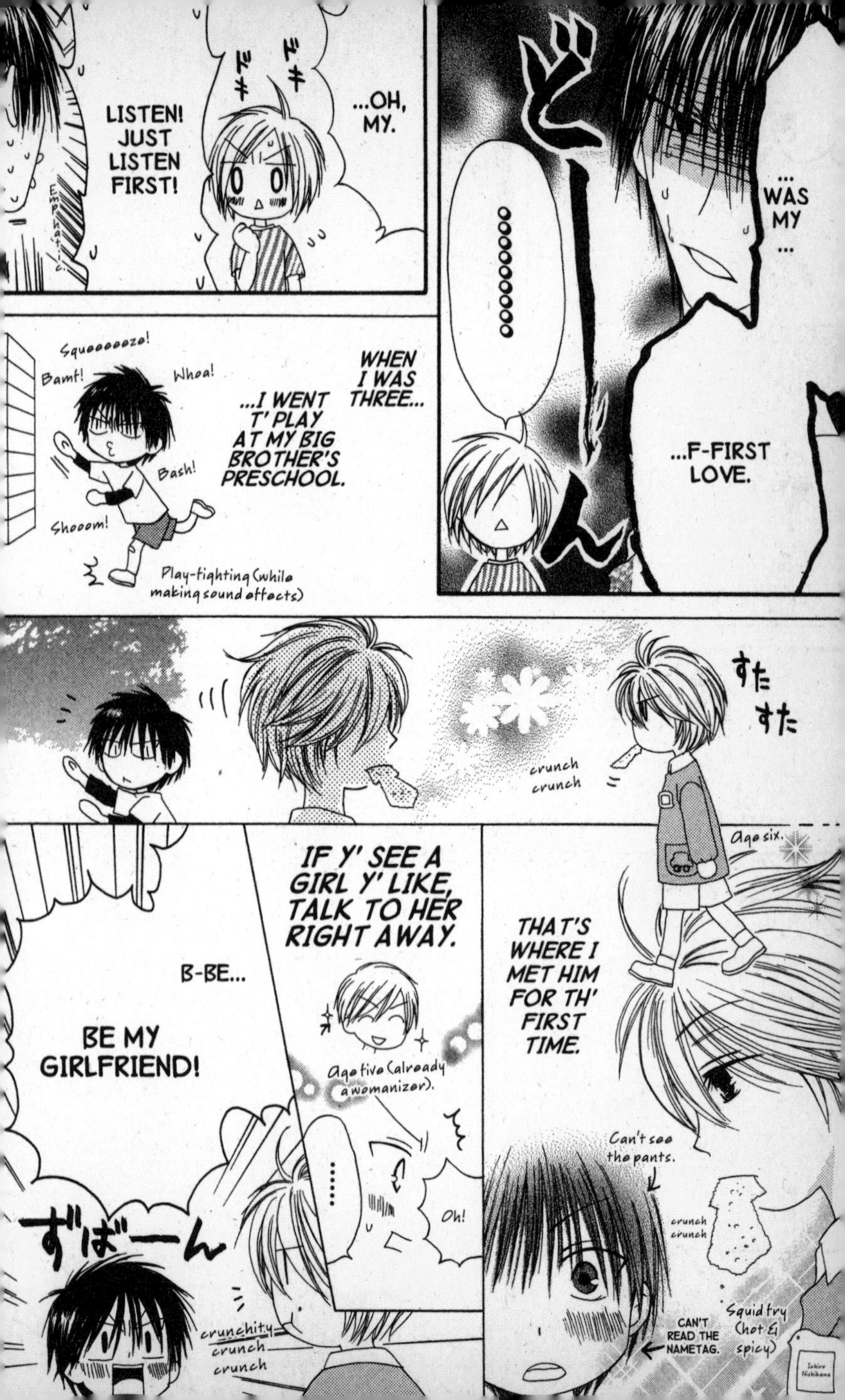

...WAS MY ...
...F-FIRST LOVE.
....
どーん
...OH, MY.
ドキドキ
LISTEN! JUST LISTEN FIRST!
Emphatic.
WHEN I WAS THREE...
...I WENT T' PLAY AT MY BIG BROTHER'S PRESCHOOL.
Squeeeeeze!
Whoa!
Bamf!
Bash!
Shooom!
Play-fighting (while making sound effects)
すたすた
crunch crunch
Age six.
THAT'S WHERE I MET HIM FOR TH' FIRST TIME.
Can't see the pants.
crunch crunch
Squid fry (hot & spicy)
CAN'T READ THE NAMETAG.
IF Y' SEE A GIRL Y' LIKE, TALK TO HER RIGHT AWAY.
Age five (already a womanizer).
......
Oh!
B-BE...
BE MY GIRLFRIEND!
ずばーん
crunchity crunch crunch

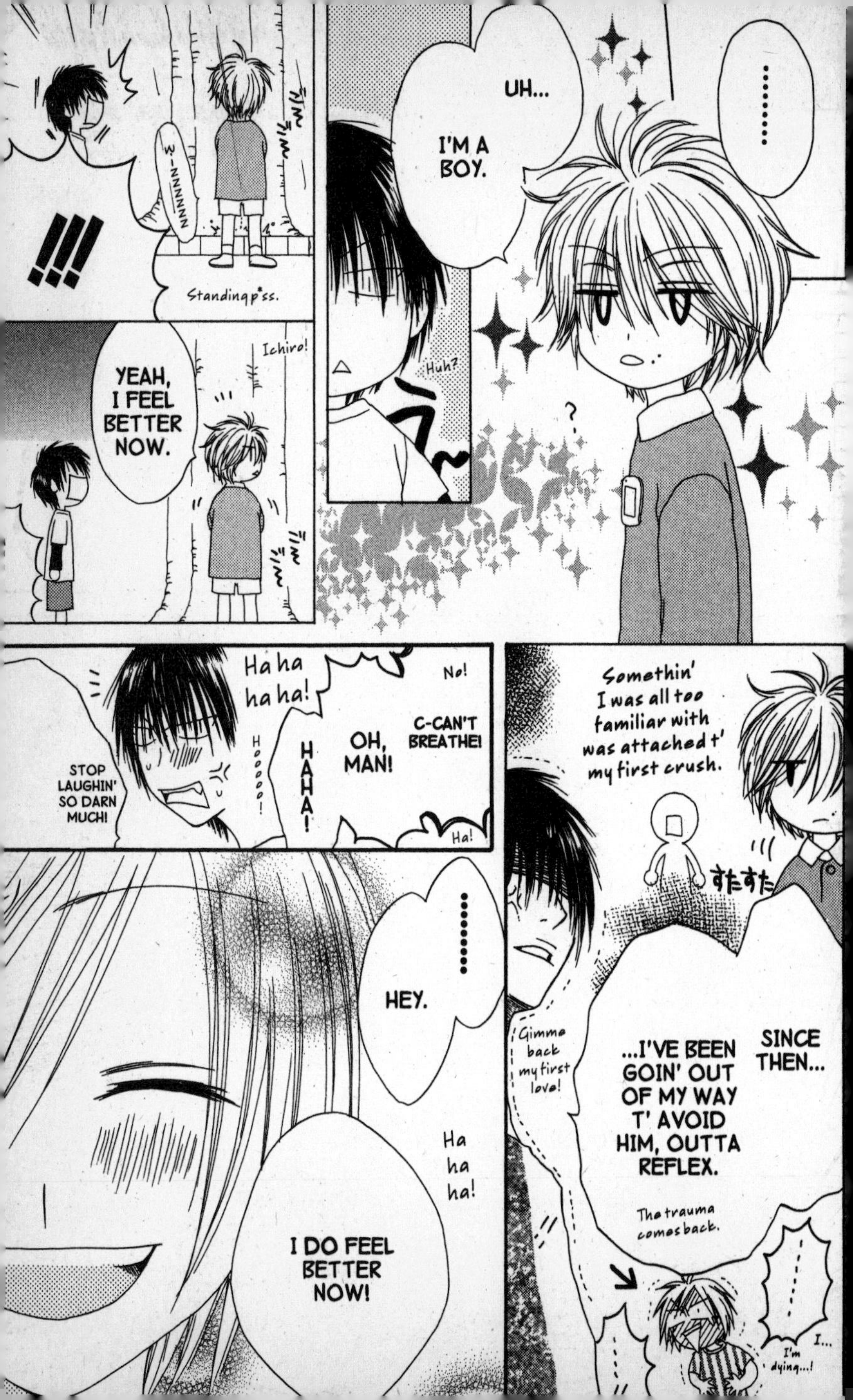
......
UH...
I'M A BOY.
Huh?
W-NNNNNN
!!!!
Standingp*ss.
Ichiro!
YEAH, I FEEL BETTER NOW.
Somethin' I was all too familiar with was attached t' my first crush.
すたすた
SINCE THEN...
...I'VE BEEN GOIN' OUT OF MY WAY T' AVOID HIM, OUTTA REFLEX.
Gimme back my first love!
The trauma comes back.
I...
I'm dying...!
No!
C-CAN'T BREATHE!
OH, MAN!
Ha ha ha ha!
HAHA!
Hoooooo!
STOP LAUGHIN' SO DARN MUCH!
Ha!
......
HEY.
Ha ha ha!
I DO FEEL BETTER NOW!

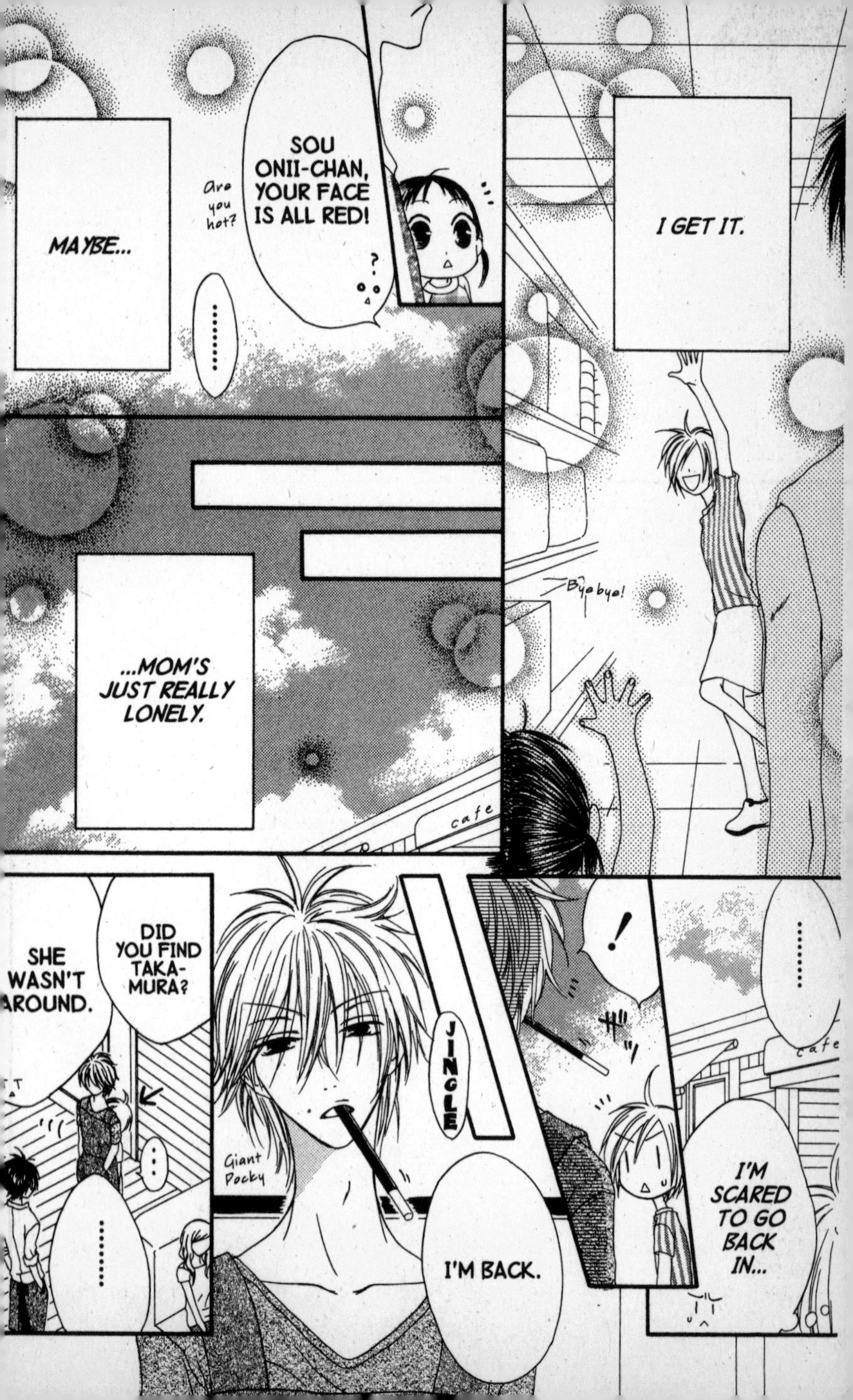
I GET IT.
Byebye!
SOU ONII-CHAN, YOUR FACE IS ALL RED!
Are you hot?
....
MAYBE...
...MOM'S JUST REALLY LONELY.
cafe
......
!
cafe
I'M SCARED TO GO BACK IN...
JINGLE
Giant Pocky
I'M BACK.
DID YOU FIND TAKAMURA?
SHE WASN'T AROUND.
...
......

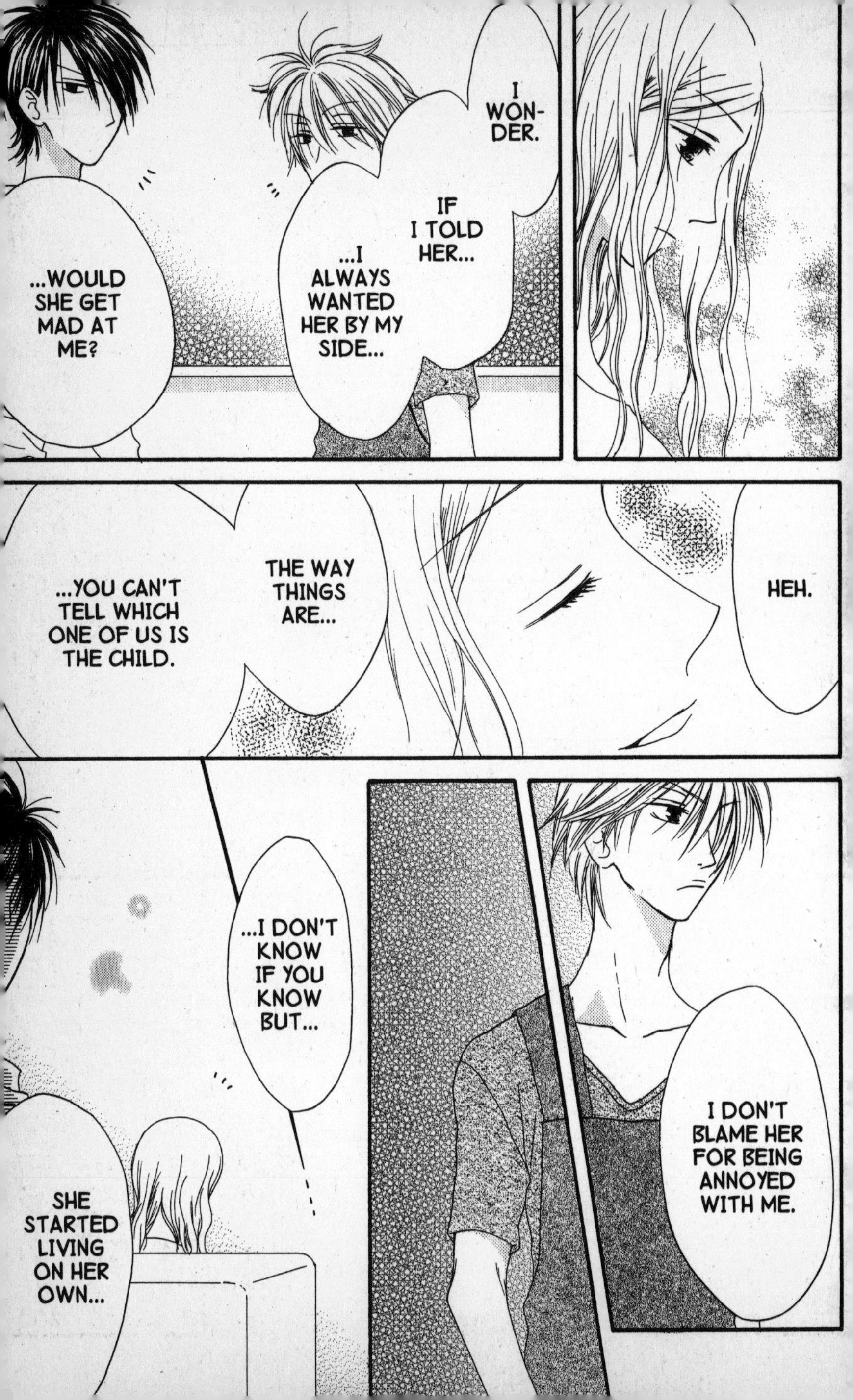
I WONDER.
IF I TOLD HER...
...I ALWAYS WANTED HER BY MY SIDE...
...WOULD SHE GET MAD AT ME?
HEH.
THE WAY THINGS ARE...
...YOU CAN'T TELL WHICH ONE OF US IS THE CHILD.
I DON'T BLAME HER FOR BEING ANNOYED WITH ME.
...I DON'T KNOW IF YOU KNOW BUT...
SHE STARTED LIVING ON HER OWN...

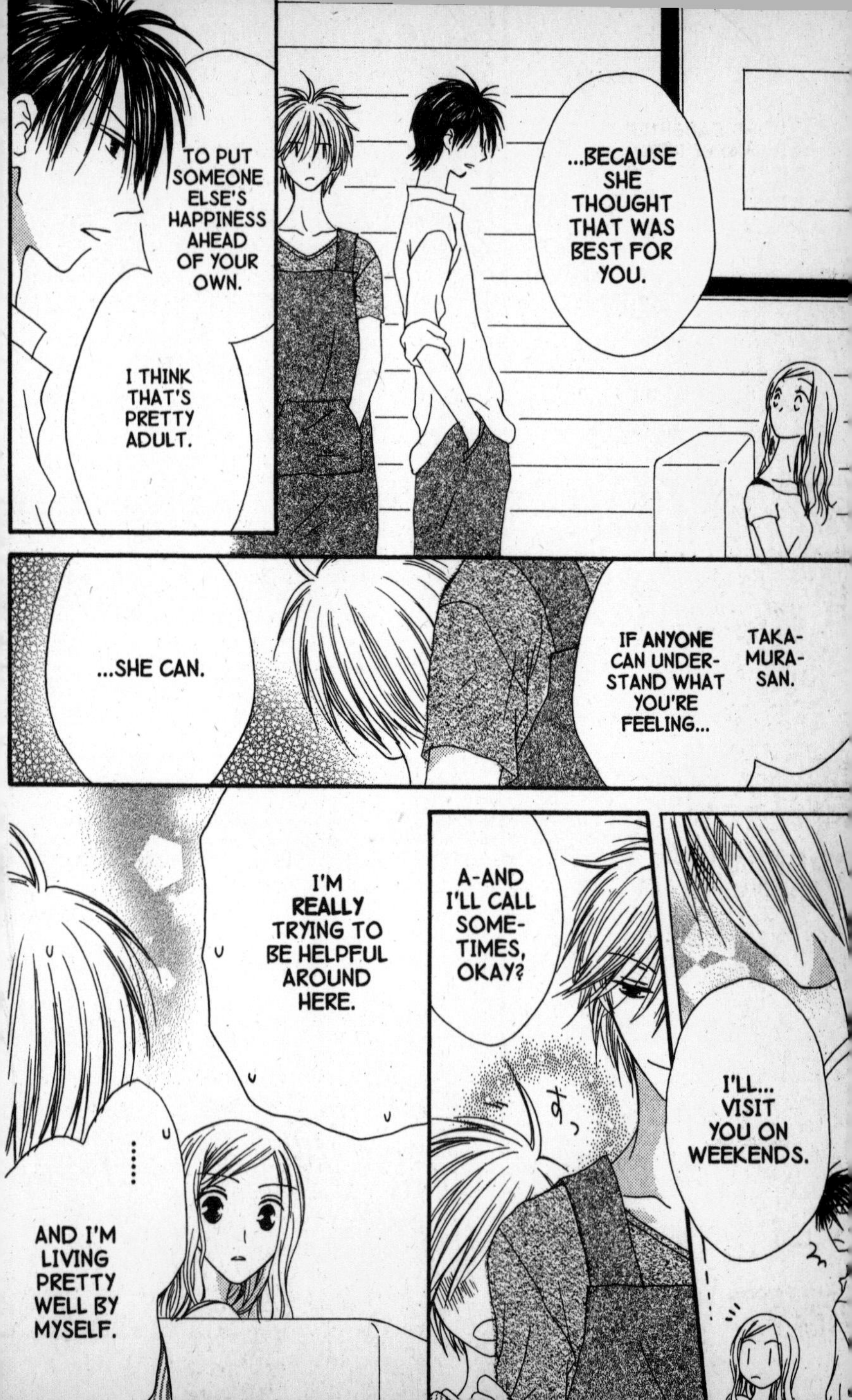
...BECAUSE SHE THOUGHT THAT WAS BEST FOR YOU.
TO PUT SOMEONE ELSE'S HAPPINESS AHEAD OF YOUR OWN.
I THINK THAT'S PRETTY ADULT.
TAKA-MURA-SAN.
IF ANYONE CAN UNDER-STAND WHAT YOU'RE FEELING...
...SHE CAN.
I'LL... VISIT YOU ON WEEKENDS.
A-AND I'LL CALL SOME-TIMES, OKAY?
すっ
I'M REALLY TRYING TO BE HELPFUL AROUND HERE.
......
AND I'M LIVING PRETTY WELL BY MYSELF.

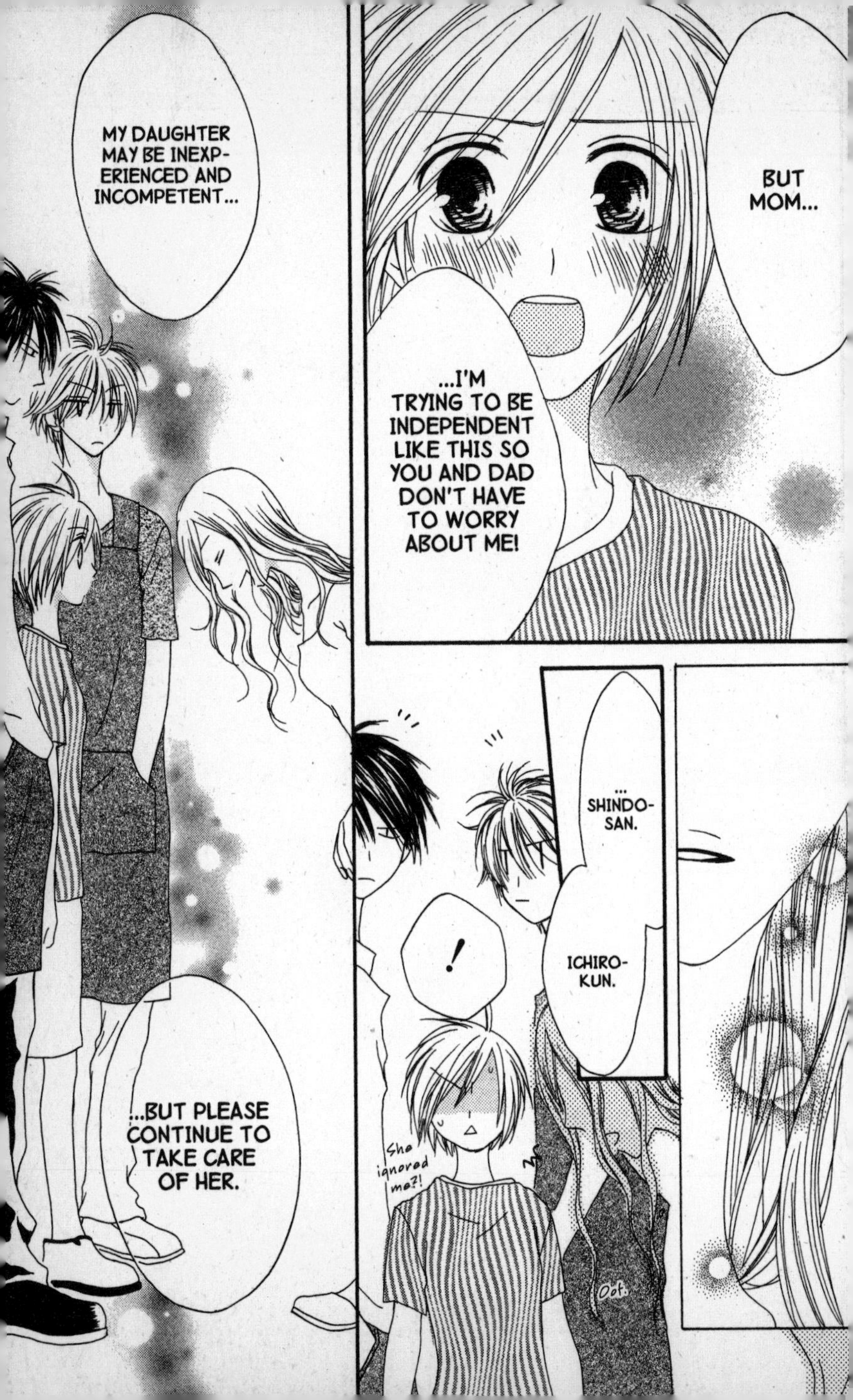

BUT MOM...
...I'M TRYING TO BE INDEPENDENT LIKE THIS SO YOU AND DAD DON'T HAVE TO WORRY ABOUT ME!
... SHINDO-SAN.
ICHIRO-KUN.
!
She ignored me?!
Oof.
MY DAUGHTER MAY BE INEXPERIENCED AND INCOMPETENT...
...BUT PLEASE CONTINUE TO TAKE CARE OF HER.

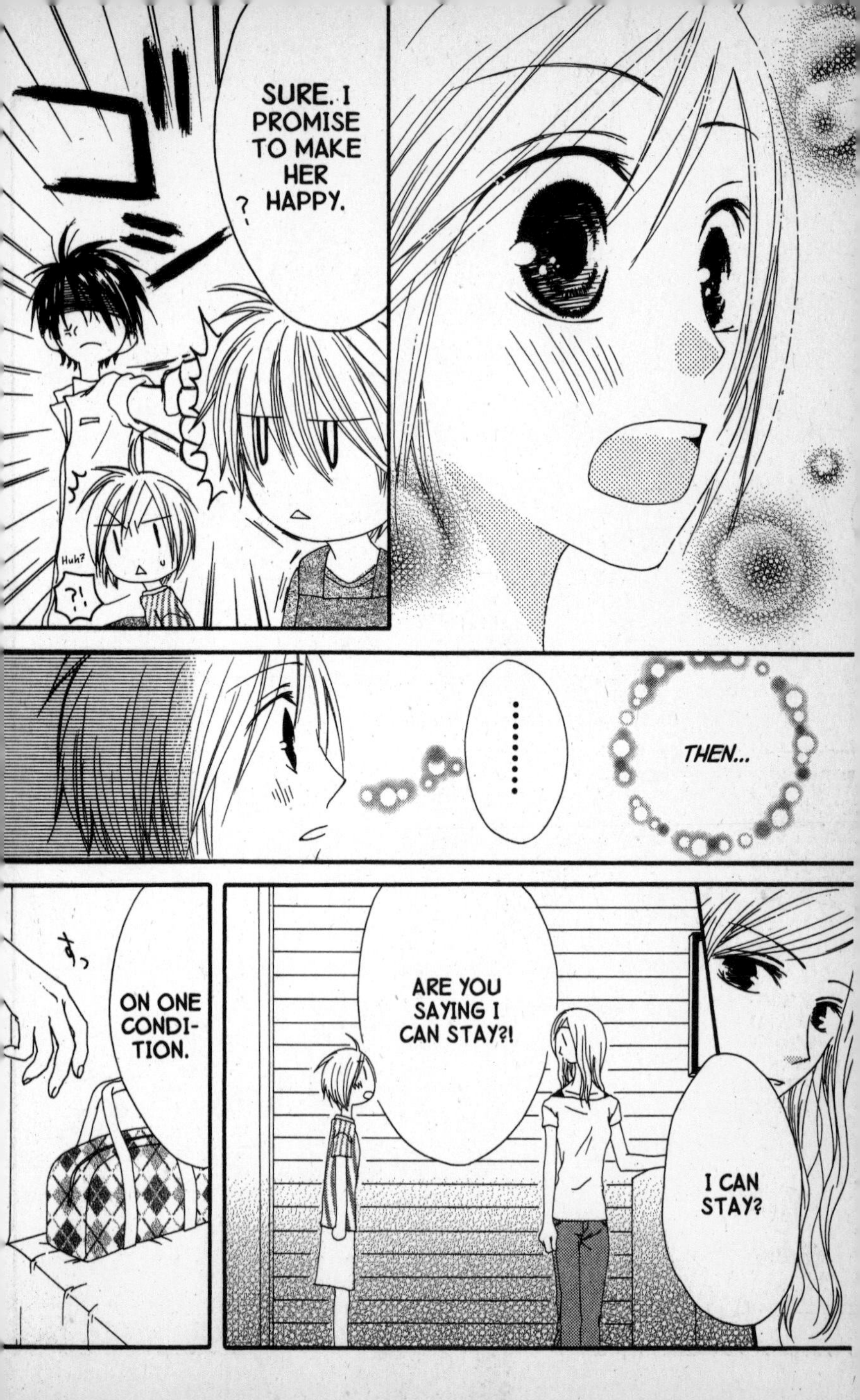
SURE. I PROMISE TO MAKE HER HAPPY.
?
Huh?
?!
THEN...
....
I CAN STAY?
ARE YOU SAYING I CAN STAY?!
すっ
ON ONE CONDITION.

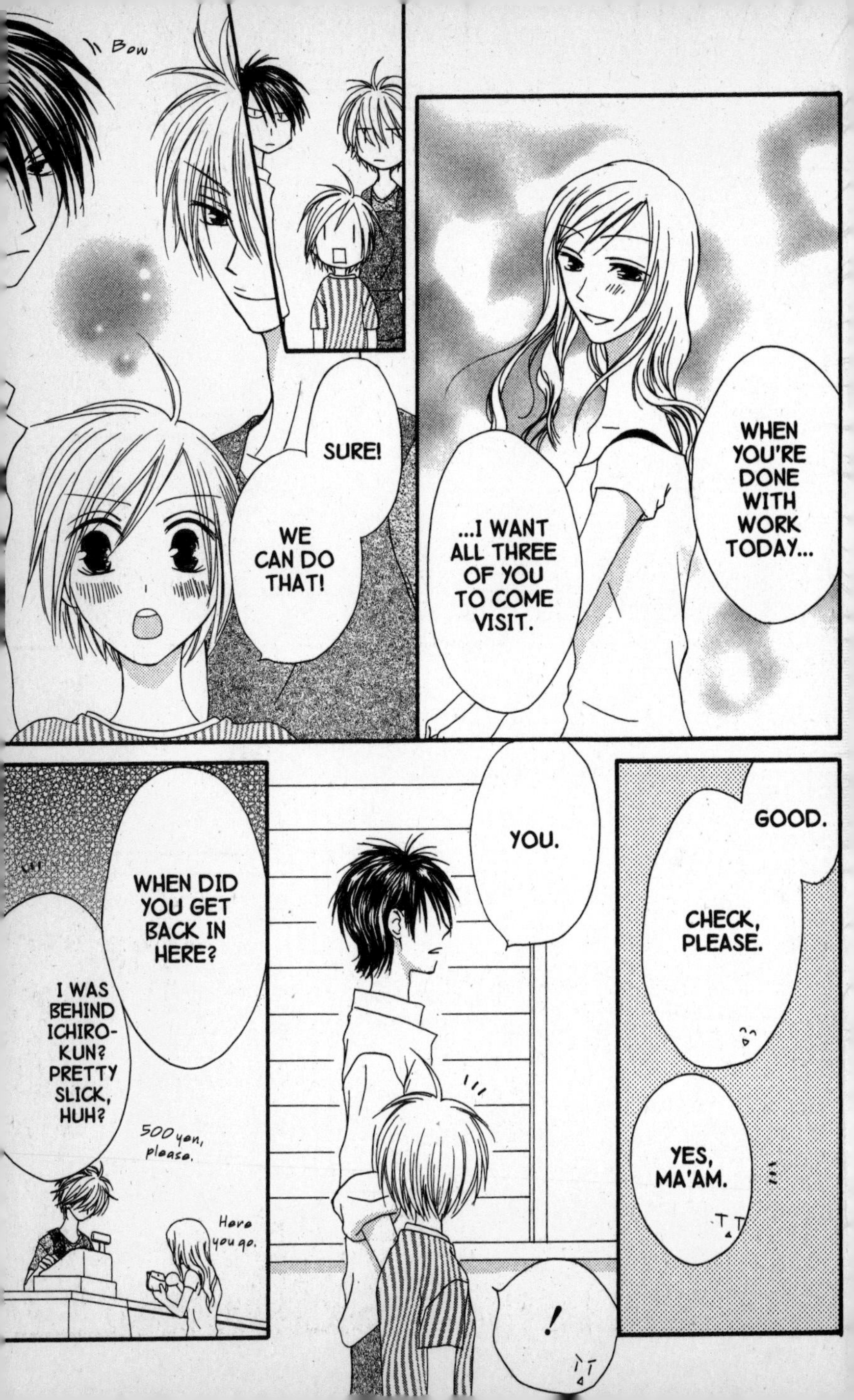
WHEN YOU'RE DONE WITH WORK TODAY...
...I WANT ALL THREE OF YOU TO COME VISIT.
Bow
SURE!
WE CAN DO THAT!
GOOD.
CHECK, PLEASE.
YES, MA'AM.
YOU.
!
WHEN DID YOU GET BACK IN HERE?
I WAS BEHIND ICHIRO-KUN? PRETTY SLICK, HUH?
500 yen, please.
Here you go.

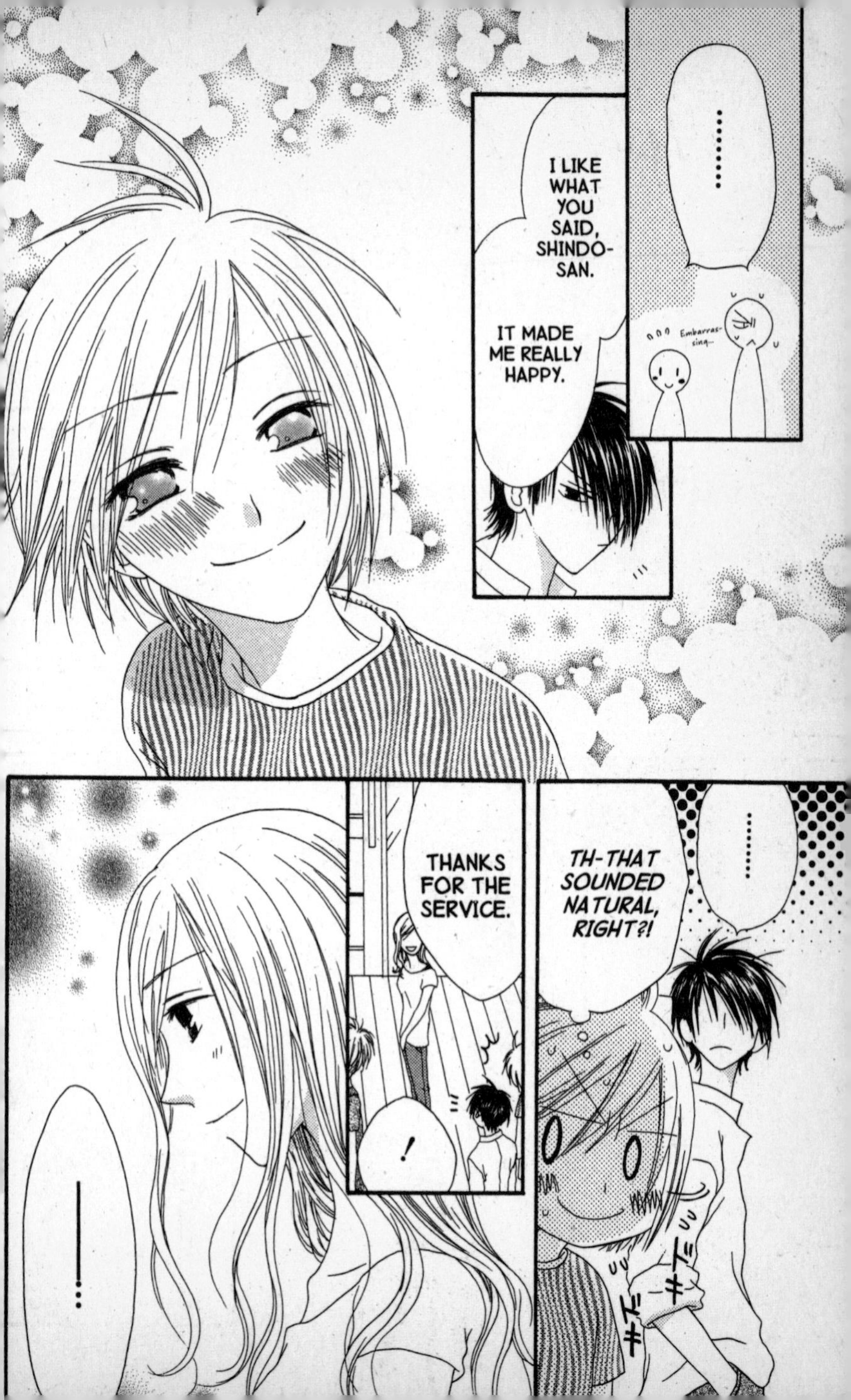
......
Embarrassing...
I LIKE WHAT YOU SAID, SHINDO-SAN.
IT MADE ME REALLY HAPPY.
......
TH-THAT SOUNDED NATURAL, RIGHT?!
THANKS FOR THE SERVICE.
!
—...

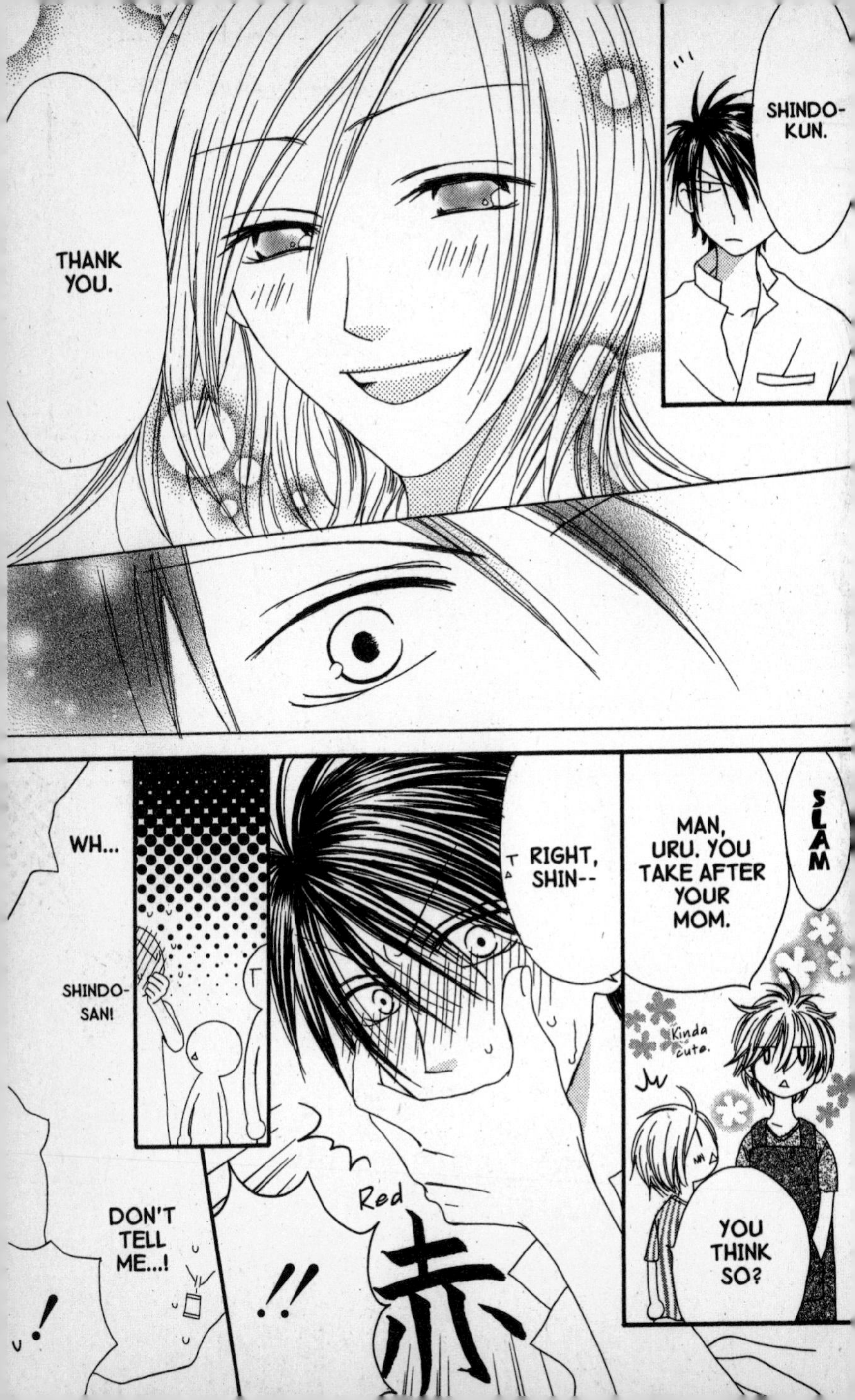
SHINDO-KUN.
THANK YOU.
SLAM
MAN, URU. YOU TAKE AFTER YOUR MOM.
Kinda cute.
YOU THINK SO?
RIGHT, SHIN--
Red
赤
SHINDO-SAN!
WH...
DON'T TELL ME...!

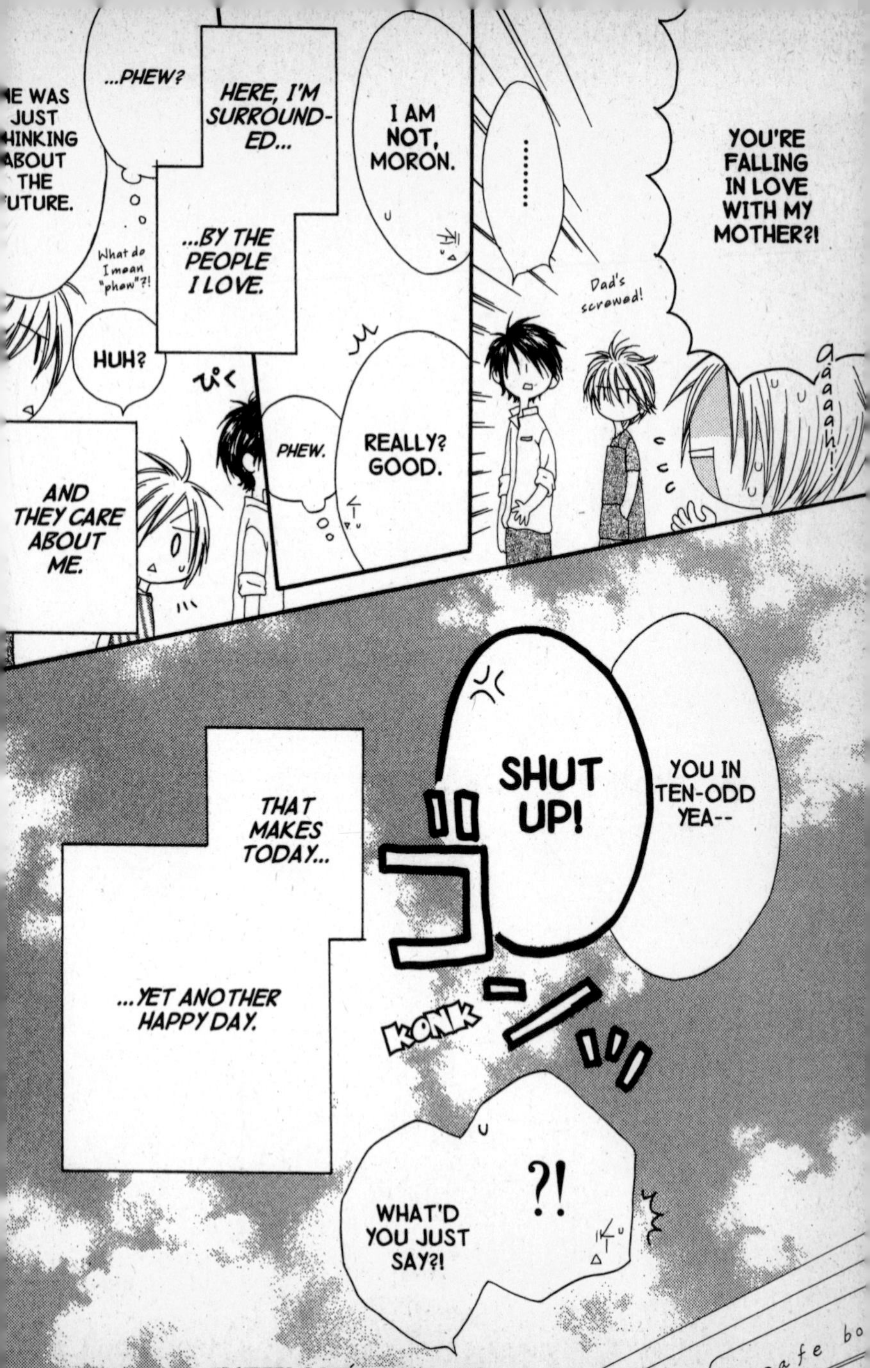
YOU'RE FALLING IN LOVE WITH MY MOTHER?!
aaaaah!
Dad's screwed!
......
I AM NOT, MORON.
REALLY? GOOD.
PHEW.
HERE, I'M SURROUNDED...
...BY THE PEOPLE I LOVE.
...PHEW?
E WAS JUST HINKING ABOUT THE UTURE.
What do I mean "phew"?!
HUH?
ぴく
AND THEY CARE ABOUT ME.
YOU IN TEN-ODD YEA--
SHUT UP!
KONK
?!
WHAT'D YOU JUST SAY?!
THAT MAKES TODAY...
...YET ANOTHER HAPPY DAY.

HAPPY CAFÉ VOL. 2 / END

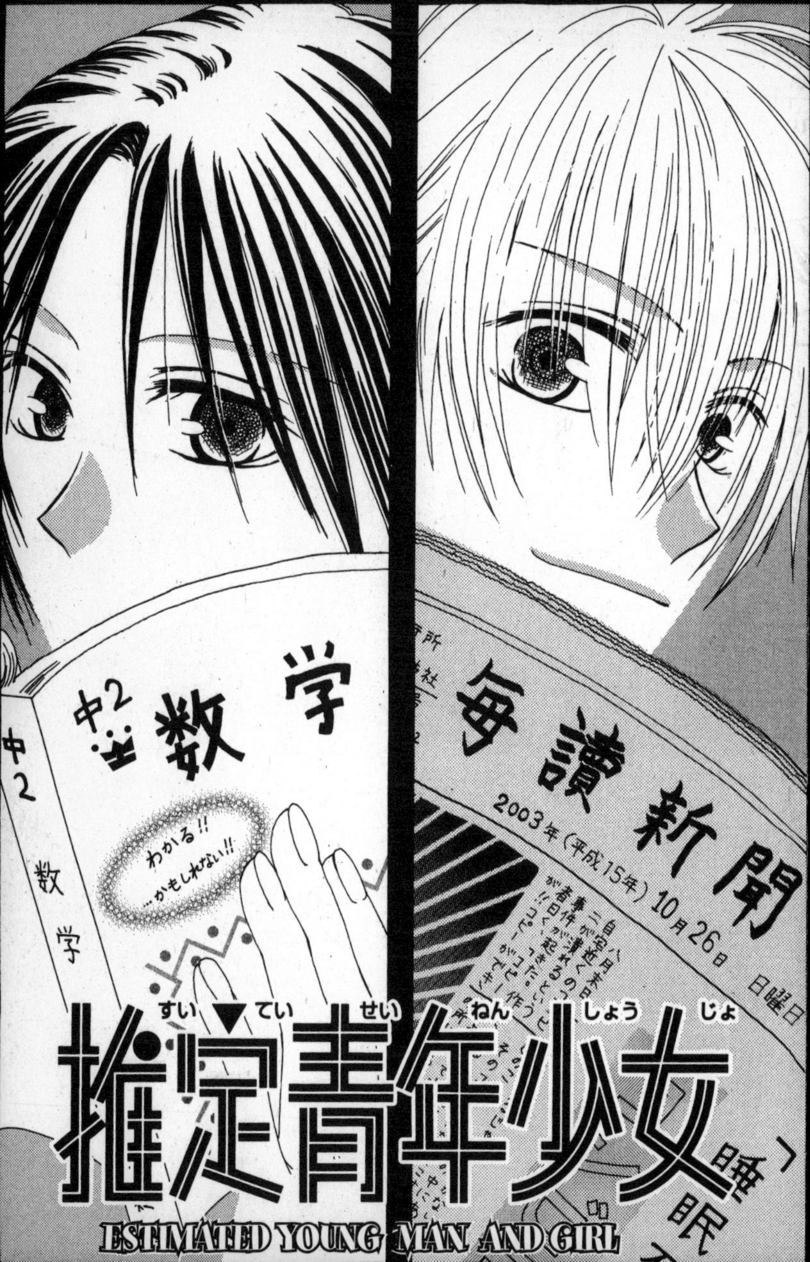
毎讀新聞
2003年(平成15年)10月26日 日曜日
中2 数学
中2 数学
わかる!!
…かもしれない!!
すい▼てい せい ねん しょう じょ
推定青年少女
ESTIMATED YOUNG MAN AND GIRL

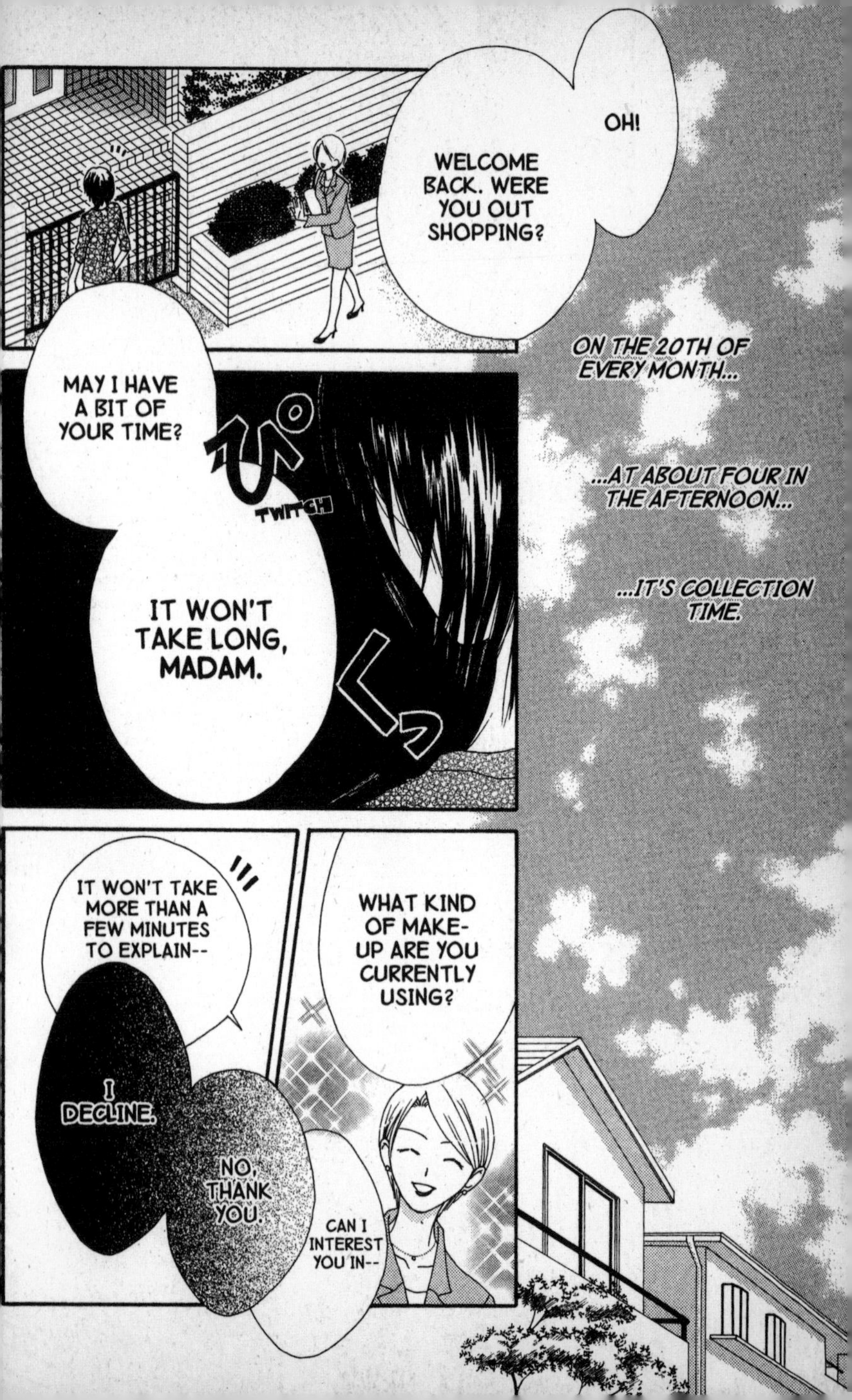
ON THE 20TH OF EVERY MONTH...
...AT ABOUT FOUR IN THE AFTERNOON...
...IT'S COLLECTION TIME.
OH!
WELCOME BACK. WERE YOU OUT SHOPPING?
MAY I HAVE A BIT OF YOUR TIME?
TWITCH
IT WON'T TAKE LONG, MADAM.
WHAT KIND OF MAKE-UP ARE YOU CURRENTLY USING?
CAN I INTEREST YOU IN--
IT WON'T TAKE MORE THAN A FEW MINUTES TO EXPLAIN--
I DECLINE.
NO, THANK YOU.

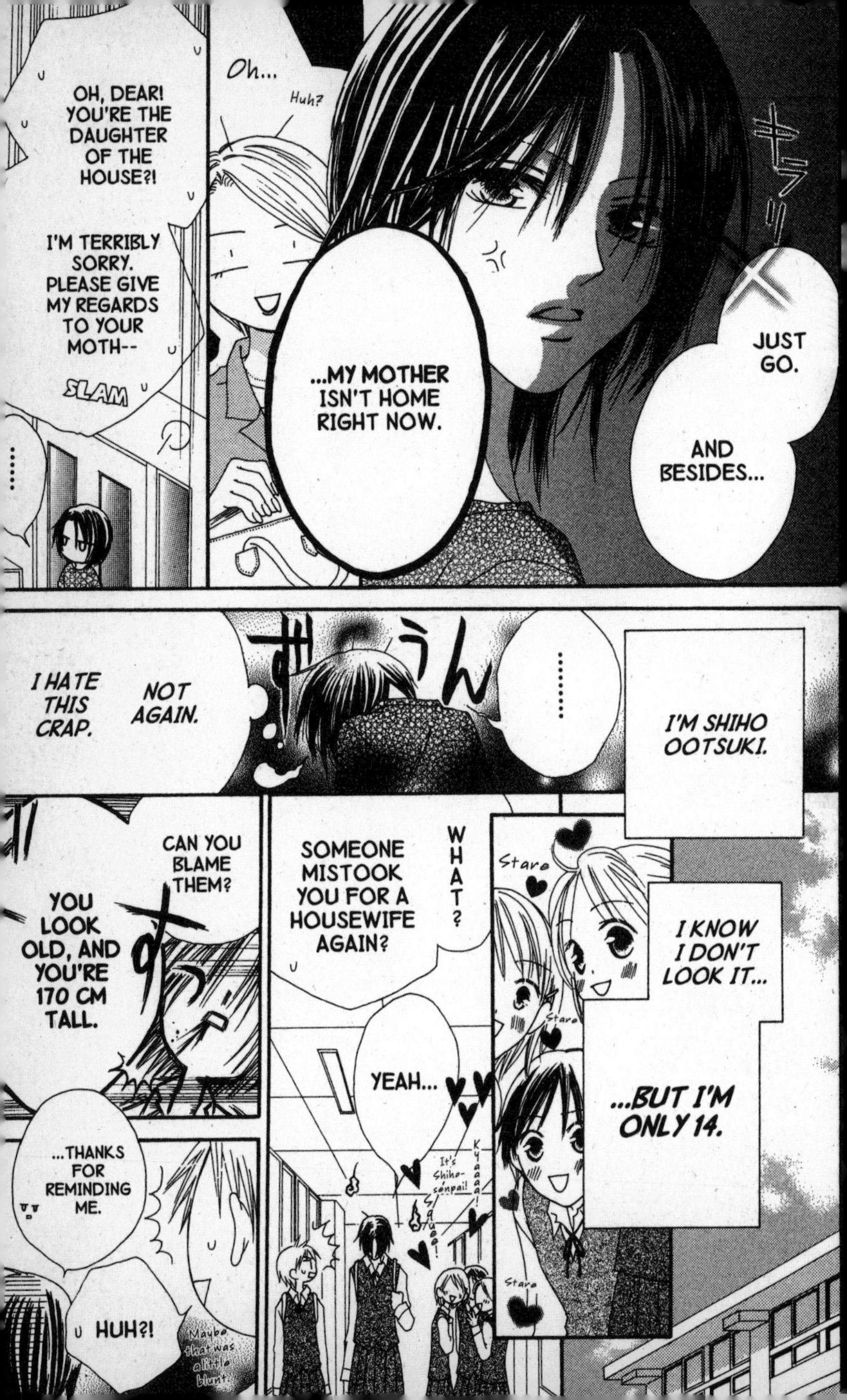
Oh...
Huh?
...MY MOTHER ISN'T HOME RIGHT NOW.
JUST GO.
AND BESIDES...
OH, DEAR! YOU'RE THE DAUGHTER OF THE HOUSE?!
I'M TERRIBLY SORRY. PLEASE GIVE MY REGARDS TO YOUR MOTH--
SLAM
......
I'M SHIHO OOTSUKI.
......
NOT AGAIN.
I HATE THIS CRAP.
I KNOW I DON'T LOOK IT...
...BUT I'M ONLY 14.
Stare
Stare
Stare
WHAT?
SOMEONE MISTOOK YOU FOR A HOUSEWIFE AGAIN?
YEAH...
It's Shiho-senpai!
Kyaaaa!
Squee!
CAN YOU BLAME THEM?
YOU LOOK OLD, AND YOU'RE 170 CM TALL.
...THANKS FOR REMINDING ME.
HUH?!
Maybe that was a little blunt.

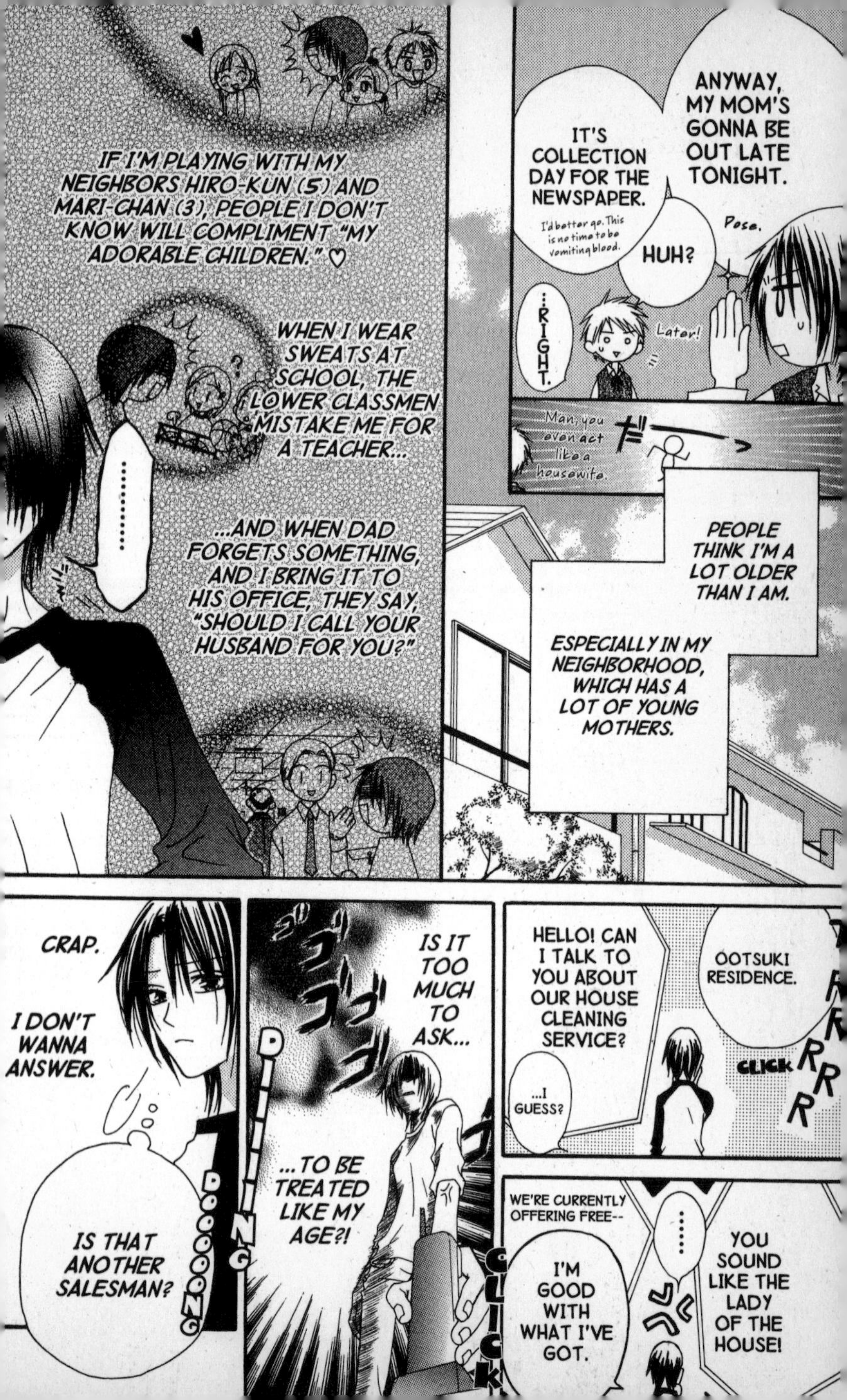
ANYWAY, MY MOM'S GONNA BE OUT LATE TONIGHT.
Pose.
IT'S COLLECTION DAY FOR THE NEWSPAPER.
HUH?
I'd better go. This is no time to be vomiting blood.
Later!
...RIGHT.
Man, you even act like a housewife.
PEOPLE THINK I'M A LOT OLDER THAN I AM.
ESPECIALLY IN MY NEIGHBORHOOD, WHICH HAS A LOT OF YOUNG MOTHERS.
IF I'M PLAYING WITH MY NEIGHBORS HIRO-KUN (5) AND MARI-CHAN (3), PEOPLE I DON'T KNOW WILL COMPLIMENT "MY ADORABLE CHILDREN." ♡
WHEN I WEAR SWEATS AT SCHOOL, THE LOWER CLASSMEN MISTAKE ME FOR A TEACHER...
....
...AND WHEN DAD FORGETS SOMETHING, AND I BRING IT TO HIS OFFICE, THEY SAY, "SHOULD I CALL YOUR HUSBAND FOR YOU?"
RRRRR
CLICK
OOTSUKI RESIDENCE.
HELLO! CAN I TALK TO YOU ABOUT OUR HOUSE CLEANING SERVICE?
...I GUESS?
WE'RE CURRENTLY OFFERING FREE--
YOU SOUND LIKE THE LADY OF THE HOUSE!
......
I'M GOOD WITH WHAT I'VE GOT.
IS IT TOO MUCH TO ASK...
...TO BE TREATED LIKE MY AGE?!
DIIIIIING
CLICK
CRAP.
I DON'T WANNA ANSWER.
IS THAT ANOTHER SALESMAN?
DOOOOOONG

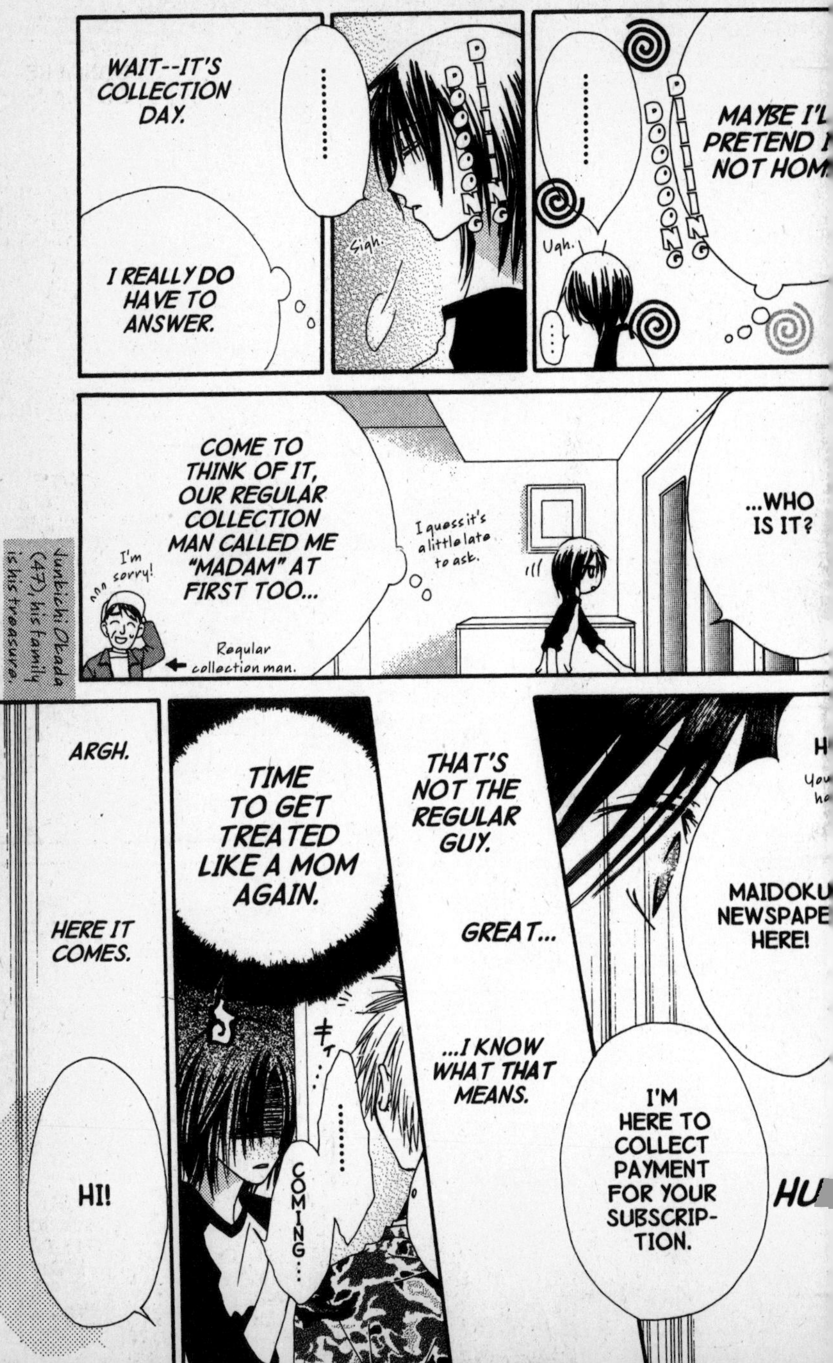
MAYBE I'L PRETEND I NOT HOM
DIIIING DOOOONG
Ugh.
......
...
DIIIING DOOOONG
......
Sigh.
WAIT--IT'S COLLECTION DAY.
I REALLY DO HAVE TO ANSWER.
...WHO IS IT?
I guess it's a little late to ask.
COME TO THINK OF IT, OUR REGULAR COLLECTION MAN CALLED ME "MADAM" AT FIRST TOO...
I'm sorry!
Regular collection man.
Junkichi Okada (47), his family is his treasure.
MAIDOKU NEWSPAPE HERE!
I'M HERE TO COLLECT PAYMENT FOR YOUR SUBSCRIPTION.
THAT'S NOT THE REGULAR GUY.
GREAT...
...I KNOW WHAT THAT MEANS.
TIME TO GET TREATED LIKE A MOM AGAIN.
......
COMING...
ARGH.
HERE IT COMES.
HI!

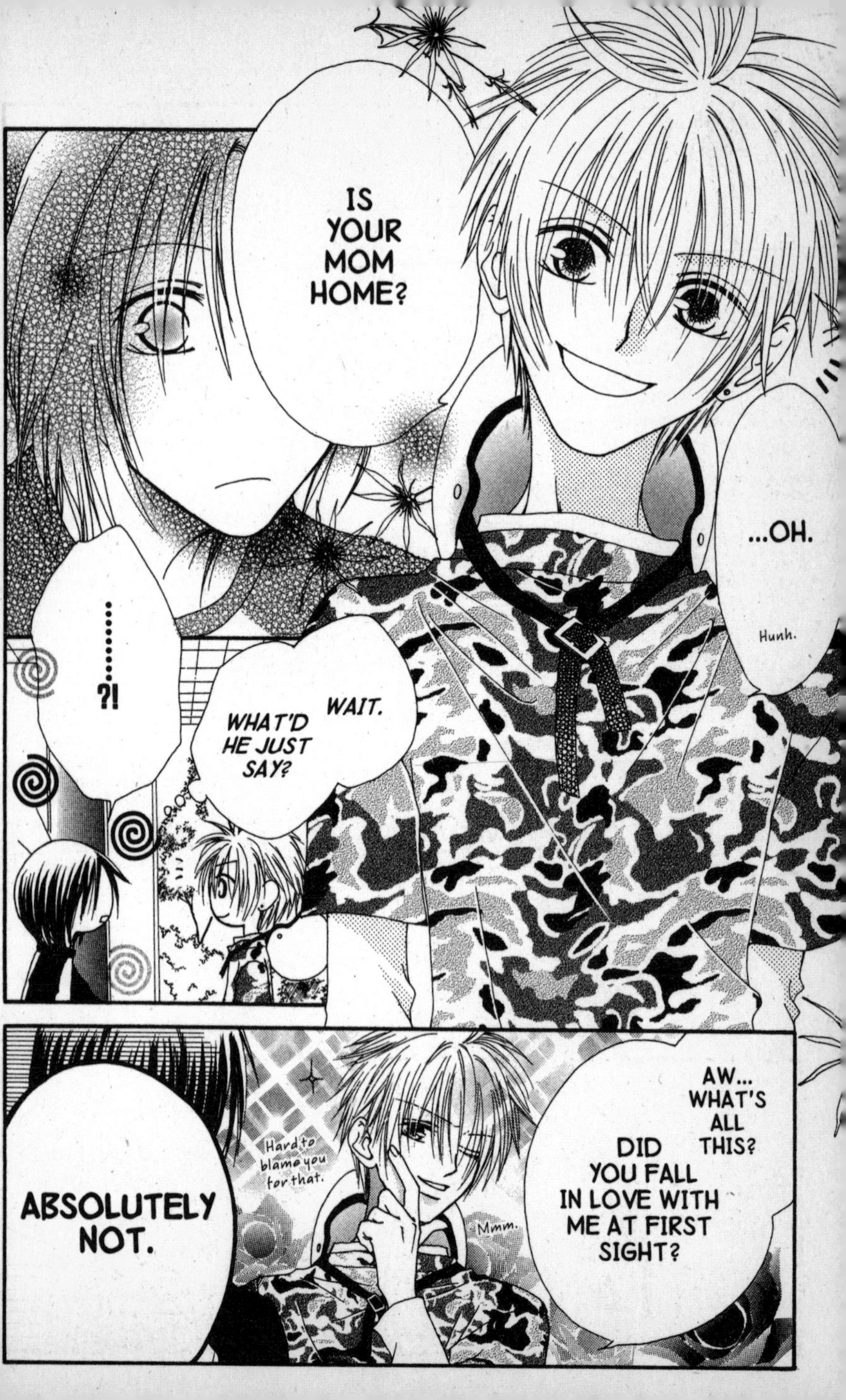

IS YOUR MOM HOME?
...OH.
Hunh.
......?!
WAIT. WHAT'D HE JUST SAY?
AW... WHAT'S ALL THIS?
DID YOU FALL IN LOVE WITH ME AT FIRST SIGHT?
Mmm.
Hard to blame you for that.
ABSOLUTELY NOT.

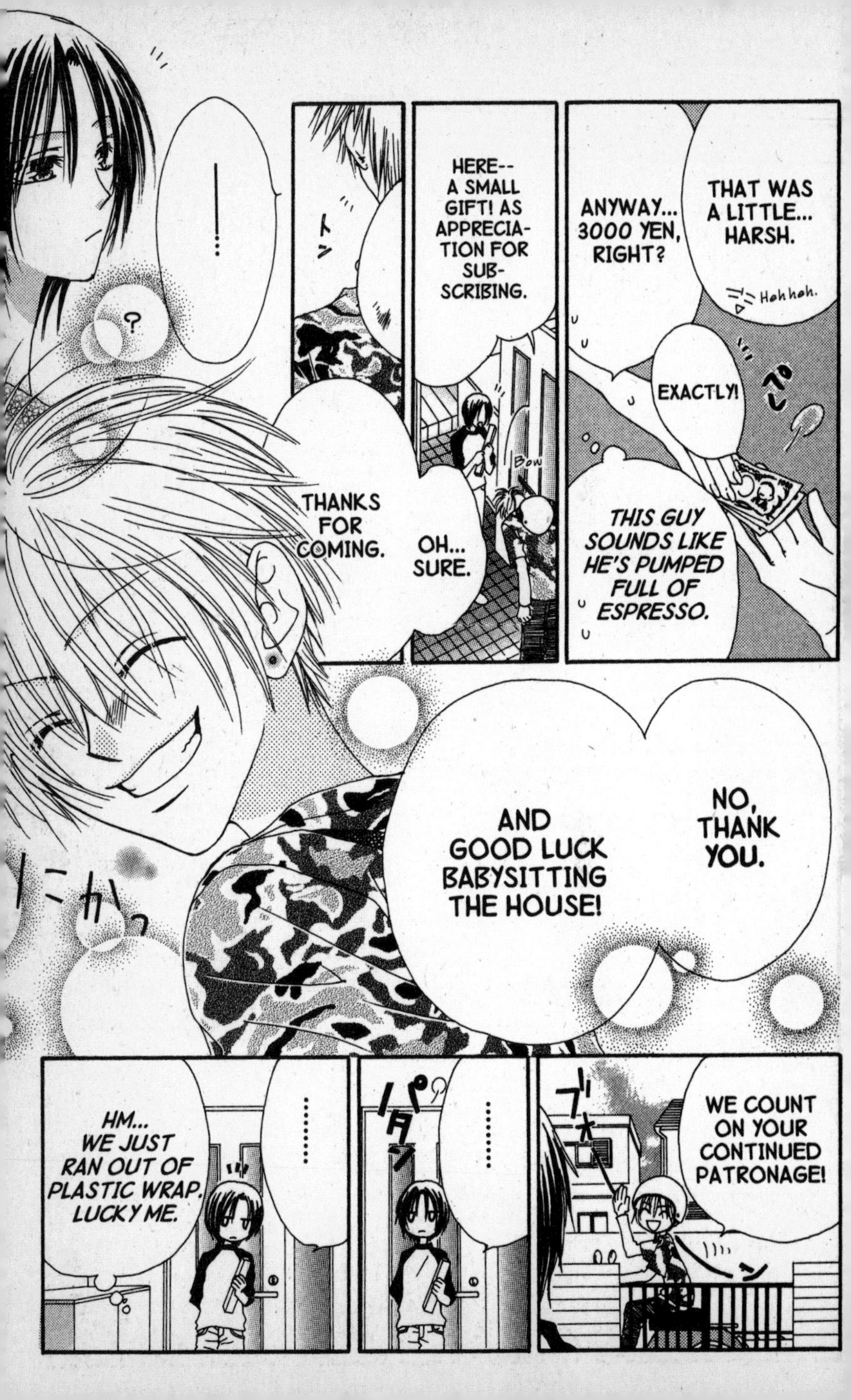
THAT WAS A LITTLE... HARSH.
Hehheh.
ANYWAY... 3000 YEN, RIGHT?
EXACTLY!
THIS GUY SOUNDS LIKE HE'S PUMPED FULL OF ESPRESSO.
HERE-- A SMALL GIFT! AS APPRECIATION FOR SUBSCRIBING.
Bow
OH... SURE.
THANKS FOR COMING.
......!
?
NO, THANK YOU.
AND GOOD LUCK BABYSITTING THE HOUSE!
WE COUNT ON YOUR CONTINUED PATRONAGE!
......
......
HM... WE JUST RAN OUT OF PLASTIC WRAP. LUCKY ME.

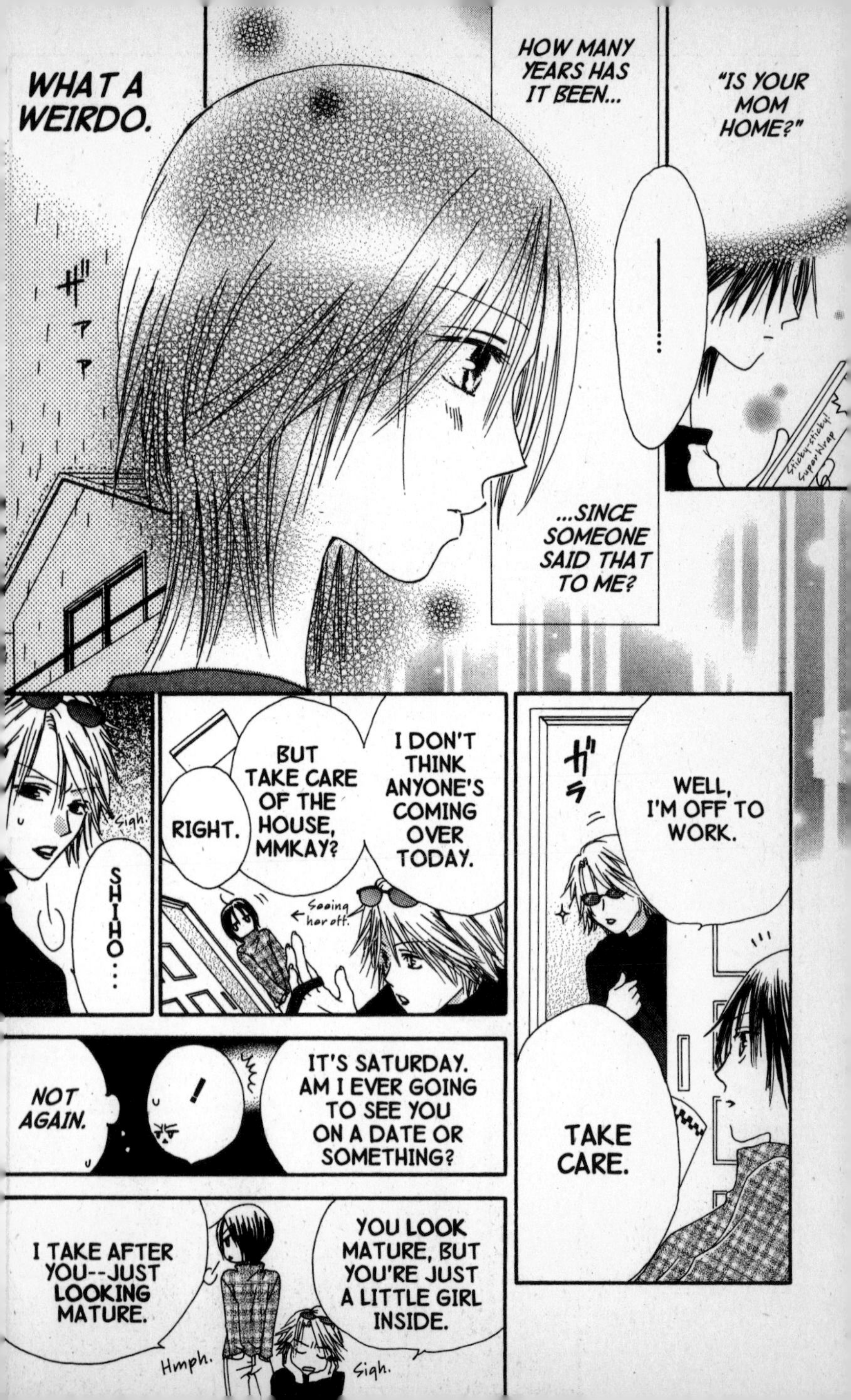
"IS YOUR MOM HOME?"
......
Sticky-sticky! Super Wrap
HOW MANY YEARS HAS IT BEEN...
...SINCE SOMEONE SAID THAT TO ME?
WHAT A WEIRDO.
ザァァ
WELL, I'M OFF TO WORK.
ガラ
TAKE CARE.
I DON'T THINK ANYONE'S COMING OVER TODAY.
BUT TAKE CARE OF THE HOUSE, MMKAY?
RIGHT.
Seeing her off.
SHIHO...
Sigh.
IT'S SATURDAY. AM I EVER GOING TO SEE YOU ON A DATE OR SOMETHING?
!
NOT AGAIN.
YOU LOOK MATURE, BUT YOU'RE JUST A LITTLE GIRL INSIDE.
Sigh.
I TAKE AFTER YOU--JUST LOOKING MATURE.
Hmph.

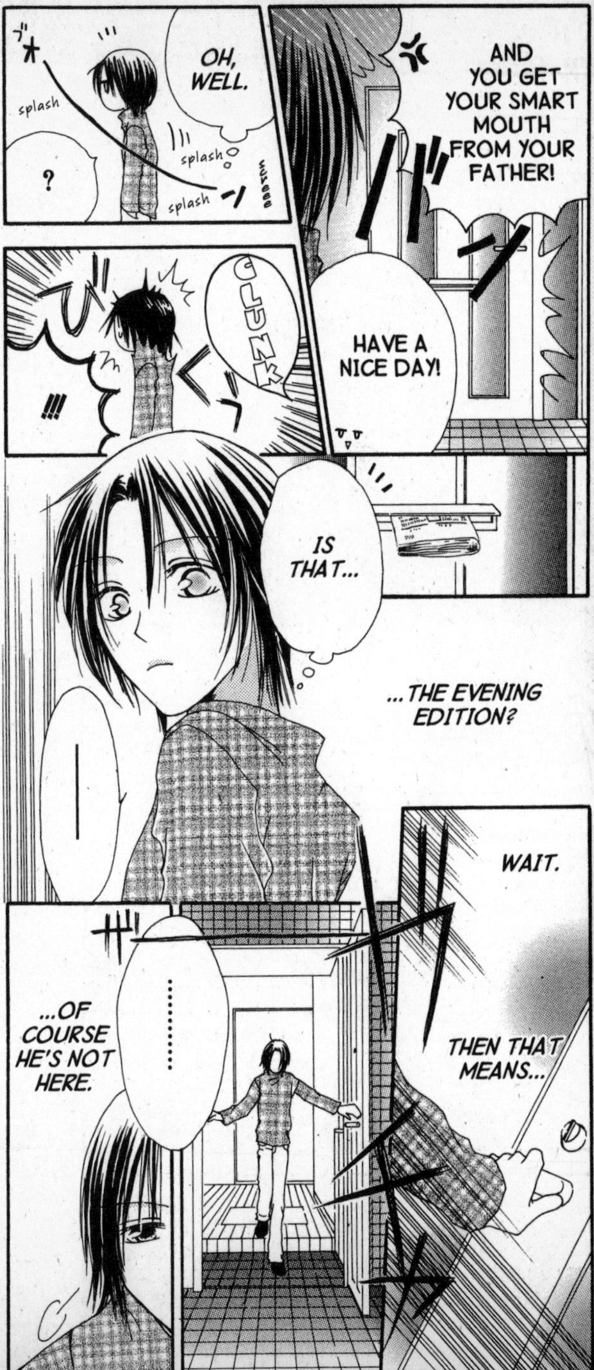
AND YOU GET YOUR SMART MOUTH FROM YOUR FATHER!
HAVE A NICE DAY!
OH, WELL.
?
splash
splash
splash
screee
CLUNK
IS THAT...
...THE EVENING EDITION?
WAIT.
THEN THAT MEANS...
...OF COURSE HE'S NOT HERE.

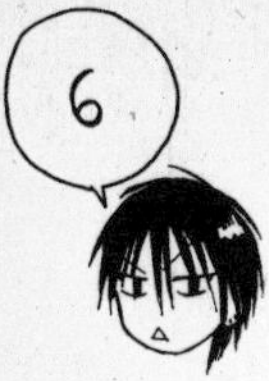
6

Now we're at the last 1/4 space.

If you have any thoughts or feelings, please send them along.

↓

TOKYOPOP-Editorial Department 5900 Wilshire Blvd., Suite 2000 Los Angeles, CA 90036

I'll be waiting!

See you at the end of the book!

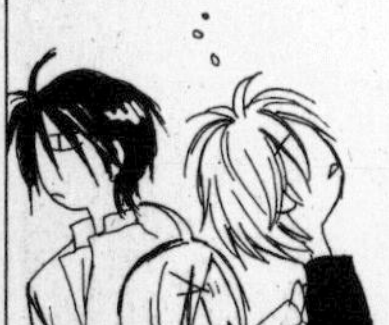

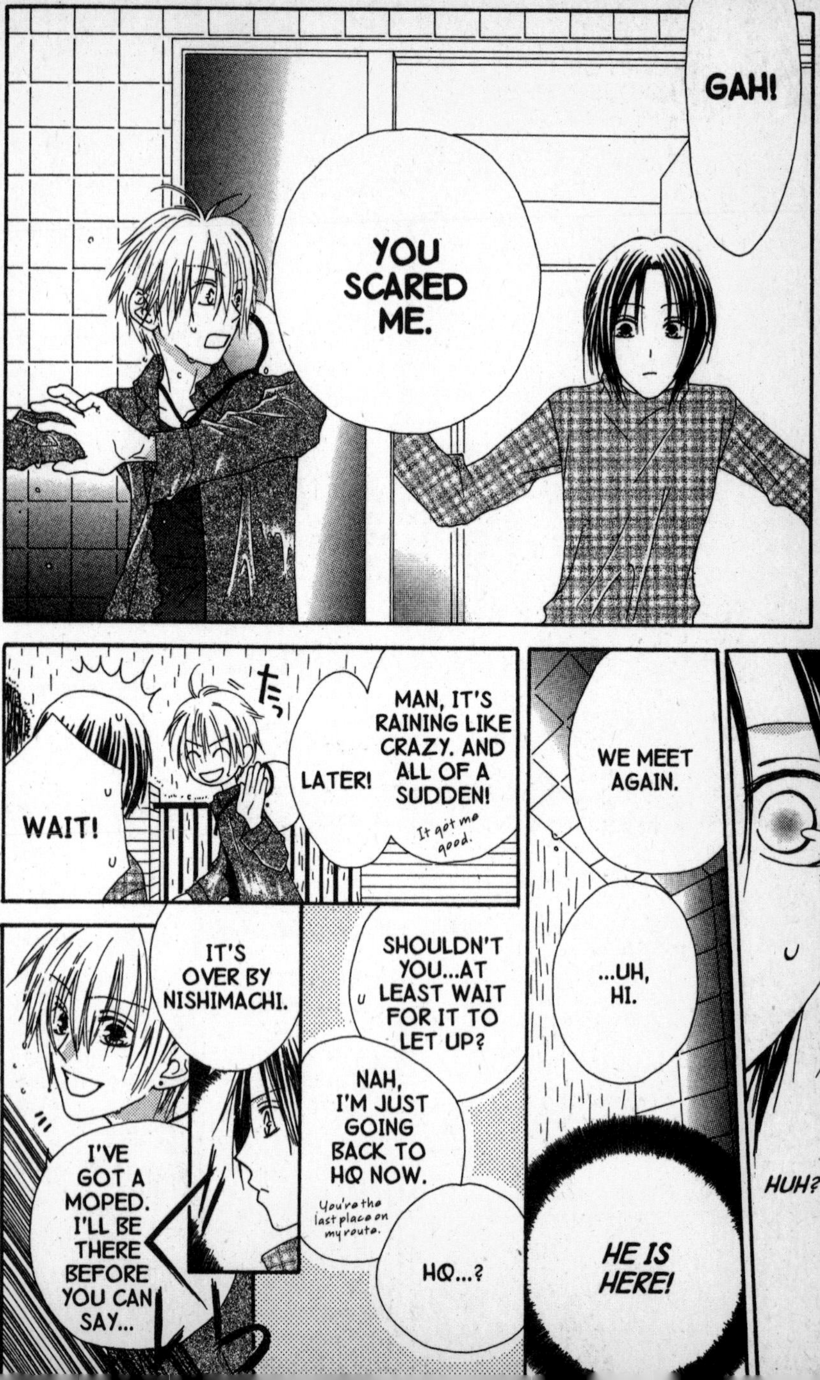
GAH!
YOU SCARED ME.
HUH?
WE MEET AGAIN.
...UH, HI.
HE IS HERE!
MAN, IT'S RAINING LIKE CRAZY. AND ALL OF A SUDDEN!
It got me good.
LATER!
WAIT!
SHOULDN'T YOU...AT LEAST WAIT FOR IT TO LET UP?
IT'S OVER BY NISHIMACHI.
NAH, I'M JUST GOING BACK TO HQ NOW.
You're the last place on my route.
HQ...?
I'VE GOT A MOPED. I'LL BE THERE BEFORE YOU CAN SAY...

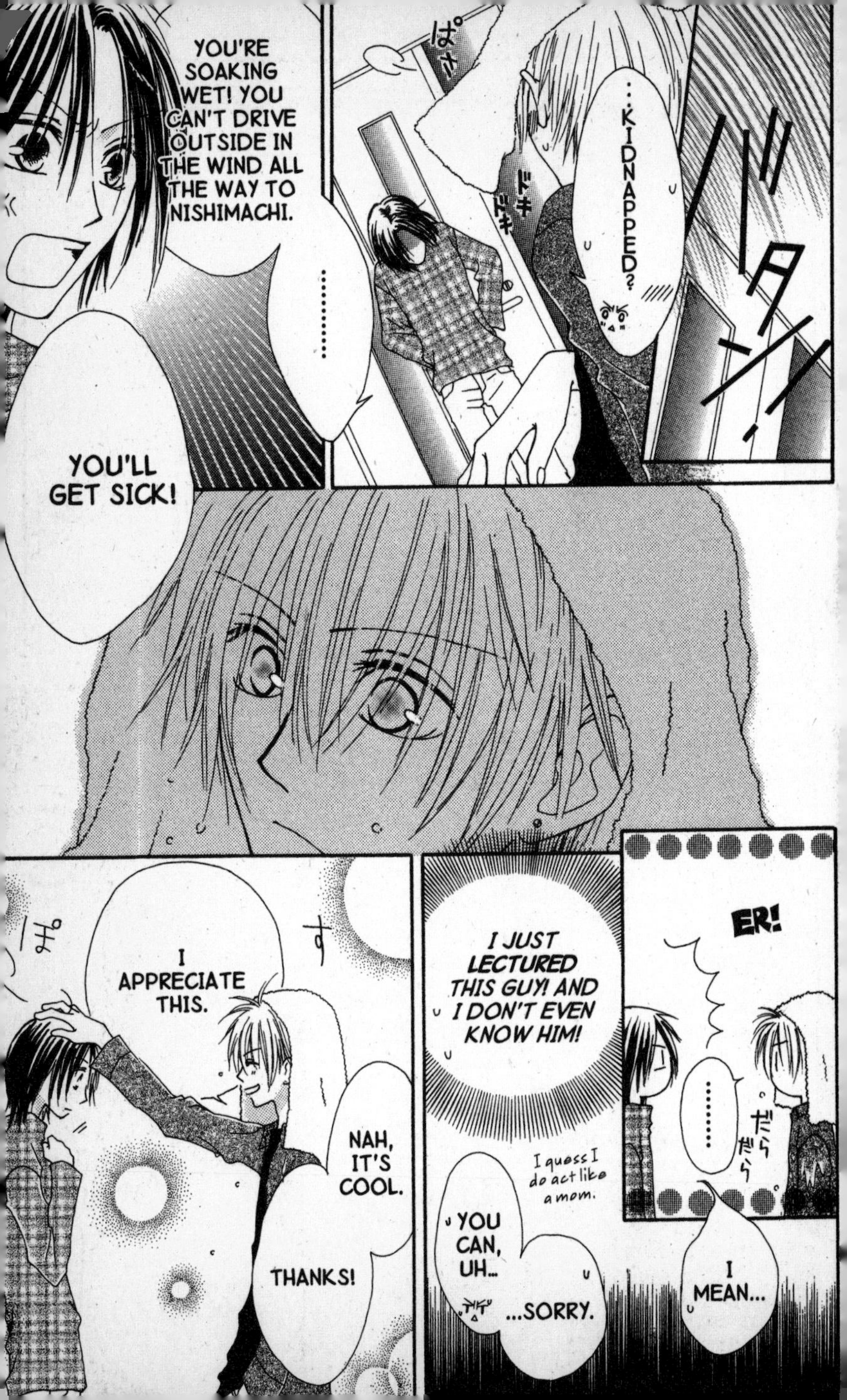

バタン
ぱさ
...KIDNAPPED?
ドキドキ
YOU'RE SOAKING WET! YOU CAN'T DRIVE OUTSIDE IN THE WIND ALL THE WAY TO NISHIMACHI.
......
YOU'LL GET SICK!
ER!
......
だらだら
I MEAN...
I JUST LECTURED THIS GUY! AND I DON'T EVEN KNOW HIM!
I guess I do act like a mom.
YOU CAN, UH...
...SORRY.
I APPRECIATE THIS.
す
NAH, IT'S COOL.
THANKS!

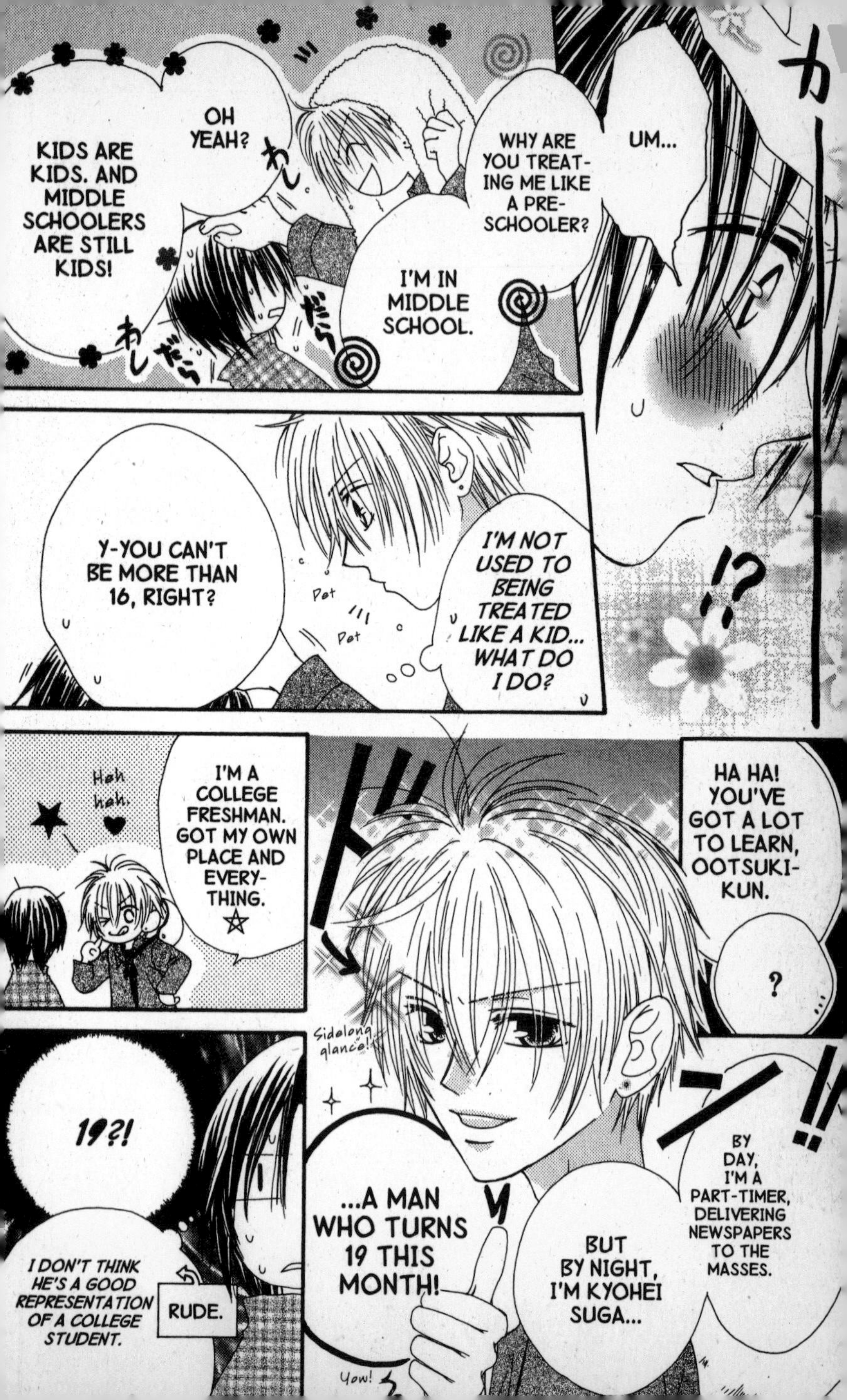
UM...
!?
WHY ARE YOU TREATING ME LIKE A PRESCHOOLER?
I'M IN MIDDLE SCHOOL.
OH YEAH?
KIDS ARE KIDS. AND MIDDLE SCHOOLERS ARE STILL KIDS!
I'M NOT USED TO BEING TREATED LIKE A KID... WHAT DO I DO?
Pet Pet
Y-YOU CAN'T BE MORE THAN 16, RIGHT?
HA HA! YOU'VE GOT A LOT TO LEARN, OOTSUKI-KUN.
?
BY DAY, I'M A PART-TIMER, DELIVERING NEWSPAPERS TO THE MASSES.
BUT BY NIGHT, I'M KYOHEI SUGA...
...A MAN WHO TURNS 19 THIS MONTH!
Sidelong glance!
Yow!
I'M A COLLEGE FRESHMAN. GOT MY OWN PLACE AND EVERYTHING. ☆
Heh heh.
19?!
RUDE.
I DON'T THINK HE'S A GOOD REPRESENTATION OF A COLLEGE STUDENT.

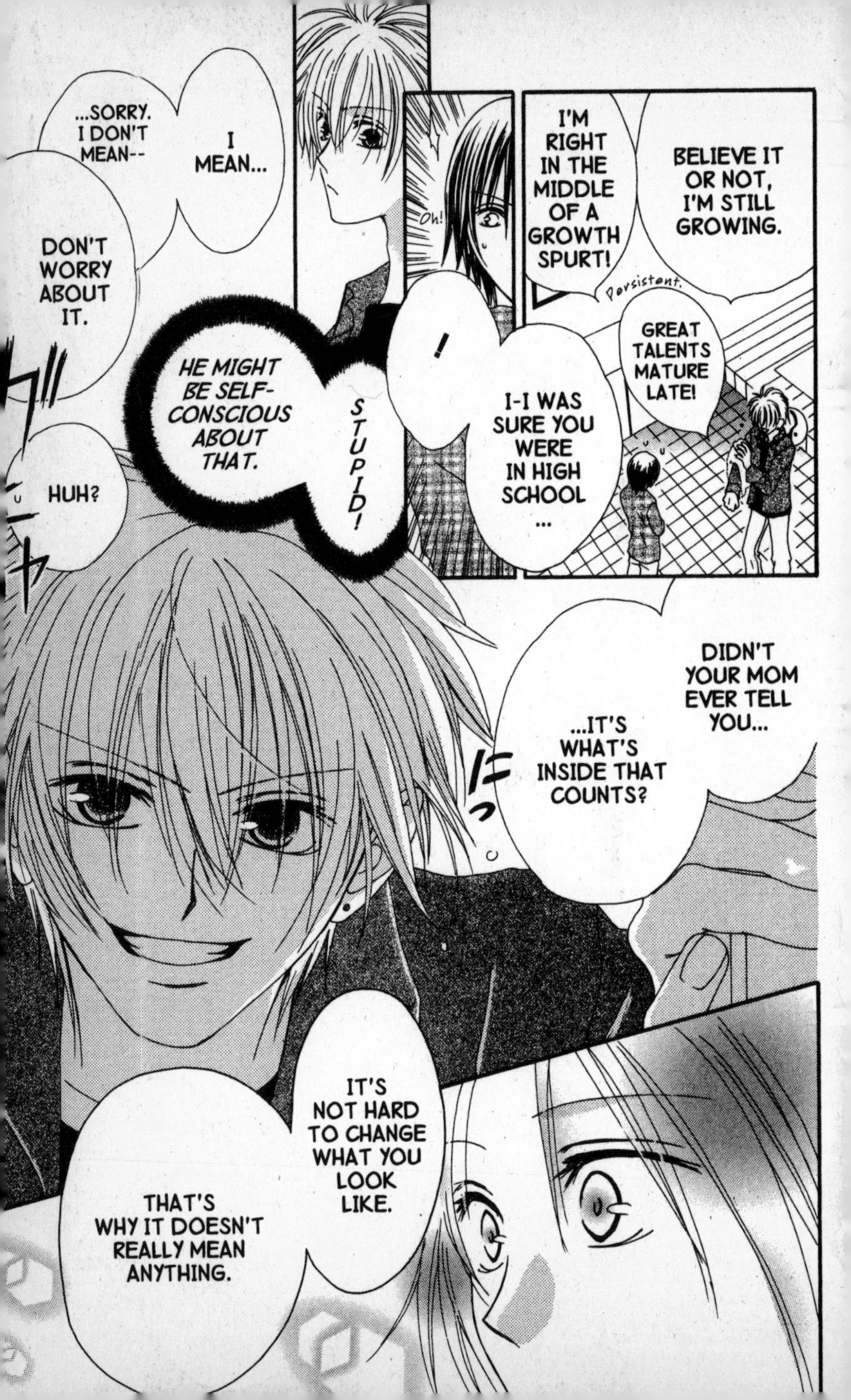
BELIEVE IT OR NOT, I'M STILL GROWING.
I'M RIGHT IN THE MIDDLE OF A GROWTH SPURT!
Persistent.
GREAT TALENTS MATURE LATE!
Oh!
!
I-I WAS SURE YOU WERE IN HIGH SCHOOL ...
STUPID!
HE MIGHT BE SELF-CONSCIOUS ABOUT THAT.
I MEAN...
...SORRY. I DON'T MEAN--
DON'T WORRY ABOUT IT.
HUH?
DIDN'T YOUR MOM EVER TELL YOU...
...IT'S WHAT'S INSIDE THAT COUNTS?
IT'S NOT HARD TO CHANGE WHAT YOU LOOK LIKE.
THAT'S WHY IT DOESN'T REALLY MEAN ANYTHING.

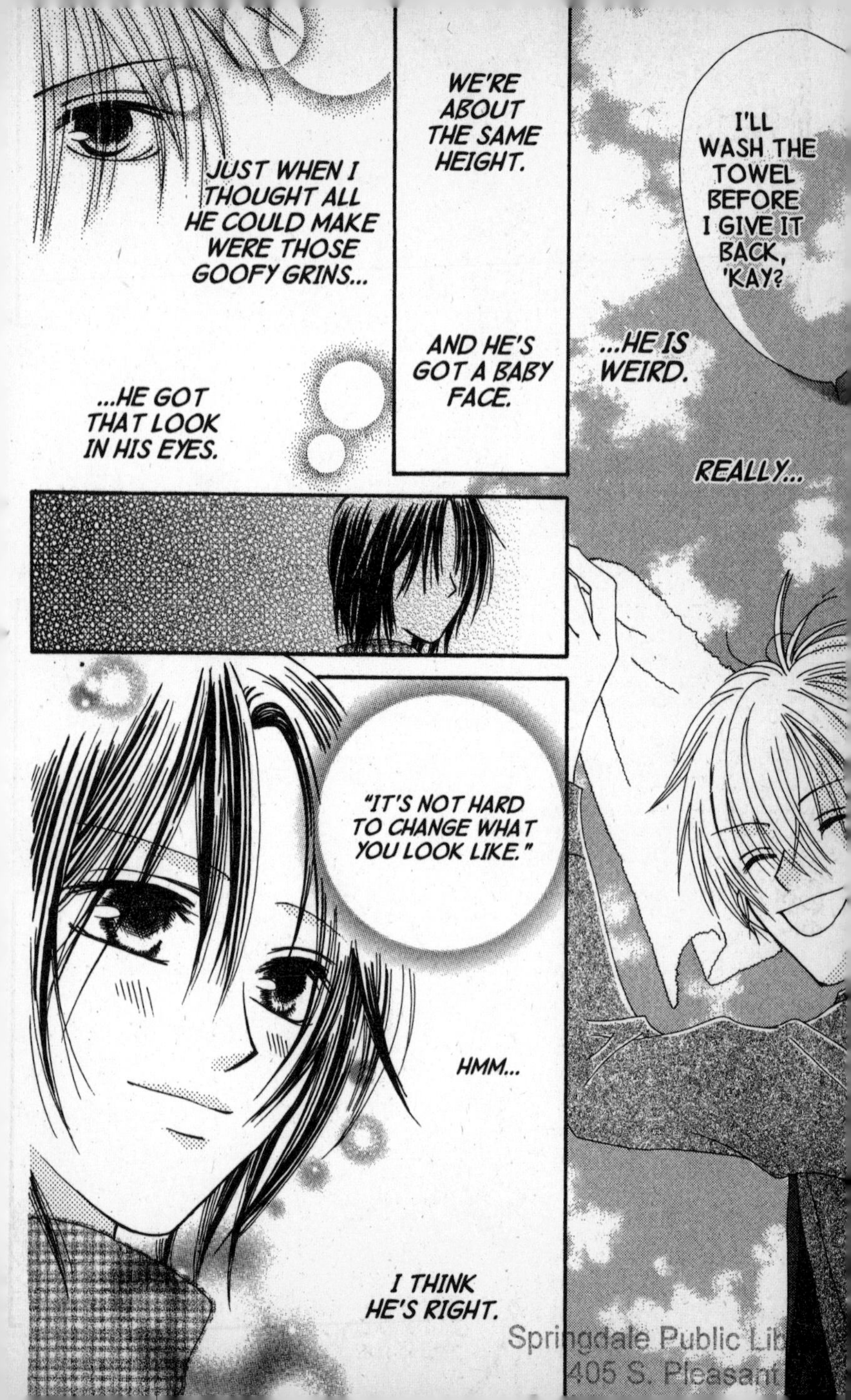
I'LL WASH THE TOWEL BEFORE I GIVE IT BACK, 'KAY?
...HE IS WEIRD.
REALLY...
WE'RE ABOUT THE SAME HEIGHT.
AND HE'S GOT A BABY FACE.
JUST WHEN I THOUGHT ALL HE COULD MAKE WERE THOSE GOOFY GRINS...
...HE GOT THAT LOOK IN HIS EYES.
"IT'S NOT HARD TO CHANGE WHAT YOU LOOK LIKE."
HMM...
I THINK HE'S RIGHT.

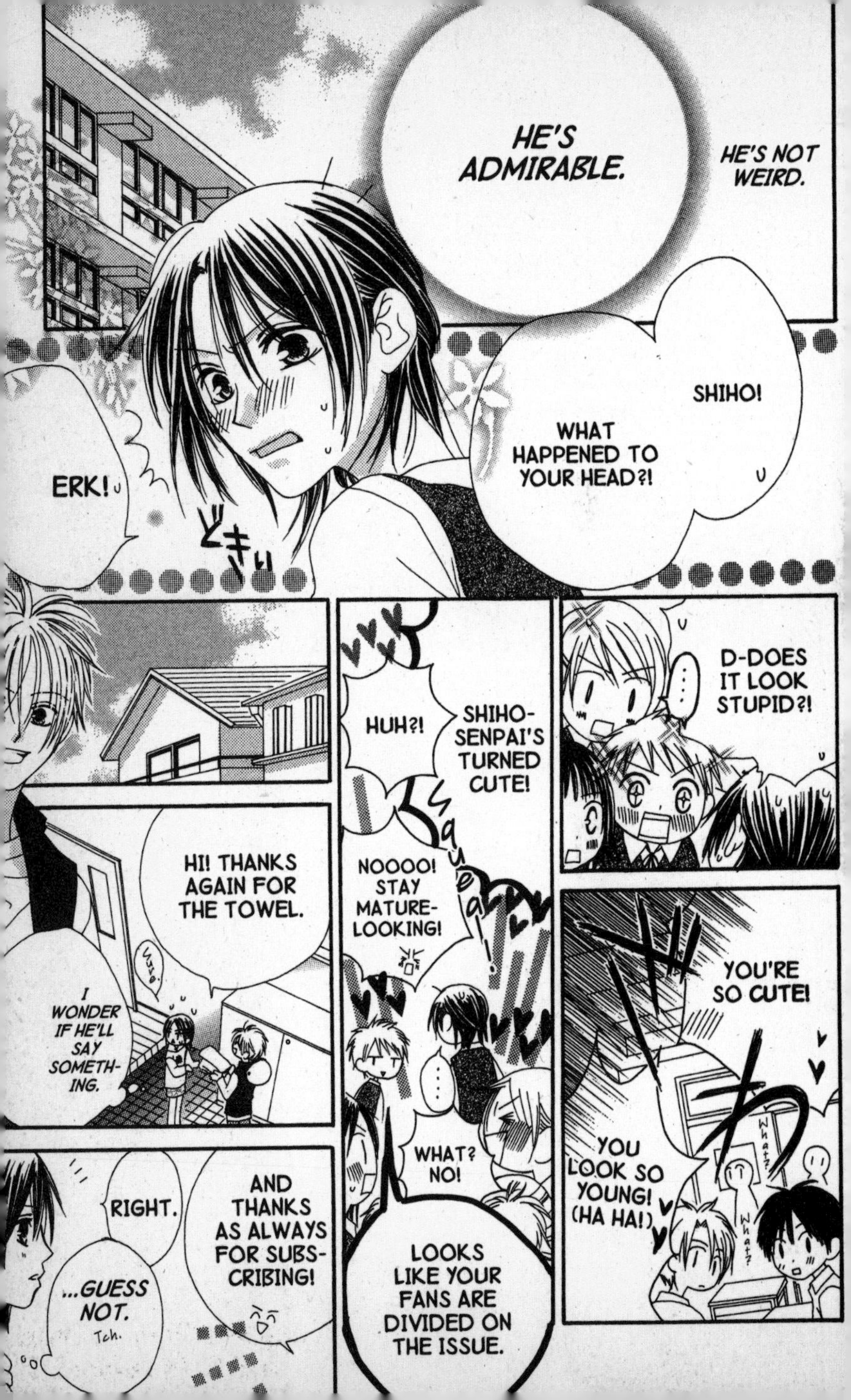

HE'S NOT WEIRD.
HE'S ADMIRABLE.
SHIHO!
WHAT HAPPENED TO YOUR HEAD?!
どきぃ
ERK!
...
D-DOES IT LOOK STUPID?!
YOU'RE SO CUTE!
YOU LOOK SO YOUNG! (HA HA!)
What?
What?
SHIHO-SENPAI'S TURNED CUTE!
HUH?!
Squeal!
NOOOO! STAY MATURE-LOOKING!
...
WHAT? NO!
LOOKS LIKE YOUR FANS ARE DIVIDED ON THE ISSUE.
HI! THANKS AGAIN FOR THE TOWEL.
Sure.
I WONDER IF HE'LL SAY SOMETHING.
AND THANKS AS ALWAYS FOR SUBSCRIBING!
RIGHT.
...GUESS NOT.
Tch.

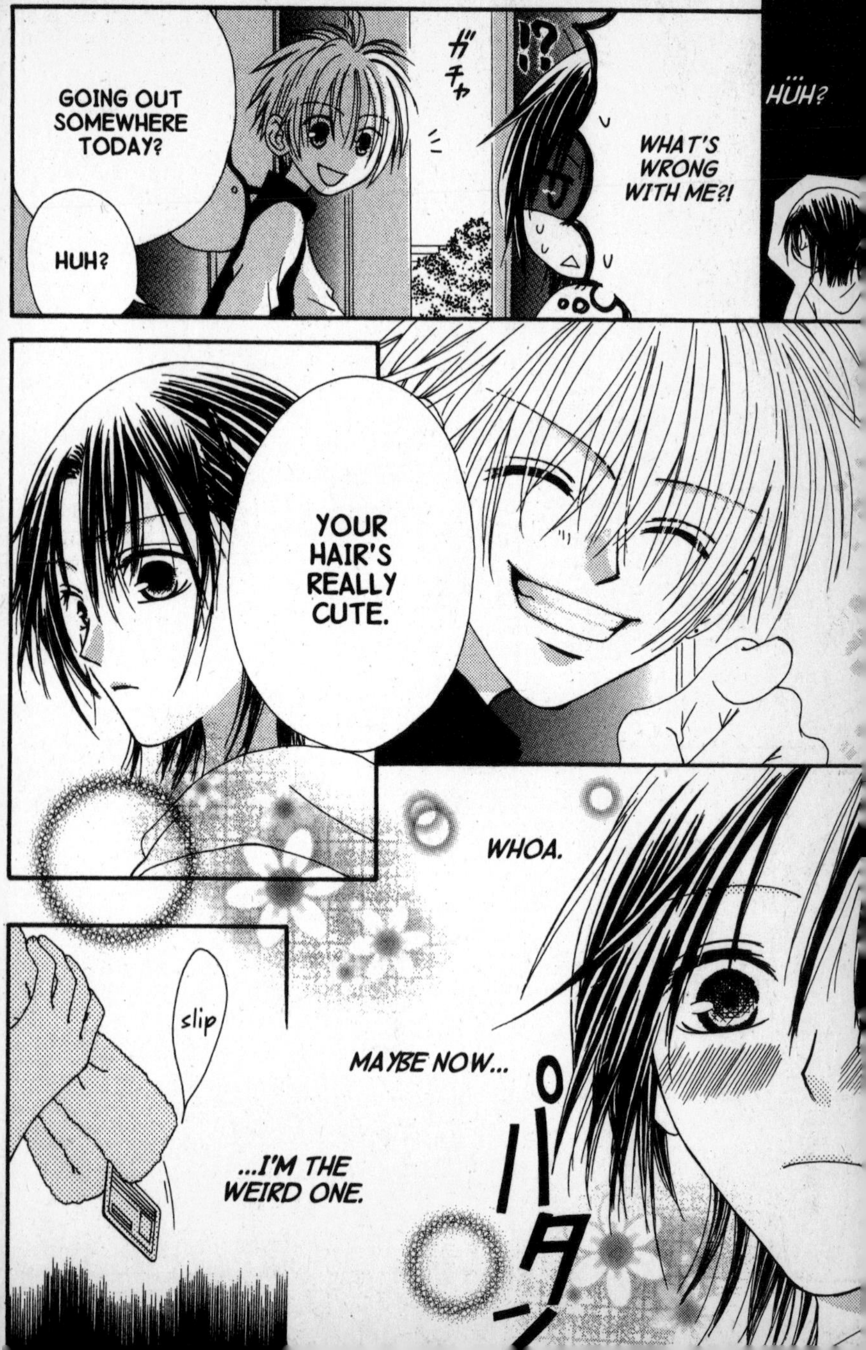
HÜH?
!?
WHAT'S WRONG WITH ME?!
ガチャ
GOING OUT SOMEWHERE TODAY?
HUH?
YOUR HAIR'S REALLY CUTE.
WHOA.
MAYBE NOW...
...I'M THE WEIRD ONE.
パタン
slip

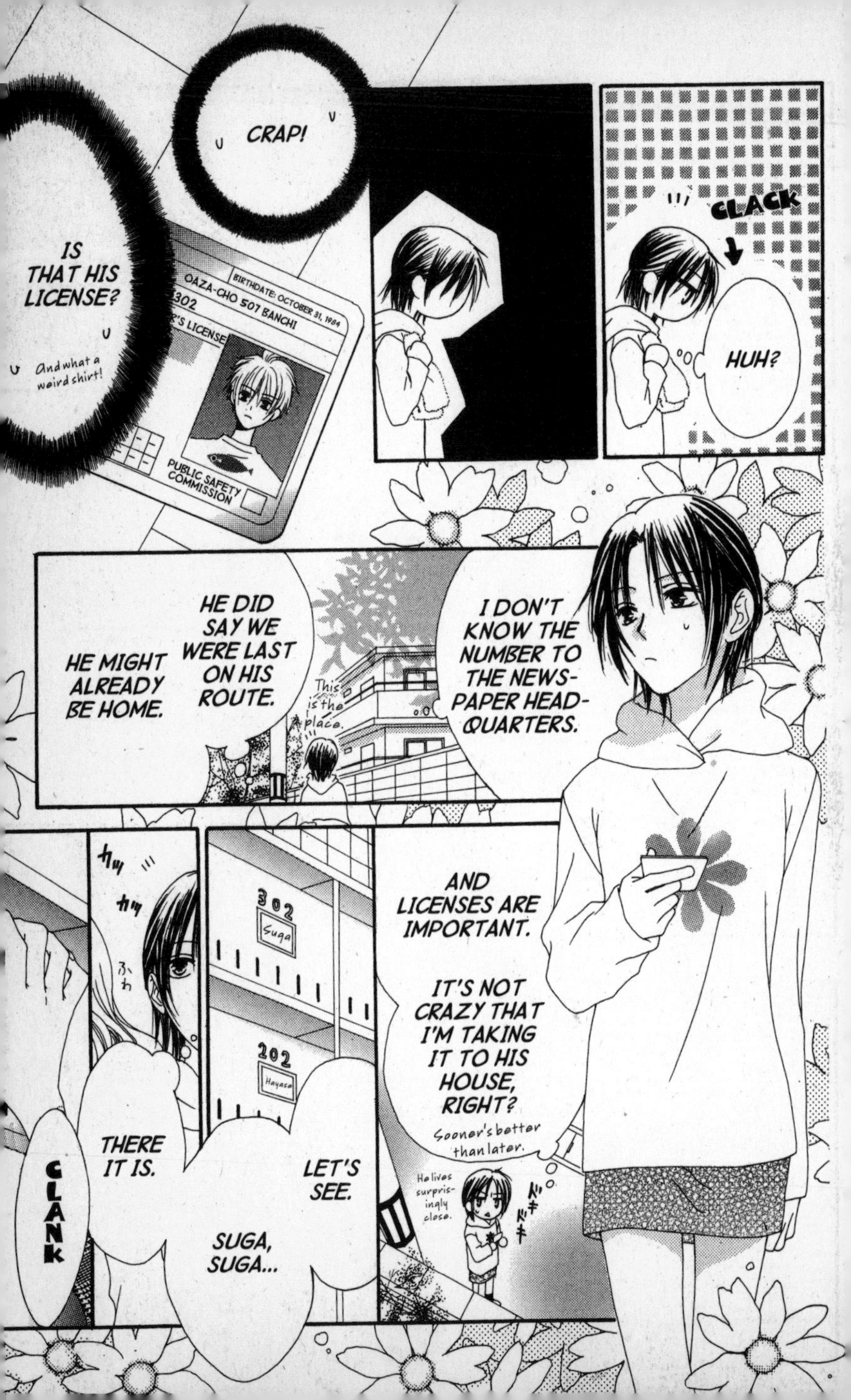
CLACK
HUH?
CRAP!
IS THAT HIS LICENSE?
And what a weird shirt!
BIRTHDATE: OCTOBER 31, 1984
OAZA-CHO 507 BANCHI
302
R'S LICENSE
PUBLIC SAFETY COMMISSION
I DON'T KNOW THE NUMBER TO THE NEWS-PAPER HEAD-QUARTERS.
HE DID SAY WE WERE LAST ON HIS ROUTE.
HE MIGHT ALREADY BE HOME.
This is the place.
AND LICENSES ARE IMPORTANT.
IT'S NOT CRAZY THAT I'M TAKING IT TO HIS HOUSE, RIGHT?
Sooner's better than later.
He lives surprisingly close.
ドキドキ
302
Suga
202
Hayase
LET'S SEE.
SUGA, SUGA...
カツ
カツ
ふわ
THERE IT IS.
CLANK

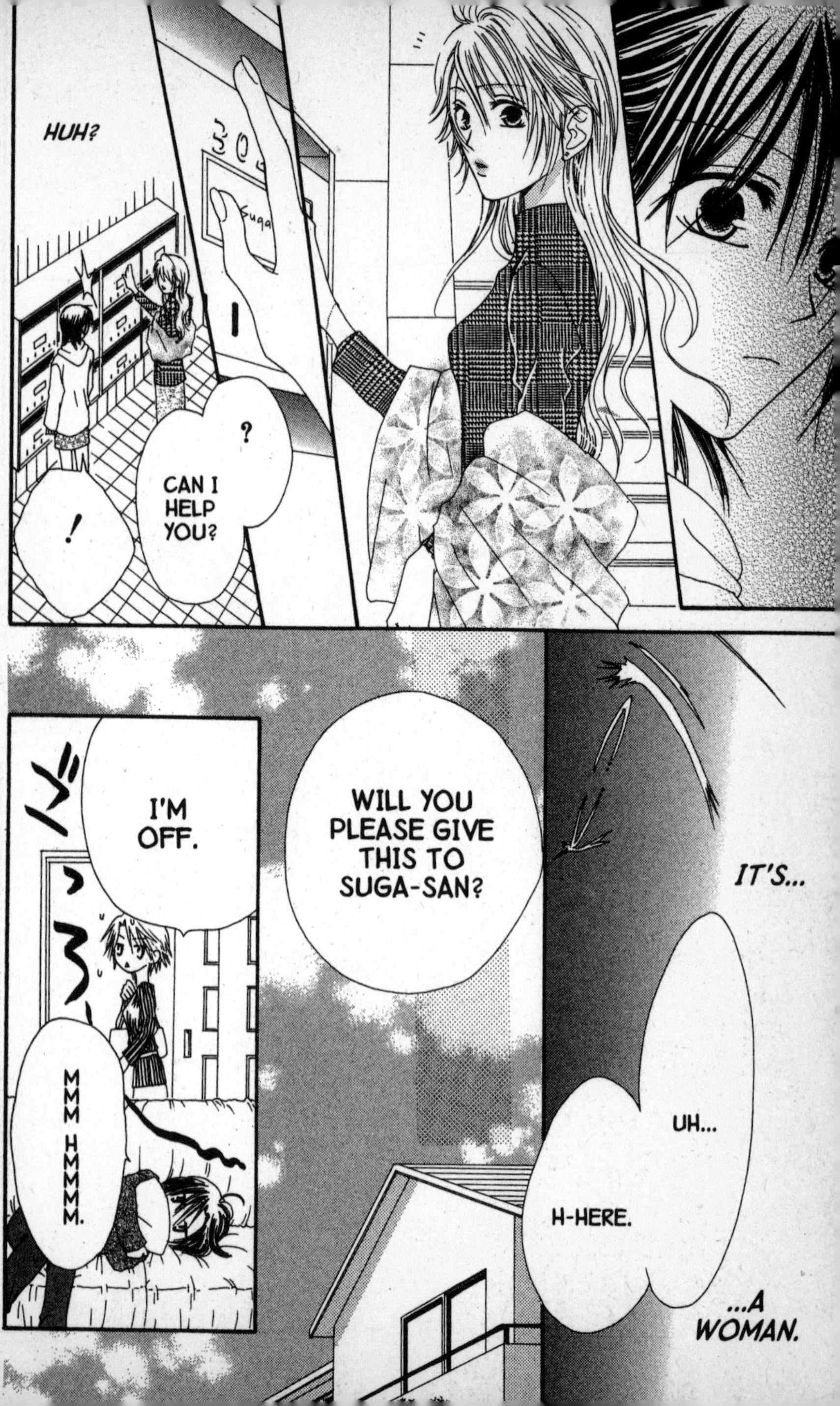

Suga
?
CAN I HELP YOU?
HUH?
!
IT'S...
...A WOMAN.
WILL YOU PLEASE GIVE THIS TO SUGA-SAN?
UH...
H-HERE.
I'M OFF.
MMM HMMMM.

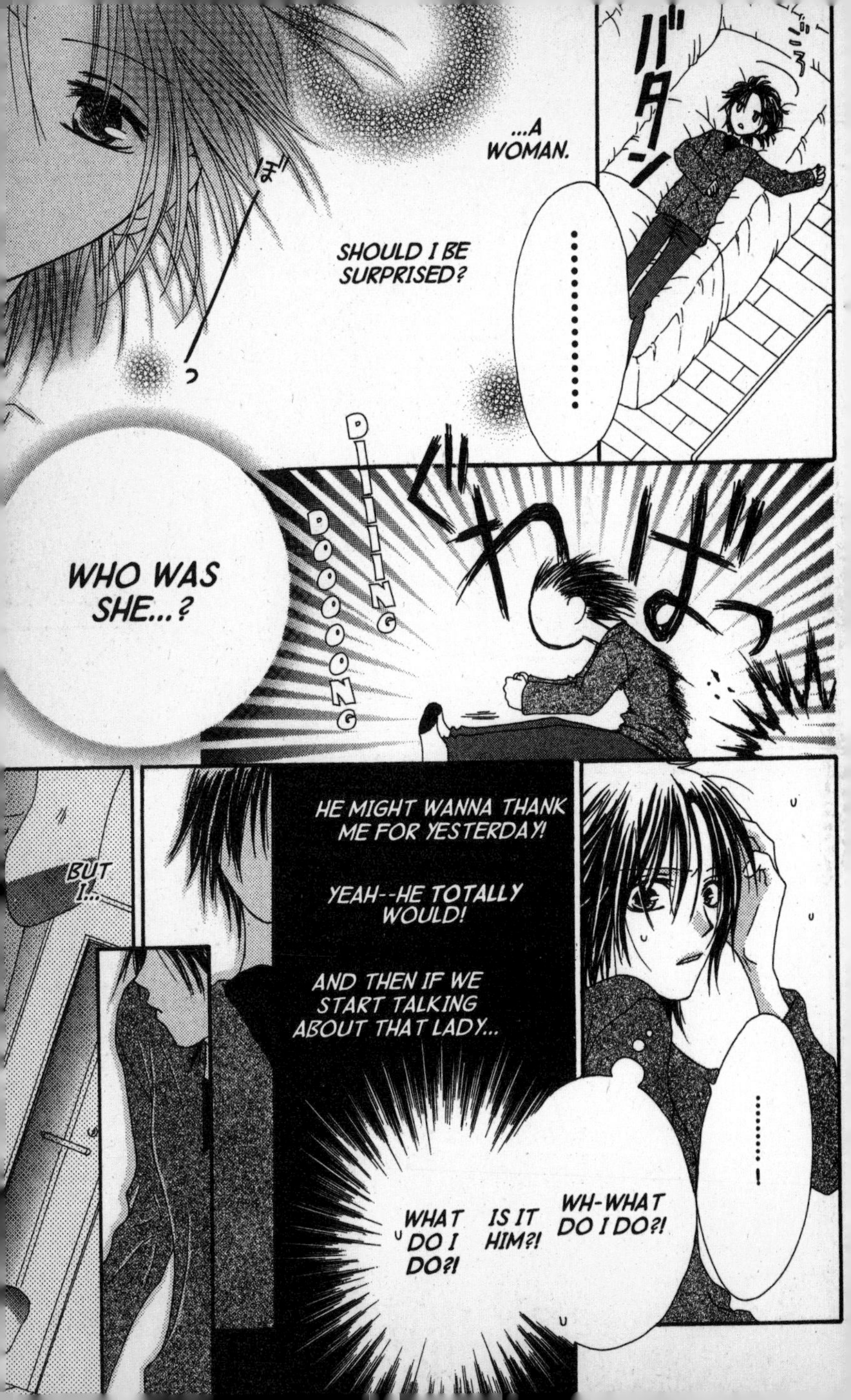

バターン
ごろ
......
...A WOMAN.
SHOULD I BE SURPRISED?
ほっ
WHO WAS SHE...?
がばっ
DIIIING
DOOOOONG
......!
WH-WHAT DO I DO?!
IS IT HIM?!
WHAT DO I DO?!
HE MIGHT WANNA THANK ME FOR YESTERDAY!
YEAH--HE TOTALLY WOULD!
AND THEN IF WE START TALKING ABOUT THAT LADY...
BUT I...

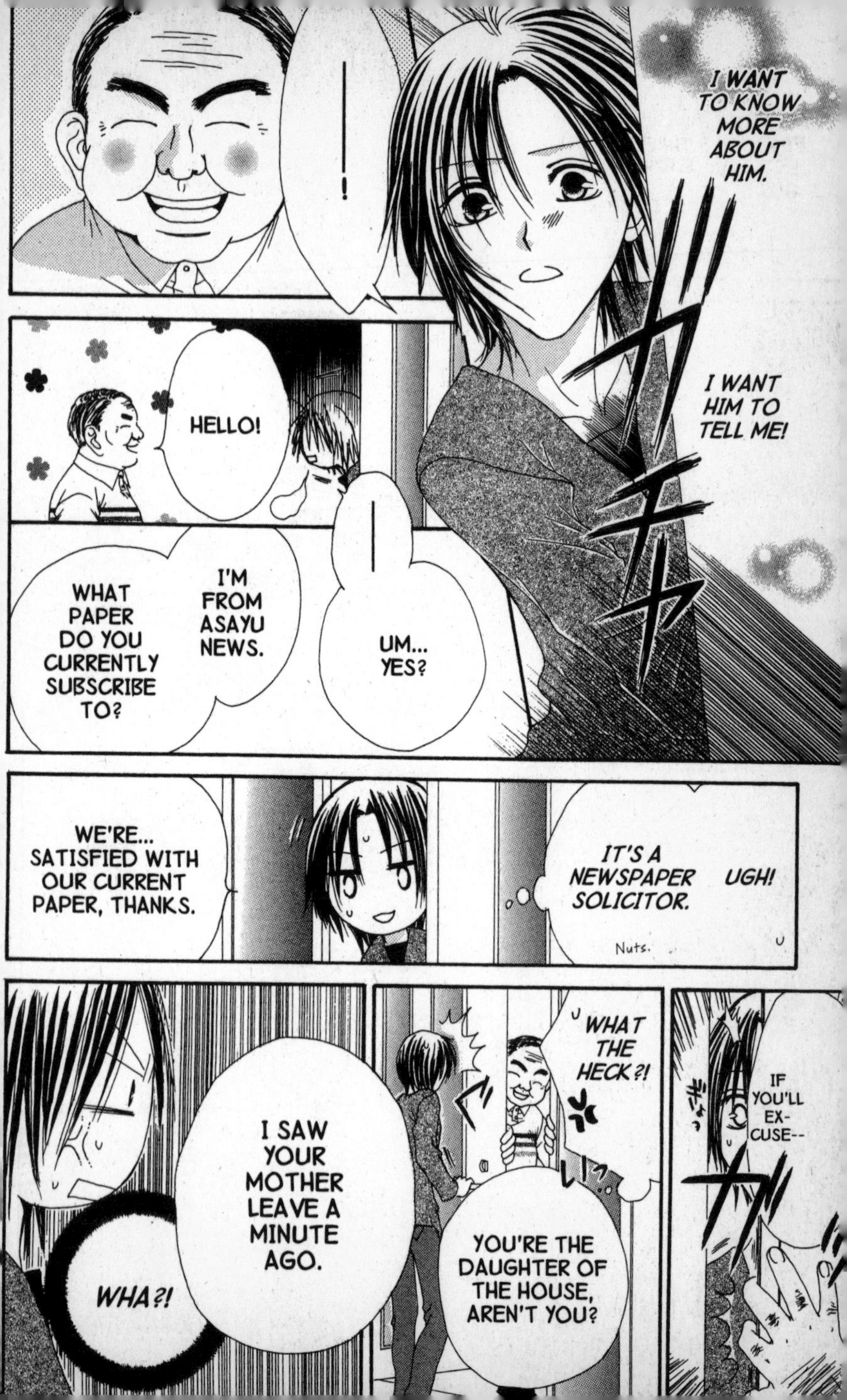
I WANT TO KNOW MORE ABOUT HIM.
I WANT HIM TO TELL ME!
—!
HELLO!
UM... YES?
I'M FROM ASAYU NEWS.
WHAT PAPER DO YOU CURRENTLY SUBSCRIBE TO?
UGH!
IT'S A NEWSPAPER SOLICITOR.
Nuts.
WE'RE... SATISFIED WITH OUR CURRENT PAPER, THANKS.
IF YOU'LL EX-CUSE--
WHAT THE HECK?!
YOU'RE THE DAUGHTER OF THE HOUSE, AREN'T YOU?
I SAW YOUR MOTHER LEAVE A MINUTE AGO.
WHA?!

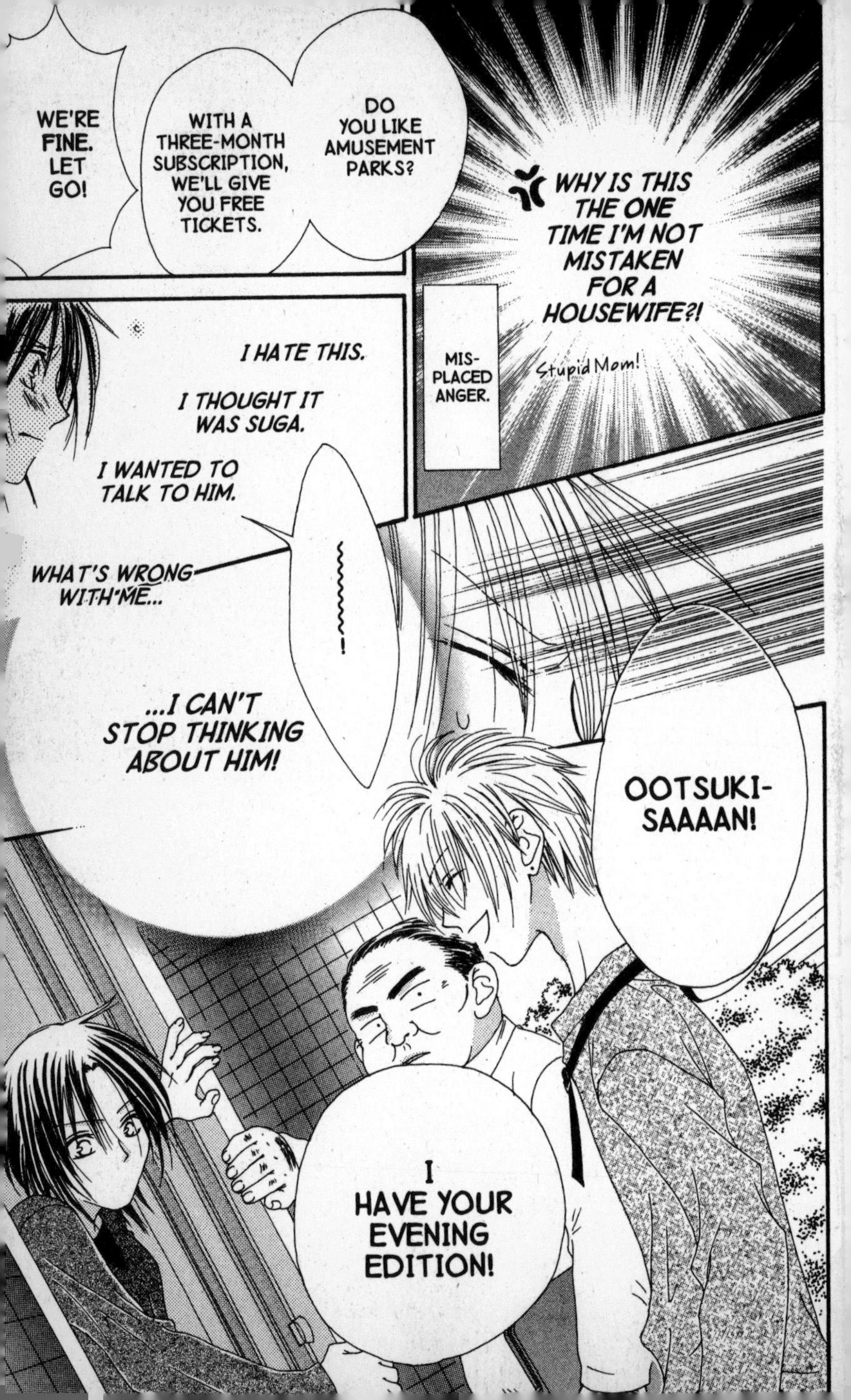
WHY IS THIS THE ONE TIME I'M NOT MISTAKEN FOR A HOUSEWIFE?!
Stupid Mom!
MIS-PLACED ANGER.
DO YOU LIKE AMUSEMENT PARKS?
WITH A THREE-MONTH SUBSCRIPTION, WE'LL GIVE YOU FREE TICKETS.
WE'RE FINE. LET GO!
I HATE THIS.
I THOUGHT IT WAS SUGA.
I WANTED TO TALK TO HIM.
~~~!
WHAT'S WRONG WITH ME...
...I CAN'T STOP THINKING ABOUT HIM!
OOTSUKI-SAAAAN!
I HAVE YOUR EVENING EDITION!
~~~

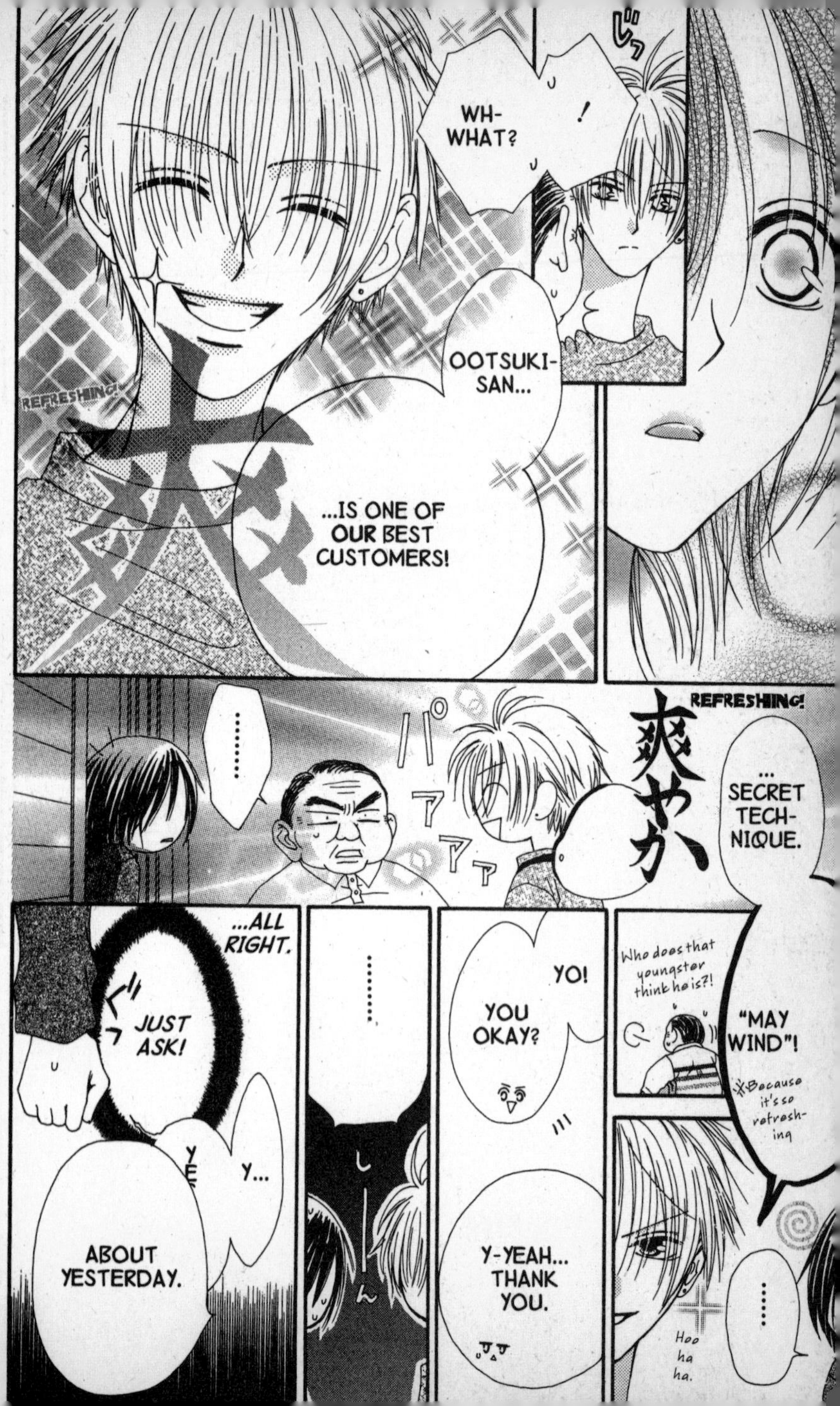
じっ
WH- WHAT?
REFRESHING!
OOTSUKI-SAN...
...IS ONE OF OUR BEST CUSTOMERS!
REFRESHING!
爽やか、
... SECRET TECH- NIQUE.
......
パァァァ
"MAY WIND"!
※Because it's so refresh- ing
Who does that youngster think he is?!
......
Hoo ha ha.
YO!
YOU OKAY?
Y-YEAH... THANK YOU.
....
しーん
...ALL RIGHT.
ぐっ
JUST ASK!
YE
Y...
ABOUT YESTERDAY.

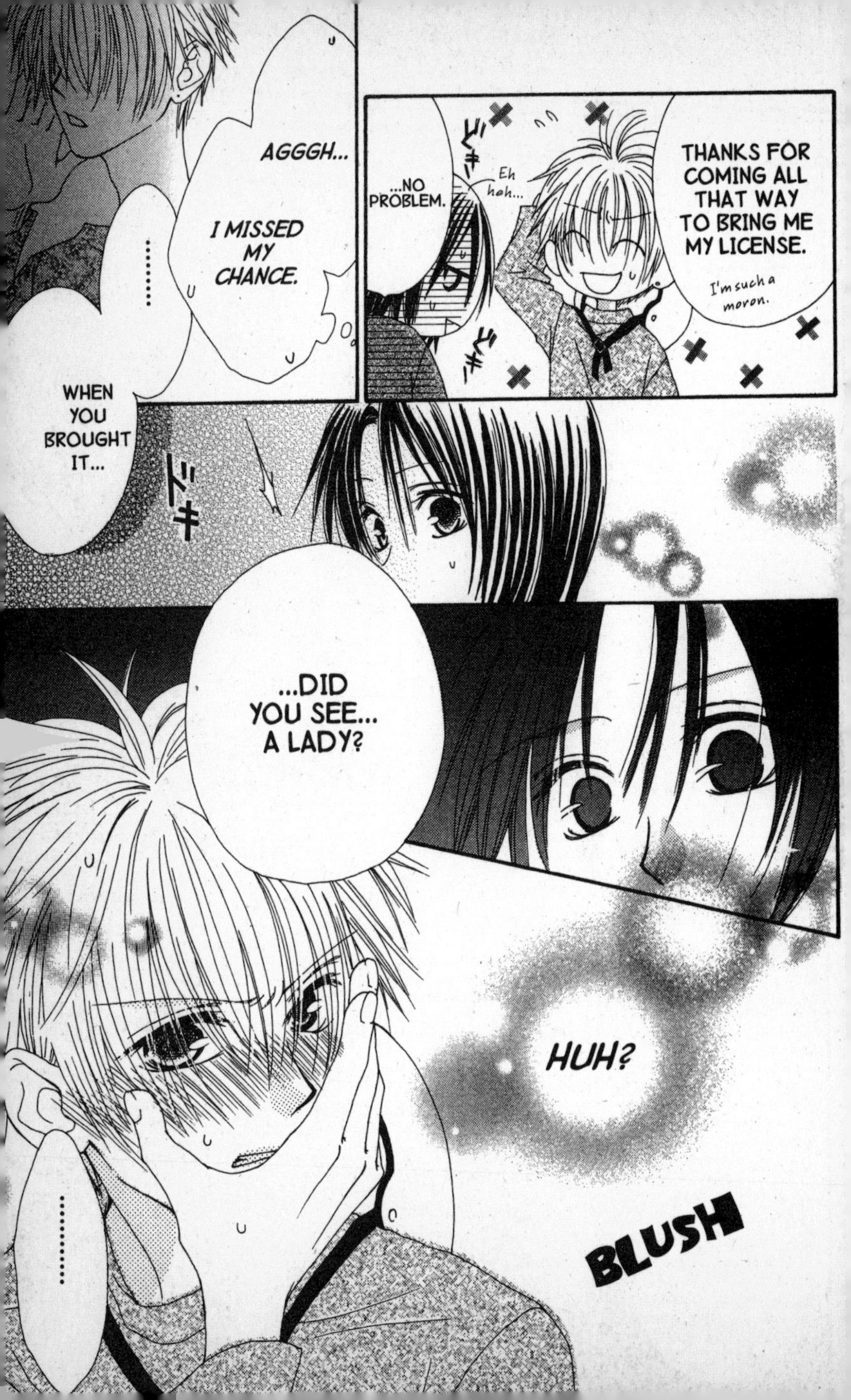
THANKS FOR COMING ALL THAT WAY TO BRING ME MY LICENSE.
I'm such a moron.
Eh heh...
...NO PROBLEM.
AGGGH...
I MISSED MY CHANCE.
......
WHEN YOU BROUGHT IT...
ドキ
...DID YOU SEE... A LADY?
HUH?
BLUSH
......

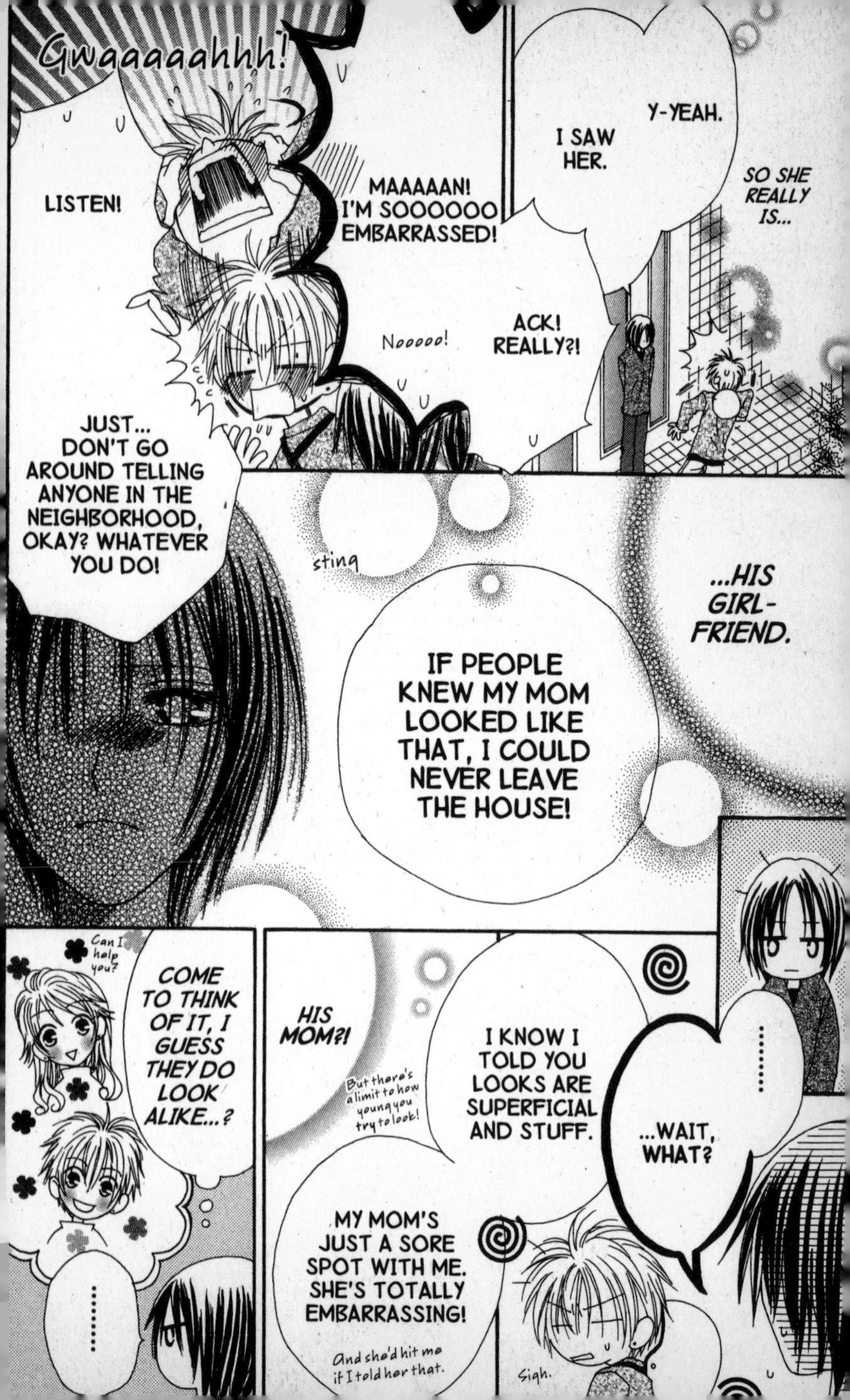
Y-YEAH.
I SAW HER.
SO SHE REALLY IS...
ACK! REALLY?!
Gwaaaaahhh!
MAAAAAN! I'M SOOOOOO EMBARRASSED!
LISTEN!
Nooooo!
JUST... DON'T GO AROUND TELLING ANYONE IN THE NEIGHBORHOOD, OKAY? WHATEVER YOU DO!
...HIS GIRL-FRIEND.
sting
IF PEOPLE KNEW MY MOM LOOKED LIKE THAT, I COULD NEVER LEAVE THE HOUSE!
......
...WAIT, WHAT?
I KNOW I TOLD YOU LOOKS ARE SUPERFICIAL AND STUFF.
HIS MOM?!
But there's a limit to how young you try to look!
MY MOM'S JUST A SORE SPOT WITH ME. SHE'S TOTALLY EMBARRASSING!
And she'd hit me if I told her that.
Sigh.
Can I help you?
COME TO THINK OF IT, I GUESS THEY DO LOOK ALIKE...?
......

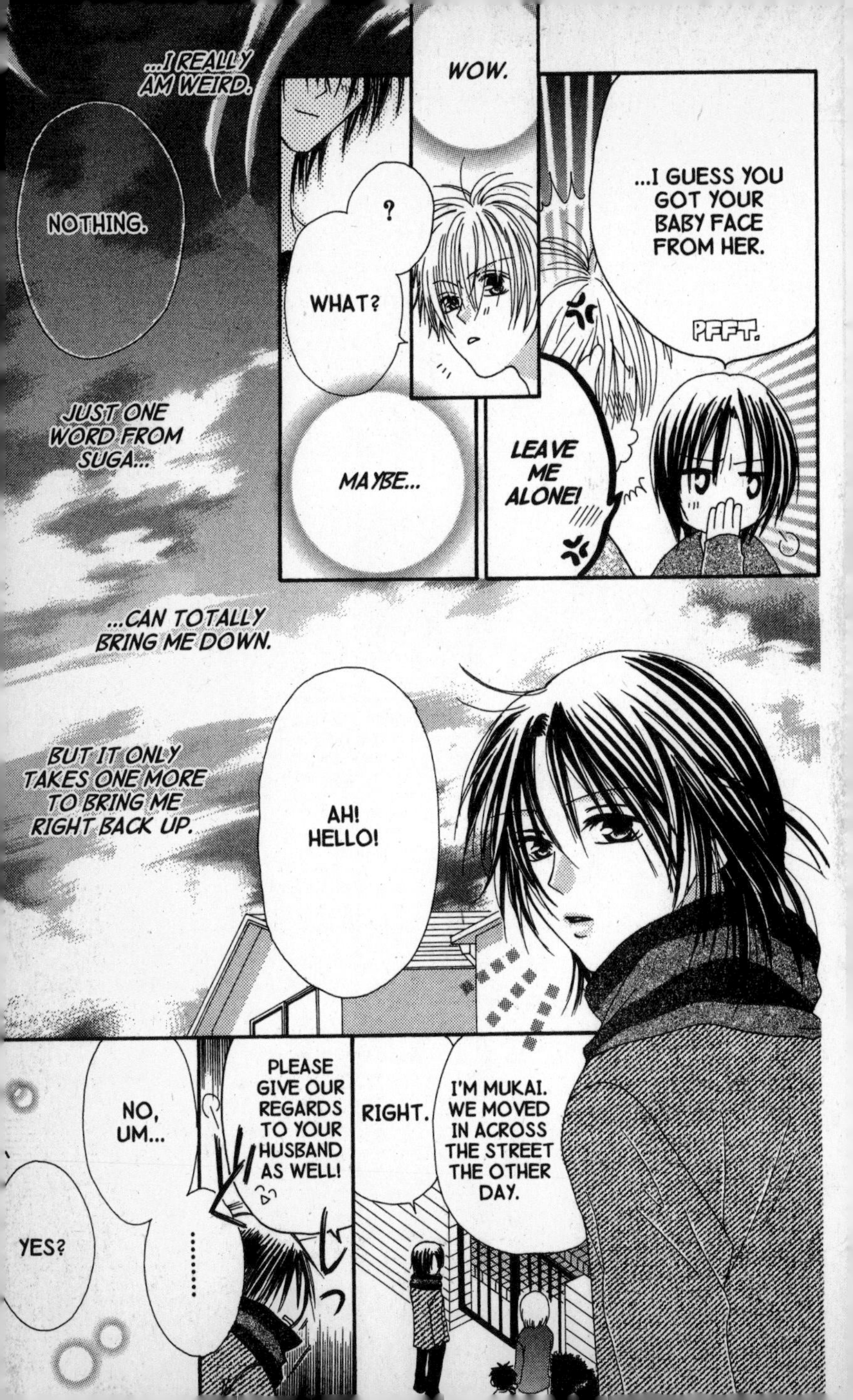
...I GUESS YOU GOT YOUR BABY FACE FROM HER.
PFFT.
LEAVE ME ALONE!
WOW.
?
WHAT?
MAYBE...
...I REALLY AM WEIRD.
NOTHING.
JUST ONE WORD FROM SUGA...
...CAN TOTALLY BRING ME DOWN.
BUT IT ONLY TAKES ONE MORE TO BRING ME RIGHT BACK UP.
AH! HELLO!
I'M MUKAI. WE MOVED IN ACROSS THE STREET THE OTHER DAY.
RIGHT.
PLEASE GIVE OUR REGARDS TO YOUR HUSBAND AS WELL!
NO, UM...
......
YES?

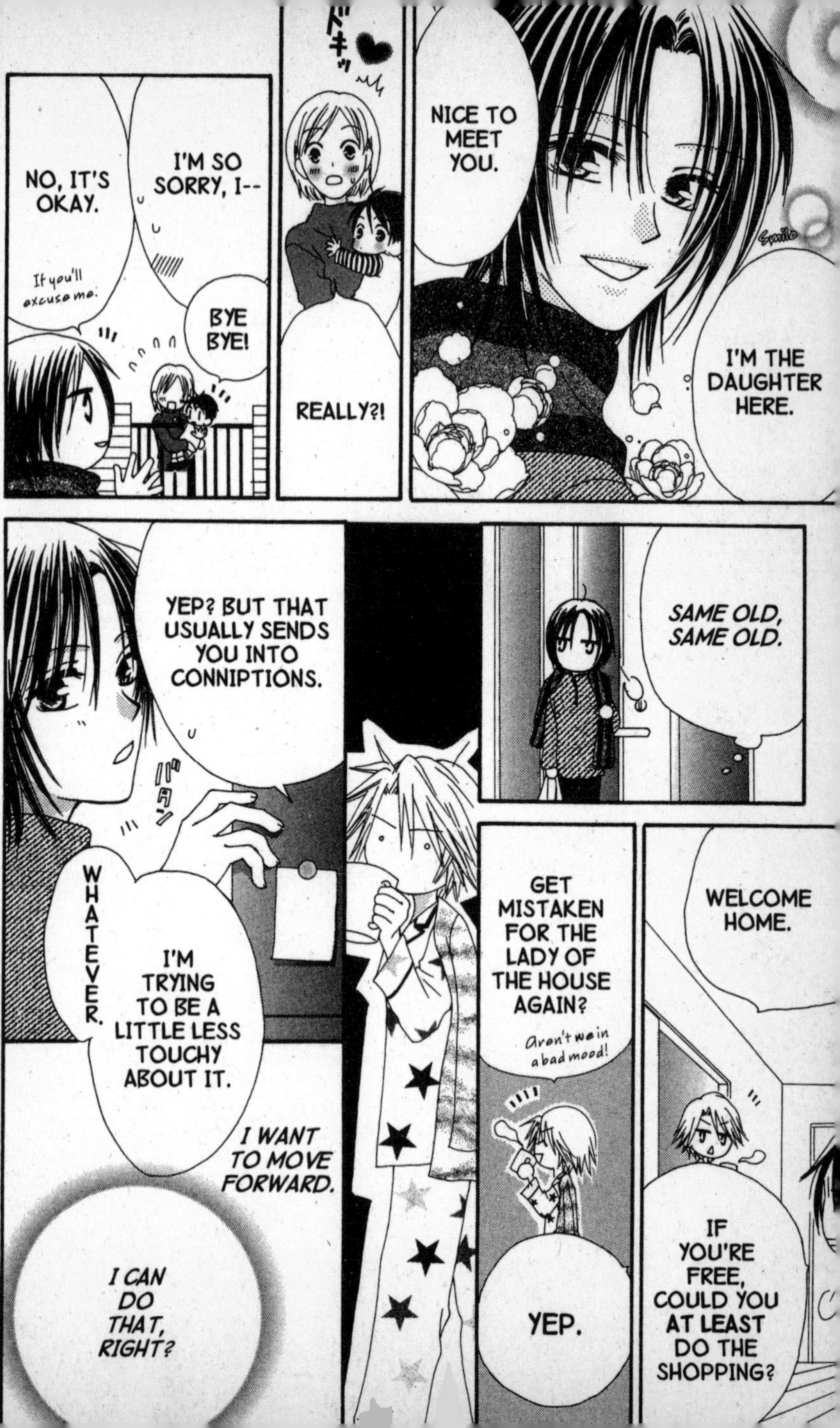
NICE TO MEET YOU.
Smile
I'M THE DAUGHTER HERE.
ドキッ
REALLY?!
I'M SO SORRY, I--
NO, IT'S OKAY.
If you'll excuse me.
BYE BYE!
SAME OLD, SAME OLD.
WELCOME HOME.
IF YOU'RE FREE, COULD YOU AT LEAST DO THE SHOPPING?
GET MISTAKEN FOR THE LADY OF THE HOUSE AGAIN?
Aren't we in a bad mood!
YEP.
YEP? BUT THAT USUALLY SENDS YOU INTO CONNIPTIONS.
WHATEVER.
I'M TRYING TO BE A LITTLE LESS TOUCHY ABOUT IT.
I WANT TO MOVE FORWARD.
I CAN DO THAT, RIGHT?

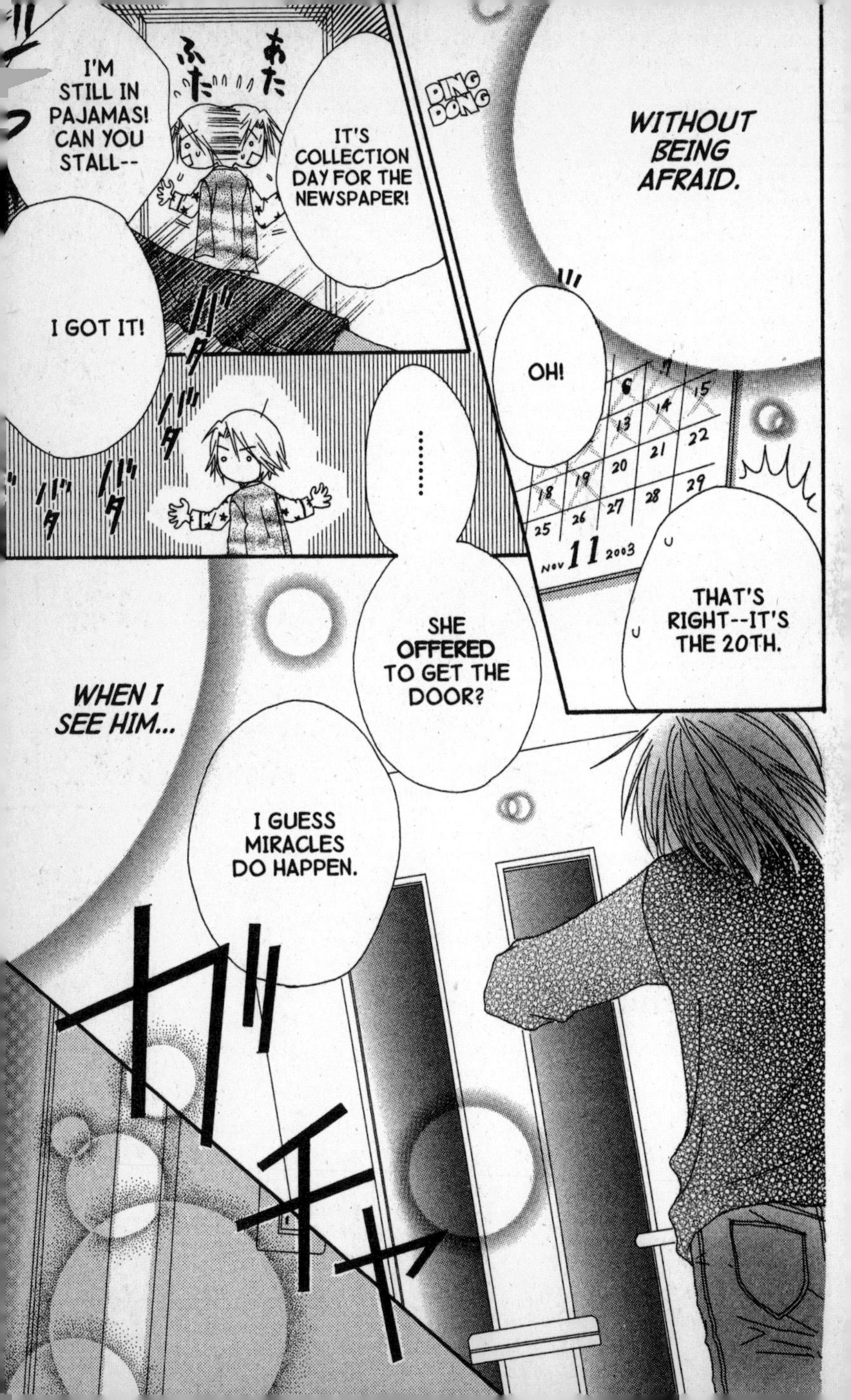
WITHOUT BEING AFRAID.
DING DONG
OH!
NOV 11 2003
THAT'S RIGHT--IT'S THE 20TH.
IT'S COLLECTION DAY FOR THE NEWSPAPER!
あたふた
I'M STILL IN PAJAMAS! CAN YOU STALL--
I GOT IT!
バタバタ
......
SHE OFFERED TO GET THE DOOR?
I GUESS MIRACLES DO HAPPEN.
WHEN I SEE HIM...
ガチャ

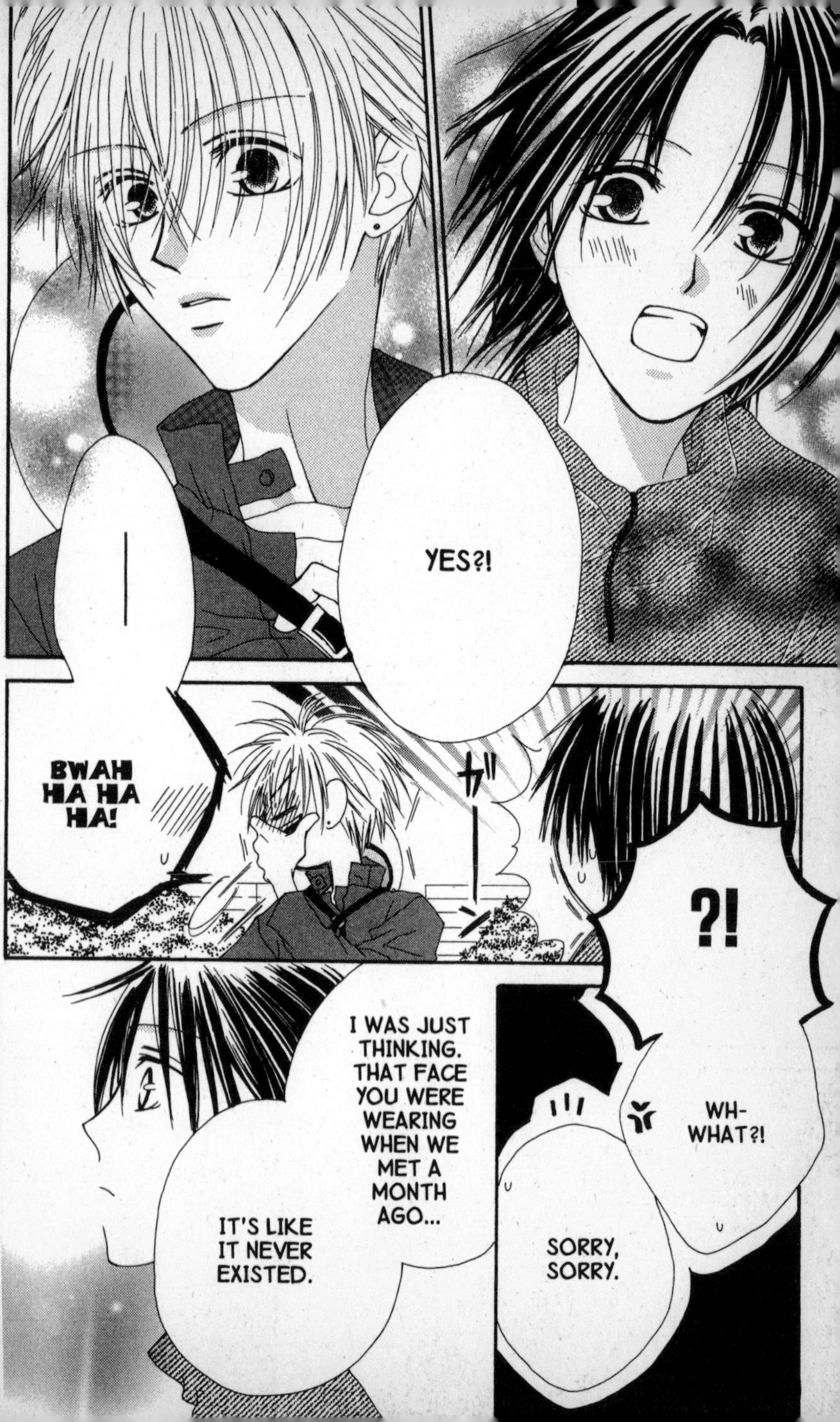
YES?!
—
?!
BWAH HA HA HA!
ガ
WH-WHAT?!
SORRY, SORRY.
I WAS JUST THINKING. THAT FACE YOU WERE WEARING WHEN WE MET A MONTH AGO...
IT'S LIKE IT NEVER EXISTED.

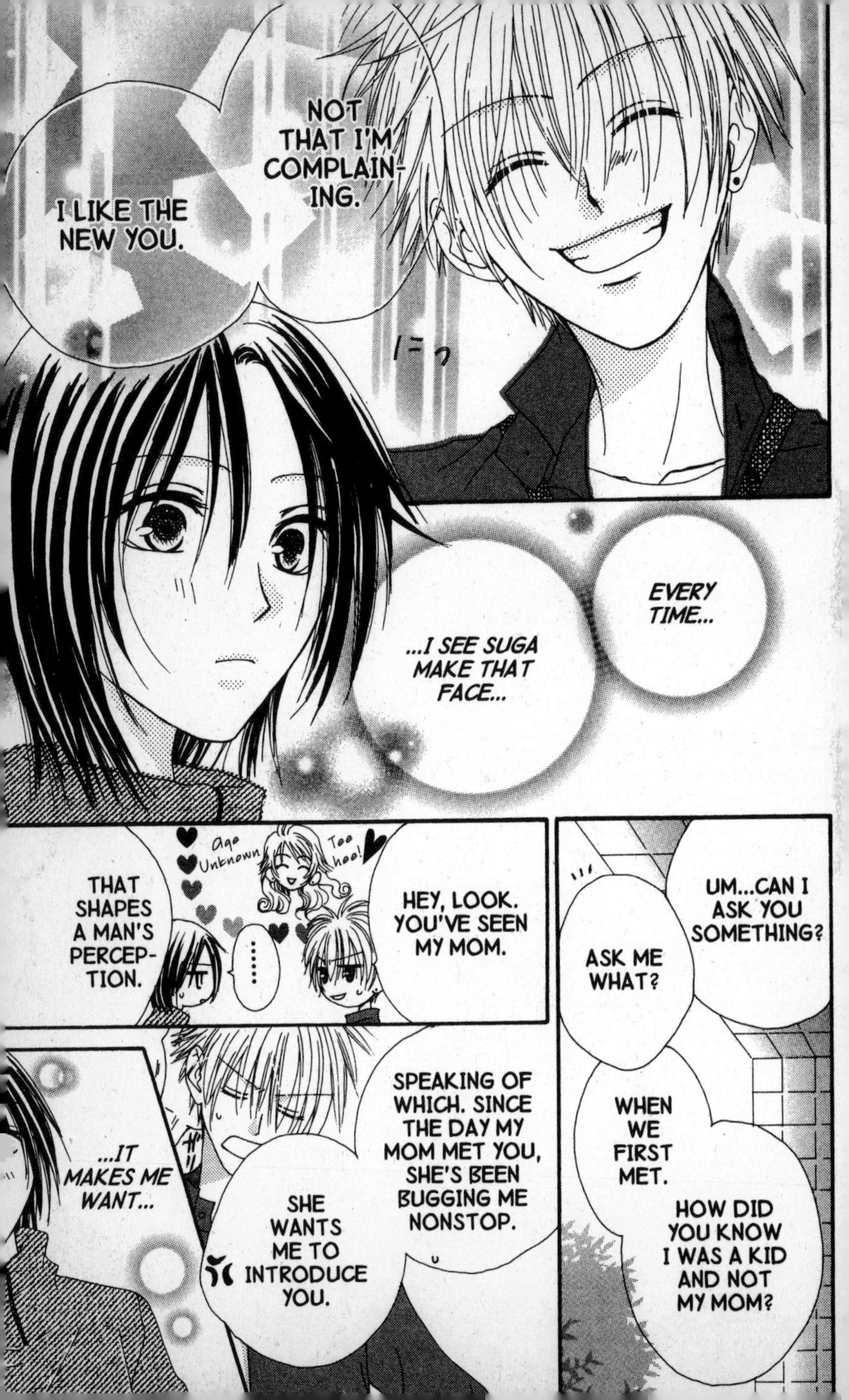
NOT THAT I'M COMPLAINING.
I LIKE THE NEW YOU.
EVERY TIME...
...I SEE SUGA MAKE THAT FACE...
UM...CAN I ASK YOU SOMETHING?
ASK ME WHAT?
WHEN WE FIRST MET.
HOW DID YOU KNOW I WAS A KID AND NOT MY MOM?
HEY, LOOK. YOU'VE SEEN MY MOM.
Age Unknown
Tee hee!
......
THAT SHAPES A MAN'S PERCEPTION.
SPEAKING OF WHICH. SINCE THE DAY MY MOM MET YOU, SHE'S BEEN BUGGING ME NONSTOP.
SHE WANTS ME TO INTRODUCE YOU.
...IT MAKES ME WANT...

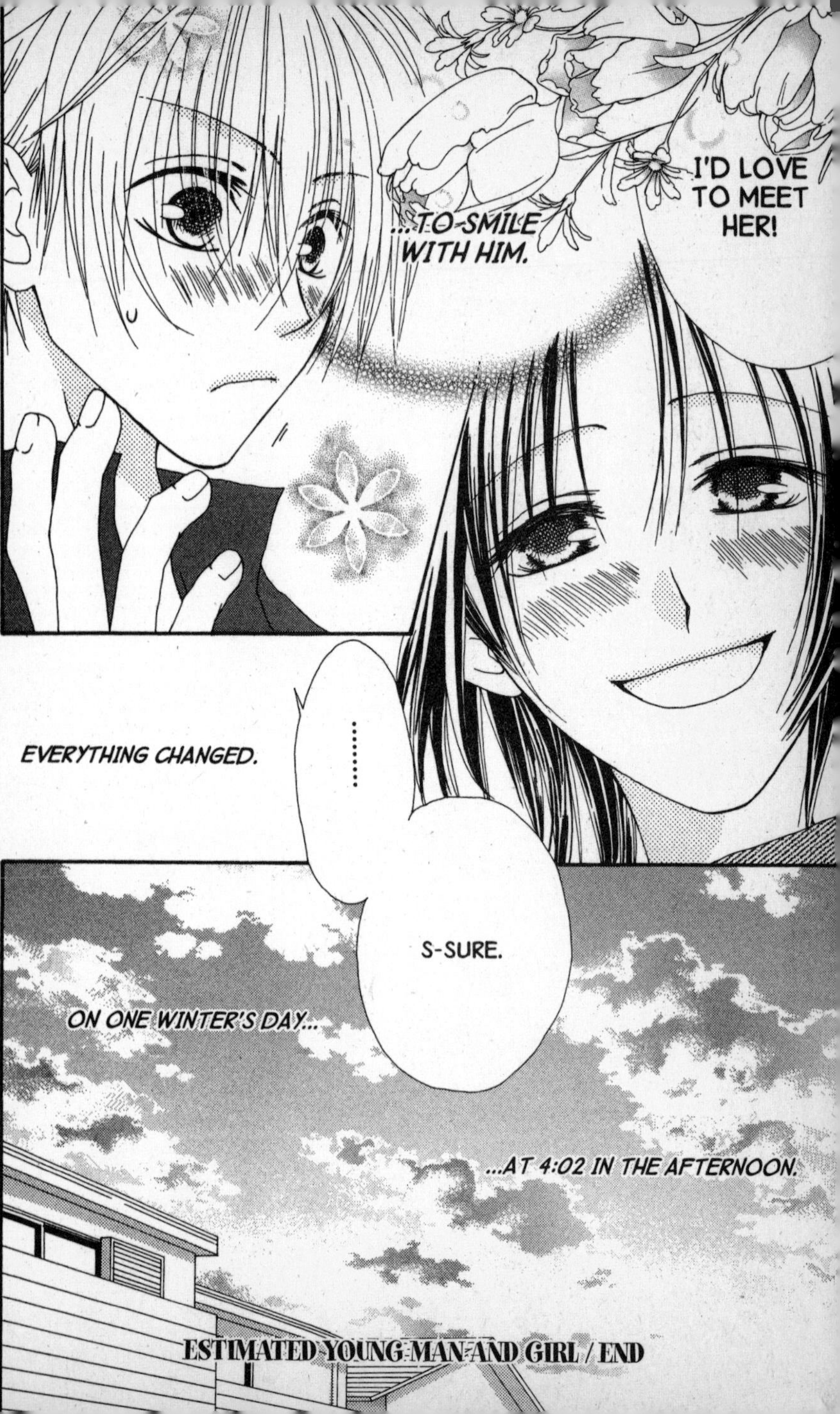
I'D LOVE TO MEET HER!
...TO-SMILE WITH HIM.
......
EVERYTHING CHANGED.
S-SURE.
ON ONE WINTER'S DAY...
...AT 4:02 IN THE AFTERNOON.
ESTIMATED YOUNG MAN AND GIRL / END

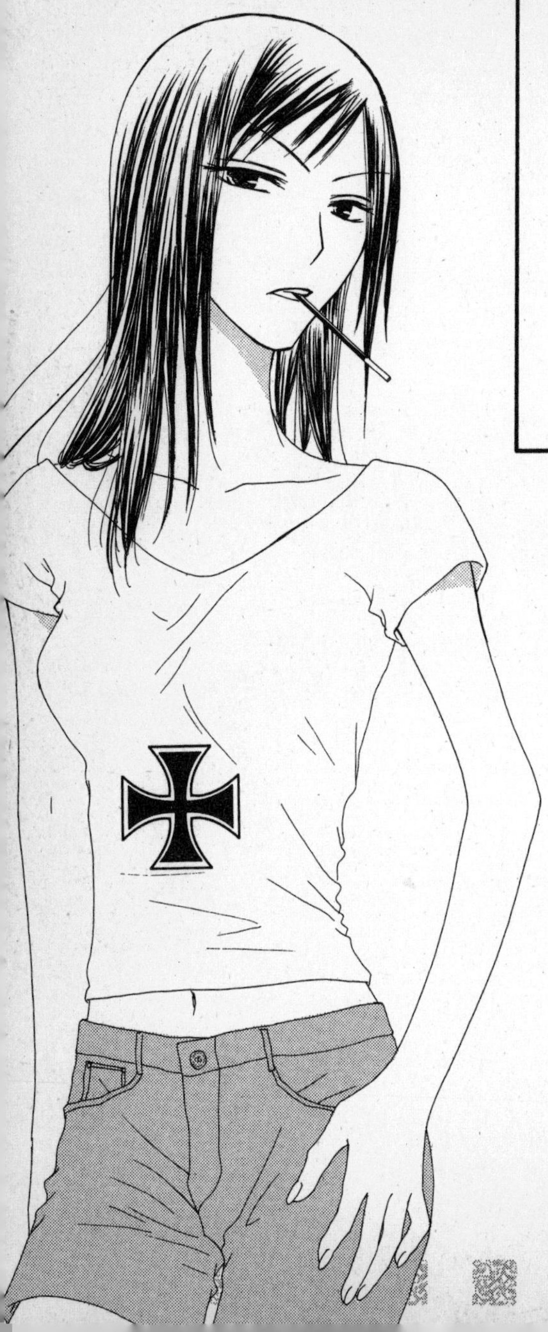

BONUS BONHEUR

Thanks for reading! This is the bonus afterword page!

MITSUKA.

I planned to only have her show up once--I never thought she'd have so many appearances. I enjoy drawing her interactions with the three from Bonheur. She's supposed to have a nice body...I guess I'll do what I can.

SOU.

It's fun drawing screaming, straight-man types. He's gotten pretty popular somehow. He's right below Uru's step-father. (laughs)

Lately, I've been drawing stories with only these brothers, but I realized that Shindo and Ichiro are really the easiest to draw.

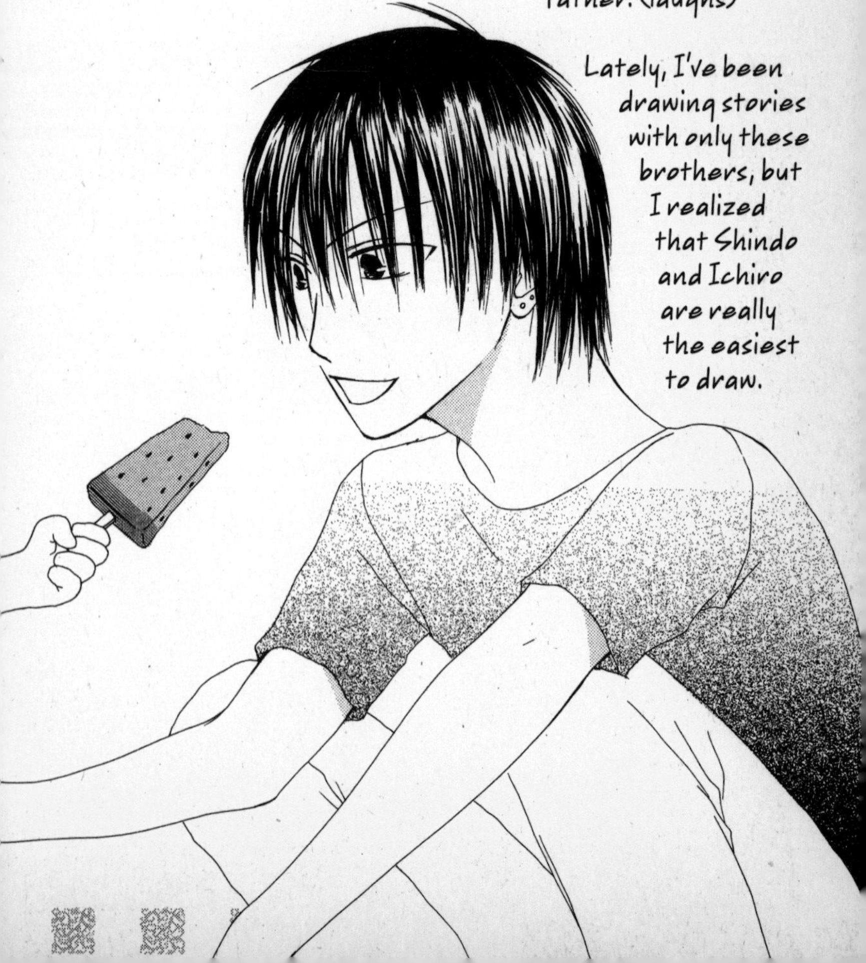

KASHIWA.

To be honest, I took all three of their names from different kinds of mochi. I justified that because of their Japanese sweet shop.

When I draw the older brother, I **try** to make his face soothing...but I get the feeling that no matter what I do, his inner pervert comes through.

SAKURA.

When I think about it, she's been in this comic since Chapter 1. Wow! At the time, I totally hadn't planned to make her the tiniest Abekawa.

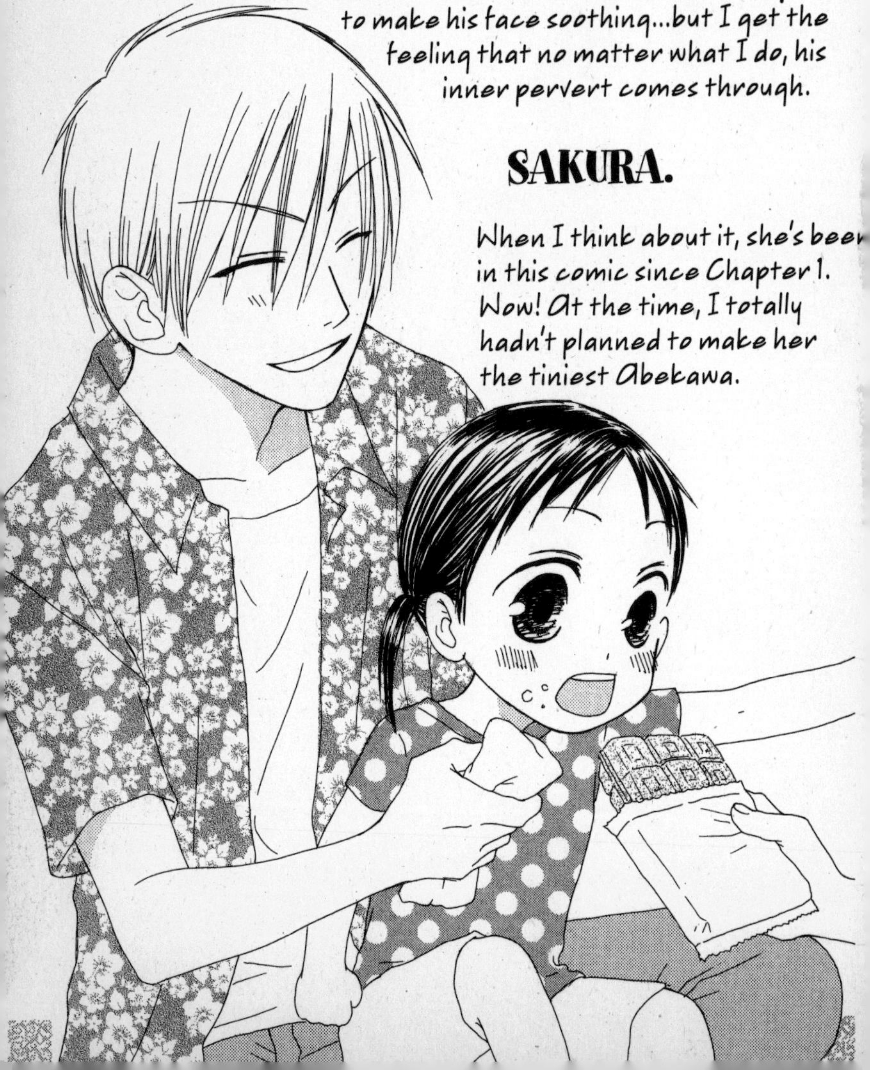

ESTIMATED YOUNG MAN AND GIRL

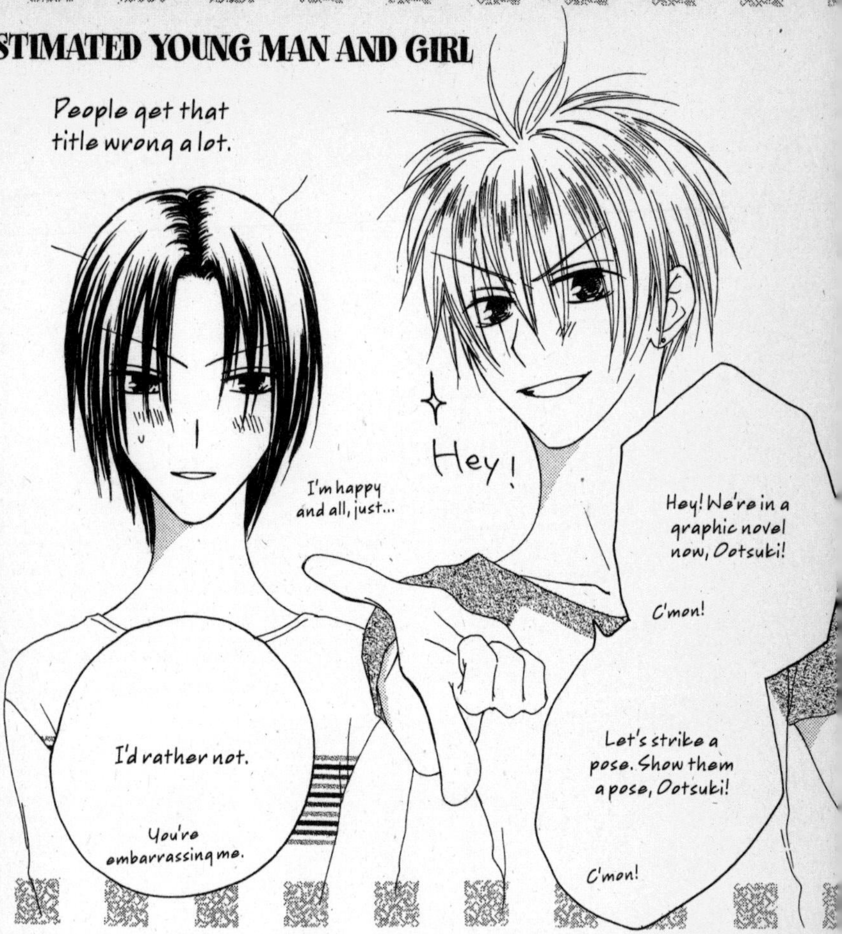
People get that title wrong a lot.
Hey!
Hey! We're in a graphic novel now, Ootsuki!
C'mon!
Let's strike a pose. Show them a pose, Ootsuki!
C'mon!
I'm happy and all, just...
I'd rather not.
You're embarrassing me.

This was my debut work. It was published in the The Hana that came out in my birth month (October). Considering it was my debut, I thought that was a pretty killer birthday present! I remember it really well. The male and female characters are complete opposites from the leads of Happy Café.

Anyway, see you again!

10/6/2005, Kou Matsuzuki

IN THE NEXT VOLUME OF...

CAFÉ BONHEUR IS BUSY! URU'S MOTHER INSISTS THAT SHINDO AND ICHIRO COME TO VISIT AFTER TESTING URU'S CAPABILITY TO WORK AND LIVE ALONE. AS ICHIRO AND URU RETURN TO SCHOOL, THE CAFE BECOMES UNEXPECTEDLY BUSY AND WITH URU TAKING MAKE-UP EXAMS AND STAYING AFTER SCHOOL, WILL CAFÉ BONHEUR BE ABLE TO FUNCTION WITHOUT HER? THINGS JUST KEEP GETTING BUSIER WHEN URU RUNS INTO HER ANGRY COUSIN ONE MINUTE AND SOU FROM ABEKAWA-YA THE NEXT! WHEN THEY FINALLY HIT A SLOW DAY, ICHIRO REVEALS THE TRUTH BEHIND HIS STRANGE SLEEPING HABITS!

THE ORIGINAL CAST OF
THE SLAYERS
IS REUNITED FOR THE FIRST TIME
IN OVER A DECADE
"At the end of the day Slayers is a great show that is about as classic as anime gets in the fantasy genre."
- DVDTalk.com
THE SLAYERS REVOLUTION
VAILABLE NOW
EPISODES ON 2 DVDS
THE SLAYERS REVOLUTION
2008 Hajime Kanzaka • Rui Araizumi / FUJIMISHOBO / SLAYERS-R COMMITTEE.
ENOKI FILMS USA, INC.
FUNIMATION ENTERTAINMENT

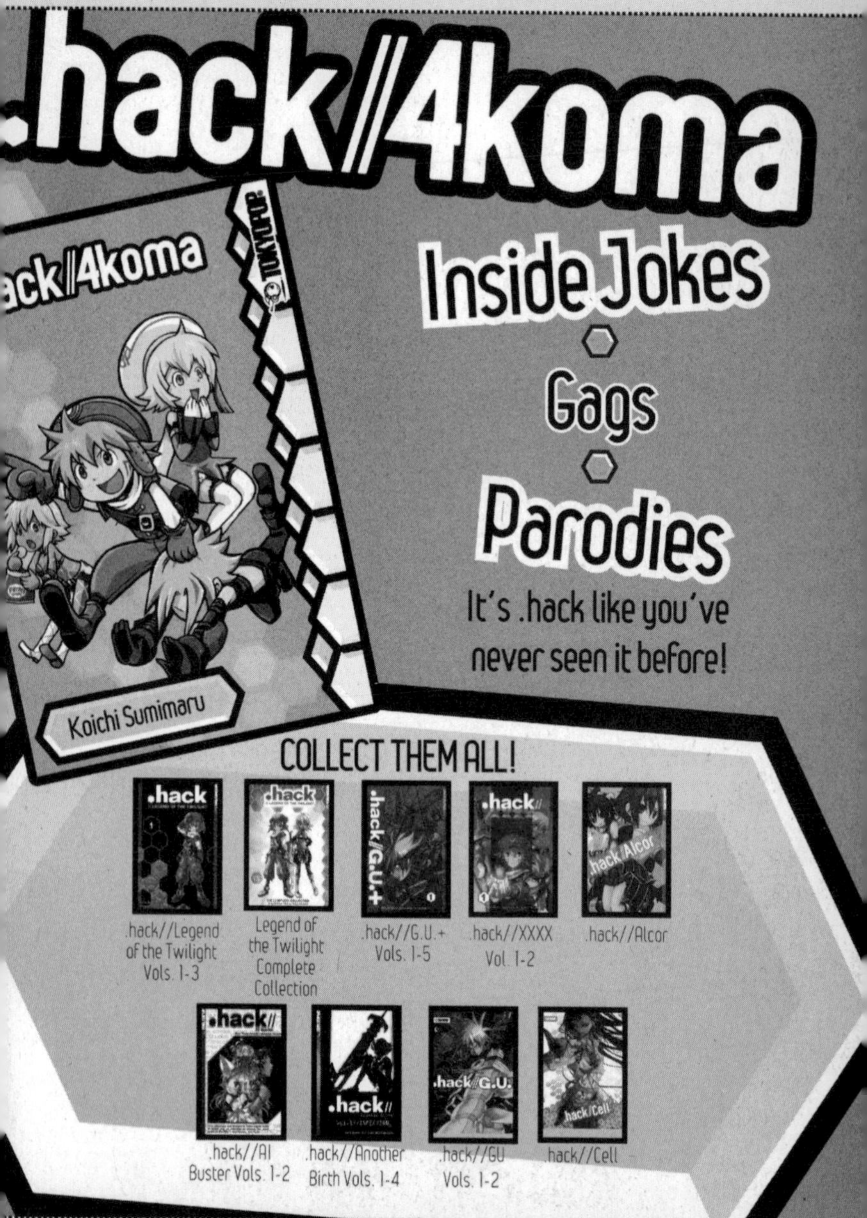
.hack//4koma
.hack//4koma
TOKYOPOP
Koichi Sumimaru
Inside Jokes
Gags
Parodies
It's .hack like you've never seen it before!
COLLECT THEM ALL!
.hack//Legend of the Twilight Vols. 1-3
Legend of the Twilight Complete Collection
.hack//G.U.+ Vols. 1-5
.hack//XXXX Vol. 1-2
.hack//Alcor
.hack//AI Buster Vols. 1-2
.hack//Another Birth Vols. 1-4
.hack//GU Vols. 1-2
.hack//Cell

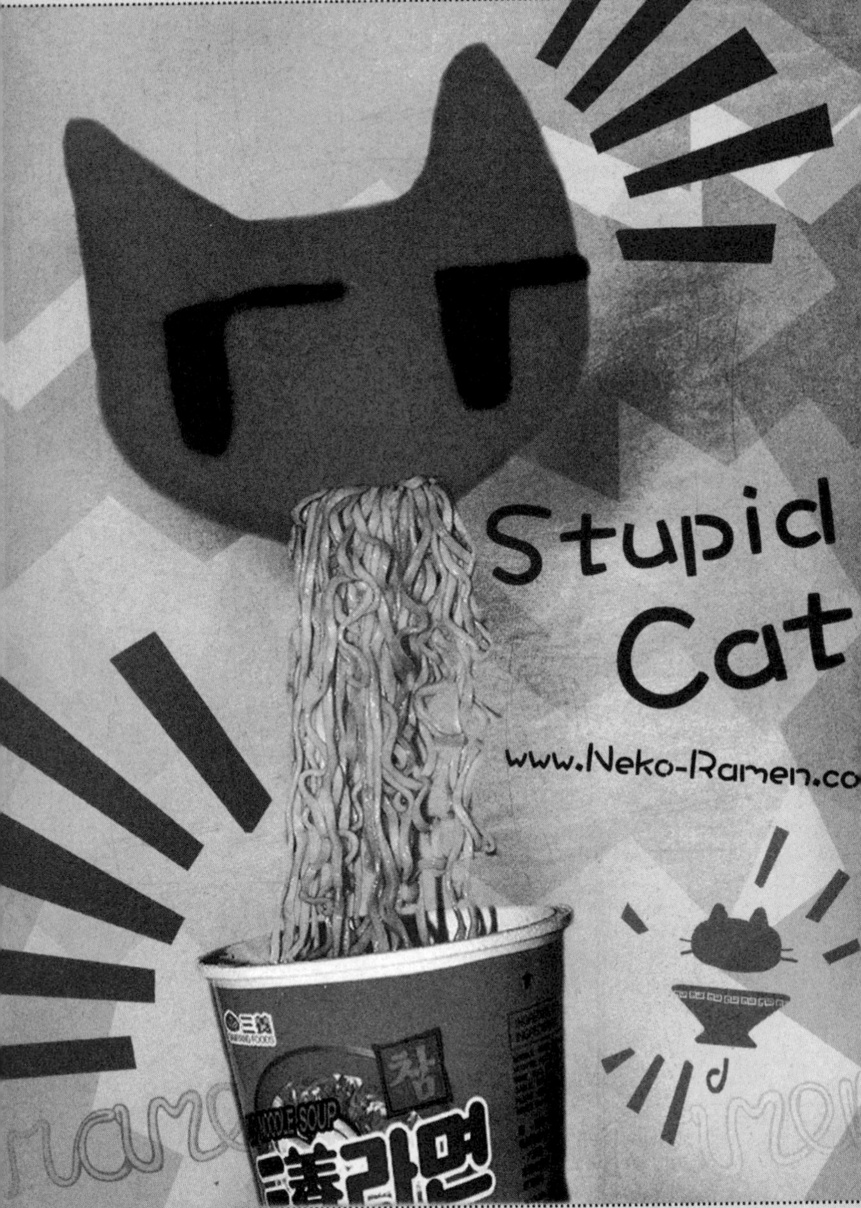
Stupid Cat
www.Neko-Ramen.co
NOODLE SOUP

The second epic trilogy continues!

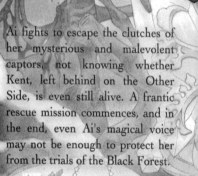

Ai fights to escape the clutches of her mysterious and malevolent captors, not knowing whether Kent, left behind on the Other Side, is even still alive. A frantic rescue mission commences, and in the end, even Ai's magical voice may not be enough to protect her from the trials of the Black Forest.

Dark secrets are revealed, and Ai must use all her strength and courage to face off against the new threat to Ai-Land. But will she ever see Kent again...?

"A very intriguing read that will satisfy old fans and create new fans, too."
— *Bookloons*

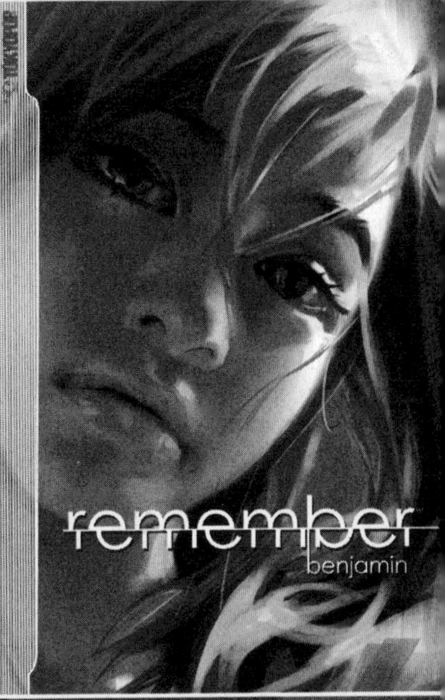
TOKYOPOP
remember
benjamin

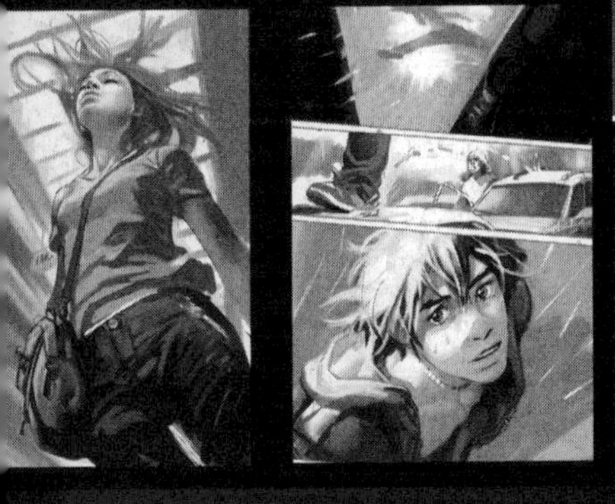

STOP!

This is the back of the book. You wouldn't want to spoil a great ending!

This book is printed "manga-style," in the authentic Japanese right-to-left format. Since none of the artwork has been flipped or altered, readers get to experience the story just as the creator intended. You've been asking for it, so TOKYOPOP® delivered: authentic, hot-off-the-press, and far more fun!

1
2
3
4
5
6
7
8
9
10

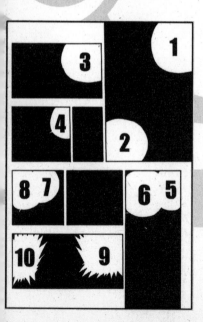

DIRECTIONS

If this is your first time reading manga-style, here's a quick guide to help you understand how it works.

It's easy... just start in the top right panel and follow the numbers. Have fun, and look for more 100% authentic manga from TOKYOPOP®!

THE MANGA REVOLUTION • LEADING 漫画革命